The Sword of Islam

O Prophet! Urge the believers to war; if there are twenty patient ones of you they shall overcome two hundred, and if there are a hundred of you they shall overcome a thousand of those who disbelieve, because they are a folk without intelligence.

The Qur'an, Sura 8:65

The Sword of Islam

From the deserts of Arabia emerges a militant new faith

In 651, a Muslim army rampaged through the ancient cities of Asia Minor and returned to Syria with five thousand Christian slaves. That same year, Byzantine forces failed to halt an invasion of Christian Armenia. More than half of Christendom would eventually fall to the expanding Muslim Empire.

Details from the illustration
by Andre Durenceau,
page 258

A.D. 565 to 740
The Muslim Onslaught all but Destroys Christendom

The Christians

THEIR FIRST TWO THOUSAND YEARS
Fifth Volume

CHP

CHRISTIAN HISTORY PROJECT

THE EDITOR:

Ted Byfield has been a journalist for fifty-eight years and a western Canadian magazine publisher since 1973, the founder of *Alberta Report* and *British Columbia Report* weekly newsmagazines, and founding editor of *Alberta in the Twentieth Century*, a twelve-volume history of Alberta. A columnist for Canada's *Sun* newspapers and sometime contributor to the *National Post* and *Globe and Mail* national newspapers, he is active in evangelical journalistic outreach. He was one of the founders of St. John's School of Alberta, an Anglican school for boys where he developed a new method of teaching history.

THE EXECUTIVE EDITOR:

Paul Stanway has been a reporter, editor and columnist for more than thirty years in both Canada and the United Kingdom. Born in Manchester, England, he began his newspaper career in 1969, and has been a regular contributor to magazines and newspapers on both sides of the Atlantic. A longtime resident of Alberta, he is the former editor-in-chief of *The Edmonton Sun* and editor of *The Calgary Sun* daily newspapers. He is also a former foreign correspondent for Canada's Sun Media newspaper group, and has written extensively on Europe and the Middle East.

COVER:

The cover illustration, by Alberta artist Dale Shuttleworth, shows the lightly armed Bedouin warriors of the Prophet Muhammad streaming out of the desert in the midst of a sandstorm: a common and highly successful tactic of the early armies of Islam.

CHRISTIAN HISTORY PROJECT LIMITED PARTNERSHIP

President and CEO	Robert W. Doull
Controller	Terry White
Contact Center Manager	Kathy Therrien
Contact Center Administrators	Bheko Dube, Larry Hill, Sameer Pandey, Peggy Roode
Marketing Manager	Leanne Nash
Vice President/Media	Brian Lehr
Credit Manager	Gloria McCullough
Distribution Coordinator	Katrina Soetaert
Customer Service	Grace De Guzman
Information Systems Manager	Michael Keast

The Sword of Islam, A.D. 565-740, The Muslim Onslaught all but Destroys Christendom

Writers:	Michael Byfield, Ted Byfield, Virginia Byfield, Calvin Demmon, Louise Henein, Paul Stanway, Jared Tkachuk, Joe Woodard
Illustrators	Richard Connor, Jamie Holloway, Dean Pickup, Dale Shuttleworth, John Smith
Volume Planner and Director of Research	Barrett Pashak
Design Director	Dean Pickup
Production Editor	Rev. David Edwards
Art Researcher	Louise Henein
Researcher	Jared Tkachuk
Proofreaders	P. A. Colwell, Faith Farthing (FinalEyes Communications)
Academic Consultants	Dr. Mateen A. Elass, Ant Greenham, Father Brian Hubka, Jack Keaschuk, Dr. Dennis Martin Dr. Jacquilyne Martin, Dr. David T. Priestley, Dr. Eugene TeSelle, Rev. Zahir Uddin

THE CHRISTIANS: Their First Two Thousand Years

(c) 2004 Christian History Project, Inc.
(c) 2004 Christian History Project Limited Partnership
Chairman, Gerald J. Maier

NATIONAL LIBRARY OF CANADA CATALOGUING IN PUBLICATION

The Sword of Islam: A.D. 565–740, The Muslim Onslaught all but Destroys Christendom

(The Christians: Their first two thousand years; 5)
Editors, Ted Byfield, Paul Stanway.
Includes bibliographical references and index.
ISBN 0-9689873-4-6

1. Christianity and other religions—Islam. 2. Islam—Relations—Christianity. 3. Islam.
I. Byfield, Ted II. Stanway, Paul, 1950- III. Christian History Project IV. Series: Christians: Their first two thousand years; 5.

BR227.S96 2004   261.2'7   C2004-901934-1

PRINTED IN CANADA BY FRIESENS CORPORATION

CONTENTS

ILLUSTRATIONS

All maps courtesy of *MapResources*, enhanced by *Dean Pickup*.

The Christian History Project is deeply indebted to the work of several nineteenth-century artists whose engravings first appeared in The Illustrated History of the World *(Ward Lock & Co., London and New York), and in Francois Guizot's* The History of France *(Estes & Lauriat, Boston). We gratefully acknowledge their contribution to this volume.*

For additional copies of this book or information on others in the series,
please contact us at:

The Christian History Project
10333 178 Street
Edmonton AB, Canada, T5S 1R5
www.christianhistoryproject.com

1-800-853-5402

FOREWORD

This series was published at a time of fervid interest in the religion called Islam. The term "9/11" had come into common parlance, referring to September 11, 2001, the date when terrorists—acting, they declared, in the name of Allah—destroyed the Twin Towers of the World Trade Center in New York City and a wing of the Pentagon in Washington, D.C., killing some twenty-eight hundred people with three hijacked airplanes. A fourth plane fell short of its mark in a field in Shanksville, Pennsylvania (near Pittsburgh), killing everyone on board.

But mass murder in the cause of Islam was not confined to America. Within a six-month period the following year, 118 people perished when police liberated the eight-hundred-plus audience held hostage in Moscow's Palace of Culture—before their captors could set off the planted bombs that would have killed them all. Two weeks later, a nightclub was blown up at Bali, island paradise of Indonesia, killing 180 young vacationers. Fifteen days after that, about two hundred people perished in Nigerian riots after Muslim terrorists began setting gasoline-soaked Christians afire to protest a beauty contest. In addition to all this, there were the "little" incidents—six murdered at a Christian school in Pakistan, and four days later, another three shot down at a Christian hospital. At Sidon in Lebanon, Bonnie Witherall, 31, of Lynden, Washington, opened the door of her Alliance Church prenatal clinic one morning and found herself confronting a strange man. He shot her first through the mouth, then put two bullets through her head.

Over all these incidents, the same cry was heard—"Allahu Akbar!"—the Muslim proclamation that "God is great!" Beyond the mere horror of these events, something else was gravely disturbing. In the popular culture of America, all great religions are the same, favoring gentleness, kindness, universal forgiveness, and unfailing mercy. So what these people were doing seemed incomprehensible.

But all the great religions are not the same. While they are remarkably in accord on many moral issues and certainly agree on the existence of God, they are not in accord on the nature of that God, nor in particular on how he would have us treat our enemies. To forgive them is a Christian idea. Comprehending such calamities as 9/11, therefore, means realizing how Islam came about, beginning with the fascinating man Muhammad himself. Such is the chief purpose of this volume.

It has a second purpose. While Christianity and Islam share a common heritage in the Old Testament, they differ dramatically in their origins. From the first Islam was not merely a spiritual movement. It was also a political and military one. In its formative centuries it spread by the sword and it took over governments. Christianity, for its first three pivotal centuries, was spread by the witness of suffering, first by the suffering of Jesus on the cross, then by the ineradicable spectacle of suffering Christian martyrs. While Christians in later years would often fail lamentably to preserve this distinction, it would always remain a standing witness to the Way, the Truth, and the Life that was its Founder.

Christians are frequently castigated in the media over the Crusades, the two hundred-year effort to establish a Christian state in Palestine. This is customarily portrayed as an unprovoked Christian attack. But the Crusades were, in fact, a counterattack, an attempt by Christians to recover the lands and peoples that had been wrested from them during the Muslim conquests three hundred years earlier—as described in this book. The story of the Crusades will be told in a future volume, but the implication of this one is clear—the Christian confrontation with Islam goes back to Islam's origins, and it is not over.

Ted Byfield

Harith ibn Jabala, the sheikh of the Monophysite Christian Banu Ghassan tribe, entertains the patriarch of Antioch with a meal of camel meat, to emphasize his utter contempt for the orthodox Sacrament.

CHAPTER 1

Success and triumph, then a terrible reversal

By the seventh century the cross rose above churches from Ireland to the Indian Ocean, but failure in Arabia leads to Christianity's worst setback in 2,000 years

For its first six centuries, the Christian story is one of strife and struggle rewarded by an undeniable success. The cross, the symbol of an ignominious death by execution, had by the year 600 risen triumphantly above churches from Ireland in the Atlantic to the shores of the Indian Ocean. Jesus' assurance that the gospel would be preached to all peoples seemed a prophecy in the course of imminent fulfillment. But then, from a direction no one expected, disaster struck Christendom. Within barely a century, more than half of the peoples who had at least nominally declared themselves Christian were lost to a new faith through military conquest—undeniably the greatest reversal Christianity would be called upon to suffer in its first two thousand years. The name of the conqueror was Islam, and its place of origin was Arabia.

Christian evangelism was to prove ineffective in Arabia, although not for lack of effort. Missions launched across the Red Sea from Christian Ethiopia had achieved brief success in the southwestern peninsula, but then largely failed. There were large Christian tribes in the northern peninsula, however, and in adjoining Syria and Iraq, the land of the wandering Bedouin. Some were allied to Persia, others to the Byzantine Empire, which still insisted upon calling itself Roman although its official and vernacular language was not Latin but Greek.

1. After the death of one fourth-century Christian Arab chief, his place was taken by his wife, the queen Mawiyya. According to no fewer than four contemporary Roman historians, she took over all Palestine before her astounded Byzantine opponents sued for peace. Mawiyya accepted, and included in the treaty a demand for a native Arab bishop. Her choice was a hermit named Moses, whose zealous ministry led the Banu Tanukh, tribal confederates of the Ghassanids, into Christianity. Mawiyya translates into western languages as Maria or Mary.

But a debilitating controversy confused and hampered the Christian allegiance of these northern tribes. Rome and Constantinople regarded all of them as heretical. Those to the west, centered in Syria, were Monophysite Christians, militantly opposed to the creed painfully hammered out at the fifth-century Council of Chalcedon. (See earlier volume, *Darkness Descends*, chapter 7.) Foremost among them were the powerful Banu Ghassan. However, Constantinople, recurrent persecutor of Monophysites elsewhere, customarily treated Arab Monophysites with great deference, since it was dependent upon them for defense against Persia, its ancient enemy.

Meanwhile to the east, Persia had a similar arrangement with the Lakhmids, based in the Mesopotamian city of Hira. They were mostly Nestorian Christians, likewise heretical in the Rome and Constantinople view. Their chiefs remained steadfastly pagan, and early in the sixth century, the incumbent Lakhmid chief was the powerful and vicious Mundhir III, who reigned like a king. His wife, Hind, was a Christian, and he was surrounded by Christian lieutenants, but he himself contemptuously rejected Christianity.

Mundhir became the scourge of the largely Monophysite Christian settlements on the Roman frontier, acquiring a reputation for savagery that was extreme even by the ferocious standards of the age. Mobile and clever, his fighters would strike without warning at the rich Syrian cities. He once reached the walls of Antioch, third city of the Roman Empire, pillaging and burning homes, butchering the older inhabitants, dragging off the young, the strong or the comely for sale on the Persian slave markets, and killing off the faltering.

An equally unpleasant fate often awaited captives who reached the Persian cities. Mundhir once reportedly amused himself, for example, by sacrificing four hundred virgins to the Persian equivalent of his preferred idol, al-Uzza, the sex goddess the Greeks called Aphrodite. When Roman armies tracked him down, he would frequently turn on them with dire consequences; he once captured two Roman generals, for whom he got enormous ransoms. But when Mundhir killed a Khinda chief—his father-in-law, in fact, and the supreme phylarch of the Roman Arabs—Constantinople decided he must be checked. They assigned the job to the Banu Ghassan, who controlled the trade routes into Bostra, capital of the old Roman province of Arabia.

The Banu Ghassan had migrated out of South Arabia in the first century A.D., when a new sea route from India made it unnecessary to haul goods from the east across the Arabian Peninsula, thus destroying the caravan business. A degree of religious and political assimilation began once they reached the Roman frontier, although the Byzantine hold on few Arab peoples was ever secure.[1]

An ornate, fourth-century Syrian ivory casket (below) decorated with biblical scenes and (along the edge of the lid) portraits of Christ and the apostles. Few such artifacts have survived to testify to the thriving Christian culture that covered much of Arabia and the Middle East before the rise of Islam. This one is housed in the Museo Civico dell'Età Christiana, Brescia, Italy.

By the turn of the sixth century the Banu Ghassan had prevailed over their tribal confederates, had abandoned the family business (i.e., pillage), and as respectable merchants had taken over the Bostra trade.

The emperor Anastasius bestowed the title of phylarch on the Banu Ghassan chief, Jabala, commissioning him to lead his affiliated tribes against Mundhir and his Lakhmids, and otherwise establish order in the Palestine area. Jabala was succeeded by his son, Harith ibn Jabala, known to Byzantine historians as Arethas. The noblest example of Christian governance the age would produce, Harith was revered by the Monophysites and also trusted by the emperor Justinian.

The sex goddess Aphrodite (above), from a sixth-century mosaic floor at Madaba, Jordan. The vicious Mundhir III, pagan chief of the powerful Lakhmid Arabs, is said to have sacrificed four hundred virgins to al-Uzza, the local equivalent of Aphrodite.

Some accounts say (and others deny) that Harith walked with a limp and was known as "the Lame." A huge man of striking appearance, he was as expert on the battlefield as he was deft at Arab diplomacy and schooled in theological debate. Within a decade of his succession, he helped suppress a revolt of the Samaritans, despised by the Jews in New Testament times but still very much in existence five hundred years later.[2]

Harith next led a federation of Christian tribes to capture and plunder Hira, the largely Christian capital of the vicious Mundhir. But the Lakhmid chief himself escaped south into the peninsula, where he brooded over his losses and schemed to put an end to Harith. By now the two had become mortal enemies in the Arab tradition. For the next forty years they would fight it out, a sideshow in the recurring clashes between the Persian and Roman armies.

In one raid, appearing as usual from nowhere, Mundhir captured a son of Harith, unwarily pasturing horses near a Ghassanid encampment. Roman accounts say the young man's life was instantly sacrificed to al-Uzza. The feud ended when the Ghassanids caught Mundhir at Qinnasrin, deep inside Syria, in June 554. When the battle was over, another of Harith's sons lay dead, but so did Mundhir. Harith's commission had been fulfilled. He buried his son as a martyr, and erected a little church on the site.

Notwithstanding his Roman affiliation, Harith continued to live Arab-fashion, moving his entire entourage as his people pursued pasturing for their livestock. Nevertheless, he and his successors may have been largely responsible for a remarkable phenomenon. Along the slopes of the Hawran district of Southwest Syria, populated today by the sect called the Druze, are the ruins of nearly three hundred towns and villages, with houses of basalt, palaces, triumphal arches, public baths, aqueducts, theaters and churches. Many of these ruins date from the sixth century.

2. As detailed in an earlier volume (*The Veil Is Torn*, page 78), the people of Samaria, which lay between Judea and Galilee, were despised as impostors by the Jews in New Testament times. Like the Jews, they gradually spread throughout the Roman Empire; in the sixth century there were Samaritan synagogues in Rome, Thessalonica and Constantinople. Their rebellion in the sixth century over Christian restrictions on their religious practice led to their mass slaughter by the Romans. Their numbers continued to decline thereafter, until by the twenty-first century only some four hundred remained, living in Tel Aviv and in Nablus, forty miles north of Jerusalem.

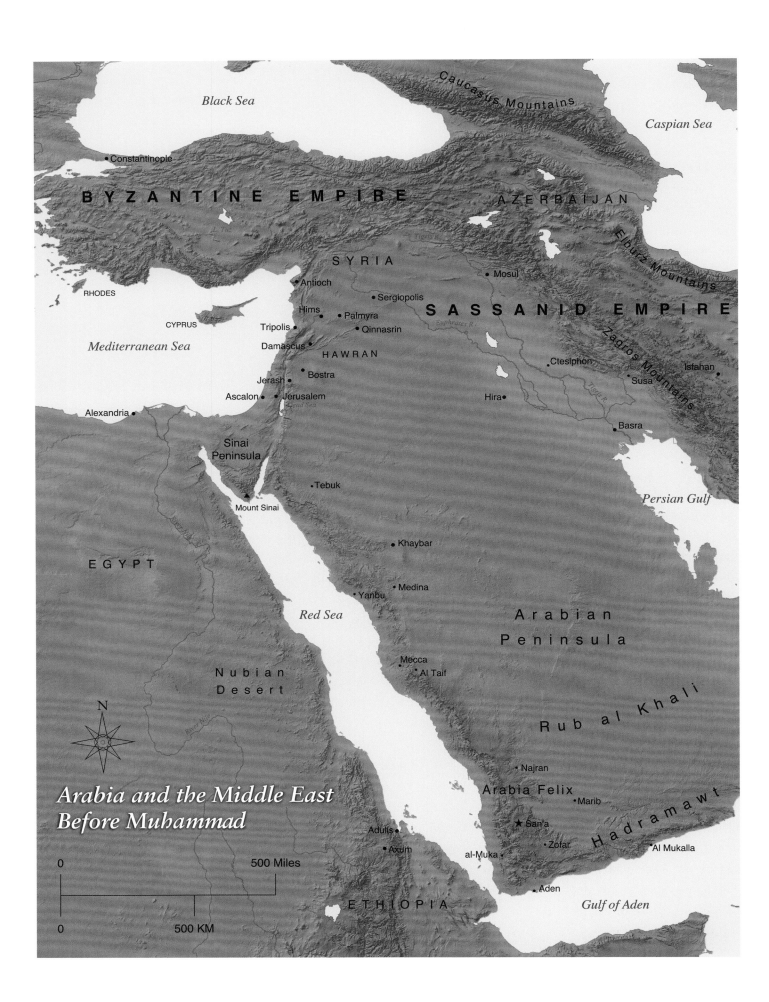

Black Sea

Caspian Sea

Caucasus Mountains

• Constantinople

B Y Z A N T I N E   E M P I R E

A Z E R B A I J A N

RHODES

S Y R I A

• Mosul

Elburz Mountains

• Antioch

• Sergiopolis

S A S S A N I D   E M P I R E

Hims •

• Palmyra

Euphrates R.

CYPRUS

Tripolis •

• Qinnasrin

Zagros Mountains

Mediterranean Sea

Damascus •

H A W R A N

• Ctesiphon

• Isfahan

• Bostra

Susa •

Jerash •

Tigris R.

Ascalon •

• Jerusalem

Hira •

Dead Sea

Alexandria •

Basra •

Sinai
Peninsula

E G Y P T

• Tebuk

Persian Gulf

▲
Mount Sinai

• Khaybar

River Nile

N u b i a n
D e s e r t

• Medina

A r a b i a n

• Yanbu

Red Sea

P e n i n s u l a

N

Mecca •

R u b   a l   K h a l i

• Al Taif

**Arabia and the Middle East
Before Muhammad**

• Najran

Arabia Felix

• Marib

H a d r a m a w t

★ San'a

Adulis •

• Zofar

• Al Mukalla

0   500 Miles

al-Muka •

• Axum

0   500 KM

• Aden

E T H I O P I A

Gulf of Aden

How was this possible in a region now utterly devoid of urban life? No one really knows, but historian Philip K. Hitti (*History of the Arabs*) ascribes much of it to the Ghassanids. Many a Monophysite church certainly rose under their direction. So did a castle in Dumayr, and there are ruins of a monastery with a magnificent tower at Qasr al-Hair al-Gharbi, fifty miles southeast of the Syrian city of Homs. But the Ghassanids' favorite center was Sergiopolis, named for the martyred Roman soldier St. Sergius, and a place of pilgrimage since pagan times. They made it an Arab Christian shrine and community, watered by cisterns and populated solely by monks, priests and pilgrims—and the endlessly migrating Ghassanids, when they were in residence. Of Sergiopolis's five churches, the greatest served them as a sort of palace, and all Arabs (even Mundhir) respected its sanctity.

Harith's commitment to Monophysite Christianity ran deep. In one celebrated incident, an aging patriarch of Antioch, loyal to Chalcedon and

Near Mount Sinai, Justinian constructed a fortress–monastery, providing a refuge for Christians amid the Muslim onslaught. Its library still houses Christendom's ancient literature.

prompted by Justinian, invited the chieftain to share in the Communion service. Harith asked the patriarch first to join the Ghassanids for dinner, and set before him a dish of camel meat, something few but Arabs can stomach. The appalled cleric retched and refused his blessing to the meal. "Know then," responded Harith, "that your food [the orthodox Sacrament] is as contemptible to us as this camel meat is to you, because hidden in yours is apostasy and the abandonment of the true faith."

However, there were limits to Harith's departure from Chalcedon doctrine. Tritheism, the belief espoused by two Monophysite bishops that Father, Son and Spirit were effectually three gods, was a heresy so repulsive to the Ghassanids that they finally asked Justinian to help them suppress it. "How can I restore you [Monophysites] to the unity of the church when you are not yourselves united?" the exasperated emperor protested.

One of Justinian's moves against the Monophysites, however, was not violent, and proved altogether durable. At the head of the Red Sea, at the apex of the V-shaped Sinai Peninsula, rises Mount Sinai, now Jebel Musa, where Moses received the codified morality that descended first to the Jews and thence to most of humanity. Here in 530—both to protect Christian monasteries and other communities against recurrent raiding from Arabia and Africa, and to provide a witness to Chalcedonian Christianity among the teeming Monophysites—Justinian erected a fortress–monastery, manned by Chalcedonian monks and soldiers of the empire.

Standing five thousand feet above the sea, it was to provide a refuge for Christians in the coming Muslim onslaught. Centuries later it would be given

The Crucifixion and Resurrection from the Rabbula Gospels *(above), an illuminated parchment manuscript from northern Syria. Located in Florence's Biblioteca Laurenziana, the manuscript is named after one of four monks who created it in 586, at the long-vanished Syrian monastery of Beth Mar John.*

the name St. Catherine's, honoring a young Alexandrian martyred in the fourth century for her faith. It stands to this day virtually unchanged, its library of ancient literature one of the world's great treasures. (See *A Pinch of Incense*, pages 36–37.) Its walls (280 feet long by 250 feet high) have for years been guarded, oddly enough, by Muslim soldiers who seem to revere it as much as do its thirty-six monks, the self-imposed limit on the number who may live there.

Justinian honored Harith with the ancient title of patrician, highest rank in the aristocracy, thus making him a symbolic kinsman of the emperor himself. Upon all this "multiculturalism," however, Constantinople society still looked with loathing. They did not like Arabs, they did not like Harith, and they liked even less the son who succeeded him, whose Monophysite Christianity was more firmly rooted even than his father's.

Harith died late in 569 or early 570, the same years favored for the birth of Muhammad. The jurisdiction of the Banu Ghassan then ran to the Wadi al-Qura, whose riverbed also marked the limit of Christian penetration from the north. Beyond it lay the Hijaz, the region of Medina and Mecca. Here almost the only Christians were merchants and other travelers, although the Ghassanids maintained a year-round establishment in Mecca, site of a big annual trading fair and pagan pilgrimage.

In South Arabia, a very different Christian endeavor had meanwhile been established and had gradually moved north, where it was destined to meet with bloody calamity. The south and the north stood in such utter contrast that their existence on the same peninsula seemed scarcely possible. Against the stark aridity of the desert, writes historian Irfan Shahid of Georgetown University, the Yemen is "a veritable cornucopia, where the vegetation is luxuriantly abundant, strikingly diversified, and comprehensively representative of all levels of use and need, from the necessities of life to its luxuries." To Herodotus, the fifth-century B.C. "Father of History," South Arabia was *Arabia Felix* (literally "Happy Arabia"), "the only country that produces frankincense, myrrh, cassia, cinnamon and laudanum."

But the contrast went beyond mere flora and fauna. The northern Arab was a nomad, the southern a sedentary farmer. The northerner spoke a Semitic language, the southerner a language akin to Ethiopian. The north consisted of tribes and tribal confederacies; the south, from the eighth century

B.C. onward, of four kingdoms. The greatest of these, and eventually the only one, was the Sabaean. Its capital was the thriving commercial city of Marib, one of whose monarchs was the famous "Queen of Sheba," captivator of (and captivated by) King Solomon.[3]

The south also had tribes, though their boundaries were defined by land-title deeds, and their chiefs acted as counselors to the king. Southerners worshiped a triad of sun, star and moon gods, and their kings in early times also served as priests. The northerners, warring always with nature, grew lean, tough, shrewd and independent. Southern life was built on luxury: the producing and marketing of spices, scents and delicate furnishings for people of taste and means. And while the northerner lived on the hazardous frontier between two great empires, the southerner dwelt within a geographic fortress, protected on three sides by a perilous and largely harborless seacoast, and on the fourth by the desert.

Finally, these two Arabias emerge from antiquity not merely different but mutually hostile. No historian has really explained this, yet it has survived through the entire fourteen centuries of the Muslim era. As the southern peoples moved northward, the conflict became one of differing family heritage as well as geography. The town of Medina identified itself with the people of the south, for example, while Mecca identified with those of the north. Whatever its origins, however, this ancient and inexplicable north–south feud would calamitously split Islam in its hour of victory, and thereby keep both the west and Christendom from total Islamic conquest.

In the south, the kingdom of the Sabaeans had fallen during the second century A.D. to the Himyarites, one of its own subject peoples, noted for a great wonder: a twenty-story castle in their city of San'a. The ancient world's only skyscraper, it was raised against recurrent Bedouin raids. However, a greater danger lay across the Red Sea, whence the Himyarites' linguistic

3. The terraces and hanging gardens in the Sabaean capital of Marib made it what the *Encyclopaedia Britannica* calls "the Paris of the Ancient World." But the most notable ancient Sabaean accomplishment lay nearby: a wall, pyramid-shaped in cross-section and eighteen hundred feet long, the famed Marib Dam. Blocking the Wadi Sadd, its sluice gates feed water to four thousand surrounding acres.

The green terraces of Djebel Sabir, Yemen (below), located in what the Romans referred to as "Arabia Felix," or Happy Arabia. At the time of Muhammad, the fertile lands of Arabia Felix were home to powerful and prosperous communities of Christians, Jews and pagans.

Lonely warriors for Christ

What impressed the tough-as-nails desert Bedouin were the hermits and monks who rejected the world and took to the wilderness to live on dates, berries, and God

As Christianity reached outward, it naturally reached the Arabs. What most impressed the Bedouin, however, was not the idyllic social Elysium portrayed by its urban congregations, nor certainly its influence upon those of high imperial office. Rather it was the Christians of the desert, the hermits and monks, who captivated the desert travelers and are spoken of with awe in Arab poetry:

> A nature is theirs,
> God gives the like to no other men,
> A wisdom that never sleeps, a bounty that never fails.
>
> Their home is God's own land,
> His chosen of old:
> Their faith is steadfast:
> Their hope is set on nought
> But the world to come.
>
> Their sandals are soft and fine,
> And girded with chastity;
> They welcome with garlands sweet
> The dawn of the Feast of Palms.

Similarly an Arab, finding the site of a former camp, is reminded in his nostalgia of the monks.

> Stay, let us weep at the remembrance
> Of a loved one and favor (bestowed),
> At the mark of a camp whose lines
> Have long ago been obliterated.
> Years have passed over it since I knew it,
> And it has become
> Like the writing of the Psalms
> In the books of the monks.

These hermits and monks were in part a reaction to the increasing social and political acceptability of Christianity. In the fourth century, some men, and women, too, followed the example of Anthony, and rejected the world by taking to the desert to live alone on dates, berries, grasshoppers and God, to weep for their irresistible sinfulness, and to contemplate the beauty of the Christ who had delivered them from its consequences. (See earlier volume, *Darkness Descends*, page 68.)

The fascinated Bedouin regularly brought Anthony bread and asked him about Christ. Hundreds, even thousands, followed his example, and the caves and tents of hermits soon dotted the Sinai Peninsula.

In Syria, the phenomenon was the same. Throughout the country, the hermits gradually came together to form monastic communities. One pupil and emulator of Anthony was Hilarion, child of pagan parents, raised near the trading town of Gaza on the Palestine coast, who, after several years, returned to lead his own solitary life near his hometown. He, too, was attended frequently by Bedouin who were said to have received healing at his hand. "Bless us," shouted a crowd of them on their way into Gaza for the pagan worship of the morning

The most famous of the column-sitting hermit monks, Saint Simeon spent thirty-six years living atop his perch in the Syrian Desert. This depiction of the hermit saint (above) is from a thirteenth-century doorframe in Istanbul's famed Hagia Sophia church. One of the very few stylite towers still standing, this sixth-century structure and small chapel (right) can be seen at Umm al-Rasas, Jordan.

star. Hilarion's sermon to them seemed so full of love that the whole band suddenly offered themselves to Christ. Their pagan priest bowed for baptism, the wreath of his forsaken office still about his head.

To a group of such solitaries, living eight miles northeast of Jerusalem, came the twenty-nine-year-old Euthymius of Melitene on the Euphrates in 405. He later moved with another monk to some caves in a hillside close to the Dead Sea. A whole community of monks grew up around them. One day, a notable pagan sheikh named Aspebet arrived with his clan from the Persian frontier, and told how he had incurred the wrath of the Persian authorities by facilitating the escape of Christians from persecution.

The bane of Aspebet's life, however, was not the Persians. It was the pitiful condition of his son, paralyzed down the right side and pronounced hopeless by all who had sought to cure him. The Christians had told Aspebet to pray to Christ for the boy and nothing had happened. But he had subsequently seen in a vision an old white-bearded monk, whom he realized was Euthymius, by now aged. The prayers of Euthymius cured the son, and the grateful sheikh ordered his whole band baptized, he himself taking the new name "Boutros" in Arabic, which translates into English as "Peter."

The recovered son became a sheikh, and Peter became a Christian missionary—later, in fact, first "Bishop of the Camps" and a delegate to the Christian Council of Ephesus in 431. The office, Bishop of the Camps, remained for centuries.

Of all the monks and hermits, however, none fascinated the Bedouin more than the "stylites" (from *stylos* the Greek word for a pillar), who sought the presence of God by perching themselves on pillars, away from the world, a practice that persisted in the Middle East for more than two hundred years. And of all the stylites, none proved more intriguing than Simeon, atop his eighty-foot structure at Telanissos (now Qalat Siman in Syria, where a large church was erected on the pillar's site). Simeon was sought out by the sick, the distressed, whole tribes from the desert,

The call of the solitary lifestyle of the hermit remains strong in some parts of the Christian world. This hermit monk at Lalibela, Ethiopia, (above) has enlarged an existing hole in a sandstone cliff into a refuge from the world.

and officers of government for his healing and advice. Whether Simeon was himself an Arab is not known, though there were Arabs in the monastery where he spent his youth.

The power of such holy men did not, in the popular view, die with them. Their bones were considered likewise beneficent, resulting, much to the disgust of church authorities, in an unseemly brawl among the village Arabs over the remains of forty hermits martyred near the Dead Sea. When similar disturbances broke out over the corpse of St. Simeon, the army had to be called out to guard it.

The sites of martyrdoms sometimes became shrines to the Christian Bedouin. For example, in the Sinjar region (seventy miles east of the Iraqi city of Mosul on the Tigris) legend held that a Jewish lad, Abd al-Masih, had decided to dedicate himself to Christ and been baptized in a certain spring, considered sacred since the earliest times. His wrathful father put him to death as a human sacrifice on the very spot. So the spring's sanctity was renewed, becoming useful, it was said, for healing disease and discovering the whereabouts of stray camels.

Until the christological conflicts of the fifth century, most monks attended the local church and respected the local bishop. While it was true that few became priests, that was rarely because they were anti-clerical or opposed the hierarchy of the church; rather, they simply did not sense a vocation to the priesthood.

After the Council of Chalcedon in 451, however, this congeniality changed sharply in Syria, Palestine and Egypt. The monks of the desert rejected Chalcedon. When the patriarch of Jerusalem declared his acceptance they denounced him, too, and ran him out of town, until the imperial troops escorted him back and ordered the desert dwellers to pay him their respects. Almost none did. Instead, many abandoned their monasteries for the road, denouncing the Chalcedon doctrine in every town and encampment. There were, however, exceptions. The revered Simeon Stylites, for one, became an influential figure in support of the Council of Chalcedon. ∎

cousins, the Ethiopians, launched successive expeditions against them. With the Ethiopians in the fifth century came a "foreign" religion: Christianity. (See Ethiopia sidebar page 66.)

By the sixth, this devout Christian presence in the southern peninsula stood firm, although resented as a foreign intrusion. There were Christian missions along the Yemen coast, and the Ethiopian garrisons were Christian, but their chief concentration was in Najran. Most northerly of the Himyarite towns, it centered a lush and well-watered valley, and was the prosperous junction point of a "Y" in the trade routes. The main trail from the south was its trunk; one arm stretched to Persian Hira, the other to Roman Syria.[4]

Christianity was not the first non-pagan religion to reach South Arabia, however; Judaism preceded it and was better established. After the fall of Jerusalem in A.D. 70, and the failure of the Jewish rebellion six decades later, Jewish refugees had fled south into Arabia. By the mid-fifth century they had established numerous communities, even converting members of the Himyarite royal household. The two faiths remained mutually hostile, and the Christians were outnumbered by the Jews.

The cause of the catastrophe that befell the Christians, however, was in the main political. Another Ethiopian invasion seized control of the major south coast ports. The Romans, through a treaty with these invaders, took over virtually all trade—a double disaster for the Jews of South Arabia. Not only were they losing their share of the caravan business, but their country was being conquered by Christian Ethiopia, backed by Rome. All their sympathies, interest, and chance of survival consequently lay with Persia. As the Ethiopian forces moved north, the Jews naturally fought back, at first suffering military reverses.

But then, in or around 523, a new king rose among them, destroyed the army of the intruder, and proceeded to conduct at Najran one of the most fastidiously documented butcheries in late antiquity. The Arabic nickname for this new Jewish king was Dhu Nuwas ("Curlylocks"), though his official name was Yusuf (Joseph). In Christian accounts, he is "Musruq," an execration meaning roughly "Worthless," which the monkish copiers doubly emphasized by printing his name upside down and in a different color from the rest of the script.

Dhu Nuwas's origins are obscure, but whether he was descended from converts

The ruins of the ancient South Arabian city of Marib (right), capital of the Sabaean kingdom in pre-Islamic times. A thriving commercial and religious center for millennia, it was finally abandoned in the late-twentieth century, a victim of modern tribal and political conflict.

or Israelites, his mother was probably a slave captured by Christian Arabs and sold to the Himyarite court. He apparently was raised a Jew. Arab accounts claim he was homosexual. One says he gained the throne after killing another contender who was trying to force him to be his lover. One chronicle says he escaped the Ethiopian invasion by hiding in the mountains; another that he disguised himself as a Christian; still another that it was not a disguise, that he had accepted baptism.

In any event, his national alliance of Jewish, pagan, and some Nestorian Christians against the Monophysite Ethiopians achieved rapid success. He besieged Zofar, the Himyarite capital, lured out the mostly Christian defenders with a pledge of clemency, then herded them into their new church and burned it. Much the same was reportedly done at Mukha, a port city on the Red Sea coast. Dhu Nuwas then turned his attention to Najran, a formidable prospect militarily, financially and psychologically.

The city's *kabir* (akin to a feudal lord, though he apparently required consensual support of some kind from his subjects) was a tough old warrior.

The saintly Ruhayma, although a grandmother, remained a beauty who was revered by Christians and Jews alike for her generosity toward all good causes in her trade-rich Arabian city.

Victor in some thirteen battles, he was a wealthy merchant as well. His name was Harith (the same name as the Ghassanid king, his remote kinsman). His wife, Ruhayma, is reputed a saintly woman who, though a grandmother, remained a striking beauty and was revered by Christians and Jews alike for her kindness and generosity in all local causes. She had for instance once loaned money to Dhu Nuwas's father, it was said, and had subsequently forgiven him the debt.

Najran was intensely Christian. A start had been made on producing an Arabic Bible and an Arabic Liturgy. An order of laypeople, called the Sons and Daughters of the Covenant, was noted for their devotion and zeal for Jesus Christ. Najranite children were taught from the dawn of their understanding that they must, if need be, die for their faith. Dhu Nuwas obviously did not count on the depth of this conviction. His operation against Najran was, in fact, a series of miscalculations.

He sent three units of his army against the city; the defenders under Harith met them in the field and routed all three. He laid siege to the place, but could not penetrate its defenses. Baffled, he finally sent an emissary with an offer. If the city surrendered, he would swear on the Torah that its people would suffer no physical harm, and that Christians would be free to practice their faith. This proposal divided the defenders; most urged acceptance. How could a Jew renege on such an oath? Harith, however, was adamantly opposed. He simply did not trust the man, he said, and Najran was withstanding the siege. But the old man was talked down, and Dhu Nuwas's army moved in.

The accounts of what followed are so lurid that one nineteenth-century archaeologist dismissed the two definitive sources as pure fiction, although

The ornate adobe Palace of Ibn Madi, at Najran, Saudi Arabia (top). The present picturesque town is built on the ruins of the ancient Christian community put to the sword by the Jewish chieftain, Dhu Nuwas. Najran is located in a fertile valley (above), at the junction of important trade routes, which continue to guarantee its prosperity.

reputable historians had long accepted the record. Twentieth-century textual discoveries have put the massacre beyond all serious doubt, however, actually naming many of the victims. Corroborating inscriptions on stone from the period have also been found. The story, however repulsive, cannot be dismissed.

Dhu Nuwas, according to these sources, ordered the execution of every Christian not prepared to renounce his faith and embrace Judaism. The property of anyone found concealing a Christian was to be confiscated, and his house burned. A cross was thrust into the ground. "Listen to my words," said Dhu Nuwas to the Najranite leaders. "Deny Jesus Christ, the son of Mary, because he was of mankind and a mortal of all men. And spit upon this cross and be Jews with us, and you shall live." Not one man complied, so next day they were all herded into the city's biggest church. Wood was stacked about the walls and set afire. None survived.

A woman who pleaded with Dhu Nuwas for her husband's life was told to recant her faith or join him. She responded by calling him "Satan," and was flung into the fire—but her defiance was a signal that shock and horror had failed to terrify the city into submission. Moreover, the aged Harith had escaped and was still at large, as was his wife Ruhayma. But they were soon captured, along with 340 determined followers. "Spare yourself in your old age," said Dhu Nuwas. "Deny that deceiver and his cross and you shall live."

The measured tones of the old man's reply come through even in translation. He had told his people not to trust Dhu Nuwas, and he had been proven right, he told the conqueror. "Now in my old age you seek to alienate me from Christ my Lord, in whom I have believed from my youth, in whose name I was baptized, whose cross I adore, and for whose sake I die. I am indeed blessed. I have lived a long time in this world through the bounty of Christ my Lord. I have lived happily. I have lacked nothing. Children, grandchildren, lineage, all these things has Christ my Lord given me abundantly. I have been victorious in many battles through the power of his cross. And I am sure that the memory of me will not fail in this city, nor among my family, and I know that I shall not die forever."

With that, Harith urged those around him to follow his example, made the sign of the cross, and submitted himself to his adversary. "Behold," he said, "the moment of eternal life." The furious Dhu Nuwas ordered him stripped naked, and with all his followers, he was marched to a nearby valley, where one by one they were beheaded.

Almost all Najran's leaders were now dead; it remained to dispose of their wives and children. With the men gone, Dhu Nuwas assumed they would be tractable. But the following day, a servant in Harith's household, Mahya by name, appeared

If Najran's women would spit on a crucifix and embrace Judaism, they and their children would be released. Not one complied. 'Forgive us our sins,' they prayed as the killing began.

suddenly in the streets. This woman, whose ill repute included "mannishness" (probably lesbianism), insolence, and flagrant exhibitionism, was universally loathed. Now she unaccountably began, with hitherto unevidenced Christian zeal, to urge further defiance. "Look at that," scoffed Dhu Nuwas's officers. "The Satan of the Christians herself. There's no vice that she hasn't practiced."

"Here I am, butcher," taunted Mahya, "a servant of Harith. And if you think you've defeated him, you're mistaken. After all, you lied in the name of your God. He died for Christ. And if he'd wanted to, he could have swatted you like a fly." Dhu Nuwas ordered her stripped. "What does this mean to me?" sneered Mahya. "I'm not ashamed of this, I've done it many times before both men and women. This is the way God made me." At that, his soldiers tied one of her legs to a donkey, the other to an ox, and beat the animals until they pulled her to pieces. What was left of Mahya they hung head down from a tamarack tree opposite Harith's house, where the archers used it for target practice.

Meanwhile, Dhu Nuwas's senior commander brought together all the women and children of the dead, and likewise challenged the women. If they would spit on the cross and embrace the new state religion, they would be free to go home with their children, and husbands could be found for them from among his troops. But not a single woman complied. So the soldiers were ordered to herd women and children; and archers sent hails of arrows into their midst. "Christ God, come to our help. . . . Forgive us our sins and accept the sacrifice of our lives," they cried as they fell. Any still alive were dispatched with swords.

Ruhayma had been arrested with the other women, but then released on Dhu Nuwas's orders. He now sent word to her that if she recanted her religion and embraced Judaism, her fortune—great in its own right apart from that of her martyred husband—would be preserved, and she could be remarried to a high official of his realm. Instead, she publicly appealed to any other women still alive to follow her example, and spat in Dhu Nuwas's face. So she too was beheaded, along with one of her daughters and a little granddaughter.

For the Christians of Najran it was over, but not for Dhu Nuwas. The treatment accorded Ruhayma, it is said, rapidly caused disaffection and rebellion among his supporters. They taxed him with reminders of Ruhayma's generosity to his father, of her legendary popularity among people of all faiths, and of the fact that she had not even been given decent burial. For this, and probably other reasons as well, dissension soon spread in his army. Much alarmed, he sent a messenger north to the Lakhmid court of Mundhir, urging that he too kill all the Christians in his jurisdiction. The Christian faith, Dhu Nuwas assured him, was obviously perishing.

This proved to be his last miscalculation. Mundhir's best general was a Nestorian Christian, and through the Lakhmid court, the story of the Najran massacre reached Constantinople. A counteroffensive was launched from Ethiopia, in which Dhu Nuwas was killed. The Arab account says he mounted his horse and plunged to his death in the sea. Syrian records say the Ethiopians captured him, took him in a boat, tied heavy pots and crockery around his neck, and dumped him overboard. But of his last stand, or his final words to his followers, nothing is known. With Dhu Nuwas perished the last Jewish state in the Middle East until the founding of Israel more than fourteen hundred years later.[5]

5. Among the first settlers in the state of Israel were one hundred thousand Jews airlifted from the Yemen. Many of them were probably descendants of Dhu Nuwas's Himyarites.

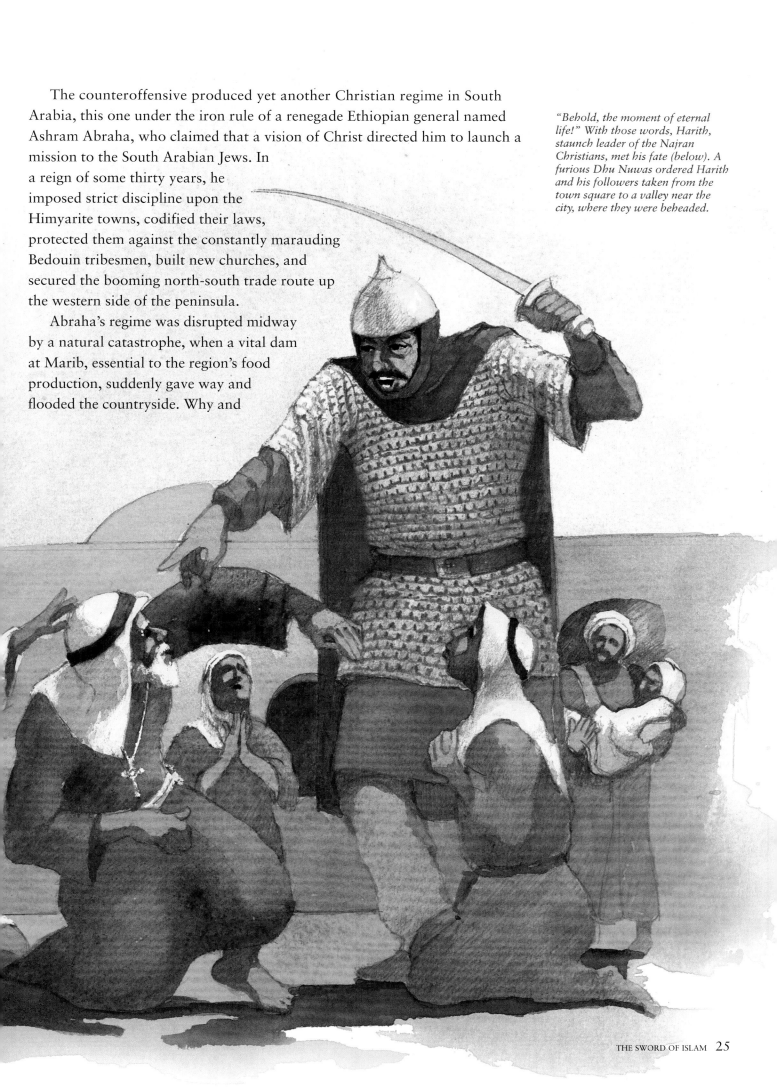

The counteroffensive produced yet another Christian regime in South Arabia, this one under the iron rule of a renegade Ethiopian general named Ashram Abraha, who claimed that a vision of Christ directed him to launch a mission to the South Arabian Jews. In a reign of some thirty years, he imposed strict discipline upon the Himyarite towns, codified their laws, protected them against the constantly marauding Bedouin tribesmen, built new churches, and secured the booming north-south trade route up the western side of the peninsula.

Abraha's regime was disrupted midway by a natural catastrophe, when a vital dam at Marib, essential to the region's food production, suddenly gave way and flooded the countryside. Why and

"Behold, the moment of eternal life!" With those words, Harith, staunch leader of the Najran Christians, met his fate (below). A furious Dhu Nuwas ordered Harith and his followers taken from the town square to a valley near the city, where they were beheaded.

Ruins of the dam at Marib, Yemen (above). A marvel of the ancient world, it was twice the span of the Hoover Dam and provided water for the irrigation of thousands of acres of farmland, supporting a population of fifty thousand. Damage to the dam in 570 was followed by a gradual depopulation of the region.

how it happened is not known, though archaeological evidence of the break is still plain. (Arab legend attributes it to a rat that somehow dislodged a huge stone that fifty men could not have moved.) In a rare instance of cooperation, however, the desert chiefs offered a truce, and worked with Abraha's men to repair the damage.

Abraha unfortunately failed to secure his succession, however, and at his death the country degenerated into lawless disorder. The Persians, invited in by the old party of Dhu Nuwas, overcame what was left of Abraha's army, and South Arabia became an adjunct of the Persian Empire. A thirteen-hundred-year history came to an end.

Neither did Najran ever become the Christian capital envisioned by the valiant Harith. When a subsequent Ethiopian invasion force, again backed by the Byzantine Empire, liberated the city, the people applied to Justinian to send them a bishop. The cleric he sent was a "Melkite" (meaning "a king's man") who opposed the Monophysite church, and thus split the town. Under a later Persian occupation, it eventually settled into Nestorianism.

In the next century, the Muslim caliph Umar would transport most of Najran's Christians to Iraq, where they would establish a town of the same name. Some of their descendants are still there—and still Christian after more than thirteen centuries, in the midst of an Islamic sea. A few somehow hung on in old Najran, which still had a bishop in the ninth century. Today the place is a city of about fifty thousand near the Yemen frontier.[6]

Historians have long pondered the causes of the Christian failure to convert pre-Muslim Arabia. Some point to the grievous theological conflicts that set both Monophysites and Nestorians at odds with Constantinople. Others say that this alone cannot account for the failure. In the north, some have contended, the Bedouin seemed impervious to all proselytizing, and their adherence to Islam would prove as insubstantial as it had been to Christianity.

Again, the Christian monks and hermits of the desert (see sidebar page 18), although they certainly impressed the Arabs, may have discouraged them from deep commitment to the faith by making it seem something that only "holy men" did. Moreover, so many Arabs spoke Aramaic and Syrian that there was no real need to translate the New Testament into Arabic. Hence the Christians could not offer the Arabs their own "holy book," a deficiency Muhammad would notably remedy.

In reality, says historian Richard Bell in *The Origin of Islam in its Christian Environment*, the Christian infusion was largely confined to cosmopolitan cities where the Arabs were one of many resident peoples. In purely Arab centers like Mecca and Medina in the Hijaz, Christianity was the religion of the passerby only. The historian Laurence E. Browne, in *The Eclipse of Christianity in Asia*, quotes at length the disheartened explanation of a sixth-century monk. His colleagues, he notes, perform few cures anymore, maybe because it would reduce the death rate and thereby deprive the kingdom of heaven of too many souls. Neither are Christians any longer interested in making converts, he adds.

John Spencer Trimingham, whose *Christianity Among the Arabs in Pre-Islamic Times* is probably the most thorough twentieth-century work on the subject in English, offers a more complex and somewhat more convincing explanation. For the Aramaic-speaking peoples, he says, religion was essentially something that arose from within the soul of man, not something imposed from without by divine revelation. Christianity assuredly possesses strong elements of both. But as it became dominated by the analytical predilections of the Greeks, Trimingham contends, their insistence upon doctrinal consistency failed to speak convincingly to either nomad or peasant.

Other historians, however, see the Christian failure in Arabia, not so much as a rejection of doctrine as such, but rather as a rejection of the complexities of Trinitarian doctrine. That is, they found the dogma of a single God, rigorously maintained, superior to the dogma of God as three-in-one and Christ as a union of divine and human nature.

Whatever the cause, the result was a void and a hunger in the minds and hearts of many people of Arabia—a void and a hunger that a man named Muhammad would soon arrive to fill. ■

6. Torn throughout its history by inter-tribal strife, Najran was also a center of controversy in the 1960s, when Yemen disputed the 1934 boundary treaty that put it on the Saudi side. Nothing survives of its Christian era—nothing, that is, but the record of its darkest hour, when it was called upon to choose between faith and physical life, and by its response gave testament to the ages to come.

An impressive, multi-story apartment house in San'a, the capital of Yemen (below). The region's distinctive architecture and tall buildings date back to pre-Islamic times, and are unique to this part of southern Arabia.

Ill-tempered and indispensable

The camel provides the desert nomad with wealth, transport, food, fuel, and clothing, all in an irascible package that can go as long as seventeen days without water

The Bedouin conquest of the desert, and for that matter much of the adjacent world, was made possible by the arrival on the Arabian Peninsula about 1100 B.C. of one of nature's most amazing creatures: the camel. Two hundred years later, when the Arabs were already making formidable military use of this creature against the Assyrians, the camel had also enabled them to launch themselves in the trans-desert cartage business, and they had become zealous camel breeders.

Small wonder. The camel's back provided the Arab with his means of transport. Its milk quenched his thirst, and its flesh his appetite. Its droppings fueled his cook fire, and its skin clothed his back. Its urine made, it was widely agreed, an excellent hair tonic, and had other medicinal qualities. Finally, it gave him a medium of exchange. Estates, dowries, gambling debts, fines and compensations were usually calculated in camels, and the number of his camels expressed a man's worth. The noted nineteenth-century desert traveler Charles Montagu Doughty, apparently an early nutritional theorist, concluded it was camel milk that gave the Bedouin his vigorous spirit. What his first drink of it gave Doughty himself was a stomach cramp.

A camel caravan moved at two-and-a-third to three miles an hour, and made twenty-five to thirty miles in a night. The average load was three hundred pounds per animal, though four hundred was common and six hundred was known. Express camels, working in relays and carrying only mail early in the twentieth century, regularly covered the four hundred miles between Basra, Iraq, and Riyadh in Saudi Arabia in three days.

The *Encyclopedia of Islam* notes that a camel can go seventeen days without water in hundred-degree heat, then drink thirty gallons at a time. It can tolerate eleven Fahrenheit degrees above its body temperature without sweating. The female will persist longer than the male without pasture or water; in fact, during the mating season, the males are easily exhausted.

After long, tiring journeys, camels need several months rest, the Bedouin found. On spring pasture, they will go two months without water, deriving moisture from vegetation, and in winter, they can pass a full week waterless without discomfort, even shunning water when they've been without it for four days. When on a long pasture, the Arabs sometimes bind a camel's jaws so it can't overeat, because excessive fat causes the hump to break down, resulting in the animal's death. (Arabian camels are one-humped; the two-humped animal, known as the Bactrian, is found in central Asia.)

On the road, the camel will eat shrubs and bushes that even goats won't touch, and its diet is enriched with crushed date stones. Lady Anne Blunt speaks of camels at Damascus being fed something called *aliek*, a compound of peas and lentils mixed with flour and water and kneaded into egg-shaped balls, six of which constitutes its daily ration. Camels, she noticed, were also especially fond of garbage, which in the city was everywhere abundant.

The camel's bridle consists of a single woollen rope attached by a short chain to a ring in its headstall, which in turn consists of two leather thongs, one around its nose, another passing behind its ears. A rope running from the neck to the leg is used to hobble the animal during stops. Each Bedouin herdsman develops his own song to call his camels when they have joined others at a waterhole, because they tend to become lost in crowds.

They can nevertheless prove highly individualistic, and Lady Anne recalls one as especially single-minded: "He is an artful old wretch, and chose his moment for wandering off whenever we were looking the other way, and wherever a bit of uneven ground favored his escape. Once or twice, he very nearly gave us the slip. He wants to get back to his family, for we bought him out of a herd where he was lord and master, a sultan among camels."

Gradually, the Arabs developed individual breeds of camels. There were heavy transport animals for the

desert caravans, which were changed for sure-footed mountain camels when the caravans passed through the high country. There were fast racing camels used in warfare that could travel 120 miles a day carrying a soldier. The camels of Mecca were smaller and faster. Oman developed a midget camel. South Arabia tended to favor black camels, much despised in the north as ill-behaved and sometimes downright vicious. The northern camels were usually dun-colored. But all prized the occasional pure white she-camel, ridden by the clan chief, perhaps dangerously, since it was highly conspicuous in a raid.

Some six centuries after the camel, another animal appeared in the peninsula that would one day give the Arabs greater international renown than the camel. That was the horse, which the Arabs skillfully bred into the small, fast, intelligent, durable and devoted companion of its owner, which became the world's first recognized breed and bears the proud name Arabian.[1] When the transportation capability of the camel was combined with the speed of the Arabian horse, the Bedouin became a fearsome enemy and a powerful ally.

But the horse was a luxury, and unlike the camel, it played no decisive part in the Arab onslaught that was about to descend upon the world. The Arabs, gratefully aware that they owed their very existence to the desert-crossing animal with the hump, rejoiced to call themselves "the People of the Camel." ■

1. All thoroughbreds are descended from three Arabian stallions: the Byerly Turk, the Darley Arabian, or the Godolphin Barb. They were all imported to England between 1689 and 1729. A son of the Darley Arabian, Bulle Rock, was brought to Virginia in 1730, the first thoroughbred in America.

Notoriously ill-tempered and unsociable (top), the camel became the key to trade and transportation across the deserts of Arabia—and a source of wealth, food, drink, and even hair tonic for the peninsula's inhabitants. It was the humble camel, not the highly prized Arabian horse, that provided the basic mobility of the Muslim armies at the time of Muhammad—as in this rare depiction of a camel-mounted Islamic warrior (above) from the Bibliothèque Nationale, Paris. Among the modern Bedouin, such as these three tribesmen (left) on the Red Sea coast at Neweiba, in Egypt's Sinai Peninsula, the unlovable beast continues to play its traditional, central role in everyday life.

Democrats of the desert

The biggest economic boom the Arabian Peninsula had ever experienced brought the people known as Arabs bursting onto the stage of world affairs

Into affluent sixth-century Constantinople, with its expensive tastes, poured a steady avalanche of Oriental goods. Its host of imperial courtiers were clothed in Chinese silk. The pomp and ritual of its great cathedral and churches required huge quantities of incense and other fine Oriental materials. The wood of the palace's interior walls was impregnated with aloe to afford a pleasant scent for the occupants. Food required rare spices, people rare perfumes. Bribes and gifts to barbarian chieftains required exotic cloth, precious stones, pepper and other products from India.

Early on, these luxuries reached the west via an overland route from the valley of the Indus, through the Khyber Pass, Afghanistan, the Caspian coast and Persia. Then sea routes were developed across the Indian Ocean to the Red Sea and the Greeks built a canal connecting the Red Sea to the Nile, so that waterborne transport could run all the way from China and India to the Mediterranean. However, the Romans neglected the canal because of its high upkeep costs, so that by the fifth century the cargoes were carried only as far as the South Arabian ports, then by caravan northward. This created the biggest economic boom the Arabian Peninsula had ever seen, and in turn brought that strangely fascinating people known as the Arabs bursting irreversibly onto the stage of world affairs.

The Arabs were neither a race nor a nation, however. In fact, the only denominators common among them were a uniform clan and tribal system, and a passionate interest in a certain style of poetry.

The nomads of northern Arabia emerge in English and French as "the Bedouin," from the Arabic word for desert-dweller. Hard, sinewy and lean like the desert itself, they held in the nineteenth and twentieth centuries a peculiar fascination for Europeans, especially Englishmen, and occasionally Englishwomen. The addiction was distinctly upper crust: Thomas Edward Lawrence "of Arabia," who organized a motley Bedouin army against the Turks during the First World War; Sir Harry St. John Philby, who

By the fifth century, the caravan trade from the southern Arabian ports northwards across the desert had created an economic boom. Spices, perfumes, and all manner of Oriental imports were carried in camel trains like this one (below), from a painting by Paul Lazerges.

was the first European to make it across the Empty Quarter east to west, and later became himself a Muslim;[1] Sir John Bagot Glubb, otherwise "Glubb Pasha," who organized the Arab Legion against Germany during the Second World War, and against the Israelis after it, only to be dismissed in 1956, when the Arab forces were purged of British influence; and Lady Anne Noel Blunt, who lived with the Bedouin while searching out Arab living habits to embellish her diary and Arabian horses to improve her stable.

To describe Bedouin life in the early twentieth century is to describe it in the sixth, for it scarcely changed. The nomad still ate, traveled, slept and traded much as he did in the age of the Roman emperors Constantine or Justinian. But Bedouin life does not reach back into antiquity. It probably developed during the first century as a utilitarian means of gaining a livelihood out of the advancing desert. For the Bedouin was not a barbarian. To move herds of sheep, goats and camels to wherever there was moisture enough to water and pasture them required a sophisticated expertise, just as dry-dirt cattle ranching does today.

In winter and spring the Bedouin followed the elusive rainfall, in summer he remained close to the sources of permanent water. Every aspect of his life was fashioned to make such an existence possible. His diet of dates and camel or goat's milk and goat meat was varied in good times with flour from the cultivated areas in South Arabia, or on occasion with the delicacy of locusts baked in salt. What water he found went to the livestock.

His clothing—an undershirt to the knees and a robe to the ankles—hung loose upon him so that the air insulated him against the heat. A shawl wound about his face and tied with a cord to his head shielded eyes against sun—and ears, nose, mouth and eyes against sand and dust. His goat-hair tent was a technological triumph. In summer, its top shaded him from the sun and the sides were raised to admit the cooling breeze. In winter, the sides came down, and when the rare rains descended violently upon it, the loosely woven fibers would rapidly swell and waterproof the dwelling.

The family tent was partitioned, a section for the women and children and one where the family head entertained his male guests. The chief or sheikh had a special tent, a *diwan*, or reception hall, used for tribal business and "occasions of state." All tools and utensils and the tents themselves were portable, with boxes and carrying cases into which everything fit. Rapid mobility was essential.

All of this could work only if the social unit was both cohesive and small. Each tent in a Bedouin camp represented a family unit. Several closely related family units might pasture their flocks together in winter, then join other such groups around an oasis in the summer. All these family groupings together formed the clan, the central factor in Bedouin life.

The clan constituted every Bedouin's society. It provided his means of livelihood; it represented his law and government; it served as his school, private club, labor union, insurance company, and the executor of his estate. The clan also defined the

1. Sir Harry St. John Philby's son, Kim, gained a greater if dubious distinction by converting to Communism during his Cambridge days and later enlisting as a Soviet spy, in which capacity he served diligently while also first secretary of the British Embassy in Washington, with special responsibility for liaison with the CIA. He fled to Russia in 1963 and retired as a general in the KGB.

limits of the *tha'r*, the rule of vendetta that was universal throughout the desert. Murder of a clansman by an outsider demanded money or blood, and the resulting feud might go on for half a century.

The chief or *sayyid* of the clan was chosen at a meeting of all the members, at which anyone could speak and everyone held a veto. He came, however, from what was regarded as the clan's noblest family, and was picked for his ability, generosity, affluence, eloquence and sense of justice. His term of office lasted as long as he could demonstrate these qualities, and no longer. Other clan members addressed him as an equal. "There is no king on the desert," the saying went. "The Bedouin," says the historian Philip K. Hitti in his classic *History of the Arabs*, "is a born democrat."

The chief could make treaties on behalf of the clan, ransom members made prisoner, and settle internal disputes. He must care for the clan's poor, and he could claim one-fourth of anything won in the Bedouin national sport, *razzia*, raiding other clans and robbing them, if possible without loss of life. Few relished the inescapable tha'r if a life were claimed. Finally, a powerful chief could pledge his protection to an individual, or a weaker clan, or—for a price—to a caravan passing through his territory. Such a pledge was expensive, inviolate, and consistently fulfilled.

The clans banded together into tribes that, nominally anyway, claimed one common ancestor, as often did the individual clan. Thus the word *banu* (sons of) might designate a tribe or a clan. The clans in the great Banu Ghassan, the Christian allies of Constantinople, considered themselves descendants of Ghassan. The tribes, in turn, often combined for purposes of war or diplomacy into confederacies. But these were ephemeral, and frequently dissolved or regrouped in new ways. Even the tribes would split when they became too large, or ally themselves to other tribes when they became weak. What did not change was the clan, and Sir William Muir, whose definitive nineteenth-century biography of Muhammad was the first in the English language and remains unsurpassed, noted that the same clan groups that lived around Mecca in Muhammad's day were still there twelve hundred years later.[2]

Crimes within the clan might be punished by the loss of a hand or even execution. But the clan's greatest power over the individual lay in its ability to expel him. In the desert, where any stranger was an enemy, such a prospect was unthinkable. The ostracized Bedouin lived alone. His family rejected him. Every hand was turned against him. Other clans, regarding him as flawed, would not take him in. Death by starvation or thirst was slow and almost inevitable. Expulsion therefore was rare, and social individualism was virtually non-existent.

Though democrats, the Bedouin

> *Poetry was a mystical, supernatural thing, one of the few bonds between all Arabs.*

2. Sir William Muir (1819–1905) was a pioneer Arabic scholar in the west, and made a careful study of the history of Muhammad he called *The Life of Mohammed From Original Sources*. Two other Muir books cover the early caliphate. In 1837, he entered the Bengal Civil Service, rising in 1868 to become lieutenant governor of the North-West Provinces of British India. It was chiefly through his exertions that the central college at Allahabad, known as Muir's College, was built and endowed. In 1885, he was elected principal of Edinburgh University and held the post until 1903, when he retired.

were also socially stratified. Many had slaves they had captured through raiding. And running within the system, then and now, were the equivalent of the Hindu castes. Some families were permanently laborers, some blacksmiths, some shepherds. Others, known as the "noble" Bedouin, disdained menial work and confined themselves to riding the camels, herding the livestock, plotting the raids and leading the frequent battles over grazing grounds. To take a wife above one's social status invited reprisals from her family. To marry beneath one's station was to risk expulsion from your own.[3]

The term *Arab*, probably deriving from an Arabic word meaning "nomad," in the sixth century designated the six million or so inhabitants of the vast peninsula that lies between the Red Sea, the Indian Ocean and the Persian Gulf, along with those in and around the arid tongue of the Syro-Mesopotamian Desert that reaches out of the peninsula to the north.[4] The peninsula, a quarter the area of Europe and a third of the continental United States, was regarded as (and in the main still is) an arid, riverless, harborless, treeless, trackless waste—until the twentieth century, that is, when the "waste" was discovered to be accommodating the world's largest and most easily productive oil reserves.

Oil or no oil, however, some parts of it can go rainless for ten years at a time. When the rain does come, it often deluges the dried riverbeds called *wadis* in torrential flash floods. Long before it can reach the sea, the water vanishes into the ground, where the inhabitants sink wells, five hundred feet deep or more, to find it. Occasionally, it springs to the surface in an oasis, around which grow settlements, towns and a hundred varieties of date palm, whose fruit, along with camel milk, was until recent times the almost total diet of most inhabitants.

Within this million-square-mile landmass, several features distinguish themselves. In the north spreads the

3. Anthony Nutting, in his 1964 history *The Arabs*, cites the case of a governor of Baghdad who was shot dead in 1932 by the noble relatives of a girl whom the governor, a member of a lesser tribe, had taken as his wife.

4. Muhammad applied the word "Arab" only to the nomads of the peninsula, not the town-dwellers. Today, the word Arab has a broader meaning, and is usually applied to the people of the peninsula, plus those of Iraq, Syria, Lebanon, Transjordan, Egypt and the states of North Africa. Though there are Christian Arabs, nearly all are Muslim.

Great Nefud, a forty-thousand-square-mile tract of reddish-white sand, which infrequent winter rains sometimes turn green with a thin carpet of grass, a joy and a bonanza for the nomads who eke a pastoral living out of it. Spreading south from the Nefud and then sprawling east and west lies the "Empty Quarter," the largest continuous body of sand in the world, where winds can sweep the dunes to the height of a forty-story building, sometimes three to four miles in length.

To the south, conditions ease. Oman, guarding the peninsula's southeast corner, gets rain enough to support rice agriculture. The topsoil of Hadramawt along the south coast produces a dependable crop. Near the southwest corner, a very different world appears. The high mountains of Yemen

The hard life of the desert nomad changed little from pre-Islamic times until recent decades. In this photograph (below), taken early in the last century, a group of nomadic women and children are preparing food in front of a traditional Bedouin tent, its flaps opened to permit the entry of any passing breeze.

are lush with rich foliage, the valleys thick with livestock. Yet it is in the west that history unfolds. Ridge upon ridge of gloomy sandstone and porphyritic mountains line the Red Sea coast. In the flinty valleys between them lies the long strip called the Hijaz, where nestles Mecca, transfer point for all northbound caravans, and in the sixth century, foremost beneficiary of the new boom. Here Muhammad was born and here too would lie, for centuries to come, the heart place of the faith known as Islam.

The Arabs were Semites, a term used to distinguish the ancient Babylonians, Assyrians, Aramaeans, Chaldeans, Phoenicians, Amorites, Abyssinians, Arabs and Hebrews, all of whom appear to share a common root language. The Arabs, says the historian

Hitti, preserve more of the original Semitic features than do the Jews. Biblically, they are viewed as the descendants of Shem, one of the three sons of Noah. Long before Muhammad, the Arabs considered themselves cousins of the Jews. The latter, they said, descended from Abraham via his wife Sarah and their son Isaac, they from Abraham via the handmaid Hagar and their son Ishmael. Hence in the Old Testament, the Arabs appear as Ishmaelites.[5]

To the Romans, the Arabs were *Saraceni* and to the Greeks *Sarakenoi*, possibly derived from the Greek corruption of an Arabic word meaning "east," hence the English synonym for Arab, "Saracen." Throughout their history, they moved northward in waves from the peninsula into the fringes of the settled regions of Egypt, Palestine, Syria, and Mesopotamia, where they preyed upon the townspeople and farmers, eventually supplanting them to become townspeople and farmers themselves. Here they became bilingual, learning the Aramaic language that from 1200 B.C. on had been the common parlance of farmers and townsmen alike throughout Syria and Mesopotamia. But they retained their Arabic as well, no great difficulty since the two languages are much the same.[6]

From its desert origins, Arabic emerged as a language rich with subtlety and gradations of meaning. Its lilting cadences made it a superb medium for lyrical verse, and it sounds better recited than spoken. Its ancient poetry was preserved solely by recitation. It revels in war, in the thrill of stalking an unsuspecting enemy,

bursting in upon him to steal his livestock, women, and children, and then vanishing without trace into the trackless sands. It relishes alike the insufferable heat of the sun and the tranquil cool beneath the moon. Beyond being a warrior, a great man must also be an orator and a lavishly generous host. Woman, though man's chattel, is celebrated as his companion and business partner. The poet was more than an entertainer. He was a tribal functionary. His verse must raise the tribe's spirits and utterly dishearten the enemy. There were single-combat contests between poets, just as between warriors. To the Arab, whether townsman or Bedouin, poetry was a mystical, supernatural thing, a common bond among all Arabs.

The distinction between town-Arab and nomad was not sharp. Some bands lived in the towns during one season, on the desert in another. Many eventually abandoned the desert permanently, retaining, however, their Arab names and genealogy, their family law and customs, and their language. Having settled in the towns, they might become farmers or traders, financing and organizing trans-desert caravans of merchandise. In all these pursuits, their worst problem was those Arabs who remained nomadic. The nomads needed the products of the towns, and acquired them either by raiding and stealing them, or by contract in exchange for "protection"—protection, that is, from yet other desert raiders. The arrangement sometimes reduced the townspeople to virtual bondage to the nomads whom the townspeople sometimes despised as wanton

5. Some Arab historians say that Arabism pre-dates Abraham, that Abraham himself was a typical Arab tribal leader or sheikh, that the girl whose beauty is celebrated in the Song of Solomon is unquestionably Arab, and that the biblical accounts of Job in fact describe an Arab sheikh, not a Jew, whose home was North Arabia.

6. The Aramaeans, another Semitic people, dominated the region from their capital at Damascus, Syria, until the ninth century B.C. when they were overthrown by the Assyrians. Their language, however, survived for about eighteen hundred years as the universal linguistic vehicle of the Middle East. It was the language of Galilee and of Jesus Christ. While Hellenistic Greek, spoken in the west, was the medium in which the New Testament was written, a version of Aramaic, called Syriac, became the language of Christians in the east. The Syriac Scriptures, however, were translated from the Greek. There is no reliable record of Syriac writings derived directly from Jesus' own Aramaic teachings.

An imposing Syrian Bedouin herdsman (above). The historian Ammianus Marcellinus compared the desert Arabs to birds of prey, striking suddenly and disappearing quickly.

barbarians. To the macho desert people, on the other hand, the townsmen were mere wimps who had rejected manliness, the prized virtue of the nomad.

The only way to stop the incessant raids on the communities along the edges of the desert was to bribe the tribes who were doing it, and to use them instead to fight off others who wanted to do it. Therefore, both of the great ancient empires established protective spheres of influence beyond their frontiers, the Roman embracing the hinterlands of Syria, Palestine and Egypt, the Persian the western borderlands of Mesopotamia, plus Bahrain and Oman down the peninsula's east coast. Within these, each empire established client kingdoms and tribal federations, bestowing upon their chiefs the imperial authority and (in the case of the Romans) the title *phylarch*. In exchange for an annual subsidy, the phylarchs, when called upon, reinforced the Roman army with cavalry and camel units.

The Arabs, both within the cities and without, called themselves "the People of the Camel," and only one other word in their language had more synonyms and derivatives than the thousand that applied to the camel. That was the word for sword. The Bedouin slept by his sword, and often uneasily, for all his kin and property were at the constant risk of a raid by another clan. If he did not lie awake worrying about who might attack him, he lay scheming about whom he himself might attack.

This was razzia, which Hitti describes as the Arabs' "chronic

mental condition." It was as old, or older, than Bedouin life. The geographer Strabo observed in the first century B.C., "Every Arab is a tradesman and a robber." The Syrian historian Ammianus Marcellinus compared the Saraceni to birds of prey. "Whenever they have caught sight of any prey from on high, they seize it with a swift swoop and directly make off." He observes that they are usually leaderless; that they ride their swift horses or slender camels half-nude, clad only to the loins, that no farmer between the Tigris and the Nile was safe from them, and that they are "without homes, without fixed abodes, and without law."

St. Jerome recalls the chagrin of a monk who told him of a party of men, women, and children on a public highway between Syria and Mesopotamia that crossed through the desert. "Suddenly these Ishmaelites," said the monk, "riding upon horses and camels, descended upon us in a startling attack, with their long hair flying from under their headbands. They wore cloaks over their half-naked bodies, and broad boots. Quivers hung from their shoulders; their unstrung bows dangled at their sides; they carried long spears. They had come not for battle but for plunder. We were seized, scattered

and carried off in different directions." The monk subsequently escaped. Others would have been sold back to their families, or on the open slave market.

Razzia, however, was more than mere sport. Even the scant rain that the desert expected would often fail, and the dilemma facing the Bedouin was to either steal or starve. They chose the former, and by the sixth century, though few realized it, their lifestyle had made the Arab nomads the most dangerous assault troops in the world.

To both the Romans and Greeks, they were an object of contempt. The Byzantine Romans, who distrusted all tradesmen, especially distrusted Arabs, and very especially Bedouin, whom they regarded as cynical, materialistic, avaricious to the point of addiction, insubordinate, lawless, and particularly treacherous to any who had been fool enough to befriend them. Though they could rarely satiate it, their appetite for food, wine and women was voracious, even gluttonous, as events were soon to prove.

It was untrue, however, that they lacked scruples. Their greatest enemy was nature itself, and a man caught on the desert without water and food could count on their boundless hospitality. The young lad who was expelled by his father for slaughtering the family's only three camels to feed some starving wayfarers is a hero in Arab poetry. (He was, as it happens, a Christian.) Guarantees of protection were rigidly observed, and the

A group of Bedouin men in a photograph taken in the 1870s (below). The tightly knit clan was the heart of traditional Bedouin society. It provided security and organization, and served as a club, school, and labor union for these fiercely independent "democrats of the desert."

Bedouin's courage and readiness to die for the honor of the clan was instant.

The role of women in pre-Islamic Arabia is a subject of confusion and dispute. Some early tribes were undoubtedly matrilineal. A woman would spend a few days with her husband if he happened to be camped nearby, but would raise her children in her own family group. Whether she could have more than one husband is not clear, but divorce was easy, and some women over time certainly had several husbands. In the towns, prior to Islam, women led an active business life, some of them financing and organizing caravans just as men did. At the same time, female infanticide also seems to have been practiced, because the Qur'an had to prohibit it specifically. Men certainly had numerous wives, and on the death of the father, the eldest son added all his father's wives to his own.

Bedouin morality did not arise out of religion. Here the Bedouin has always been a skeptic. He embraced, if it served his purposes, Christianity, then—with some notable exceptions—paid it little real heed. When Islam came, he did the same. Though Allah entered into his poetry, it was always obliquely, referring to what religious people did, rather than enjoining religion upon the hearer.

Even before Muhammad, the Bedouin had words, it is true, that meant "prayer," and "worship," and "ascribe glory to," but their gods mostly derived from

nature. And their worship of the sun, moon, trees and stones consisted of appeals for natural benefits and for propitiation against natural disaster. Since surviving each day wholly preoccupied them, they had no time for philosophic speculation. Their ultimate realities were birth, marriage, food, rain, death, goats, sheep and camels. Their poetry contemplated fate, usually as a dismal observation of its injustice.

The Bedouin, however fearsome, were necessary to both the Romans and Persians. For one thing, only they could run the trans-desert caravans. They knew the trails and the watering places, and how to avoid trouble. For another, they could not be controlled. Their homeland, the desert, proved unassailable. Caesar Augustus's efforts to invade the peninsula with ten thousand men down the Red Sea coast at the time of Christ had proved such a serial calamity of disease, hunger, toil, treachery and death that no one tried it again for more than five hundred years. ■

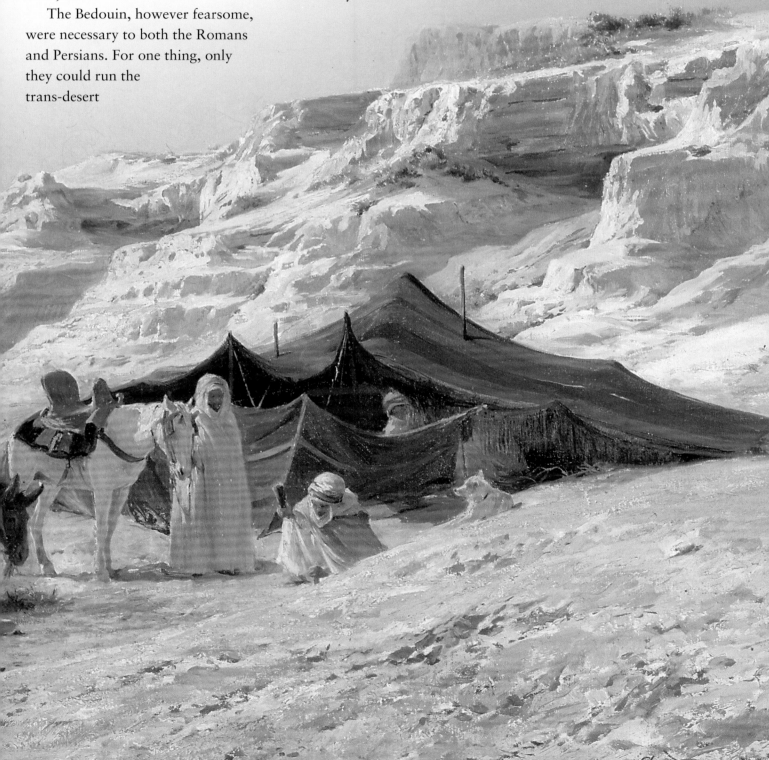

A Bedouin encampment in the lee of a desert outcrop (below), from a painting by Eugene Girardet. Survival in the harsh desert environment was the constant preoccupation of the nomad, but the Bedouin's arid homeland also proved an insurmountable obstacle to invasion and control by the great powers of the pre-Islamic Middle East.

Abraham is revered by Muslims, Christians and Jews alike as the father of monotheism. He left his native city of Ur in Mesopotamia after rejecting his people's polytheistic practices, and eventually settled in Egypt. He is said to have banished a handmaid, Hagar, and their son, Ishmael (seen here in a painting by Giovanni Francesco Guercino), to a desolate valley in Arabia, trusting in God's promise to care for them. The valley became the site of Mecca, and Ishmael the father of the Arabs.

CHAPTER 2

Ishmael's well becomes the birthplace of Islam

From Mecca, a dusty town jammed between flinty hills, emerges the single-minded prophet of a militant faith

In or about the year 570, the Christian ruler of Yemen launched an offensive against Mecca. His soldiers seized the camels pastured outside the town, and ordered the city to surrender. They meant no injury to anyone, said their commander—only to destroy the strange little box-like building called the *Ka'ba*, which drew thousands of Arab pilgrims each year to sexual and other degenerate rites characteristic of some pagan worship. A dignified elderly man delivered Meccans' response. They would pay a third of all their camels, he said, but they would not surrender the Ka'ba. He was courteously received, but his terms were refused. He returned to the town to prepare for the attack, pausing before the Ka'ba to pray: "Defend, O Lord, thy house, and suffer not the cross to triumph over the Ka'ba."

That night, so the story goes, sickness broke out among the Christian forces, probably smallpox, and they withdrew in disorder. Some died by the wayside, covered with sores, their commander among them. Others were swept away by an equally fortuitous flood. Their fate figures prominently in Islamic folklore, as having miraculously saved Mecca from Christianity. Moreover, in Muslim tradition, the old man who spoke for Mecca was to be blessed again, perhaps in that very year, with the birth of a grandson, a boy they named Muhammad.[1]

1. The year of Muhammad's birth is not precisely known. The historian Maxime Rodinson says it must have occurred between 567 and 573. Arab tradition assigns it to the "Year of the Elephant," i.e., 570 or 571.

Whatever moved the Christians to attack Mecca, it could hardly have been the town's beauty. It lies in one of the flinty valleys that crease the mountain range along Arabia's Red Sea coast, the sunbaked rock of its flanking hills sharp with jagged granite and quartz. The windblown dust of spring, summer and fall is relieved only by December rains that can create torrential floods, leaving a residue of slime, animal corpses and disease.

In the sixth century, the crescent-shaped city itself, crowded between the hills, was as ugly as its environs, with buildings wedged so close together that from a distance they seemed one large mass. The poor lived in hovels or caves on the outskirts. Most Meccans were artisans (carpenters, veterinarians, butchers, blacksmiths) and most shared a common proclivity. From poorest to richest, they gambled: on the success of the caravans, on crops two years before they were planted, on camel prices, on exchange rates, on the outcome of tribal conflicts, on the weather.

If speculation was Mecca's civic sport, commerce was its soul. Himyarite caravans brought goods from South Arabian ports for shipment north, making it a boomtown. Caravan profits soared, with leading families, all bankers, charging up to four-hundred-percent interest. The poor rushed to borrow, pledging even

Rich or poor, most Meccans gambled on the success of caravans, on crops two years before they were planted, on camel prices, on exchange rates, on tribal conflicts and the weather.

their freedom as collateral, while poets extolled the exhilarating joy of making money. Caravan investors could afford to hire dependable mercenary protection against the constantly marauding Bedouin, effectively reducing once fearsome tribesmen into hirelings. Thus Meccan grandees would make frequent and profitable excursions to the vast market outside the town, where a polyglot humanity of bawling hawkers clawed out a living by peddling weapons, clothing, camels, jewelry and secondhand goods—anything that would sell. They included refugees, tribal renegades, hooligans, hit men, thieves, prostitutes, Byzantine and Persian commercial agents, spies, slave traders and Christian missionary monks, all talking an Arabic diluted by a dozen other tongues.

The caravan industry remained elaborate, risky, but exceedingly lucrative. Guards and drivers had to be carefully selected, and skilled leaders to pilot them through the hordes of desert cutthroats, legal and otherwise. Any tribe along the way had to be paid a steep levy. At the Roman frontier there were heavy customs duties, with fines or whipping for smugglers. Successful caravan masters became civic heroes. At Palmyra, 125 miles northeast of Damascus in the Syrian Desert, archaeologists have found more statues of caravan leaders than of poets or generals. But women ran businesses too. Muhammad's first wife financed and organized caravans; another dealt in slaves. The wife of a rival ran a big jewelry business. The pre-Islamic Arab woman could be, in short, very active in the world.

The Jesuit historian Henri Lammens surmises that Mecca was a "merchant republic" governed by an oligarchy of clan chiefs, the big financiers who sat as a senate or council. But the new wealth, he says, corrupted age-old desert values. Honor no longer mattered as much as advantage, or family as much as profit, which created a social disruption ignored by the "upwardly mobile." Widows and orphans were left destitute. The proud tribesmen of the desert, who although they didn't yet know it were among the world's best soldiers, became enslaved by debt to their prosperous town cousins. The kindling, in other words, lay dry. All that was required was the spark—and that would be provided by the boy born in this seething commercial town about 570: Muhammad.

The Mecca in which Muhammad grew up was also in the business of religion. People worshiped sun, moon, stars and other gods, usually embodied in idols. They feared the *jinn* or *genii*, wild spirit-creatures considered evil. Allah, a kind of general-manager god whose name appears in inscriptions five centuries before Islam, was also widely recognized, although not the object of worship. And to Mecca's Ka'ba, Arabs traveled each year by the thousands.

According to Islamic tradition, the angel Gabriel answered Hagar's prayers by opening a gushing spring at the feet of her son, Ishmael. The spring, known as Zam Zam, became the water source upon which Mecca's prosperity was founded. It runs to this day.

In Muslim story, this curious little structure goes back to Abraham, patriarch of the Jews through his wife Sarah, and of the Arabs through the handmaiden Hagar. The exiled Hagar is said to have crossed the blazing sands, with her little son Ishmael, to an arid valley. Gasping for water, she set the child down and rushed frantically back and forth in search of a spring. Meanwhile Ishmael, thrashing in the sand, liberated a fountain of clear, sweet water. He had found Zam Zam, the spring that created the oasis around which Mecca would rise, and there Abraham built the Ka'ba.

Thus the legend. The sacred "Black Stone," probably a meteorite, was set into its wall. Around it were at least three female goddesses: al-Uzza, a sex goddess to whom human sacrifices were sometimes made; al-Lat, the sun goddess; and al-Manat, goddess of fate or doom. Associated with them was Hubal, an idol in the form of a human male. Some wall paintings reputedly depicted Mary and Joseph, suggesting that the place may once have been a church. Cleansed by Muhammad of its pagan past, this building would become Islam's central shrine.

The Ka'ba proved peculiarly vulnerable to the forces of nature however. For many centuries, a fifteen-minute downpour could flood the place; pilgrims sometimes had to swim for their lives. Hence it frequently had to be rebuilt, once during Muhammad's lifetime; the present structure dates from the seventeenth century. And even before Muhammad's day the well Zam Zam had either dried up or caved in. But still the pilgrims came, to enact a ritual so old that no one knew (or knows) its origins.

About the sixth day of the pilgrimage, the devout Arab donned the prescribed holy garment, then entered the Ka'ba and kissed the sacred Black Stone. Next he made seven circuits around the Ka'ba while other devotees clapped and sang, and then hastened back and forth seven times between two hills, Safa and Merwa, representing Hagar's desperate search. As an act of purification, he shaved his head and pared his nails. Finally, he journeyed twelve miles to another hill, Arafat, and returned by the Mina Valley, where he collected pebbles. These he cast at various designated objects, in a symbolic "stoning of the devil." The entire procedure was to be adopted as Islam's most sacred rite.

Arab tradition says that when Ishmael was about thirteen years old, he and his father, Abraham, constructed the Ka'ba (below), as a place of worship. Muhammad would declare it Islam's holy of holies.

Custodians of the Ka'ba at that time were the Banu Quraysh—shepherds, robbers and caravanners from the north country. An adventurous Quraysh chief, a certain Kosai, came south and conquered Mecca around 400. He built a council house beside the Ka'ba, and corrected certain defects in the old Arab calendar to stabilize the pilgrimage season. This made the food concessions, which he controlled, more manageable. Kosai was Muhammad's great-great-great-grandfather.

Some Quraysh continued to live as Bedouin, ranging the desert and preserving their old ways and virtues. The town-dwelling Quraysh bankers and merchants became so prosperous, however, that hardworking farmers of the Medina district, north of Mecca, regarded them as kings. The word *Quraysh* meant "shark," and from their arrival in Mecca, they had a well-deserved reputation for supple-minded decisiveness. Under Muhammad, they would emerge from this narrow background to conquer and govern much of the known world.

Kosai's descendants did not always get along amicably, of course. A dispute between two of his sons over the food concession was settled only at the last minute, with both families lined up for battle. Another family quarrel would never be settled—and would have momentous consequences. A rich and philanthropic grandson, Hashem, made the pilgrimage into a grandiose event, lavishing food upon the pilgrims and building water cisterns on their route. This gained Hashem wide admiration, but angry resentment from his nephew Umayya. Enduring conflict between the Hashemite and Umayyad factions would divide the Islamic movement at a critical point, saving Europe and Christianity. It still divides Islam today.

Late in life, Hashem beheld at a Medina trade fair an elegant merchant woman named Selma, graceful, wealthy and divorced. Wholly smitten, he married her. The child of this union, Abbas ibn Abdul Muttalib, disinherited through another family wrangle, was left impoverished, until through diligence or good fortune he made an amazing discovery. He uncovered the old well Zam Zam, still flowing with

Enduring conflict between the Hashemite and Umayyad Arabs would divide the Islamic movement at a critical point, thereby saving Europe and Christianity.

abundant sweet water, and largely on this account became in time Mecca's chieftain. It was he, Muhammad's grandfather, who confronted the invading Christian army.

The Christian invasion was not the only crisis in Abbas ibn Abdul Muttalib's life. In the despair of his early poverty, he had vowed that if the gods gave him ten sons he would offer one as a sacrifice. After his tenth son was born, he evaded the pledge for years until, stricken by conscience and full of grief, he led his ten sons into the Ka'ba and drew lots to determine which should die. It fell upon the youngest, Abdallah.

His daughters pleaded with him to spare their brother, so he picked out ten camels, and again drew lots: the camels or the baby? Again the lot fell on little Abdallah. In vain, Abbas ibn Abdul Muttalib offered ten more. Not until the ante stood at one hundred camels did the lot finally fall upon them instead. Gratefully, the old man sacrificed the camels, and Abdallah was saved. He would one day father Muhammad, although he did not live to see his son's birth. Illness claimed him at age twenty-four, and when his widow presented the baby to her father-in-law, the old man carried the infant into the Ka'ba and named him Muhammad. Rarely heard then, the name has since been conferred upon hundreds of millions of baby boys.[2]

The infant Muhammad was placed in the care of a poor Bedouin wet nurse whose family fortunes, say the traditions, immediately and amazingly improved. Their sheep grew plump, and their barren camels burst with milk, as did the woman herself. "By God," declared her husband, "you've taken on a blessed

2. Within a generation of Muhammad, so many Muslim boys had been given the name Muhammad that the caliph Umar tried to prohibit its use in order to preserve respect for it. In Arabic, the name "Ahmed" translates as "praised one," prompting Muslims to conclude that Christ, when he promised the coming of the Paraclete (John 14:16, 14:26, 15:26, 16:7), was prophesying the coming of Muhammad.

creature." The blessed creature grew up active and robust, although twice he suffered alarming seizures (prompting skeptics to dismiss his future moments of visionary ecstasy as epileptic fits). At six he was returned to his mother, who soon after fell ill and died. Some fifty years later, her son, ruler of most of Arabia, would weep bitterly over her grave.

Now Muhammad was entrusted to his doting eighty-year-old grandfather, and after his death to the poorest but most beloved of his uncles, Abu Talib, working for a time as a shepherd. Later, as a youth in booming Mecca, he observed the decline of ancient Arab propriety, particularly in the shameless profiteering of the Quraysh who managed the Ka'ba. They were forcing poor pilgrims to eat only expensive food supplied by them, and for the ceremonial circling either to purchase a pricey ritual garment or wear no clothes at all. Appalled at the spectacle of penniless women performing the ritual naked, Muhammad vowed that he would one day ban this practice. Another such was female infanticide.

Meanwhile, the fortunes of the Hashemite branch of Muhammad's family had steadily declined in favor of the rival Umayyads. He himself was too poor to

Appalled at poor women having to dance the Ka'ba rituals naked, young Muhammad vowed to ban the practice of forcing pilgrims to buy food and religious garments at inflated prices.

marry, until he caught the eye of the twice-widowed Khadeja, forty years old, wellborn, dignified and rich. Owner of a flourishing caravan business, she hired him at double the usual pay. Then, after he eminently succeeded with his first caravan, she made a marriage offer through an intermediary, to which Muhammad enthusiastically assented.

Their marriage was blissful and fruitful. In Muslim tradition, Khadeja, despite her age, bore him two sons and four daughters. Though the sons did not survive, the daughters did; the fourth, Fatima, would provide the name and credentials for one of the great Muslim dynasties. Moreover, Khadeja became Muhammad's confidant, counsel and devoted supporter.

Together they adopted Ali, son of Uncle Abu Talib, who was too poor to support him. Ali's descendants would form another dynastic empire. And upon Muhammad Khadeja also conferred the slave Zayd, captured from Christian Arabs and eventually traced to Mecca by his grieving father. Muhammad, ever generous, freed Zayd, who chose to remain as his secretary. Zayd's loyalty to his erstwhile owner would carry him eventually to a heroic death.

Muhammad always regarded his days with Khadeja as the happiest of his life, and during her lifetime married no other woman. Afterward, when he had ten wives, and according to some Muslim historians, several concubines, her memory would still haunt him. The fiery A'isha, favored of all his harem, once screamed at him: "Why do you always have to be remembering that toothless old Qurayshite with her red mouth?"

Meanwhile, his biographers write, Muhammad was earning distinction in the community. When he was about thirty-five, for instance, seasonal flooding had left the Ka'ba an open ruin and a haunt of thieves. The Quraysh, having rebuilt it, began disputing which of their four clans should have the honor of reinstalling the sacred Black Stone. Deadlocked, they agreed it should go to the next man who entered the building.

This was Muhammad, who diplomatically decided to lay the stone on a blanket and have the chief of each clan take a corner and lift it, while he himself pushed it into position. Later on, the Ka'ba was significantly improved. Its walls were raised, the idol Hubal presided in the center, and a sacred precinct was defined around it as a "place of prostration" (*mosque* in Arabic).

But in the following five years, Muhammad's hitherto conventional life took a strange turn. He began making long sojourns in the hills, sometimes accompanied by Khadeja, but usually alone. Often he was gone for days, dwelling in particular at a cave on Mount Hira, a cone-shaped hill less than a mile from town.[3] He became, like John the Baptist, possessed of the grim conviction that mankind was doomed because of its rejection of goodness and of God. Some of these reflections survive as the earliest *sura* (chapters) of the Qur'an. Man is "in the way of ruin" (Sura 103:2). The "wrath is kindled" against "those that walk in error" (Sura 92:14–16). "They that deny our signs . . . around them shall the fire come" (Sura 90:19–20).

During one such sojourn, there occurred an event of catastrophic impact. He suddenly became aware, say the biographers, of an alarming presence. The fifty-third sura describes "one terrible in power" that "drew near and suspended, two bows' lengths away, or nearer." Muhammad concluded that this must be Gabriel, God's courier angel. Gabriel delivered to him again and again three Arabic words destined to change his life, and that of much of the world. English requires six words to translate them: "Thou art the Messenger of God." From that time forth, Muhammad saw the Almighty as the source of his thoughts, and himself as uniquely entrusted to convey them to men:

> Say: O men, I am the Messenger of Allah to you all, from him who rules over earth and sky. There is no God but he. He ordains life and death. Believe in Allah and in his Messenger, the unlettered Prophet (Sura 7:158).

In this Persian manuscript illumination (above) from the Bibliothèque Nationale, Paris, Muhammad, astride a camel, bids farewell to his fiancée, the influential and wealthy businesswoman, Khadeja.

3. The Swiss adventurer John Lewis Burckhardt (1784–1817), who explored the Mecca country in the guise of an "Egyptian gentleman" twelve hundred years after Muhammad, described a "small cavern" in the red granite rock of Hira where Muhammad is believed to have meditated. A little above it is a cleft in the rock, about the size of a man, where he is said to have "stretched himself out" and implored the help of God against his many foes in the town below.

The experience is said to have reduced Muhammad to trembling incoherence. Was it really Gabriel? he wondered. Or could it be one of the notorious jinn, the evil spirits who haunted the outskirts of heaven trying to pick up gossip with which to work mischief?

The Muslim historians Ibn Hisham and al-Tabari say this fear that his vision was diabolically inspired drove Muhammad to the brink of suicide, but when he resolved to hurl himself off a cliff, Gabriel reappeared to stop him. Thereafter, the visions became less onerous for Muhammad. Within ten or so years he would experience them almost routinely, full of directions on the day-to-day problems of municipal administration.

Whatever the explanation for his visions, their credibility within Muhammad's immediate family was unquestioned. Khadeja became a believer from the start, and therefore the first Muslim. She was closely followed by their son, Ali, then about thirteen, and Muhammad's secretary Zayd. His cherished uncle Abu Talib never did accept Islam, but he did extend to the fledgling cult the crucial protection of the Hashemite branch of the family.

Muhammad's first approach beyond his family was to Abu Bakr, a merchant two years his junior, whose mild nature concealed an iron determination and unwavering fidelity, which in a dark hour many years later would save Islam. Abu Bakr, respected everywhere, brought the movement a new credibility, and his fortune of forty thousand silver pieces. He also attracted several distinguished converts, including Uthman, who was regarded in Mecca as a kind of seer.[4] Soon the group consisted of thirteen men and twenty wives and children. The terms were elementary then as now. The convert must recognize that God is One and that Muhammad speaks for him. In accepting this, the convert surrenders himself to the Almighty. The word for such a surrender is "Islam."

In the sixth year (615), there came two more key converts. One was another of Muhammad's uncles, Hamza, who was poor, quick-tempered, and fond of strong drink, but well known and respected, chiefly for his huge size. His subsequent bravery in Islam's early battles would earn him the title "Lion of God."

More significant still was the other convert, whose contribution would be second only to that of Muhammad himself, and whose conversion story is part of Islamic lore. Umar ibn al-Khattab was, like Hamza, an enormous and impetuous man, but far more disciplined. A resolute opponent of the Muslims, he was appalled to learn that his own sister and brother-in-law had converted. Descending in fury upon their home, he overheard them reciting verses from the Qur'an. While the brother-in-law fled, Umar smacked his sister in the face. Although bleeding profusely, she defiantly confessed her new religion.

Muhammad's experience in the cave at Hira outside Mecca (pictured below in a nineteenth-century engraving) changed his life and that of much of the world.

The tradition continues: Angrily Umar took up the text. His eyes widened. His hands gripped it. He read intensely, utterly engrossed. His brother-in-law then cautiously emerged, stammering that only yesterday Muhammad had prayed for Umar's conversion. (The problem with this account is, of course, that the Qur'an, as such, did not yet exist. The sura, however, were often memorized or recorded by the faithful before the book was compiled.)

Without a word, Umar strode out the door and marched, sword at his side, to the Prophet's house. Muhammad greeted him kindly, put his hand on Umar's sword hilt, and asked: "Wilt thou not refrain from persecuting until the Lord send some calamity upon thee?" "Truly I testify," replied Umar, "that you are the Prophet of God." He would become the second and greatest of all the caliphs.

The traditions abound in other conversion stories, many of them replete with marvels. There was the shepherd who joined after seeing a thirsty Muhammad get milk from an unbred ewe, and the pilgrim who stuffed his ears with wool yet heard Muhammad's message anyway. Some Meccans viewed him as a harmless half-wit, however, and some parodied his name as "Mudhammam" (signifying a reprobate). Others were more tolerant. The Romans, after all, had a prophet in Jesus. The Jews had numerous prophets. Why shouldn't the Arabs have a prophet?

Before long, all Mecca was taking sides, as Muhammad began to be seen as something more than merely quaint. It became clear that he was either a prophet

4. Uthman proved a dubious gain—a rival visionary of sorts to Muhammad. He was later dispatched with his family and other Muslim refugees to Ethiopia. An ascetic, he is said to have denounced all display of lavish luxury (something to which those Arabs who could afford it were much given), and to have sworn off sex, a self-denial bitterly resented by his wife, who complained to Abu Bakr's daughter. Finally, say the traditions, he asked Muhammad for permission to castrate himself. The request was rejected in horror.

What would Muhammad's constant harangues against idolatry do to the pilgrimage? Would the pious thronging to Mecca want to hear a stream of abuse against their gods?

or actively seditious. He was upsetting the whole familial structure of Meccan society; a father would become a mortal enemy of Islam while several of his sons and daughters joined it.

Moreover, Islam seemed to pose a challenge to the entire Arab status quo. Lavish generosity, unfailing courage and absolute fidelity to one's word—this was what proper Arabs cared about. While Muhammad didn't exactly repudiate these virtues, he seemed to consider this religious surrender of his far more crucial. And what would his interminable harangues against idolatry do to the pilgrimage? Would the thousands who swarmed annually to Mecca want to listen to a stream of abuse against its gods? Sentries were posted on the roads to warn pilgrims about the lunatic impostor.

A rich uncle of Muhammad, Abu Lahib, was foremost among his foes. At first he merely jeered; later his attacks became virulent. One of Umar's uncles waged an even more sweeping campaign. He would charge a convert who was devoted to his Arabic heritage with betraying his ancestors, for example, and a merchant convert with imperiling business. More ominous yet,

Muhammad's cousin and foster brother, Abu Sufyan, became chief of the rival Umayyads. Once his closest friend, Abu Sufyan was now an implacable opponent, and this added tribal rivalry to the religious controversy. Moreover, Abu Sufyan's wife was a fierce and vicious woman named Hind, destined to play a bloody role in future events.

The most vulnerable converts were the slaves, completely in their masters' power. The traditions tell of Abu Bakr's pity for them. One slave's master had tied him prostrate and naked in the sun, where he lay stammering, "One God! One God!"—determined not to recant. Abu Bakr bought and freed him, as he did five or six others. This particular slave, a black man named Bilal, would be renowned as Muhammad's *muezzin* (crier) who called the faithful to prayer from atop the mosque.

Muhammad himself did not altogether escape persecution. We are told that his neighbors and Uncle Abu Lahib not only subjected him to invective, but repeatedly threw "unclean things" at his house. When some goat entrails landed

Muhammad, becoming uneasy over his approval of the three idols, consulted Gabriel, and he disowned the two fateful verses. They had been whispered by Satan, the angel warned.

in front of him as he cooked dinner, for instance, he is said to have picked them up with a stick and thrown them into the street, wondering aloud "what sort of good neighborhood this is."

The Quraysh reportedly tried bribery, too, offering to make Muhammad Mecca's richest and most-honored citizen if only he would give up his mission. He contemptuously refused, and the emissary who delivered the offer was so mesmerized by hearing the Qur'an that his colleagues concluded he had been "bewitched."

When the Quraysh further demanded that the Prophet authenticate himself by working a few miracles, Muhammad replied that he had not been sent to work miracles. However, say the traditions, he once relented, and for the benefit of the doubtful caused the moon to briefly split in two. Again, we are told that when a skeptic held a bone before his face, challenging him to bring it to life, Muhammad smiled disdainfully, crumbled it in his hand, and replied that God would one day bring it back to life. He would bring the skeptic back to life as well, the Prophet added, preparatory to consigning him to hellfire. Such an attitude was not conducive to universal popularity. Mecca sneered and raged, while Muhammad remained resolutely censorious.

He himself still had some protection from the Hashemites, however reluctant, but this was not true for his followers. He therefore urged them to take refuge across the Red Sea in Christian Ethiopia. They departed, most accounts agree, in two expeditions, in total ninety-four men and twenty-two women, and were cordially received by the *negus* (king), Ethiopia's Christian ruler.

The Quraysh followed them there. Possibly fearing another Ethiopian invasion of Arabia, they were laden with diplomatic gifts, and they demanded that the fugitives be sent home. The Negus summoned both groups before a council of his bishops. A cousin of Muhammad, acting as spokesman for the refugees, described the moral reform Muhammad was working, and how he had condemned idolatry, and done away with cannibalism and lewd living.

Maybe so, countered the Quraysh, but the bishops should know that Muslims reject Jesus as Son of God, dismissing him as a mere slave. A slave of God, replied Muhammad's cousin, and also the son of Mary in whose virgin womb the Spirit had placed the Word of God. Thereupon, report al-Tabari and Hisham, the Christian bishops burst into tears. Arabia, they joyfully concluded, had at last come into the Christian fold! Thus the Quraysh returned home in failure. Muslim historians also speculate that the Negus himself embraced Islam—but Ethiopia, far from becoming Muslim, would remain an African bulwark against Islam from that day to this.

Most of the refugees eventually returned to Mecca, although the reasons remain controversial among Muslims. The story told by the historians Wakidi and al-Tabari, but rejected by others, is that the Prophet, weary of the whole conflict, met the Quraysh leaders and compromised on the question of idolatry. He agreed to let the goddesses al-Lat, al-Uzza and al-Manat remain in the Ka'ba, though in an inferior status to Allah. Gabriel, he said, had told him: "These are exalted females whose intercession verily is to be sought after." The Quraysh, ecstatic that the strife was over, all bowed in reverence to Allah. But Muhammad, becoming unhappy with this whole development, again consulted Gabriel, and he disowned the fateful verses. They had been whispered by Satan, he said, not by him. (They would become known as the "satanic verses.")

Muhammad thereupon repudiated the concession, and the conflict grew worse. So the Quraysh next approached Muhammad's patient uncle Abu Talib, demanding that he withdraw tribal protection. This would virtually assure Muhammad's assassination. When Abu Talib refused, the

The freed slave, Bilal, became the first muezzin, or crier, to call Muslims to prayer five times a day. He is said to have roused the faithful at dawn with the admonition "Prayer is better than sleep!" Generations of criers, like this one (below) in Paris, have since performed the same duties at mosques around the world.

exasperated Quraysh formed a league of Mecca's other families against the Hashemites. No business was to be done with them, no daughters betrothed to them, and no supplies provided to them. This became known as the "Boycott," and because of it, the Hashemites were forced to withdraw into an isolated quarter on the city's eastern outskirts, where famine tightened upon them.

The Boycott presented Muhammad with a crucial question. He could end it by renouncing the protection of his family, delivering himself unresisting to his adversaries, and face almost certain death. Or he could somehow mobilize his followers to resist, to survive and to prevail, which would involve first politics and then war. During the Boycott, he appears to have made his choice, thereby defining one of the fundamental differences between the founder of Christianity and the founder of Islam.

As their ministries gained support, both Jesus and Muhammad faced dangerous hostility from their respective governments, but their response was profoundly different. Jesus surrendered himself and was crucified. This is foreshadowed in the third of three temptations he undergoes at the outset of his ministry, as portrayed in the Gospel of Matthew.[5] He is shown the kingdoms of the earth spread before him. Evil beckons him. All this can be his, if only he will submit to the prince of this world—that is, adopt the world's ways, head up a political movement, and conquer by the power of the sword.

Jesus rejects the offer. Satan, he says, is an impostor—the world is not his to give. It belongs to Jesus' Father. He thus becomes the suffering servant envisioned in the fifty-third chapter of the prophet Isaiah. But in so doing, Christians affirm, he rises triumphant over this world and its satanic prince, thus ensuring the salvation of mankind.

As events in Muhammad's life unfold, however, he will take the other path, in effect yielding to the third temptation. The idea of a theocratic state, with all that this implies, becomes increasingly attractive to him, until he unreservedly embraces it. As though to underline this distinction, Muslims accept Jesus as both a prophet and as the Jewish Messiah—but indignantly deny that he was crucified. To Muhammad himself the cross became a hated symbol, whose very sight he could not endure. The eighth-century Arabian historian al-Wakidi describes how he would search his house for every instance where two boards crossed one another, and smash them.[6]

An even more crucial difference between the two, however, lies in their theology. Muhammad's claim is essentially that of a prophet. God, he says, has revealed the truth to him through Gabriel. Jesus, by contrast, on occasion speaks as God himself, the Creator of the world, who now has actually come into it as one of his own creatures, to effect an entirely new creation. "Behold, I make all things new," says God in the Book of the Revelation (21:5).

The Meccan Boycott, which increasingly offended the town's tribal allegiances, failed. After two years, Abu Talib, discovering that the Boycott document had been largely consumed by termites in the Ka'ba, challenged Muhammad's adversaries to produce it. Unable to do so, they became so

5. The three temptations of Jesus Christ are described both in Matthew 4:3–11 and in Luke 4:3–13. The order is slightly different in Luke.

6. Muslims point out that, whatever Jesus did and taught, Christians from Constantine onward began to take over the government and establish the same kind of theocracy that Muhammad established. Even today, they correctly observe, Christians seek to exert decisive influence on governmental policy and law. In effect, therefore, Muhammad confronted a reality that Jesus left to his followers to confront. To this, Christians would reply that, by distinguishing what the individual owes to Caesar (i.e., the government) from what he owes to God (Matt. 22:21; Mk. 12:17; Lk. 20:25), Jesus established two realms, leaving it to Christians in each age to decide where the line between them lies. In Islam, there is no such line.

unnerved that his sympathizers were able to get the edict revoked. The Hashemites, all fully armed, were escorted triumphantly home. Far from being the end of the conflict, however, this was no more than the beginning.

Two sharp reversals now struck Muhammad. In the year 619 Khadeja died at age sixty-five. Not only did he lose thereby his wife and first supporter, speculates the nineteenth-century German historian Aloys Sprenger, he may also have lost the inspiration for the deeply spiritual early chapters of the Qur'an, which hereafter becomes increasingly administrative, in fact dull. Soon afterward Abu Talib also died, striving to the end to reconcile his nephew's strange convictions with his people's ancient traditions. At the end, Muhammad pressed him to affirm that there was no God but Allah, and the old man's mouth seemed to move. "I heard him say it," declared his brother Abbas. "I heard him not," rejoined Muhammad.

Three months after Khadeja's death, Muhammad married Sauda, widow of a Muslim refugee who had turned Christian. More housekeeper than wife, she was running to fat. Far more interesting to him was the child bride who followed Sauda as his second wife: six-year-old A'isha, daughter of Abu Bakr. Precocious and pert, A'isha grew up quickly and the marriage reportedly was consummated when she was nine.

Without Abu Talib's protection, the Muslims were more than ever vulnerable to the assassin and the mob. Ibn Ishaq tells how Abu Bakr, his wealth largely gone, was set upon and left bound outside the city, but managed to free himself. Nor was the credibility of the movement much enhanced when Muhammad started talking of his "Night Journey," a visionary episode much celebrated in

Like so many later paintings of Muhammad, this miniature (below), belonging to London's Royal Asiatic Society, pictures the Prophet and his followers as prosperous and well armed, yet in the early years, this was far from the case. The Muslims were often impoverished and shunned by their fellow Meccans.

Muslim tradition, in which he was taken by winged horse to Jerusalem and back, accompanied by Gabriel. When Muhammad told a cousin about this, she advised him to keep it to himself because it wouldn't help the cause, and in the Qur'an it merits only a single verse (Sura 17:1).

But the traditions are lavish with detail. For example, they say that from the Temple, Muhammad climbed to the seventh heaven, where he encountered Jesus, Moses and Abraham, and led them in prayer. Jesus, he noted, was "a reddish man of medium height, with lank hair and many freckles on his face, as though he had just come from a bath." Muhammad told them he had resolved to teach mankind to pray fifty times a day. Too many, said Moses, considering the frailty of man's faith. The proposal was cut to forty, then thirty, and finally five. Moses was dubious even about this, but Muhammad said he was ashamed to ask for less. Therefore, Muslims pray five times daily.

Such talk did strain the credulity of many. Conversions virtually ceased, and defections increased. But a new note appeared in the Qur'an: No longer was Muhammad merely history's latest prophet. He now became *the* Prophet, prophecy's final fulfillment, the bearer of a message without which all men were doomed. "Whosoever disobeyeth God and his Prophet, for him is prepared the

For the very first time the world heard the cry that still echoes: "There is no God but Allah and Muhammad is his Prophet," a single sentence which became the creed of Islam.

fire of hell" (Sura 72:23). Rules and order rapidly became essential to the new faith, including dietary laws. Animal flesh might be eaten only if "killed in the name of the Lord," and pork not at all. The Ka'ba monopoly was denounced; Islam would countenance no naked dancing around the sacred shrine.

And now for the first time, the world heard the cry that would echo through history: "There is no God but Allah, and Muhammad is his Prophet," which was to become the creed of Islam. Beside the complex Christian formulary of Nicea, it did have a refreshing simplicity. But why, the puzzled Greeks would later protest, should we expect the nature of God, Creator of the whole bafflingly complex physical universe, to be simple?

To most Meccans, Muhammad's cause must have seemed lost, but in fact, his fortunes were about to turn. During the next pilgrimage, he chatted about God and Islam with pilgrims from Medina, who proved to be reassuringly attentive. A thought struck him: Could he and his followers secure refuge at Medina? The implications of such a move were very dark, he knew. In view of the ancient antipathies between the tribes of the two centers, for one to harbor dissidents from the other was an open invitation to war. But six of his listeners seemed particularly enthralled by his message. Would they carry Islam to Medina? he asked. They would return with an answer, they replied, in one year.

Medina, earlier known to the Arabs as Yathrib, was as ancient as Mecca.

Since Nebuchadnezzar's invasion of Palestine in the sixth century B.C., Jewish refugees had been finding their way to its green and well-watered environs, and had named it Medina. It became a settlement of three tribes that had acquired Judaism either by descent or conversion. In the fourth century, two southern Arab tribes, the Khazraj and the Aus, conquered the city, invited the Jewish leaders to a banquet of reconciliation, and then gleefully butchered all their guests. But the Khazraj and the Aus were soon at war with each other, and the remaining Jews survived by alliances with one or the other. Thus Medina became a collection of isolated and heavily armed agricultural settlements, three of them Jewish.

Moses and Muhammad (face veiled) conversing with the angel Gabriel during the Prophet's "Night Journey," in a detail from a sixteenth-century Turkish manuscript. Moses is said to have convinced Muhammad that requiring Muslims to pray fifty times a day was, perhaps, asking too much.

Into this volatile uncertainty the Medina pilgrims returned, some of them enthusiastically talking of Islam and of its message of strength through Arab unity. Interest grew mightily in Medina, and at the next year's pilgrimage, twelve prominent Medinians met the Prophet secretly outside Mecca, in a glen called Aqaba. "We will not worship any but the one God," they promised. "We will not steal, neither will we commit adultery, nor kill our children; we will not slander in any wise; nor will we disobey the Prophet in anything that is right."

Known in Muslim history as "the First Pledge of Aqaba," this is sometimes called "the Pledge of Women," because it notably omits any commitment to take up arms. The twelve agreed to meet at the same place next year, and returned more zealous than ever to Medina, where from house to Arab house the message spread. Tribal animosities vanished before it, and the Jews looked on amazed at the disappearance of the idolatry they had long deplored among the Gentiles.

It was in 622 that the event occurred that completed the rupture between the Prophet and his native city. As the annual festival ended, the Medinians traveled in small groups to the gully of Aqaba. To the amazement even of the Prophet, seventy-five people gathered there: sixty-two Khazraji, eleven Aus and two women. Perhaps to keep the meeting secret even from his followers, Muhammad was accompanied only by his Uncle Abbas, a non-Muslim whose presence has intrigued Muslim historians ever since.

"We have listened to your words," said a Medina elder. "Our resolution is unshaken. Our lives are at the Prophet's service." The seventy-three men pledged to defend him as they would their own families; the women were not required to swear. "Whoever you war against, him I war against. Whoever you make peace with, him I make peace with," the Prophet told them at this "Second Pledge of Aqaba."

Secrecy notwithstanding, news of the meeting spread rapidly in Mecca. The die was now cast. Muhammad ordered his followers to leave for Medina on a date generally acknowledged as July 16, 622 (which now became year one on the Islamic calendar). He himself remained in Mecca, some say to protect the dwindling number that had stayed behind, others to make sure that all was ready at Medina for his reception. The Quraysh, perhaps perceiving only one chance to prevent a war engendered by this treasonous activity, took council to consider assassinating him. If one representative of each Qurayshite tribe plunged one fatal wound into his body, one chief argued, no single tribe would bear the responsibility. "May God reward this man!" shouted an old sheikh from Nejd. "This is the right advice and none other." This man was Satan attending in disguise, the historian Ibn Hisham assures us.[7]

But Muhammad, forewarned, sent word to Abu Bakr, the only other senior Muslim left in Mecca, who had kept two swift camels in readiness. Their escape is one of the thrillers of Islamic lore. Exchanging cloaks with his willing foster son Ali, the Prophet crept out a rear window into the darkness. He and Abu Bakr then stole through the town to Mount Thawr, about ninety minutes south on the Yemen road. The sentries were deceived by Ali's cloak (and by the fact, adds the pious Hisham, that the Prophet had thrown magical dust in their eyes to temporarily blind them.)

Up the rocky and thorny slope of Thawr the pair struggled, to a cave that

7. The nineteenth-century British historian William Muir doubts the whole assassination story. Had it actually happened, he writes, much more would have been made of it in traditional records and also in the Qur'an, where it is merely implied: "And call to mind when the unbelievers plotted against thee, that they might detain thee, or slay thee, or expel thee. Yea, they plotted; but God plotted likewise. And God is the best of plotters" (Sura 8:30).

The road from Mecca to Medina (below), photographed in 1914. Muhammad himself took a less direct route when he fled his home in 622, possibly one step ahead of assassins bent upon his murder.

both tradition and archaeology can still identify, known to Islam as the "Glorious Cave." The Quraysh, discovering the deception next morning, offered a hundred-camel reward for the Prophet's discovery, and launched a massive three-day search. (Curiously, they did not hold Ali hostage.) A servant of Abu Bakr carried daily food to the cave. On the third day, his daughter Asama brought news that the search had been abandoned, and also supplies for a journey.[8] Swiftly, the two fugitives moved from Mecca west to the Red Sea coast, then north, then east again, guided by a non-Muslim hired by Abu Bakr. Ali meanwhile tidied up the Prophet's affairs and also left for Medina.

When they reached the encampment of expatriate Muslims at Quba, outside Medina, there was great rejoicing. The Prophet remained there four days, helping to begin construction of the "Mosque of Godly Fear," which would become a beloved Islamic shrine. On the fifth, a Friday, he mounted his camel with Abu Bakr behind him, and began a solemn procession into the city, escorted by more than a hundred Medinians in full fighting array, a triumphal entry that would thereafter make Friday the holy day of the new faith.

Thus ended the *hijra*, a word popularly mistranslated as "flight." It actually means, Muslims explain, "the migration," and refers not to the Prophet's journey, but to that of all the faithful.

All the faithful pitched in to raise a rude but enormous building, with stone foundations, walls of unburned brick, palm trunk rafters and palm leaf roof, roughly 150 feet to a side. Its eastern flank provided rooms for the Prophet's wives, Sauda and A'isha. More were added later as needed for new wives. The eastern side of a mosque is known to this day as the "Women's Porch." On the north side a niche, or *qibla*, indicated the direction of Jerusalem, towards which all faithful monotheists faced in prayer.

The workmen burst into poetry as they raised the building,
Muhammad joining in discordantly—demonstrating,
say his biographers, that he had no

8. Having forgotten to bring a cord to tie the supply bundle, however, Asama had to tear a strip from her cloak. She has been known ever since in Muslim history as "She of the Two Shreds."

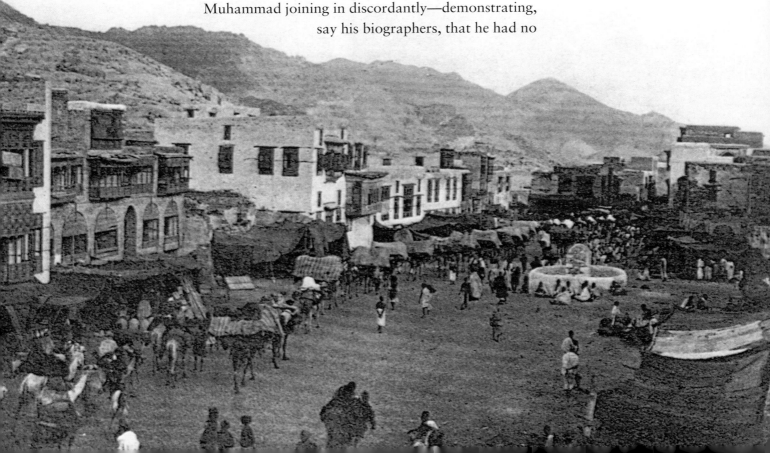

*Muhammad and his followers on the road to
Medina, where he built his model theocratic state
and began the conversion of much of Arabia;
from an 1845 engraving.*

great gift for verse, and hence that the eloquence of the Qur'an came, not from him, but from God through Gabriel. The Qur'an's eloquence, however, lay in the verses already written. The sura still to be revealed lack eloquence—demonstrating, say some skeptics, that the eloquence came from neither Muhammad nor from God, but from Khadeja. Elements in the design of that first Medina mosque would survive in every building of Islam, whether a makeshift stucco structure in Hoboken or the Taj Mahal.

During the seven-month construction period, believers Abu and Um Ayyub delightedly gave up the ground floor of their house to the Prophet, moving themselves upstairs, and preparing his meals as well. Ishaq records the Ayyubs' reminiscence of their honored guest. Once they sent him a dinner of garlic vegetables. It came back untouched with a delicate explanation: "He had perceived the smell of the vegetables," Ishaq quotes the Prophet's host,

Elements in the design of the first mosque at Medina would survive in every future building of Islam, whether makeshift stucco or the Taj Mahal.

"and as he was a man who had to speak confidentially to people, his host and hostess should eat them themselves." They did, and sent him no more garlic. Abu Ayyub was to die carrying the sword of Islam against Constantinople, capital of the Roman world.

The building complete, Muhammad decided to move in, along with A'isha, now nine. This marriage to a child is explained by some historians as intended merely to cement relations with Abu Bakr, and was not unusual among sixth-century Arabs. Although the union was childless, A'isha became and remained queen of the harem, and later played a role in the bloody politics of the caliphate period that was, says the *Cambridge Medieval History*, "by no means honorable."

Medina's climate is unhealthy—cold in winter, very hot in summer, rain intermittent, highly conducive to disease. Fever struck the Muslims hard, disabling almost all but the Prophet himself; many died. The Prophet prayed that his flock should come to love Medina as much as Mecca, and that God should take away the fever and visit it instead upon rival al-Juhfa, through which caravans often bypassed Medina. God apparently obliged. The survivors regained their strength.

Within a year, Muhammad may have gained sufficient control over Medina to begin legislating for the whole town. A municipal "constitution" has been preserved, though of dubious origin. In this period also, the Qur'an seems to have set out many principles of Muslim morality, ritual and law. Drinking wine is formally condemned. Restrictions are placed on blood feuding. Female infanticide is banned. A woman can no longer be bequeathed as part of her husband's estate. Usury is prohibited. Theft is discouraged by the proviso that the hands of thieves will be amputated. Fighting among Medinians is condemned; all wars are to be undertaken by the city as a whole. Giving aid to or communicating with the Quraysh at Mecca is forbidden. An alms tax is established, payable to the Prophet, to be used for relief to the poor. Disputes are to be referred to the Prophet for final arbitration. Current scholarship, however, prefers to date the origins of definitive Islamic law at least a century later.

Upon equally uncertain grounds, tradition ascribes to the early years in Medina the development of Islamic religious ritual as well. The five daily prayers, it says, were set for dawn, midday, afternoon, sunset and nightfall. Friday was established as the day of a more complete service, with a sermon preached by the Prophet. He would begin with the Tekbir, "God is most great!" then ritualistically prostrate himself. All these customs survive today.

Much thought was eventually given to the summons to prayer. The Jewish trumpet was considered, and the Christian bell, until someone proposed simply using the human voice. So Muhammad directed his big servant Bilal to stand on a high roof at the five appointed hours, beginning with the first light of dawn, and cry: "Great is the Lord! Great is the Lord! I bear witness that there is no God but the Lord: I bear witness that Muhammad is the Prophet of God. Come unto prayer. Come unto salvation. God is great! God is great! There is no God but the Lord!" For emphasis, Bilal is said to have added to his morning call: "Prayer is better than sleep! Prayer is better than sleep!"

Thus began the office of *muezzin*; for the next fourteen hundred years at mosques all over the Muslim world, the cry has first been heard at daybreak from the minaret tower. Bilal himself would become as well a great warrior in the Muslim cause, and be rewarded with an estate at Damascus where his tomb has been preserved.

In these days also, Muhammad instituted the fast of Ramadan, apparently adopted from the Jewish Atonement, but having more in common with Christian Lent. The fast continues for a lunar month, and the faithful at first tried to deny themselves all food and drink, but the Prophet restricted it to daylight hours only (also exempting travelers and the sick). Consequently, in Ramadan nothing is consumed in daylight, but big meals tend to

Muhammad's triumphant entry into Medina (below left) marked the official establishment of Islam, created a starting point for a new Muslim calendar, and confirmed Friday as the new religion's day of prayer. Within a year of the Prophet's arrival, the Muslims had become the effective government of the town, and were able to use it as a base of operations.

occur after dark and before dawn. It can still be very onerous, however, when the calendrical flaw carries it out of winter and into the heat of summer—especially in the higher latitudes where days are inordinately long.[9] Finally, Islam adopted the peculiar rite of circumcision common to other Semitic cultures, although the Qur'an does not mention it and there is no evidence that the Prophet himself was circumcised.

Since religious and secular authority were inseparable, it was universally recognized that whoever led the prayers led the state. Hence, as Muhammad aged, he sometimes absented himself and named Abu Bakr as his substitute. Once, when Abu Bakr was also absent, Umar automatically took over. Hisham records the Prophet's alarm over this precedent, calling from his apartment: "No! No! No! None but Abu Bakr. Let no one lead the prayers but he!" Perhaps he foresaw the problems of succession that would divide Islam just as fiercely as the problems of doctrine divide Christianity.

Much of Medina society accepted Muhammad as preferable to the interminable civil war that had preceded him, while quietly scoffing at all this talk of God and moral duty. These people go down in Muslim history as the

Unlike Christianity, religious and secular authority in Islam was inseparable from the beginning, and it was recognized that whoever led the prayers also led the state.

"Hypocrites," carefully distinguished from the *Ansar* or "Helpers," who actively aided the Muslim cause. However, far more serious resistance developed among the Medina Jews, who saw clearly that accepting the Prophet's message meant rejecting Judaism. Islam contended not only that the Jewish Messiah had already arrived in the person of Jesus, but that one greater than Jesus was now on the scene—and he was not even Jewish, but Arab.

The Jews' rejection of his message came as a bitter blow to Muhammad. He had counted on their help and had made an early treaty with them, guaranteeing them continued use of their synagogues and mutual support of Muslim for Jew and Jew for Muslim in event of war. Their growing opposition carried a dangerous implication. Since he himself had recognized them as the original people of God, must their opposition not mean that God was against, not for, the Prophet? Moreover, they knew their Scriptures as well or better than he, and increasingly heckled him with tough questions during his sermons. Why, they wondered, could he not cure As'ad, one of the original six from Aqaba, now stricken with a sore throat and dying? The Prophet's reply, even echoed through his own biographers, sounds a curiously frantic note: "I have no power of the Lord over even my own life, or over that of my followers. Let the Lord destroy the Jews that speak thus."

Another question, designed by the Jews to test the Prophet's allegiance to the Law of Moses, again reveals the startling gulf between his teachings and those of Jesus.

9. The Muslim calendar begins with the year of the hijra. In effect, Muhammad restored the old Arab calendar, abolishing Kosai's thirteenth "short month." Based on twelve lunar months, it is eleven and a quarter days short of the solar year. This dating system guaranteed an ongoing problem, and once again the season of the pilgrimage began to stray wildly. Modern Islamic states now have to recognize two calendars, the Islamic one and a solar version consisting of months with Persian, Syrian and Coptic names.

'Like the ringing of a bell'

Muslims believe the holy Qur'an contains the final and absolute word of God,
revealed to the Prophet Muhammad in 114 infallible messages called 'sura'

Non-Muslims often assume that the Qur'an is Islam's equivalent of the Christian New Testament. In reality, however, the two scriptures are quite different. The Qur'an consists of commandments and warnings, along with concise explanations and anecdotes. Not even a basic description of Muhammad's own life appears in its pages. The New Testament, in contrast, consists of four accounts of Jesus' life, a chronological history of the first Christians, letters from the Christian apostles, and a heavenly vision in Revelation.

The Qur'an (Arabic for "recitation") is made up of 114 individual messages, each known as a "sura," the original text of which, say the faithful, is preserved on a tablet in heaven. They believe that most suras were delivered to Muhammad by the angel Gabriel in a mountain cave. Other messages came, he said, "like the ringing of a bell, penetrating my very heart, and rending me." To the faithful, only the Arabic version is valid, and it must be accepted as inerrant.

Seventh-century Arabs, like many preliterate peoples, could preserve epics and poems for generations through simple memorization. In early Islamic assemblies, oral repetition of the Qur'an was obligatory. Some Muslims within the Prophet's lifetime could recite the entire opus.

It is not certain whether Muhammad could read or write, but he definitely did not authorize a complete edition. Within a year of his death, however, textual variations began creeping into Qur'anic verses written on palm leaves and thin white stones. Alarmed, the caliph Abu Bakr commissioned Zayd, Muhammad's secretary, to complete a reliable version.

But this did not resolve all the problems. Besides accuracy, the young man faced another issue. In what order would the suras appear? Should the holy messages be organized by subjects? Or should the Qur'an proceed chronologically from the Prophet's first revelation to the last? Zayd opted for a third choice. After a brief opening, he began with the longest sura (two hundred eighty-six verses) and progressed with little variation to the shortest, just six concise lines.

This approach has awkward aspects. Muhammad's earliest pronouncements were often poetic, vigorous and brief. As he aged, the suras typically grew more complex, frequently dealing with social issues faced by his growing community. By placing the longest suras first, Zayd tends to present the messages in reverse chronological order. Also, subjects are addressed in no particular order whatever. Thanks in part to this confusing composition, few non-Muslims read the Qur'an, despite its relative brevity (its word count is similar to the New Testament).

In any event, new variations continued to appear in the text. So Uthman, the third caliph, instructed Zayd to authenticate a perfect edition. Three Meccans, experts in Muhammad's own regional dialect, ruled on language usage. Around 650, Uthman dispatched copies of the authorized Qur'an throughout the Arab empire, ordering all rival scripts destroyed. The decree proved effective, and as intended, the authorized Qur'an has proven to be a crucial unifying factor within a frequently fragmented religion. "There is probably no other work in the world that has remained twelve centuries with so pure a text," concludes British historian William Muir.

Christians, in contrast, have never forced an all-encompassing official recension of their scriptures. Gospels not included in the official biblical canon have not been physically eliminated. Regarding the authorized books, variant records are never annihilated in Muslim fashion. Instead, Christian scholars have striven century upon century to evaluate all evidence and preserve both the original wording and its underlying meaning. Controversies within this relatively free-spirited transmission process have been minor, and modern archaeological discoveries testify to the remarkable textual precision of today's Bible.

But the Qur'an alone could not satisfy the natural yearning of the faithful to know the actual history of their religion's foundation, and the human context in which the divine laws had been laid down. So the Prophet's Companions (any believer who knew him) gave personal accounts describing the *sunna*—principles and practices approved by Muhammad through his own words and deeds. These "Hadith" (traditions) carry scriptural weight, albeit distinctly second to the Qur'an, and they underlie the Muslim legal code.

Two centuries after Muhammad's death, specialists began to weed out false traditions and compile authoritative collections. Al-Bukhari is considered the most rigorous in ensuring the authenticity of his 2,602 Hadith. Even so, valid questions of reliability remain, and some Hadith appear outlandish today. Modern readers cannot help questioning whether God really made women deficient in intelligence, if a mixture of camel urine and milk makes an effective medicine, and whether a child's gender is determined by which partner reaches sexual climax first.

A few modern Muslims, noting that Muhammad did not proclaim his opinions and behavior as a personal model, think the Hadith may need reevaluation. But most scholars continue to employ Hadith in interpreting the Qur'an itself, as well as legal questions. And beyond the traditions, the Prophet's own scriptural witness continues to weather the test of time for all the faithful. As the Qur'an in its second sura avows about itself: "This book, there is no doubt in it. . . ." ∎

The Jews had caught a couple in the act of adultery. What, they asked the Prophet, should be done with them? To demonstrate his devotion to Mosaic Law, the Prophet declared that they must be stoned to death. The record preserves a piteous scene, the man vainly trying to protect the woman as the rocks cascade upon them. This tale, cited to reassure Muslims of the Prophet's determined fidelity to Scripture, stands in sharp contrast to Christ's response in an almost identical situation. "Let him who has not sinned cast the first stone" (John 8:7) Jesus replied, thus convicting the accusers with their own consciences, so that none could throw a stone.

That New Testament incident demonstrates more than Christ's mercy, however. Its underlying point is that few if any people truly keep the Mosaic Law, or meet even the minimum rules imposed by their own consciences. Hence, if a man's salvation depends upon his unaided performance of the moral code, he is lost. How then can he be saved? Only by God himself, reply the Christians—by God the Son, assuming the nature of a man and meeting the demands of the Law on behalf of every human being.

These examples of adultery illustrate, in short, both the pitiful futility of unaided human moral effort, and the compelling appeal of Christ's doctrine of salvation. Christians contend that they represent a problem, and a solution, which neither Muhammad nor the Qur'an ever satisfactorily addresses. Some also theorize that this is the principal reason why Islam prohibits, on pain of death, the preaching of the Christian gospel in some Muslim countries, and the

Mecca (below), the birthplace of Muhammad, in a photograph from 1889. The arid, dusty town is larger but otherwise little changed from the early Middle Ages. It had few of the natural advantages possessed by the more fertile district surrounding Medina, which by 622 had become the Prophet's new home.

conversion of a Muslim to Christianity.

Muhammad's taxes, imposed in the name of God, provoked further trouble. If Allah required their tax money, jeered the Jews, then they must be richer than Allah. God is aware of such Jewish blasphemy, the Prophet later told Abu Bakr. "They shall taste the punishment of burning," promises the Qur'an (Sura 3:116). Later, following the Muslim victory at Badr, the language of the Qur'an would become even more specific: "You will be defeated and gathered into hell, a wretched resting place" (Sura 3:12).

At last, one final symbolic and historic gesture completed the rupture with Judaism. About seventeen months after his arrival in Medina, the Prophet paused in the midst of the Friday service. Following his prostrations towards Jerusalem, he abruptly turned and finished the service facing instead towards Mecca and the Ka'ba. Said the Qur'an: "Turn . . . thy face toward the Holy Temple of Mecca. Wheresoever ye be, when ye pray, turn towards the same" (Sura 2:144).

This gesture and promulgation destroyed any hope of reconciliation with the Jews. Mortified and estranged, they charged that with this decision, Muhammad had returned the Arabs to idolatry. His response in the days immediately ahead would entail bloodshed and mass slaughter. ∎

Ethiopia's enduring faith

Surrounded on all sides by enemies, Christians of the north-east African kingdom have resisted colonization and Muslim domination for more than sixteen centuries

A Coptic priest (below) holds an ornate cross outside his church in Lalibela, Ethiopia. Christianity in the region can trace its roots back to the fourth century, and the mighty empire of Axum.

Early in the fourth century, a big Roman merchant ship, probably bound for India, put in at Adulis on the African coast of the Red Sea. A riot broke out, in which the local people put to death the entire crew and all the passengers, save for two boys, Frumentius and Edesius. They were traveling with their uncle, a Christian philosopher from Tyre on the east coast of the Mediterranean. Taken as slaves, the pair were sent inland to the royal court at Axum. By a swirl of circumstance, the stranded lads would become Christ's first popular evangelists to black Africa.

The trek to Axum was short but exhausting, just eighty miles inland, but a climb of seventy-two hundred feet from the sea. Axum was the name of both the capital city and the kingdom, but its ruling dynasty was founding a state that would be known to history as Abyssinia, and later Ethiopia. Its Christian population would resist both European colonization and Muslim domination from that time to this, an achievement unmatched on the African continent. Crucial to that success was its topography. The Ethiopian heartland consists of high, generally fertile plateaus, surrounded by searing deserts and thinly settled prairies. It was a natural fortress whose unique civilization was already well known to the world when Frumentius and Edesius clambered unwillingly into its majestic confines.

At least two peoples provided its earliest recorded population. First came the dark-skinned inhabitants of Kush (later Nubia, and later still Meroe), in the Middle and Upper Nile Valley, south of Egypt, whom the Old Testament deemed the descendants of Noah's son Ham. These merged with the Semites who arrived from South Arabia, bringing with them the plough, an alphabet and a religion called Judaism, a radical departure from the polytheism and witchcraft they had known.

The Jewish Ethiopians believe themselves descendants of a secret union between Solomon and the Queen of Sheba (1 Kings 10:1–13) that the Bible does not record. This produced a son, Menelik I, founder of the Axumite dynasty, whose heirs would call themselves descendants of Solomon, until the Ethiopian monarchy was extinguished in the late-twentieth century. They add another touch. Visiting Jerusalem for his father's blessing, Menelik made a duplicate of the Ark of the Covenant, substituted it, and brought the real one home, where it lies to this day in the Cathedral of St. Mary of Zion at Axum, they say. Though none of this is historically verifiable, two facts stand in its favor. What became of the Ark of the Covenant is unknown; it is believed to have been spirited away from Jerusalem to protect it from invaders. Second, the Axumite kingdom repeatedly invaded South Arabia, including Sabea (Sheba), so a royal connection is tenable.

Ethiopian history records that Menelik brought twelve thousand Hebrew settlers with him from Jerusalem, and that devotion to Jehovah soon replaced sun and moon worship. A considerable Jewish population has lived in Ethiopia ever since, known popularly as Falashas ("exiles"), but calling itself Beta Israel (House of Israel).[1] That an Ethiopian eunuch, an official of state, should have been visiting Jerusalem for Passover early in the first Christian century was therefore altogether likely, and the deacon Philip's successful preaching to him of the Christian gospel altogether possible (Acts 8:26–40).

But whether the Ethiopia referred to was Axum or the neighboring kingdom of Nubia is debatable, since it too was sometimes referred to as Ethiopia by the often-vague geographers of the time. Even so, the Ethiopian church has always claimed the eunuch for its own, and his influence on the monarchy made Ethiopia the world's first specifically Christian government, says Archbishop L. M. Mandefro, author of *The Ethiopian Tewahedo Church*. The new faith saw the Great Synagogue of Axum rededicated as the Cathedral of St. Mary of Zion, he writes, resting place of the Ark of the Covenant and Ethiopia's holiest sanctuary. The claim to be the first Christian nation,

however, is disputed.[2]

When the captured Frumentius and Edesius were presented at the royal court more than two centuries later, Mandefro acknowledges, Christianity had not established itself at the popular level in eastern Africa. The Axumites were still erecting monolithic towers to the moon god, one of them over one hundred feet high, possibly the largest block of stone quarried in the ancient world.

The boys made a fine impression. Edesius eventually became the royal cupbearer, Frumentius the royal secretary and treasurer who, encouraged by the king, began baptizing people in significant numbers. When the king died, his widowed queen as regent made Frumentius tutor to her son, Ezana, and gave the former slave senior administrative duties.

Edesius returned to Tyre, became a priest, and told his story to a writer named Rufinus, who recorded it for posterity. But Frumentius, yearning to see the Ethiopians brought to the Lord, descended the Nile to Alexandria, met with the patriarch Athanasius, who consecrated him as a bishop, and returned to Ethiopia, where he became known as *Abba Selama*, Father of Peace, as well as *Abuna* (Father), still the title of Ethiopia's patriarchs. He then produced the first Ethiopian translation of the New Testament. When Ezana became king, he helped spread the Word throughout Axum, and invaded pagan Nubia on the Upper Nile, bringing the faith with him. Thus Christianity sank deep and permanent roots in eastern Africa.

Toward the end of the fifth century, African Christianity surged again

An ornate and priceless cross (above) is displayed to the faithful during the colorful traditional feast of Timkey, the Ethiopian Orthodox celebration of Epiphany.

1. In 1983 and 1991, about thirty thousand Falashas were airlifted to Israel. The community, now numbering eighty thousand, remains among the poorest in their adopted homeland, where they face some discrimination. In 2003, after years of rejection, Israel admitted three thousand more Falashas, and seventeen thousand Falash Mura (Jews who had been forcibly converted to Christianity).

2. Armenia is widely recognized as the first Christian state, dating from 301, the year that its king, Tiridates, was baptized by Gregory the Illuminator, the man responsible for the conversion of the entire nation. (See earlier volume, *By This Sign*, chapter 7.)

under the auspices of foreigners known as the Nine Saints, probably Monophysite refugees fleeing Byzantine persecution in Syria after the Council of Chalcedon. These nine individuals fueled an Ethiopian monastic movement, marked by severe austerity and a tendency toward eremitical (desert-style) practice. It saw some 850 Ethiopian monasteries founded, and the position of head monk established as first office under the patriarch, a post unique to the Ethiopian church.

Due to its Solomonic heritage, the Ethiopian church has retained a particularly Judaic outlook. Saturday, the Jewish Sabbath, remains a day nearly as sacred as Sunday. Boys are circumcised. Many Mosaic laws regarding food, cleanliness, and purification are respected. Following the model of the Jewish Temple, an Ethiopian church has a compartment protected by a veil that shelters a model of the Ark of the Covenant, carved from wood, and inscribed with the Ten Commandments, as in the Hebrew Temple. Only a specially authorized priest may enter this holiest of places. When the Ark is carried out during festivals, it rests on a cupboard-like container with an open cupola at the top. In greeting it, priests play primitive musical instruments and

An Ethiopian monk greets the sunrise overlooking the spectacular scenery of the country's central highlands (below). Ethiopia's rugged landscape has helped keep potential invaders at bay, but also guaranteed its continuing remoteness and isolation.

dance, again reflecting Hebrew customs. The people shout "ellel" (the Hebrew word *haliel* means "praise," familiar to other Christians as *halleluja*).

As well, the Ethiopian church retained until the twentieth century its ancient connection with Alexandria. The Alexandrian patriarchate reserved the right to assign an Egyptian monk as the bishop of Axum and its successor states. And like Egypt, Axum remained staunchly opposed to the Council of Chalcedon, in fact becoming the numerically largest church to maintain that position. Its official name is the Ethiopian Tewahedo Church, *tewahedo* meaning "oneness" or "one nature."

Ethiopia unwittingly played a key role in the rise of Islam, since it was Negus Armah of Axum who sheltered refugees from Mecca during the critical first years of the Muslim movement. (See page 50.) Upon their victory, the appreciative Muslims consequently kept the peace for decades with these neighbors across the Red Sea. However, in the early eighth century, the Muslims gained control of Adulis, Axum's big port, and the trade-oriented country began a sharp decline. Incessant warfare followed between the Muslims on the coast and Christians in the highlands.

"Encompassed on all sides by the enemies of its religion, the Ethiopians slept near a thousand years, forgetful of the world by which they were forgotten," writes Edward Gibbon in his *The Decline and Fall of the Roman Empire*.

Ethiopia was not alone in this long sleep. Also Christian was Nubia, the country to the west and north of Ethiopia that straddles the Nile Valley, which would one day form part of modern Sudan and southern Egypt. "It is often forgotten that for nearly a thousand years, Christianity was the official religion of the greater portion of the middle Nile basin," writes Osbert Crawford, a British archaeologist, in *Antiquity* magazine.

Nubia's relations with the Ethiopian highlands were minimal both before and after Ezana's invasion from Axum in the fourth century.[3] Bishop John of Ephesus reports that the emperor Justinian sent an orthodox mission there in about 540, while his wife Theodora quietly dispatched a competing Monophysite one. The Monophysite emissary found this furnace-like region staggeringly hot. "He used to say," writes Bishop John, "that from nine o'clock until four in the afternoon he was obliged to take refuge in caverns, full of water, where he sat undressed and girt only in a linen garment, such as the people of the country wear."

The Muslim invaders of Egypt first assaulted the Nubians in 641, but when they encountered Nubia's skilled archers, they lost all interest in the job. The Arabs called them "pupil-smiters" because they habitually and accurately aimed their arrows at the eyes of the enemy. In 745,

when the Muslims imprisoned the patriarch of Alexandria, the pupil-smiters attacked northward into Egypt and reached Cairo, before the Muslims released the patriarch and withdrew. Though centuries of periodic warfare followed, Nubia held Islam in check well into the second millennium. A tenth-century Arab visitor describes the Nubian city of Soba as having "fine buildings, spacious houses, churches with much gold and gardens . . . their bishops come from the patriarch of Alexandria . . . and their books are in Greek, which they translate into their own language."

Nubia's last Christian king died in 1323, but its Christianity does not appear to have vanished entirely into Islam. Some scholars theorize that the faith had always been confined largely to the upper class, whose interest may have ebbed when Christian Nubian dynasties intermarried with their Islamic counterparts. Another factor seems to have been immigration from the burgeoning Muslim population in Egypt. Despite the challenges, pockets of Christians survived in Nubian lands, and others would come. The dawn of the third millennium found their spiritual heirs in modern Sudan fighting for their lives against Muslim oppression. ∎

At Lalibela, Ethiopia (above), priests shaded by richly colored umbrellas lead a procession in which the holy Tabots—cupboard-like structures that contain a model of the Ark of the Covenant—are carried from the town's churches and paraded through the streets.

3. Inscriptions on coins and monuments reflect the changing beliefs of eastern Africa. Where King Ezana's first victories are credited to a household god ("unconquered Mahrem"), later credits cite "the Lord of Heaven and the Lord of Earth." The monarch's first coins carry the pagan crescent and disk, the later ones a cross.

A Bedouin caravan crossing the Arabian Desert (above),
from a painting by the French artist Jean Leon Gerome
(1824-1904). Preying upon the caravan trade became a
lucrative source of income for the impoverished early
followers of the Prophet.

CHAPTER 3

Victory after victory fires the Muslim cause

From bandits to veteran soldiers, in seven short years Muhammad's refugees become a formidable army

I t was 623 on the Christian calendar, Year Two on the Islamic one, and Muhammad was about fifty-three years old. His Muslims, settled in Medina, were rapidly taking over the town. As yet they had little thought to spare for Mecca, two hundred miles to the south, their hometown and their enemy in a war as yet undeclared. Muhammad's most pressing problem was the desperate poverty of the refugees who accompanied him to Medina. Unskilled in its basic industry, agriculture, they were hiring themselves out to Medina's landed gentry as laborers.

What these impoverished Meccans understood very well, however, was the caravan business, and how penurious Bedouin tribesmen customarily preyed upon it through bandit raids known as *razzias*. As Muhammad quickly realized, a program of efficiently run razzias could convert this Bedouin sub-trade into a kind of Muslim state enterprise, handily solving the refugees' financial problem. Medina was an excellent base for attack and retreat. Moreover, this would constitute a holy mission, performed for God; participants could kill without qualm. If they themselves perished, heaven awaited them. If they survived, they prospered.

The first Muslim razzias did poorly, however, probably because people at Medina tipped off the caravans. When Muhammad's towering and tough Uncle

Hamza set an ambush for one particularly enticing shipment, he found it unexpectedly guarded by 250 soldiers, and the next three attempts were similarly foiled. The fifth went worse yet; a Bedouin chief raided the raiders, stealing some of their camels and sheep. The sixth target, a caravan headed by Abu Sufyan, once Muhammad's friend but now an implacable enemy, eluded the ambush on the way north, and on its return trip would set off a battle pivotal to the history of Islam and the world.

In that interim, however, the seventh Muslim razzia gloriously succeeded. Riding far south, the raiders caught a northbound caravan headed for Mecca, loaded with wine, raisins and leather. It was almost unguarded, since the southern routes were considered relatively safe, and since this was the month of pilgrimage when fighting was forbidden. Thus the entire shipment fell to the Muslims.

Troubled at this attack during the sacred month, however, Muhammad berated the razzia leader. All right then, the chastened culprit wondered, should they therefore return the goods? Muhammad hastened to consult Gabriel, who thought not. Warring during a sacred month is "grievous," said he, but "to obstruct the way of God and deny him is more grievous still" (Sura 2:217). This would prove a helpful principle in razzias and other matters too. If accepted moral rules need not apply to the servants of God, Muhammad now discerned, his Muslims could justifiably lie, rob or kill to accomplish any holy purpose, thus confounding an enemy whose mind was still darkened by ignorance and thought himself safe.

Once this matter was resolved, four-fifths of the booty was distributed to the raiders and one-fifth given to Muhammad, which became the customary split. The Prophet used his share not only for his own family, but also for the poverty-stricken refugees. Thus, pillage became an expression of devotion, even charity. "War is ordained for you even if it be irksome," the Qur'an advises (Sura 2:216). Furthermore, it adds: "They that are slain in the way of God, he will not suffer their work to perish. . . . He will lead them into

paradise whereof he hath told them" (Sura 47:4–6).

Several weeks later, Abu Sufyan's return caravan approached the little town of Badr, later to give its name to Islam's first great battle—the first of thousands. Some three hundred Muslims lay in wait as Abu Sufyan rode ahead into the town. Had anyone from Medina been around lately? he inquired. No one, said the townspeople. But beside the oasis, he noticed camel dung containing date seeds—and camels with dates in their diets came from only one place: Medina.

Abu Sufyan therefore instantly rerouted his caravan, and hastily requested help from Mecca. With the fate of the caravan from the south fresh in their minds, nearly all able-bodied Meccan men responded. Towards Badr they marched, their women preceding them and clanging tambourines to raise their courage, an old Arab custom. After the battle, they would embrace their menfolk if they were victorious, or likely become enemy prizes if they lost. Foremost among them was Abu Sufyan's own wife, the fierce and wildly beautiful Hind, who would play a ferocious if unromantic role in the days ahead.

Ultimately nine hundred Meccans, determined to eliminate this trouble-making Muhammad once and for all, camped behind a hill near the Badr oasis. Around the oasis Muhammad and his raiders waited, expecting a lightly defended caravan, but were actually outnumbered three to one. As the Meccans emerged over the hilltop, led by their most distinguished chiefs, Muhammad prayed by name for their destruction. "Mecca has thrown you the best morsels of her liver," he assured his men.

A fast camel was tethered nearby, says one account, in case the day went badly. Events now moved swiftly. A party of Meccans, discerning the numerical frailty of the opposition, charged the oasis, but the huge Hamza cut them down. Two Meccan brothers and a son of one of them, all kinfolk of Hind, then stepped forward and challenged any three Muslims to take them on. Three of Muhammad's immediate family—his foster son Ali, Hamza, and a sixty-five-

A trading caravan (below) nears the Red Sea in this evocative painting by Alberto Pasini (1826–1899). An attempt by the Meccans to prevent Muhammad's followers from seizing such a caravan led to armed confrontation and the Battle of Badr, the Muslim's first military victory.

The battle at the Badr oasis (above), from the Siyar-e-Nabi (Life of the Prophet), *a sixteenth-century Turkish-illustrated manuscript by Mustafa Darir. Muhammad can be seen directing his troops (top right), while the angel Gabriel dictates a portion of the Qur'an.*

year-old cousin—volunteered. The three Meccans were soon dead, along with Muhammad's cousin. Hind, who thereby lost her father, uncle and brother, pledged a terrible vengeance. She would not wash nor comb her hair, she vowed, until she had eaten Hamza's liver.

Fighting then became general. Striding sword in hand behind the line according to some accounts, praying fervently according to others, Muhammad urged on his fighters. At the height of conflict, Muslim records agree, a roaring wind blasted the scene. "It is Gabriel!" cried the Prophet. "Attack!" The Muslim warriors rushed forward, driving the Meccans back upon each other.

One Muslim hacked his way to a Meccan chief, a particularly fervid foe of Muhammad, and cut off his head. With his own arm almost severed in the process, this warrior is said to have placed his foot on the dangling limb and torn it from his body—and then continued fighting with his good arm. This one-armed hero would survive into the reign of Muhammad's third successor. The Meccans, with fifty of their warriors dead and fifty more taken prisoner, fled for home.

How greatly the Battle of Badr enhanced the Islamic cause can scarcely be exaggerated. With few casualties of their own, the Muslims had exterminated many leading enemies, and to have fought at Badr became a coveted distinction among the faithful. A theological principle had also been established: Islam's credibility depended upon Islam's ascendancy. It became a case of "We're right because we're winning," which would work splendidly so long as they did indeed win—but reversals would necessitate serious reexamination of this basis for the faith.

Meanwhile, consternation spread through Mecca. Abu Sufyan was now the Quraysh chieftain-elect, nearly every other leader having perished. He banned all public display of grief for a month, foreswore all cooked food himself, and said he would not approach his wives until a counterattack had been made.[1] When the month ended, all Mecca gave over to wild grieving.

At Medina, however, the Hypocrites (the Islamic term for Medina residents who tolerated the Muslims as a practical necessity but scoffed at their religion) remained sullenly skeptical, and the Jews were increasingly alarmed. It behooved Muhammad to find ways to consolidate the power conferred by Badr.

1. Abu Sufyan's vow not to "approach" his wives is ridiculed by Muslim tradition, because, although he had children, he was by reputation a homosexual. It should be remembered, however, that the early Muslim biographies were largely written by later chroniclers belonging to the powerful Abbasid dynasty, whose primary concern would not be to enhance the reputation of Abu Sufyan, ancestor of the rival Umayyad caliphs.

God seemingly had assured the faithful that they could serve him well by killing in battle. But why just in battle, when battles could be avoided, or even won in advance, by selective extermination. Thus assassination became a recognized means to win the favor of both God and his Prophet.

There was, for example, the poetess Asma, whose verses heaped scorn on the entire Muslim movement. Asma's blind husband, who detested her anyway, became a Muslim and stabbed her to death in her bed. Muhammad commended him from the pulpit as "a man who has assisted the Lord and his Prophet." Another enemy, an Arab chief from al-Taif, assembled a force to march on Medina. A Muslim convert won his confidence, cut off his head, and escaped to present this grisly trophy to Muhammad. As reward, the Prophet presented him with his own staff, which the assassin carried all his life.

Another problematic poet, half Jewish, was murdered in his marriage bed by his foster brother, secretly a Muslim convert. This man, conscience-stricken later on, confessed to Muhammad that he had had to lie and dissemble. The Prophet told him not to worry about it. The incident further signaled that no Jew was safe in Medina. Indeed, says the Muslim historian, Ibn Ishaq, the Prophet shortly gave orders to kill any who came into Muslim hands—and thus began the Medina pogrom.

Of Medina's three Jewish tribal communities, the most vulnerable was the Banu Qainuqa. Unlike the other two, it lacked territory of its own—its members were artisans and soldiers—but Medina's titular chieftain, although nominally a Muslim, was heavily in debt to this tribe, and had sworn a mutual defence pact. Now Muhammad abruptly demanded that the Qainuqa recognize him forthwith as the Prophet of God. They refused, and warned him not to infer too much from his victory at Badr, which they said was "against men who had no knowledge of war." A war with the Qainuqa would not be another Badr. Muhammad withdrew, and the Qainuqa congratulated themselves on calling his bluff.

But they had misjudged their man. A few days later there occurred an "incident." A Jewish boy was accused of lifting the skirts of a Muslim girl. Her Muslim kinsman killed the lad, and in the resulting uproar was himself slain. That was excuse enough. Muhammad invaded the Qainuqa quarter at the head of his army. The Qainuqa withdrew into their fortified enclosure and appealed to Medina's chieftain to come to their aid. The chieftain seized Muhammad by the breastplate, threatening him. "Let me go, wretch!" shouted Muhammad, but he knew he was not yet strong enough to challenge Medina's old establishment. As a compromise he agreed that the Qainuqa should merely be deported, and their store of arms become Muslim booty.

This windfall was nothing, however, compared with the bonanza that fell to a hundred-man raiding party organized about this time by Zayd, the former Christian slave who served as Muhammad's secretary. Because the old route to Syria was now too

A bronze water ewer (below)— from New York's Metropolitan Museum of Art—dating from the time of Muhammad, with a spout in the shape of a crowing rooster. Since Arabs ate with their fingers, such pitchers and a basin for washing were common items in all but the poorest households.

2. During the fighting, Arab women would perch themselves behind the warriors, shaking their timbrels to accompany their songs of encouragement. A sample verse:

> Daughters fair of Tariq are we,
> Attack—we'll give you our kisses free,
> Our perfumed beds will ready be.
> But we'll desert you if you flee,
> Our love for braver men will be.

A list of the names of the fallen in the Battle of Badr (below), from a nineteenth-century manuscript by Muhammad as-Sadi. Islam's first "martyrs" continue to be revered fourteen centuries after the fight.

dangerous for Meccan caravans, an enormous expedition, rich with silver bars and vessels, had decided to follow an arid back route to Iraq, along the east side of the Arabian Peninsula. Word leaked to Medina, and Zayd's raiders easily overpowered its escort. They returned triumphant with eight hundred pieces of silver for each man, and twenty thousand for Muhammad's household. The message was unmistakable. Not only was Islam spiritually comforting—it also paid handsomely.

To survive the reversal they were about to suffer, however, the Muslims would require all the fervor they could command. At Mecca the canny Abu Sufyan, preparing for one gigantic assault upon Medina and Muhammad, appealed to every available ally. Uncle Abbas, Muhammad's chief informant in the enemy camp, sent him word that the force arrayed against him would number three thousand. In January 625, this army set out from Mecca in splendor, led by the customary contingent of timbrel-banging women.[2]

Hind, wife of Abu Sufyan, had an additional plan. She brought along a huge black Ethiopian slave named Wahshi, renowned as an expert with the javelin. He must watch the melee from a distance until he spotted Muhammad's Uncle Hamza, Hind told Wahshi, and bring him down. His reward would be his freedom and a share in any booty. The Muslim force of about seven hundred was outnumbered more than four to one by the advancing Meccans, who encamped in a valley behind a hill called Uhud, three miles north of Medina's outskirts. At dawn, Muhammad placed his men around the hill, keeping it at his back as a refuge should things go badly. This precaution would save the lives of most of his army, and the future of Islam.

Commanding the Meccan cavalry was Khalid ibn al-Walid, a formidable tactician who was destined to convert to Islam, and over the next thirty years would establish himself as one of the great attack generals of history. Khalid noted that the Muslims' left flank might be vulnerable to a concerted cavalry attack. The Prophet had stationed a squad of crack bowmen on the hill with strict orders never to leave their position under any circumstance. In the event, however, an overwhelming temptation would lure them away: sex.

As the armies confronted one another a Meccan fighter named Talha loudly challenged any Muslim to combat. The Prophet's son Ali stepped forward and with a single sword blow sliced through Talha's helmet and skull. Then Talha's brother was struck dead by Hamza, and in the next few minutes Hamza, Ali, and another Muslim put an end to two more brothers and three sons of the perished Talha. These single-combat encounters, though much in the Arab tradition, robbed the Meccans of the benefit of their numerical advantage. Hamza's conspicuous performance made his identity unmistakable, however, and sealed his fate. The Ethiopian Wahshi spotted his target and hurled his javelin. Hamza fell dead, and Wahshi left. "I had no further business there," he observed.

Meanwhile, the magnificent feats of their champions so cheered the Muslims that, as at Badr, they charged wildly forward. When the Meccan front rank again collapsed, the Muslims broke through to the Meccan camp, and began making free with the women. Rape on the battlefield was within Arab rules and was little mitigated by Islamic morality, which merely ritualized it. This time, however, it brought disaster. The spectacle proved too enticing for the archers, who were missing it all. Forgetting Muhammad's orders, they rushed to join in, and sharp-eyed Khalid ibn al-Walid loosed upon the Muslim flank every available cavalryman. A seeming Muslim victory suddenly became a rout.

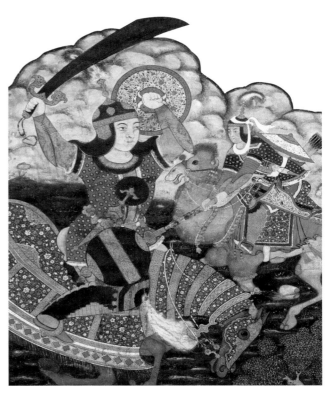

The more fortunate were able to scramble to the safety of the hill above, but Muhammad himself was one of the first to fall. He had stood screaming at his fleeing soldiery: "Come back! I am the Apostle of the Lord! Return!" This proving futile, he hurled rocks at the enemy until a Meccan blow smashed his helmet down onto his head, so hard that the rings of the earpieces sank deep into his cheek.

Neck and forehead gashed, lip cut and a tooth broken, the Prophet reeled backward and disappeared from sight. But then he regained his feet and climbed the hill to safety, and when his men cheered to see him, he quickly silenced them. If the enemy knew he was alive, he warned, they would attack again. Meanwhile, his wounds seemed to enrage him, and he hurled a curse upon his assailants: "Let the wrath of God burn against the men that have sprinkled the face of his Apostle with his own blood!"[3]

With Muhammad presumed dead, the Meccans did indeed call off their attack. If he was gone, Mecca had no quarrel with Medina. Abu Sufyan loudly declared that Badr was avenged, and proclaimed the glory of the Meccan idols. This was too much for the Prophet's stalwart follower Umar ibn al-Khattab. "The Lord is ours, not yours," Umar roared. "Our slain are in paradise; yours are in the fire." Abu Sufyan responded with a challenge for a showdown at Badr one year hence, and when Umar accepted, the Meccan army began moving for home.

One further scene bears mention. Wahshi, the javelin thrower, had conducted the vengeful Hind to Hamza's body. She tore out the liver, nibbled at it, swallowed, and sickened, spat out the rest. Other Meccan women helped her to carve up the body, fashioning armlets, bracelets and anklets from the ears, nose, and, says the record delicately, "other parts."

The Meccans reportedly lost twenty men at the Battle of Uhud, and the Muslims seventy-four, but the principal Muslim loss was in credibility. In Medina, the Jews proclaimed the obvious implications. If victory at Badr proved God was with Muhammad, then surely defeat at Uhud must prove the reverse. Muhammad's interesting answer appears in the Qur'an's third sura.

An incredible oral tradition developed around the imaginary exploits of Muhammad's Uncle Hamza, which over the centuries grew into elaborate tales of fantastic derring-do involving a host of giants, sorcerers, demons and dragons. The young Indian Mughal Emperor Akbar (1556–1605) was so taken with the stories that he ordered them written down. His epic Hamzanama *eventually comprised fourteen volumes, accompanied by fourteen hundred unbound paintings. About two hundred of the paintings (including this one, above) have survived.*

3. Muhammad's bitter curse upon those who had wounded him in the Battle of Uhud makes an interesting contrast with Jesus' response to those who had nailed him to a cross: "Father, forgive them, for they know not what they do" (Lk. 23:34).

Reversals are necessary, it explains, to separate true believers from the merely opportunistic: "This various success we cause to alternate among men, that God may know those that believe . . . and annihilate the infidels. What! Did ye think to enter paradise, while as yet God knew not those that fight for him, and knew not the persevering amongst you?" (Sura 3:139–142).

Nevertheless, something more was needed to allay the hostility of neighboring tribes, now challenging Muhammad. He thwarted one belligerent by attacking first, capturing and enslaving some two hundred women in the process. (Before long, the procession of female captives into Muslim slavery would number in the tens of thousands.) In two other instances, however, the Muslims were the losers.

Muhammad told his men to uproot the Jewish tribe's date palms, an act forbidden by the Law of Moses. But the Prophet revealed that Muslims enjoyed a special exemption from the rule.

4. Thus the first Muslim martyrs followed the example of Muhammad, and cursed those who inflicted violence upon them; while the first Christian martyr Stephen followed the example of Jesus and asked God to forgive his assailants (Acts 7:60).

5. Many historians doubt the story of this Jewish assassination attempt upon Muhammad. While the Qur'an wholly devotes one sura (59) to the Banu al-Nadir case, it does not mention this plot—a most improbable oversight. Nevertheless, in a very typical sermon carried on a twenty-first-century Saudi Web site, Sheikh Abd al-Muhsin al Qassem would categorically cite it as proof of the perfidy of Jewish tribes at Medina: "When our Prophet Muhammad was sent, the Jews incited the people and fought against him . . . The Jewish tribe Banu al-Nadir tried to drop a large rock on him from the roof of a house, but he was warned by the heavens." The sheikh proceeded to a denunciation of Jews as the enemies of God intent upon destroying Muslims (cited by the Middle East Research Institute, October 18, 2002).

One tribe professed interest in embracing Islam, then ambushed the seven-man mission sent to instruct them. Only one escaped, four were killed, and two were captured and sold to the Meccans. These men, refusing to recant, perished during torture as true martyrs, evidencing the defiant courage that would characterize Islam for generations to come. "Allah! Count them well," they shouted, eyeing their torturers, "then kill them all, one by one. Let none escape."[4]

Another tribe, playing the same trick, ambushed a forty-man Muslim mission and killed all but one. This incident, however, provided Muhammad with an excuse to attack their allies, the Banu al-Nadir, the region's second Jewish community. At a preliminary parley, writes the Muslim historian Ibn Ishaq, the Jews planned to murder Muhammad by dropping a huge boulder on him as he arrived. But Gabriel warned the Prophet, who returned to the town and sent a warning instead: "By your proposing to slay me, you have broken the pact I made with you . . . I give you ten days to depart from my country. Whosoever of you is seen after that, his head shall be cut off."[5]

What particularly alarmed the Banu al-Nadir was that this message was delivered by a member of the Aus tribe, supposedly their allies. As the Qainuqa had, they barricaded themselves in their fortified community. Muhammad ordered his men to destroy the date palms around their fields, thus instantly depriving them of future earnings. To destroy such trees was specifically prohibited by the Law of Moses, and by later *Shari'a* (Islamic Law); but Muhammad explained that it did not apply to Muslims, to whom Gabriel had provided special dispensation.

The Banu al-Nadir, having nothing left to defend, then surrendered on condition that they could leave safely, with all their possessions except weapons. These possessions proved of significantly greater value than the Muslims had estimated; however, they had to watch in frustration as mesmerizing quantities of gold and goods were taken north to Khaybar, a big Jewish settlement. Also impressive were the beauty and luxury of the women, laden with ornaments of finest gold set with precious stones. Only one Jewish tribe, the Banu Qurayza, still remained at Medina.

One year after Badr, marking the end of the truce between Mecca and Medina, neither side appeared ready to fight. Muhammad's appeals for recruits reportedly went largely unheeded until he announced he would face the enemy by himself if need be, which brought fifteen hundred volunteers. At Mecca, Abu Sufyan assembled two thousand foot soldiers and fifty horses, who marched north, came within sight of Medina, halted, and returned home. This non-engagement is nevertheless known as "the Second Battle of Badr."

However, the following year, the Meccans amassed their biggest force ever, reportedly ten thousand men: including four thousand soldiers on foot, fifteen hundred on camels, and three hundred on horseback. Panic seized Medina, which could muster at most three thousand. How could it possibly survive such a siege? But an Iraqi Christian slave, freed upon his conversion to Islam, offered timely advice on defensive warfare, an art unknown to the Arabs.

Deeply scored basalt plains made the city difficult to approach from three sides, he noted. Only from the north did open fields leave it vulnerable. Here they dug a huge trench, too wide for horses to jump, and deep enough that attacking foot soldiers could be shot from above. This chasm did indeed balk Abu Sufyan's horde.

The siege became a mere contest of abuse, all thirteen thousand participants hurling insults and threats for days, but the Meccan besiegers had time on their side. The biggest uncertainty was what the Jewish Banu Qurayza might do. Thus it was, say the Islamic records, that God saved Islam by providing the Muslims with a deliverer, a member of the Christian Banu Ghassan, who was serving with the Meccan army. This man, trusted by both the Meccans and the Qurayza, came to Muhammad secretly to ask how he could serve the Muslim cause. Muhammad's answer was explicit: Sow distrust between the Meccans and the Jews.

Camel-mounted warriors fighting at the Battle of Uhud (below), from Mustafa Darir's Siyar-e-Nabi (Life of the Prophet). *Lack of discipline among the Muslim troops led to a setback at the hands of the Meccan cavalry commander Khalid ibn al-Walid, who after his conversion to Islam would become the greatest general of the Muslim conquests.*

سراسیمه وحیران در میان مکشتند ورخی ازبشان سعادت شهادت قایزشدند وسح

The volunteer secret agent thereupon approached his old friends, the Banu Qurayza. If the Meccans should lose the battle, he suggested, they would simply go home—but the Jews would lose everything. To guarantee their continued participation, therefore, the Jews should demand that they provide significant hostages. This made sense to the Banu Qurayza. Then the agent went to his old friends, the Meccans. He felt it his duty to warn them, said he, that the Jews now regretted opposing Muhammad, and were about to join the Muslims. They even intended to demand high-ranking Meccan hostages, whom they planned to turn over to Muhammad.

Sure enough, a Meccan delegation sought Jewish help in an all-out attack on the Muslim rear—and was appalled when the Qurayza demanded hostages. With all trust lost, no Jewish attack occurred. Disease and discord broke out among the Meccans, fierce winds assailed their camp, Bedouin tribes began pulling out, and after two weeks, Abu Sufyan called off the siege. Muhammad was now considered invincible. If an army of ten thousand could not defeat him, who

The besieged Jews faced three terrible choices: Embrace Islam, thus betraying God. Or slaughter their own families and fight to the death. Or break the Sabbath with a surprise attack.

could? The time had come, advised the angel Gabriel (as quoted by the Prophet) to deal with the Banu Qurayza, Medina's last Jews. Muhammad did so with an act of butchery that would permanently poison Islamic–Jewish relations.

The Qurayza were barricaded within their fortress about three miles southeast of the town. As Muhammad's army approached this stronghold, flights of Jewish arrows rained hard upon them. One Muslim ventured to the fortress walls, and was killed by a huge millstone pushed upon him from above by an unidentified Jewess. But the Qurayza sensed themselves doomed.

They had three hard choices, their leader reasoned. First, they could embrace Islam and thereby betray God. Second, they could kill their wives and children to keep them from the infidels, and then fight to the death. Third, they could attack on Saturday, thus violating God's Sabbath law, but catching the Muslims off guard. His people rejected all three. They appealed instead to the Aus tribe, whom on a previous occasion they had saved from destruction. The advice of the Aus chief was unequivocal. To surrender was to perish, he said; they should fight to the death.[6]

The Qurayza nevertheless did surrender twenty-five days later, on condition that their fate be determined by the Aus. Muhammad, having agreed, then announced that the decision would not be made by their friend, the local Aus chief. Instead, he called upon the grand chief of the Aus federation, a merciless man known to deeply despise Jews. This dignitary, a grossly corpulent man, physically supported by his aides, was transported to the Qurayza fort. While his kinsmen pleaded with him to spare their allies, the Muslim army envisioned vast booty within the fortress, and speculatively eyed the Jewish women. Muhammad himself

6. Abu Lababa, the Aus chief, rushed back to his people, guilt-stricken. He had betrayed the Prophet, he said, by telling the Qurayza the truth. Was not war supposed to be deceit? As penance for his truthfulness, Abu Lababa ordered his daughter to tie him to a post in the mosque, where for some fifteen days he remained until Muhammad, informed by Gabriel that he had suffered enough, ordered him to free himself. The spot is still known as the "Pillar of Repentance."

had set his eye on one particular prize, the beautiful Reihana, aged seventeen.

"Proceed with your judgment," ordered the Prophet. "My judgment," said the gross old Aus chieftain, "is that the men shall be put to death, the women and children sold into slavery, and the spoil divided amongst the army." Wails of agony were silenced by a wave of Muhammad's hand. This, he pronounced, was "the judgment of God."

So all the male Qurayza were dragged into Medina and penned in an enclosure, where they prayed through the night, exhorting each other to remain steadfast in their faith. Muhammad, they reasoned, could not possibly behead some eight hundred men. But next morning, a Muslim soldier led away half a dozen of them, then returned for another half dozen, then another, and another. Even as their numbers dwindled, the survivors could still not bring themselves to believe these men had all in fact been killed—but such was the case. Each group was made to kneel by a deep trench, dug overnight across the town square. As their heads were severed, their bodies were pushed into the pit.

At length, it was time for the booty, and then the women. The numbers were satisfactory indeed: fifteen hundred swords, a thousand lances, five hundred shields and three hundred coats of mail, flocks of sheep and camels, gold and silver vessels, jewels and beautiful household furnishings, and about a thousand women. The four-fifths to one-fifth division was again carried out. Included in Muhammad's share, of course, was the comely Reihana.

The Prophet proposed marriage as soon as Reihana's husband, brothers and father had been executed. Muslim tradition naturally omits description of her misery, but does say that she refused to wed him. She preferred to be his concubine, she said, which she immediately became. (Devout Muslims reject this tradition, however. Muhammad, they say, had no concubines.) Some sources say she also refused to convert to Islam, others that she later did so. Reihana would die four years later, a year before Muhammad himself.

Bedouin herding camels on the arid valley floor near Medina (below) where the Muslim and Meccan armies clashed at Uhud in 625. Muhammad's forces escaped disaster by regrouping on one of the hills overlooking the valley.

MCBRIDE

Only one woman was put to death. She came forward to announce that it was she who had crushed the Muslim attacker with the millstone, and she demanded to share her husband's fate. She met her death fearless and smiling—a smile, Muhammad's wife A'isha later confessed, that haunted her all her life.

This mass extermination of the Banu Qurayza effectively terminated any possibility thereafter of peaceful relations between Judaism and Islam. Further, Muhammad's personal participation in the slaughter would stand in such stark contrast to anything in the ministry of Jesus Christ as to preclude, in the minds of many Christians, any tolerant recognition of Muhammad as a prophet. To envision Jesus of Nazareth personally presiding over the butchery of his enemies would never be feasible—nor did he ever provide legitimate grounds for anyone else to do so.

Some Christians would point out, no doubt, that to contrast what God Incarnate did with what any mortal human did is manifestly unfair. Others would reply that, even so, the example set for Christians is shockingly at odds with the example set for Muslims. Yet this, of course, would render such a deed far worse if perpetuated by Christians than by Muslims, and in the coming wars with Islam, Christians themselves would sometimes rival the Prophet's vicious early venture into genocide.

A Muslim archer and Bedouin officer from the time of Muhammad. It was soldiers like these, lightly armed and sandal-shod tribesmen from the desert and small towns of southern Arabia, who formed the backbone of an army that challenged the great powers of the seventh century.

Cultural historian Martin Lings, a lecturer at Cairo University who himself became a Muslim and who served as Keeper of Oriental Manuscripts at the British Museum, points out in defence of the massacre that Muhammad's judgment there was in perfect accord with the Jews' own code for such a situation: "When the Lord thy God hath delivered it unto thy hands, thou shalt smite every male therein with the edge of the sword: but the women and little ones, and the cattle, and all that is in the city, even all the spoil thereof, thou shalt take unto thyself." (Deut. 20:12–14) However, this was pronounced after an offer of peace and forced labor. No such offer was made to the Banu Qurayza.

Historian William Muir (*The Life of Mohammed from Original Sources*) is less understanding. "The indiscriminate slaughter of eight hundred men, and the subjugation of the whole tribe to slavery, cannot be recognized otherwise than as an act of monstrous cruelty," he writes. "The plea of divine ratification or command may allay the scruples of the Muslim; but it will be summarily rejected by those who call to mind that the same authority was now habitually produced for personal ends, and for the justification of even questionable actions. In short, the butchery of the Banu Qurayza casts an indelible blot on the life of Muhammad."

The fate of the rest of Arabia's Jewry was probably settled in August and September 628. Having negotiated a long-term truce with Mecca, Muhammad turned his attention to Khaybar, the Jewish settlement one hundred miles north

The Muslim army consisted of a mere sixteen hundred men, but Muhammad's gift for strategy, stealth and diplomacy would once again bring his followers success.

of Medina, haven for many refugees from earlier conquests. Its elimination would provide a solution to the Jewish problem, but it was known to have ten thousand men under arms, drilling daily, and among them were the most accurate archers on the peninsula.

Like Medina, Khaybar was the center of a rich agricultural area. Also like Medina, its Jewish tribes were divided. They occupied separate fortresses atop steep hills, and depended on alliances with such neighboring tribes as the Christian Ghassan to the north. The campaign against them began with a number of strategic assassinations, followed by a direct assault. The Muslim army consisted of a mere sixteen hundred men, but Muhammad's gift for strategy, stealth and tribal diplomacy would again bring success.

All seven Jewish fortresses sealed their gates and prepared for a siege. While Muhammad encircled and took each in turn, however, not once did any one of them come out to aid another. Jewish traitors, on the other hand, allegedly helped the Muslims. One showed them a cache of siege machinery, something the Arabs had scarcely heard of before, but put to immediate use. Another turncoat revealed the source of an underground water supply to one fortress. The Muslims blocked it, forcing the defenders to capitulate.

Looming large and seemingly unassailable was the al-Kamus fortress, citadel of the Banu al-Nadir whom the Muslims had expelled from Medina. Remembering the disastrous siege there, the Jews sallied into the field, their skilled archers repelling repeated Muslim attacks. Neither the veteran Abu Bakr nor Umar could make headway against their defence, say the Islamic traditions. It was Ali, charging like a man gone mad, who led a veritable rampage through their fighters, though reputedly losing only nineteen men to the Jewish ninety-three. Again the Banu al-Nadir surrendered. Again they were to be allowed to leave—but only after handing over all their weapons, land and wealth.

The wealth they produced proved suspiciously meager, however, for the disappointed Muslims vividly remembered all the fine fabric, jewels and golden utensils they had seen leave Medina. Where was it now? The Jewish chief denied there was more until torture, in the form of a small fire kindled on his naked chest, improved his memory. The remainder was seized, and the chief and a cousin decapitated. Within weeks the other Khaybar forts fell. The Jewish presence in Arabia, from that day to this, ceased to be significant. Within two decades, Judaism, along with Christianity, would be prohibited throughout the peninsula.

The wealth seized at Khaybar far exceeded that taken at Medina. Riches were increasingly becoming a reward for faith, and desire for plunder played a central role in the conquests that followed. The traditions also indicate that from then on, the Muslims had many slaves. One fifth of the Khaybar booty went to the Prophet's household. He also got half the Jewish lands, the other half being

The Prophet, having eliminated the Jewish threat to the north, could again look south to Mecca, the city that had violently rejected the divine revelation of its native son.

divided among the soldiers, and a further bonus as well. His quick eye had, as usual, spotted an especially beautiful girl. At a victory banquet that evening, seventeen-year-old Safiyah, widowed in the battle and splendidly garbed, was presented to him.

Unlike Reihana, say the traditions, Safiyah gratefully accepted her fate. She allegedly had been intrigued by Islam since childhood, and was so enamored of its Prophet that her indignant husband had recently blackened her eye for it. The ardent Muhammad consummated his latest marriage that very night, a violation of the rule he tried to impose on his followers, namely that no new wife could be entered until she had completed her current menstrual cycle, so that paternity of children was identifiable.

Zaynab, another young woman bereaved at Khaybar, appeared similarly admiring of the Prophet at the victory banquet. She presented him with a special gift, a young goat beautifully roasted, and as it turned out, thoroughly poisoned—particularly in the shoulder, Muhammad's known preference. Unsuspecting, he helped himself to shoulder, and offered the rest to Abu Bakr and to Bishr, another faithful lieutenant. These two had been first after the Prophet to turn away from Jerusalem, and towards Mecca, when that change was decreed in the mosque. (See previous chapter.)

Before Muhammad had swallowed much, however, he spat out the poisoned meat, grabbing his gut in pain. Bishr, who had wolfed down a hefty portion, collapsed, paralyzed, never to move again. Zaynab, glaring at the company, identified herself as the sister of a slain Jewish soldier. "You have inflicted grievous injuries on my people," she said. "You have killed my father, uncle, and husband.

A nineteenth-century engraving of Muhammad preaching to the faithful in Medina (above). By 629, after consolidating his hold on Medina and the surrounding region, the Prophet was secure enough to begin a final and ultimately successful campaign against his hometown of Mecca.

Therefore I said within myself, if he is a prophet he will reject the [goat] kid, knowing it is poisoned. But if he is a mere pretender, then we shall be rid of him, and the Jews will again prosper."

Modern Muslims and their liberal Western apologists, for whom the Prophet's conduct on such occasions can represent insurmountable embarrassment, like to add that he forgave the girl after this valiant confession. Unfortunately, however, all but one of the records say she was put to death. The effects of the poison were prolonged, and would be blamed by some for Muhammad's death a year later. In any case, Jews were now recognized as implacable enemies of Islam. "Alas for that which they work! Wherefore do their rabbis and their priests restrain them not from uttering wickedness, and eating that which is forbidden. Alas for that which they commit! The Jews say, 'The hand of God is tied up.' Nay, their own hands are tied up, and they are cursed for what they say" (Sura 5:62–64).

Having eliminated the Jewish threat in the north, the Prophet could again look south to Mecca, the city that had so decisively and violently rejected its native son. He had been able to concentrate his forces against Khaybar because he had made a truce with the Meccans following the desultory Battle of the Trench. But Mecca's humiliation on that occasion had caused a political upset back home. The party headed by Abu Sufyan, sponsor of that ignominiously futile siege, had lost influence to a more belligerent younger generation.

Hostilities therefore resumed with raids and counterraids, the Muslims conducting no less than seventeen in a year, and in March 628, Muhammad created a new crisis. He and his followers, he announced, would make the "lesser" annual pilgrimage to the Ka'ba at Mecca. Since the lesser pilgrimage was less widely observed, few other Arabs would be there. This presented Mecca with a dilemma. If it attacked pilgrims, even Muslim ones, all Arabia would be horrified. But if it admitted them, Muhammad might again discover that the old truce rules did not apply to him, and seize power in a sudden coup. The younger set swore to resist him.

A somewhat fanciful nineteenth-century German depiction of a triumphant Muhammad entering Mecca. Muslim history records that the town's streets were, in fact, almost deserted as the Prophet's troops occupied his birthplace. Only eleven citizens were condemned for their resistance, and seven of those were later reprieved.

How many pilgrims accompanied Muhammad is debatable, with estimates varying from seven hundred to sixteen hundred (plus a few women). The Bedouin, seeing few prospects of loot, did not answer the call, which would earn them a Qur'anic rebuke: "Those that stay behind . . . are a people that understandeth little" (Sura 48:11 and following). (But it goes on to promise them more booty in greater wars to come.)

As the extensive company, dressed in pilgrim garb, neared Mecca, they found their way blocked by a squad of horsemen under Khalid ibn al-Walid. Muhammad sent a troop of his own horses to confront them. After much parley, they worked out a ten-year truce named the Treaty of Hudaybiyya, for the locale where it was signed.

The Muslims agreed not to interfere with Meccan caravans, and to send home to Mecca any converts lacking permission from their families. But beginning with the next year, the Meccans would evacuate their city annually to

'We don't want your food,' said the Meccans. 'Be gone.' So Muhammad left, but he began to prepare his last and decisive move against his native city.

let Muslim pilgrims in. Muhammad, greatly pleased, readily assented. With Mecca neutralized, he could move against Jewish Khaybar (described above). Moreover, the pilgrimage would signify to all Arabs that Islam had not come to destroy their religion, but merely to purify it from idolatry.

The following year, two thousand Muslims, wearing pilgrim robes and armed only with sheathed swords, arrived for the lesser pilgrimage, leading sixty sacrificial camels into the strangely abandoned city, while the Meccans watched from the surrounding hills. Muhammad touched the Black Stone of the Ka'ba with his staff, and made the seven ritual circuits. His followers did the same. A few began shouting challenges at the hills. Muhammad restrained them, instructing them to shout instead the praises of God.

But when Bilal climbed to the roof of the Ka'ba and sounded the Muslim call to prayer, the listening Meccans began to think they had made a serious mistake. Three days later, Muhammad made his uncle's sister-in-law his tenth wife, and invited the Meccans to a wedding feast. "We don't want your food," said they. "Be gone." So he left, but he also began to prepare his last and decisive move against his native city.

Converts were now multiplying, and new tribes hastening to pledge allegiance. When Meccans arrived at Medina as converts, Muhammad sent them home, as agreed in the treaty, but he knew that many went instead to a razzia-financed settlement of would-be Muslims on the Red Sea. One such convert, fatally injured in a camel accident, before he died sent a letter to his brother in Mecca, urging him to embrace Islam. The recipient of this momentous letter was none other than Khalid ibn al-Walid.

Khalid's disenchantment with the Meccan cause had grown since the Battle of

Uhud, where his own sharp generalship had won Mecca its only victory. Finally he left for Medina, meeting on the way another traveler, Amr ibn As, a poet of devastating skill, whose verses had enraged Muhammad, but who was now ready to change sides. Khalid ibn al-Walid would play a key role in the conquest of Zoroastrian Persia and Christian Syria. Amr would become the conqueror of Christian Egypt.

It was time to tackle Mecca head-on, treaty or no treaty. In any case, a convenient attack by the Mecca-supported Banu Bakr on the neighboring Banu Khoza'a, who were committed to Muhammad, was deemed sufficient cause to repudiate it.[7] The alarmed Meccans sent Abu Sufyan himself to Medina to secure its reaffirmation, but the mission is recorded as a failure.

Unparalleled secrecy attended Muhammad's next move. Messages went out

Muhammad made the seven circuits around the Ka'ba and then, pointing his stick at each of the 360 idols around the shrine, commanded their immediate and complete destruction.

7. The Treaty of Hudaybiyya (630) became a major issue thirteen centuries later, when an American newsman surreptitiously taped a 1994 speech made by Palestinian leader Yasir Arafat to a Muslim audience in Johannesburg (*New York Times*, May 20, 1994). Answering Muslim criticism of his treaty with Israel, Arafat explained: "I see this agreement as being no more than the agreement signed by our Prophet Muhammad and the Quraysh in Mecca." He added: "We now accept the peace agreement, but only to continue on the road to Jerusalem." Many news media interpreted this remark as a declared intention to break the treaty when convenient, and were inundated by outraged Muslim protests. How dared they imply that God's Prophet was perfidious? This was unthinkable. Obviously, it was the Quraysh who broke the Treaty of Hudaybiyya. Appropriate media apologies followed.

to his wide constituency of allied tribes, naming a rendezvous, and the fully assembled army reportedly numbered ten thousand. At the head of the crack horsemen rode the seemingly invincible Khalid, Mecca's former champion, followed by five hundred Meccan refugees. In their midst rode the Prophet, flanked by Abu Bakr and Umar, and escorted by a bodyguard of the best cavalry—a scene intended to stir his followers' hearts. This was the climax, and God's fearsomely armed Prophet would triumph. (Here, too, the Christian equivalent provides an interesting contrast: Jesus, riding on a donkey amidst the palms and hosannas of the poor, destined through a hideous death to gain victory for humankind.)

After a day's ride, the army bivouacked above Mecca. With thousands of campfires blinking from the hills, all Arabia seemed arrayed there. Out of the city stole Uncle Abbas to formally join his nephew at last. A day later, Abbas met the Meccan chieftain Abu Sufyan on the road, and led him to Muhammad. It was a historic meeting. "Out upon thee, Abu Sufyan," declared the Prophet. "Have you not yet discovered that there is no God but the Lord alone?" Replied Abu Sufyan: "Noble and generous sir, had there been any God beside, verily he would have been of some avail to me."

So Muhammad pushed the next and critical question: "And do you not acknowledge that I am the Prophet of the Lord?" But Abu Sufyan was not quite ready for this. "Noble sir, as to this thing there is yet in my heart some hesitancy." Abbas groaned. "Woe to you," he exclaimed. "This is no time for hesitancy. Believe and testify forthwith the creed of Islam, or your neck shall be in danger!"

So Abu Sufyan thereupon acquiesced, and Muhammad's terms followed swiftly. He returned to Mecca, proclaimed the hopelessness of resistance, and guaranteed the safety of anyone who stayed inside, behind closed doors, or who took refuge in the mosque. His capitulation roused the jeers and scorn of his own wife, the inimitable Hind, who demanded his immediate execution. "Kill this fat and greasy bladder of lard," she screamed at the Meccans. "Don't let her lead you astray," expostulated Abu Sufyan. "We are confronted with the unprecedented." The panic-stricken Meccans believed him, and ran in terror for their homes. Only on the city's south side was resistance offered, by young dissenters determined to fight it out.

Three of the four columns of Muhammad's army entered the city and rode through its silent streets of shuttered houses. On the south flank, where the clatter of battle broke forth, Khalid and a Bedouin force made short work of the holdouts. One of their three leaders surrendered; the other two made good their escape to the Red Sea coast.

Muhammad formally made the seven circuits around the Ka'ba, and then pointed his stick at each of the 360 idols surrounding it, and commanded their destruction. "Truth has come!" he shouted as the great image of the god Hubal crashed down. "Truth hath come and falsehood gone. For falsehood vanisheth away." These became the words of the seventeenth sura (verse 81).

Uthman, the keeper of the Ka'ba and now a convert, opened its doors. Muhammad entered, and reportedly ordered the destruction of all but two of the images within it, one being of Abraham, the other of Mary and the child Jesus. Uthman's family was reaffirmed as keepers of the Ka'ba, as it had been for generations, and Muhammad's own family as provisioner of pilgrims. Every effort was made, that is, to preserve the ancient Arab worship, cleansed of its idolatry.

Only eleven of Mecca's citizens were condemned, and seven of them were later reprieved. (The four not pardoned included two poets whose parodies had particularly irked Muhammad.) Among the many new Muslim converts came a long line of women, one of them veiled. "O Messenger of God," said she from beneath the veil, "praise be to him who hath made triumph the religion which I herewith choose for myself." She said the Muslim creed and threw back the veil. "Hind, daughter of Utbah," she proclaimed. "Welcome," said Muhammad.

"There is no god but Allah" proclaim the banners carried by mounted musicians from this thirteenth-century illustration (right), by Mahmud al-Wasiti, of the annual pilgrimage to Mecca. Muhammad's subjugation of his hometown and his veneration of the Ka'ba shrine meant that Mecca inevitably eclipsed Medina to become the spiritual center of Islam.

8. Muslim history, much to its own discomfort, had not heard the end of Hind. Why the Prophet accepted her insolence is not explained. Some say he could not afford to offend Abu Sufyan whose support was now vital, and Hind, however ferocious, was deeply loved by her husband. In another tradition, Muhammad asked that a pot of water be brought before him. Both he and the women plunged their hands into it, thereby cementing the pledge.

This, at any rate, is the version of Hind's embrace of Islam that modern-day Muslims prefer to tell. Another version, that of Ibn Ishaq, is both older and more convincing. By his account, Muhammad charged the assembled women not to associate any created "thing" with the Deity. "By God," said a voice from beneath a veil, "you lay on us something you have not laid upon the men. But we will carry it out."

"And you shall not steal," charged Muhammad. But this, protested the same woman, would mean giving up her habit of helping herself to a little of her husband's money. Abu Sufyan, who was standing by, observed that he had never regarded this habit as morally wrong.

Muhammad continued with his charge. "Do not commit adultery," he said. "Can a free woman commit adultery, Apostle of God?" demanded the female heckler. Muhammad ignored the question. "And do not kill your children," he continued. "Indeed, I did not," said Hind. "I brought them up when they were little. Who killed them was you, on the field of Badr. So you should know all about killing children."

"You shall not disobey me in carrying out orders to do good," continued Muhammad. "Would we be sitting here like this," countered Hind, "if we were of a mind to disobey your orders?" Muhammad, who never would accept directly the pledge of a woman, then commissioned Umar to admit Hind and the other women to the faith. "Go," Muhammad commanded. "I have accepted your homage."[8]

The virtually unopposed triumph over Mecca, however, ended on a prophetically bloody note. Khalid was dispatched to subdue the Banu Jadhima, south of Mecca, enemies of his family for generations. On his approach, they laid down their arms and professed allegiance to Muhammad. Their men were thereupon bound, and Khalid and his Bedouin began a systematic annihilation, killing one after another. Only the intervention of the Medina Muslims prevented their complete annihilation.

Ibn Ishaq's description of this incident relates a touching scene in which one victim, his hands tied behind his head, asked to be taken to a group of women who stood wailing nearby. One was his wife. "May you fare well, Hubaysha," he said, "though for me my life is at an end." He was dragged back to his comrades and his head struck off. The frantic wife threw herself upon the body, kissed it frantically, and suddenly fell still. The executioners turned her over. She was dead.

The fate of the Banu Jadhima seems to have gravely distressed Muhammad. Stripping his arms bare in the Ka'ba, he cried to the heavens, "O God! O God! I am innocent before thee of what Khalid has done." He had few other regrets, however, because all Arabia now lay open before him, and beyond Arabia lay the world. ■

The Prophet's women

From fiery A'isha to Christian Mary and Jewish Safiyah, Muhammad's domestic life has a profound and lasting impact on Muslim attitudes towards sex and marriage

Managing his empire and keeping peace among the Arabs may have weighed less heavily upon Muhammad than another more intimate problem, namely managing his harem and keeping peace among his wives. He ventured throughout the last decade of his life into what the devout describe as a series of diplomatic marriages, though the early Muslim historians regarded these unions as merely evidence of a healthy and robust virility.

Muhammad remarried soon after the death of his first and probably most influential wife, Khadeja, mother of his four daughters and the only wife to bear him children, though a Christian concubine would, in his advanced years, produce a son. Khadeja's immediate successor was Sauda, middle-aged, dowdy, but well able to raise his daughters. With that done, he divorced her. But she pleaded to be retained so that she could be "numbered with his wives" on the day of resurrection. He agreed and reinstated her as wife.

Though his first step beyond monogamy came with his marriage to the nine-year-old virgin child A'isha, his taste thereafter was distinctly for previously married women. A'isha was followed by and forced to share him with eight other wives and two or more concubines. (Two other

candidates for marriage shocked the faithful by turning him down.) Though A'isha remained queen of the harem, she would turn treacherously conspiratorial after his death, helping to create a permanent schism in Islam. Since she is also the chief historical source for the affairs of his inner household, most of the countless anecdotes about it are stamped with A'isha's perspective.

A'isha's first rival on the scene was his third living wife, Hafsa, daughter of Umar. Hafsa's first husband, an early convert, had been dead for six months. Umar, keen to see her remarried, offered her to the recently widowed Uthman, who did not yet want to remarry, and to Abu Bakr, who preferred his one wife. Chagrined, Umar brought the problem to Muhammad, who offered himself as a husband. Purely, say the devout, to confer on Umar the same status already enjoyed by Abu Bakr. The early Muslim historians admiringly advance another explanation. She was eighteen, dark and ravishingly beautiful. A'isha, now thirteen, confessed herself instantly jealous. But as the harem grew more crowded and political, Hafsa became her ally.

Within a year, Muhammad had

The striking covered face of a Bedouin woman from Oman (below). Muhammad's complex home life with his ten wives and various concubines heralded increasing restrictions on the lives of Muslim women.

A traditional camel-mounted howdah (above). For highborn Arab women such as Muhammad's third wife A'isha, the tent-like covering offered protection from the elements and a degree of privacy while traveling.

agreed, and he spent the next three days exclusively with her, a favor that Muslim husbands would thereafter confer on new brides added to their harems. A'isha, Hafsa and Um Salema became the Prophet's favored companions on the march, each taking turns with him in his red leather tent.

A'isha was a forgetful young lady. On the road with the army, she lost a necklace, and the whole contingent stood by while she searched for it and found her camel had been lying on it. Since it was then too late to move on, the army had to make camp where there was no water for drinking, washing or for the evening prayer ablutions.

The necklace caused a worse problem on another march. Having lost it when she left the camp "to fulfill a need," A'isha went back to recover it, and when she returned, found the column gone. Her slaves had assumed her asleep inside when they lifted her curtained howdah onto her camel, and still asleep when they reached Medina and took it down. The next morning, she arrived in Medina atop a camel led by a Muslim soldier who had fallen behind the column, and hastening to catch up, had come upon her.

The result was a stupendous scandal. A'isha, the gossips said, was unable to have a baby by Muhammad and therefore was seeking a substitute father. Such talk, says A'isha, reached all ears but her own. She could not understand it, she said, when the Prophet suddenly became cool towards her, scarcely comforting her even when she was sick. Then one

acquired two more wives, both from the tribe of Abu Jahal, Muhammad's chief adversary slain at Badr, a family he was at pains to appease. But again the women, both widows, were young and attractive (although one, Zaynab, died soon after). For A'isha, a far graver challenge was posed by wife number five, the startlingly beautiful Um Salema, a woman of wild passion, about thirty, and already noted for her devotion to the faith. Her husband had been wounded at Uhud and died eight months later. She at first resisted Muhammad's marriage proposal, then

day, she learned what was being said from another woman in the Arab equivalent of a ladies' room discussion.[1] "I could not even finish what I was about," she wrote. "I could not stop crying until I thought my liver would burst with my sobs."

When Muhammad consulted his aide Osama and his foster son Ali, the former vouched for A'isha's unassailable fidelity. Ali was less reassuring. "Come now, Prophet," he said, "there's no shortage of women, and you wouldn't have trouble finding a substitute." That remark, later repeated to A'isha, would lead to his assassination twenty years later. Muhammad eventually terminated the gossip by denouncing it from the pulpit. The angel Gabriel assured him of his wife's innocence, he said later.

But if A'isha was innocent, that meant the gossips must be guilty. The outcome appears in the sections of suras 4 and 24 of the Qur'an, setting out the penalties for adultery (death, as the Qur'an was subsequently interpreted), for fornication (one hundred lashes), and for slandering innocent married women (eighty lashes). Adultery and fornication, however, can only be established if four witnesses testify to it, and Muslim courts later declared all four had to have actually seen it taking place. Unless, therefore, it was virtually a grandstand performance, proof is impossible, and the law usually ineffective.

A'isha's cousin Mistah and a servant girl got the lash for their slander. So did the loathsome poet Hassan, who had done much to spread the rumors. He is described as a propagandist, much favored by the Prophet for his verse, but otherwise dirty-mouthed, too cowardly to go into battle, fat, and given to combing his black hair in his eyes and dying his moustache scarlet. After the thrashing, Hassan went blind and suffered further at the hands of the now exculpated soldier who had saved A'isha. He went at Hassan with a sword, and wounded him grievously. The poet survived, however, and Muhammad compensated him with an estate outside Medina, and with a little Coptic Christian girl presented to Muhammad as a gift by the Christian ruler of Egypt. To thoroughly ingratiate himself, Hassan wrote a verse lauding the virtue, charm, wit and slenderness of A'isha, who heckled him as he recited it with jeers about his own absence of slenderness.

In the next affair of the harem, it was the Prophet himself whose virtue was brought into question. Zayd, the male Christian slave given him by Khadeja, though pug-nosed and physically repulsive, had proved exceedingly useful. He taught himself Aramaic so that Muhammad would not have to use a Jewish secretary, and was adopted by the Prophet as a son. Since in the Arab tradition an adopted son had the same status as a natural son, Zayd's wife had the full status of daughter-in-law, which was much the same as that of daughter. To cohabit with a daughter-in-law,

> The veil and seclusion within their homes would circumscribe life for millions of women.

1. "We are Arabs," Muhammad's wife A'isha explains in her memoirs, "and do not have in our houses such closets for the relief of nature as foreigners have. We loathe and we abhor them. We go out into the empty places of Medina. The women go out together every evening to relieve themselves."

therefore, was incestuous.

Zayd had married Muhammad's cousin, another Zaynab, who though in her mid-thirties had preserved a great beauty. Visiting Zayd one day, Muhammad found him absent, but Zaynab at home. On what happened next, the records disagree. Some say she dashed scantily clad from the room as he entered; others, that the wind blew aside the curtain to reveal her almost naked. Either way, the Prophet's mental turmoil is much described. "Gracious Lord! Good heavens," he said. "How thou dost turn the hearts of men." When Zayd heard about it, he offered to divorce his wife so she could marry Muhammad. "Keep your wife to yourself and fear God," the Prophet replied. Zayd divorced her anyway.

That the incident concerned Muhammad is made evident in the Qur'an where Gabriel, in Sura 33, berates him for fearing the condemnation of men. Hereafter, it says, the status of adopted sons will not be quite the same as that of real sons.[2] He should therefore take Zaynab as his sixth wife. A great banquet in the mosque celebrated the wedding.

The diplomatic or social objective of his next recruit is obscure. The beautiful seventeen-year-old Jewish girl Reihana refused the role of wife and remained a concubine. It might have been argued that the union improved relations with her tribe, were it not for the fact Muhammad had just exterminated it. Wife number seven was also acquired through a conquest, this time

the Prophet's suppression of the Banu al-Mustalik, whose forces surrendered almost without a fight. Their two hundred women were among the prizes taken by the Muslim soldiers.

One of the two hundred was Juweiraya, about twenty, a pert and forthright young woman who was the chief's wife. She was awarded to a Muslim officer who, considering her status, demanded nine ounces of gold for her return. Knowing no one in the tribe could afford that, Juweiraya asked him to take her promissory note. Refused, she took her case directly to the Prophet. "I had scarcely seen her before I detested her," said A'isha, noting her husband's fascination.

Rather than take her note, Muhammad had another idea. "And what," she asked coyly, "might that be?" That he should pay the ransom and take her himself, came the reply. Juweiraya enthusiastically agreed. "Nobody ever did more for her tribe than Juweiraya," observed A'isha. Since they were now related to the Prophet, the remaining prisoners were returned without ransom.

The eighth wife was the Jewish girl Safiyah, claimed after the fall of Khaybar—a marriage, the apologists explain, purely intended to pacify Arabia's remaining Jews. It did little to pacify A'isha, however, whose share of the Prophet's much-taxed physical estate diminished with each new acquisition. "How did you find her?" asked Muhammad, after wife number two had met wife number eight. "A Jewess," replied A'isha drily, "like all

2. The intention of the verses in Sura 33, say some modern writers, was purely to revise the restrictive Arab adoption laws. That a man of fifty-six should be carried away by a woman of thirty-five is "most unlikely," writes the historian Montgomery Watt in his biography, *Mohammed: Prophet and Statesman*. Moreover, the story of Muhammad's attraction to Zaynab does not appear in the earliest sources.

Jewesses." The Prophet was hurt, for this Jewess had become a Muslim.

Diplomacy is a more probable motive for Muhammad's marriage to wife number nine, Um Habiba, a daughter of the Meccan leader Abu Sufyan. She was in her mid-thirties, the widow of a Muslim refugee who had died as a Christian in Abyssinia. At Muhammad's request, she was married to him in absentia by Ethiopia's Christian king, who provided ships to send her and the remaining refugees home. Negotiations were then proceeding for the capitulation of Mecca, where Abu Sufyan's attitude would be crucial.

She did little herself to win her father over, however. "Don't sit on that carpet," she ordered Abu Sufyan when he visited her in Medina. "My dear daughter," he replied, "I hardly know whether you think the carpet is too good for me or I am too good for the carpet." She responded testily, "It's the Apostle's carpet, and you are an unclean polytheist." She outlived the Prophet by thirty years, into the era of her formidable brother, Mu'awiya, first of the long line of caliphs descended from her family.

Another marriage to emerge from the Meccan negotiations was the tenth and last, this one to Meimunna, sister of old Uncle Abbas's wife, but herself only twenty-five years of age. Muhammad married her when he was under a deadline to get out of the holy city, then used the marriage as a pretext for prolonging the visit. "How would it harm you if you were to let me stay, and we prepared a [wedding] banquet, and you could come, too?" he asked the Qurayshite leaders. "We

don't need your food, so get out," they replied, and he did, consummating the marriage at the first halt.

It was Gabriel who finally halted the Prophet's matrimonial endeavors at ten. "No more women are lawful unto thee after this; nor that thou shouldest exchange any of thy wives for others, even though their beauty fascinate thee, excepting such as thy right hand may possess [i.e., slaves], and God observeth all things" (Sura 33:52).

He was also exempted from the daily grind of attending to each wife in turn: "Postpone the turn of such as thou mayest please; and admit unto thyself her whom thou choosest, as well as those whom thou mayest desire of those whom thou hadst put aside; it will be no offense to thee. This will be easier, that they may be satisfied, and not repine, and be all content with that thou gavest unto them" (Sura 33:51).

Reports of endless jealousies and tearful complaints recur throughout the traditions. The chief source of them was A'isha, to whom a distinct favoritism is always shown [though it must be remembered that many of the accounts of harem life originate with her]. She likened herself to an ungrazed and verdant pasture, much in

The windows of the harem of the Palace of the Winds (above), at Jaipur, India. The harem, overlooking the city's main bazaar, is a maze of almost one thousand small openings providing ventilation and privacy, but which also allowed the women of the harem an opportunity to view the bustling outside world from which they were sequestered.

contrast to the heavily worked pastures of her rivals, a reference of course to her initial virginity. Her vicious tongue once sent the Jewish wife, Safiyah, into the Prophet's arms in a tearful rage.

Muhammad himself perhaps enjoyed the rivalry. In one revealing story, he holds a necklace before them all and says he will give it to "her whom I love the most." They murmur that it will inevitably go to A'isha. Instead, he gives it to his granddaughter Umamah. A'isha's reaction is not recorded.

The greatest crisis in harem affairs, however, was created by one of the concubines. This was Mary, Mariya in Arabic, one of two Coptic girls given Muhammad by the Roman governor of Egypt. (Her sister went to the repulsive Hassan.) She was young, delicate of feature, her fair-skinned face wreathed in curly black hair, and she immediately fascinated the Prophet, though she refused to abandon the Christian faith. She soon, however, gained a distinction not one of the wives could acquire. She became pregnant.[3]

The child would be called Ibrahim, the Arabic form of Abraham, and a special house was built for Mary that has been preserved until this day. The wives' jealousy of the young Copt knew no bounds. Muhammad, who had produced no children in twenty-five years, doted on the infant, carrying him once to show off to A'isha. "Look how much he looks like me," said the Prophet. "I do not see it," she replied

According to tradition, jealousy and complaint recurred endlessly among the ten wives.

coldly. "What! Can't you see the similarity, how fair and fat he is?" She replied that any baby would be fat who drank as much milk as this one. A special herd of goats had been established to provide him with milk.

But Ibrahim fell gravely ill at about fifteen months, reducing the father to abject sorrow. In deep and bitter grief he wept over the child's sickbed, others gently reminding him that he had warned that grief must be controlled. He had meant, he sobbed, the sort of loud ritualistic wailing that attended Arab funerals. Grief felt from the heart was permissible of expression.

"Ibrahim, O Ibrahim," he prayed, "if it were not that the promise is faithful, and hope of resurrection sure, if it were not that this is the way to be trodden by all, and that the last of us shall rejoin the first, I would grieve for you with a grief sorer than this." The child died in his arms. Muhammad followed the little bier to the graveside, and lingered over it. A solar eclipse that day darkened the earth, ascribed immediately to the Prophet's sorrow, but he repudiated the conclusion. The sun and the moon reflect the affairs of heaven, not earth, he said.

This was not the last that Muslim history hears of Mary. The story that follows has been curiously ignored by the Prophet's biographers, but western historians like Sir William Muir (*Life of Mohammed from Original Sources*) and Maxime Rodinson (*Mohammed*) derive it from the curious 66th sura of

3. Even in their prior marriages, Muhammad's wives were a surprisingly infertile lot. Though nine of the ten had had previous husbands, only Um Salema and Um Habiba had borne children to them.

the Qur'an. Muhammad, they say, carried on with his concubine not only in her little house, but even in the sacred precinct of the mosque. Wife number three, Hafsa, returned unexpectedly and found the Prophet in her bed with his concubine. Moreover, it was to have been her day.

Hafsa flew into a rage, threatening to tell the other wives what had happened. Her embarrassed husband implored her to keep the matter quiet, and promised he would see no more of Mary. Hafsa, however, was too angry to remain silent, and told A'isha, who, fevered with indignation, told all the others. All now became cold to him. The Prophet, apparently frantic, besought Gabriel, who told him to warn them all that if they didn't behave themselves, he would divorce the lot. Thus, according to historians Muir and Rodinson, the outcome of this domestic spat became part of the eternal Qur'an. Devout Muslims must therefore recite the details:

"O Prophet! Why hast thou forbidden thyself that which God hath made lawful unto thee [i.e., continuing to sleep with Mary], out of a desire to please thy wives; for God is forgiving and merciful? Verily God hath sanctioned the revocation of your oaths; and God is your master. He is knowing and wise. And when he had

Muslim women crowd the narrow streets outside a small mosque (above) at Nebi Musa in the Judean Desert, a short distance from Jericho. Worshipers make an annual pilgrimage to the site (pictured left in an aerial view), which is traditionally believed to be the burial place of A'isha, Muhammad's third wife. Moses, venerated by Muslims as well as Christians and Jews, is also said to have been buried nearby, in the hills overlooking the Jordan Valley.

4. The Muslim historian Sahih al-Bukhari, in the memoirs of A'isha, reports that Muhammad thought he had sexual relations with his wives that he did not actually have. These fantasies were the effects of magic worked on him, says A'isha, by an Arab who was an ally of the Jews (Bukhari, volume 7, book 71, number 600).

acquainted her [presumably Hafsa] with this, she said, 'Who hath told thee this?' He replied: 'He told it to me, the Knowing and the Wise. If ye both [i.e., A'isha and Hafsa] turn with repentance unto God [for verily the hearts of you both have swerved], well and good. But if ye combine with one another against him, surely God is his master; and Gabriel and all good men of the believers, and the angels, will thereafter be his supporters. Haply, his Lord, if he divorce you, will give him in your stead wives that are better than ye, submissive unto God, believers, pious, repentant, devout, fasting. Both women married previously and virgins'" (Sura 66:1 and following).[4]

This threat of divorce spread consternation not only throughout the harem, but also throughout the top echelon of the Muslim establishment,

women were becoming unruly. His own wife had taken to answering back, declaring that the Prophet's wives all did the same, and that their daughter, Hafsa, was in the same habit. Muhammad blamed the sinister influence of Persia and Byzantium. Affluence, he said, was making women harder to handle. To resolve all this, Muhammad served notice on his wives that he would not see them for a full month.[5]

When he returned to them, they said it was only day twenty-nine. He reminded them that it was, in fact, a twenty-nine-day month, and he recited to them a special revelation for the wives of the Prophet, enjoining them to live exemplary lives, refrain from exhibitionism and dedicate themselves wholly to God (Sura 33:28 and following). All was thereupon forgiven, and the incident was over—but not the problems. Harem intrigue, politics, rebellion and conspiracy would continue as a permanent aspect of imperial Islam for the next twelve centuries. ■

for the two women at the center were the daughters of Umar and Abu Bakr, his senior lieutenants. Al-Bukhari tells how Umar went to see the Prophet about it, three times being denied an audience, until Muhammad finally let him in. The Prophet would not divorce his wives, much to the relief of Umar who then unburdened himself of his own problems.

In his household, too, he said, the

5. The freedom of Western women would long remain offensive to strict Muslims. Speaking in the year 2002 at a Riyadh mosque, Sheikh Fahd bin Abd al-Rahman al-Abyan, for example, deplored the "putrid ideas (about women) spread by the infidel West," which he blamed for rampant crime, adultery, family breakdown, and illegitimacy. It is "a society in which the woman does as she pleases, even if she is married." In the West, "the woman leaves the home whenever she feels like it, goes where she wants, and wears what she wants, without her husband's permission." In fact, "in some homes, the situation has reached the point where the woman gives the orders, and that is that." (Middle East Media Research Institute, Special Report Number 10, September 26, 2002.)

Muhammad, the Prophet of Islam, from a nineteenth engraving which appeared in The Illustrated History Of The World. Vol. One, *published by Ward. Lock and Co., of London.*

CHAPTER 4

With all Arabia subdued Islam is set to unleash the conquest of the world

The democracy of tribal life vanishes with the idols, and Muhammad becomes the equal of any potentate, holds his final pilgrimage, and dies cradled by A'isha

Mecca might be conquered, but the conquest could not be secure until al-Taif, the neighboring city to the southeast, was taken as well. It was in al-Taif that Muhammad had attempted his first "foreign" mission, only to be sent home humiliated and rejected; but now, with most of Arabia supporting him, he understandably assumed that his second attempt would surely be less onerous. He was wrong. Al-Taif proved harder to subdue than Mecca.

As his army streamed out of Mecca on the al-Taif road—twelve thousand strong, proud, confident and seemingly invincible—Abu Bakr observed that they certainly wouldn't be beaten that day for lack of numbers. Confidently, the advance squad of Bedouin cavalry, led by Khalid ibn al-Walid, pranced into the narrow defile known as the Valley of Honein—and found themselves in a hail of arrows from the archers of al-Taif's twenty-thousand-man defense force.

They panicked, charging back on the ranks behind them, who also tried to turn and flee. Muhammad was left shouting, "Where are you going? Come here! The Prophet of the Lord is here!" just as he had at the Battle of Uhud. (See chapter 3.) This time, however, another figure stood beside him, trying to stem

Abu Sufyan, Muhammad's boyhood friend, and the Prophet's cousin, Abu Zayd, embrace on the road to Mecca in this thirteenth-century painting (above) from Baghdad, Iraq. Long a determined enemy of Muhammad, Abu Sufyan was reconciled with him after the conquest of Mecca.

the tide of men, horses and camels hurtling past. "Who are you?" bellowed Muhammad, peering through the dust and confusion. "I am your grandmother's grandson, O Apostle of the Lord," the stranger shouted back, and Muhammad recognized his cousin Abu Sufyan, so long his enemy and now his comrade again.

It was his Uncle Abbas who halted the rout, however. Said to have the loudest voice in Arabia, Abbas hollered loud enough to persuade about one hundred men to stand and fight, then led them back upon the enemy. Soon the whole Muslim host turned around and came screaming into the attack. Breaking through to the al-Taif camp, they gathered a vast harvest of spoils, including women, and then laid siege to the town.

This brought unexpected results. Al-Taif's initial defenders had been the Hawazin who lived round about. One captive, an elderly woman, warned the Muslim troops, "Keep your hands off me, for I am your Prophet's foster sister." Alarmed, they took her before Muhammad, and he saw it was indeed Sheima, who had cared for him in his childhood among the Bedouin. As a little boy he once bit her, and she still bore on her neck the tooth marks. He presented Sheima with a handsome gift.

She was not the only one, for these were his own people, and they now not only accepted, but adulated him. His generosity became boundless. The man who led the attack on Khalid in the Valley of Honein, captive and still uncommitted to Islam, was rewarded with a huge tract of land. The recent and reluctant convert Abu Sufyan received a hundred camels, as did both his sons.

Muhammad's veterans not unnaturally grumbled at this rewarding of enemies, while men loyal since Badr got nothing. So bitter did the animosity become that some historians suspect open rebellion broke out, during which a mob actually manhandled the Prophet. "Return my mantle," he is recorded as shouting, "for I swear by the Lord that if the sheep and camels [taken at Honein] were as many in number as the trees of the forest, I would divide them all among you. You have not heretofore found me niggardly." He plucked a hair from a camel: "Even to a hair like this I would keep back nothing but the fifth, and even that will I divide among you."

This was the kind of talk they wanted to hear, and the malcontents subsided, but still al-Taif proved painfully resistant. Days passed with no indication of surrender, as flights of arrows and cascades of red-hot iron balls cut down warriors trying to breach its walls, and when Muhammad began destroying the orchards and date palms, as he had at Medina, his own commanders insisted he desist.

Finally they had to lift the siege, but al-Taif, seeing the odds it ultimately faced, began to parley. Could they keep their goddess al-Lat for three years, they petitioned, while they accustomed themselves to the new religion? The answer: No. Two years, then? No. One year? No. Six months? No—al-Lat must go forthwith. All right, but surely they need not pray five times a day? They were frightfully busy people and not very religious. Certainly they must pray, was the implacable answer—five times.

But must they really stop loaning money at interest? Yes. And refrain from intercourse with women who were not their wives or concubines? Yes. Surely the Prophet realized, they argued, that they traveled a lot, making this rule very hard. Too bad, was the reply, but they must just put up with it. Well, all right, but could the Muslims at least protect their famous forest of Wajj as a game preserve? Yes, said the Prophet, it would be preserved, and thus did al-Taif embrace Islam.

By 631, Muhammad restricted the annual Mecca pilgrimage to Muslims, and warned idolatrous Arab tribes to embrace Islam or face the Muslim sword, which meant submitting not only to a new religious system, but also to a new political order. Legal disputes must be settled according to the Qur'an, as interpreted by a resident Muslim jurist,[1] and a system was established to collect the annual tax payable to Medina. This was bitterly unpopular, but the Qur'an's ninth sura (verse 5) prescribed a bloody fate for any tribe that resisted: "Kill the polytheists wherever you find them. Seize them, besiege them, and lie in wait for them in every ambush."[2]

Dread of Muslim military potential set off an avalanche of capitulation throughout the peninsula, with tribe after tribe sending envoys to Medina to submit. Even some Christians were tempted. As Nestorians, they were Persian in sympathy, but Persia was distracted by its death struggle with Byzantium. The Arab Christians feared Byzantium far more than they feared the Muslims, who for the moment let them retain their faith in return for protection money.

Muhammad, too, seemed worried chiefly about Byzantium. As early as 627, say various Muslim traditions, he dispatched emissaries to the Roman emperor Heraclius, the Persian emperor Chosroes, all their governors, and adjacent countries as well, demanding recognition as the Prophet of God. Islamic lore has much to say about the reception of such ultimatums, not all of it demonstrably accurate. Muslim legend claims, for example, that the Negus of Ethiopia embraced Islam forthwith. But Ethiopian raids against Muslim coastal tribes are known to have begun soon afterward, and Ethiopian Christians would raise an impregnable and lasting barrier against Islam.

The Byzantine governor of Egypt equivocated, remarking that he thought such a prophet was predicted as arising in Syria, not Arabia. But he sent a special gift of two slave girls, one of whom would later set off a horrendous row in the Prophet's household. (See sidebar, page 96.) Chosroes of Persia, now facing the approach of a Roman invasion force, is said to have torn up the Prophet's demand. "Just as his kingdom shall be torn up," Muhammad correctly prophesied.

1. Muhammad appointed one Mo'adh senior judge in South Arabia, and inquired how he intended to settle legal disputes. "By the book," replied Mo'adh, meaning the Qur'an. "And if the answer isn't in the book?" asked Muhammad. "Then by whatever precedent you set," said Mo'adh. "What if I have set no precedent?" persisted Muhammad. "Then I'll carefully form my own judgment," replied Mo'adh. Muhammad clapped him on the chest and praised God. Mo'adh left for the south, poor and deep in debt, and returned so rich that Umar, then caliph, publicly deplored his avarice. His "carefully formed judgments," that is, doubtless served the cause of Mo'adh as munificently as they did the cause of Islam. This story, however, presents a problem of credibility, since there was no "book" or Qur'an during the Prophet's lifetime. Either the story is imaginary, or perhaps Muhammad knew that such a book would come into being.

2. The new *suras* of the Qur'an became something like an army's orders of the day. "It needs the faith of the Muslims to continue to see in them an unparalleled work of universal rhetoric whose perfection is enough to demonstrate its divine origin," comments historian Maxime Rodinson. The sometimes skeptical A'isha noted Allah's readiness to conform to her husband's wishes, and Umar was amazed at the way his own purely pragmatic advice to the Prophet was so often confirmed by Gabriel.

Accounts of the reaction of Heraclius vary. One has him telling his generals: "By God, he (Muhammad) is truly the Prophet whom we expect," and saying, when the generals vehemently disagree, that he was only testing their Christian convictions. In another version, Heraclius immediately accepts Muhammad, and recommends that Syria and Egypt be given to Islam forthwith to avoid their inevitable conquest, but the inhabitants erupt in fury because they consider Arabs "an inferior people from an inferior country."

A. A. Bevan, in *The Cambridge Medieval History* doubts the veracity of all these stories. Indeed, many later historians think the Muslim vision of world conquest emerged only after Muhammad's death, when the Arab tribes, eager for loot and women, pushed north and were astonished to find themselves so

After the lost battle at Mu'ta, one warrior reportedly skulked in his home for months, unable to face his neighbors' jeers. Militant Islam had small room for military failures.

amazingly successful. Such theories understandably appall many Muslims, because they suggest that avarice and lust, rather than zeal for Allah, account for the success of Islam.

However, at the first mention of the Muslims in Western history—a brief notice in the Greek ecclesiastical chronicler Theophanes—they do not appear as victors. Four months before the taking of Mecca, when a semi-Christian border tribe attacked Muslim emissaries, Muhammad sent a three-thousand-man punitive expedition north towards Mu'ta, southeast of the Dead Sea. There his horrified warriors encountered something entirely new to them: a Roman legion drawn up rank upon rank, its implacable foot soldiers arrayed shield to shield, their officer cadre blazing in colorful pageantry, and with wildly plunging Arab cavalry on their flanks. Two hundred thousand men in all, says the Muslim account.

This last was certainly a vast exaggeration, but Muhammad lost two men dear to him in the next few minutes. One was Zayd, the slave given to him by Khadeja, who had served as his secretary. The other was Ja'far, brother of his foster son Ali. It was Zayd who died first. He hamstrung his horse, making escape impossible, then with the Bedouin hurled himself at the approaching legionaries and was hacked to pieces by their short swords. Ja'far followed him to the same fate.[3] But one Muslim soldier grabbed the endangered Islamic standard and handed it to a cavalry officer he knew could command instant respect.

This was none other than Khalid ibn al-Walid, who swiftly assembled the Bedouin in defensive formation and engineered a strategic retreat to the Arabian border. Thence the survivors of Mu'ta crept back to Medina, where crowds hurled dust at them and jeered them as "runaways" from God's battle. They would fight again, said Muhammad, but popular contempt was not mitigated. One man is said to have skulked for months in his home, unable to face his neighbors. Islam had small room for military failure.

3. Abdallah ibn Rawaha, a Muslim poet who died at Mu'ta, had prayed for his own martyrdom, to atone with his blood if the mission failed. The passion of his fervent fatalism comes through even in translation:

I ask the Merciful
Not only for pardon
But for a wide-open wound
Discharging blood,
Or a deadly lance thrust
From a zealous warrior
That will pierce
The bowels and liver;
So that men will say
When they pass my grave,
God guide him,
Fine warrior that he was;
He died well.

Within the peninsula, however, pagan tribes rapidly capitulated. The Banu Jofi were beaten into submission, but still retained an idolatrous horror of animal hearts as something accursed. Forced at sword point to eat them, they trembled, gagged them down, and became Muslim. The chief of the Banu Amr demanded to be named successor to the Prophet, and contemptuously rejected the counteroffer of a cavalry command. Striding indignantly off, he mysteriously fell dead. Gabriel got him, said the faithful.

Many tribes yielded unresisting, though some fought until they had few weapons left but clubs and rocks, and finally saw their women, children and cattle rounded up and herded back to Medina. Yemen, a center of idolatry, fell in 632, to a trick the Muslim army would use time and again. After a monthlong siege, they feigned retreat. When the defenders streamed out in pursuit, the retiring troops suddenly turned, cut them to pieces, and seized the town.

Christian tribes proved the most resistant, and not even the nearest of them, the Banu Kalb, hastened to embrace the Prophet's message. One Banu Kalb chief accepted Islam. Another refused, but his daughter was claimed for the teeming harem of Abd al-Rahman (by then numbering sixteen wives plus concubines), and became the mother of Selama, a founding Muslim jurist. The Islamization of Christian Arabia would eventually be accomplished more by raising the offspring of Christian slave women as Muslims than by direct apostasy.

San'a (below), ancient capital of Yemen, and designated a World Heritage Site by the United Nations. According to legend, San'a was founded by Shem, Noah's oldest son. The city and the remnants of the Christian Himyarite kingdom fell to the armies of Islam after a siege in 632.

Significantly, at least two Christian tribes were allowed to retain their faith, but not to baptize their children. In the north, where the extensive Banu Bakr tribe had many Christian branches, most of them rejected Muhammad's claims. Not all, however, and conversions were thorough. When the Banu Hanifa went over to Islam, it was instructed to destroy its church, purify the ground with special water furnished by Muhammad, and build a mosque.

From the big Christian community at Najran in the south, a bishop of the Banu Hanifa led a fourteen-man delegation to Medina. From his youth Muhammad had respected the Najran Christians for their determined refusal, a

One Muslim legend tells of a Christian bishop who exchanged his black robe for white, proclaiming that the prophet Ahmed had arrived. The bishop's skeptical flock beat him up.

4. The Muslim historian Ibn Ishaq implies a less than edifying motive for the conversion to Islam of the Christian chief Adi. Did Adi not feel shame for seizing a quarter of the goods of his people in taxes? asked the Prophet. Adi replied that he did indeed sense shame. Well then, said Muhammad, under Islam, such a confiscation was perfectly in order, so he need feel no further shame. Moreover, the riches of "Babylon" (i.e., the Byzantine and Persian Empires) would soon be his to share as well, and all his people would be rich beyond their imaginings.

5. The loyalty to Jesus Christ of the Banu Ghassan would for centuries be cited by Muslims as a scandalous example of religious perfidy. For instance, a dissertation attributed to Osama bin Laden, the reputed mastermind of the terrorist attack on the United States on September 11, 2001, attacked current Arab rulers for being the "new al-Ghassanid," and accused the historical tribe of "killing their brothers among the peninsula's Arabs to safeguard the interests of the Romans." (BBC News, January 5, 2004.)

half-century before his birth, to yield to a Jewish despot. (See chapter 1.) He met the delegation in the mosque, and after ceremonial posturing on both sides, awarded them a generous treaty. On payment of a tax (a certain quantity of garments and livestock in peacetime, a certain quantity of armor and horses in wartime), their buildings, land and priests would remain unmolested.

The thought, no doubt, was that the Najran Christians and others would gradually yield to Islam. In regard to the Najrans, however, the Muslims were to be disappointed; they remained resolutely Christian. By contrast, Muslims like to tell of Adi, chief of the partly Christian Banu Tayy, near the Iraqi border, whose sister was captured in a Muslim raid. Her Christian brother, she informed Muhammad, always released women prisoners. So the Prophet did likewise. He sent her back to Adi, whom she persuaded in turn to visit the kindly prince of Medina. Adi did so, and was so impressed that he joined his faith.[4]

With the Banu Ghassan, the large Christian tribe in Syria and stout allies of Byzantium, the Muslims failed in their mission; in all but a few instances the tribe remained defiantly Christian.[5] One exception was a chief called Farwa. To lure him back, the imperial authorities are said to have promised him a higher office if he would abjure his new faith. When Farwa refused, the Banu Ghassan crucified him—an Islamic martyr.

In another instance, the Banu Ghassan are said to have sent three delegates to Medina to discuss an alliance against Persia. All three converted, although on their return only one would admit it, and he not until several years after Muhammad's death, with Muslim armies already moving north. One border chief embraced Islam in return for a written deed to his lands. When he told his wife, she burned the deed.

Also recorded is the case of Okeidir, a Christian ruler captured while hunting wild cows. Brought to Medina wearing a golden cross and regal gold-embroidered brocade, Okeidir renounced the gospel, accepted the Qur'an, and surrendered his town. He was to prove a dubious convert, however. Later, on pilgrimage, he reputedly refused point blank to wear the common pilgrim garb and to treat all men as brothers. No royal personage could carry on like that, Okeidir protested, and returned to imperial territory where, he said, a king was a king.

Yet another story, probably pure legend, tells of a Christian bishop in the imperial capital itself, supposedly so impressed by Muhammad's summons to the emperor that he changed his black robes for white and loudly proclaimed that the prophet Ahmed had at last arrived. He seems to have confused Muhammad's rise with the promised coming of Ahmed (the Holy Spirit). The bishop's unappreciative flock beat him up. In general, however, at Muhammad's death Islam's great rival seemingly remained in about the same tenuous state in Arabia as it had been at his birth.

Meanwhile, by the spring of 630, rumors abounded of a massive Byzantine army poised to attack Medina. Muhammad issued a call to arms; the Bedouin, comfortable in their newfound wealth, largely ignored him. Even Medina's response was so feeble, says one account, that the furious Muhammad resolved to lead the army himself, and deal with backsliders on his return. He assembled a force of thirty thousand troops, marched to Tebuk near the Gulf of Aqaba at the head of the Red Sea—and found there was no Byzantine army. The rumors were false.

It was during this march that the Prophet's foster son Ali, left in charge at Medina, arrived breathless and pleading to join the campaign. People in Medina were describing him as undependable in battle, he explained. The Prophet's response was to gain great

The ruins of the church of Saint Theodore in the city of Jerash, Jordan (bottom), and a seventh-century Syrian ivory tablet (below) from the Louvre, Paris, depicting the prophet Joel. With a few exceptions, during Muhammad's lifetime, the thriving Christian communities on the Arabian frontier (protected by Christian Arab tribes such as the Banu Ghassan) resisted the lure of Islam.

significance in Islam's interminable dynastic wars: "O Ali, are you not content that you should be to me as Aaron was to Moses, save that after me there is no prophet?" This was taken by some as a clear directive for the succession.

When Muhammad returned to Medina after two months, rising dissidence became evident. A schismatic mosque had been built there, which Ali burned down. The Prophet severely censured any followers found to be selling their weapons. Abdallah ibn Ubay, the old chieftain he had supplanted at Medina who was chronically seditious, denied he was plotting a major insurrection, but Umar, deeply suspicious, repeatedly recommended his execution. Abdallah's own son, a fervent adherent of the new faith, offered to present Muhammad with his father's head. The Prophet refused.

Nevertheless the "Murmurers," as the disenchanted came to be called, were vigorously denounced by Gabriel. Pacifism, Gabriel said, was not merely questionable, but an incontrovertible evil. "Do ye prefer the present life before that which is to come?" demands the Qur'an's Sura 9:38. "If ye go not forth to war, he will punish you with a grievous punishment, and he will substitute another people for you." Sura 9:47 adds: "If they [i.e., those who had refused Muhammad's call] had gone forth with thee,
they had only added

In this eighteenth-century Persian miniature, the angel Gabriel instructs a veiled Muhammad during a battle. Pacifism, Muslims were told, was not merely questionable, but an incontrovertible evil: "If ye go not forth to war," warns the Qur'an's Sura 9:38, "He (Allah) will punish you with a grievous punishment."

weakness to you, and had run to and fro amongst you, stirring up sedition."

One malingerer, the poet Ka'b ibn al-Ashraf of the Prophet's inner circle, was subjected to what some strict Christian groups would one day call "shunning," which proved a terrible punishment. He had the freedom of the city, but all were commanded to ignore him. When he walked to the mosque, no one would even look at him. He threw himself before Muhammad, and the Prophet turned away. He begged his closest friend to intervene, and was ignored. So he stayed home, but had even been ordered not to speak or make love to his wife. She reported that she feared he would go blind from weeping. Yet when the chief of a nearby Christian tribe offered to take him in, Ka'b burned the letter.

But on the fiftieth night he heard, from across the hills, a voice shouting his name. He ran towards the sound, and a man told him his punishment was over. As he walked toward the mosque, tears streaming down his face, everyone greeted him warmly, and Muhammad declared him forgiven. "This is good news," said the Prophet. "From you or from God?" asked Ka'b. "From God, of course," said Muhammad. Ka'b, his face shining, offered to give away all his property. "Keep some," Muhammad advised. "You might need it."

When Muhammad returned from Tebuk, he had about three years left to live,

Sadder still, Muhammad's children tended to die at some moment of his worldly triumph, so that exultation over earthly victory was dampened by simultaneous grief over his loss.

during which his wives posed a continuing problem, and his children recurring tragedy. His first wife, Khadeja, bore him six children: two sons, who died in infancy, and four daughters—Zaynab, Rokeiya, Um Kulthum and Fatima—of whom only Fatima outlived Muhammad. Sadder still, each died at some hour of his worldly triumph, so that exultation over the victory was dampened by grief over his loss.

Of the four daughters, by far the most noted for loyalty, faith, determination and intelligence was the eldest, Zaynab, who also seems the one most influenced by her mother, Khadeja.[6] Khadeja urged that Zaynab be given in marriage to her favorite nephew, al-As ibn al-Rabeah, a trader widely reputed for honesty and astuteness. But he did not embrace Islam, and at the hijra he and Zaynab consequently remained in Mecca. He was equally resolute, however, in resisting the demands of the Meccans that he divorce her and marry one of their women instead. Zaynab, he said, was his wife, and he loved her dearly.

This love apparently was mutual. Al-Rabeah was captured at Badr, and to ransom him Zaynab sent the Prophet something she knew would touch his heart: a necklace given to her by her mother. Muhammad burst into tears at the sight of it, and returned al-Rabeah to Mecca, on condition that he send Zaynab to Medina. So Zaynab, now pregnant, departed for Medina in the care of her husband's brother, but they were overtaken by a party of Meccan fanatics, led by one Hamsar, determined to bring her back. The resulting melee so terrified her that she miscarried.

6. No fewer than five Zaynabs play a part in the Prophet's life. Zaynab was the name of his fourth and sixth wives, of his eldest daughter, of Fatima's third child (who was Muhammad's eldest granddaughter), and ironically, of the Jewess who poisoned him (see previous chapter), possibly contributing to his death.

Back in Mecca, however, she was secretly released by Abu Sufyan, who said Mecca had no interest in separating father and daughter.[7] Later still, al-Rabeah was again captured, and again brought captive to Medina. This time, Zaynab defiantly and publicly shouted out in the mosque that she had put him under her protection. The startled Muhammad stopped the service. "Did you hear what I heard?" he asked the congregation. There was a murmur of assent. This, he declared, was his daughter's doing, not his; however, he had no choice but to acquiesce.

So his son-in-law was freed, although Muhammad warned Zaynab not to sleep with him, because he was not a Muslim. Al-Rabeah thereupon returned to Mecca, settled his affairs, and came back to Medina as a convert. He and Zaynab lived happily ever after, though ever after was not very long; she died a year later. It was the year of the Prophet's greatest triumph, the conquest of Mecca, and grief once more attended victory.

Similarly, after the Byzantine threat at Tebuk proved groundless, Muhammad had returned to news of the death of his fourth daughter, Um Kulthum. If he had

Muhammad mended his own sandals and clothes, tended goats, and helped his wives with the household chores. He dressed in plain white cotton except on festive occasions.

another unwed daughter, he assured her grieving husband, Uthman, now bereaved of a wife for the second time, he would gladly give her to him. Meanwhile, only Fatima presented him with grandsons, Hassan and Hussein, and a granddaughter, Zaynab.

Muhammad's style of living gradually rose with the fortunes of Islam, although it never approached the luxury in which his Muslims would later indulge. In the early days at Medina, said his wife A'isha, she could remember not a single meal when she had enough to eat. The family would go for months without cooked food, she said, the Prophet himself eating almost nothing for days on end because they had so little. "The food of one is enough for two," he would say, "the food of two enough for four, and the food of four enough for eight." Often they ate in the dark, because there was no oil for the lamps.

His wives' apartments were little more than twelve-by-fourteen-foot huts of unburned brick, thatched with palm branches. A screen of goatskin or camel hair hung over the doorway; a simple leather mattress and pillow, stuffed with palm coir, lay on the floor; waterskins hung on the walls. Some huts had a kind of veranda. A'isha's had a closet where the Prophet prayed, and contained his bed of teak and palm cords. Once, as he lay on it with an injured hand, the pitying Umar contrasted his crude furnishings with those of Heraclius or Chosroes. "They have their portion [reward] in this world," Muhammad replied. When the cords left marks on his skin, a servant offered to cover them with a soft blanket. Muhammad objected that such comforts were of the world, and the world was like a tree by the wayside. It provided only brief comfort for the passerby, and

7. Some accounts say that Muhammad's daughter Zaynab was kicked in the encounter with Hamsar. Abu Sufyan's wife, the inimitable Hind, had a few well-chosen words for the woman beater Hamsar. "In time of peace, you are very fierce and brave against the weak and unprotected," she scoffed, "but in battle, you speak as gently as a bunch of women." Muhammad at first gave instructions that Hamsar, if taken, was to be burned alive, and when Mecca fell, Hamsar hid himself for days. But then he emerged as a penitent convert to Islam, and Muhammad forgave him.

would soon be left behind. When his wife Um Salema made an addition to her hut during his absence on campaign, he deplored it. "Nothing will eat up the wealth of a believer more than buildings," he told her.[8]

The living conditions of his other relatives were no better. Ali, hero of so many battles, earned a living by carrying water, and his wife Fatima by grinding corn. Often exhausted, they once hesitantly approached Muhammad and asked for a captive to help with their chores. He refused. He had to think first, he said, of the poor, the "People of the Bench," so called because they crowded the mosque, sleeping on its benches. All captives must be sold, he said, to support the poor.

He himself mended his own sandals and clothes, tended his own goats, and helped his wives with the household chores. Also, he usually dressed in plain white cotton, although on festive occasions he wore linen striped with red, gold, and yellow, and on entering Mecca at the pinnacle of his ministry, is said to have worn a black turban.

Nevertheless, as the prophet in him yielded to the warrior prince, so too did frugality yield to luxury, and equality to ostentation. Gradually but noticeably, his lifestyle changed. People must rise when he entered a room. They must address him only in low tones. They must not crowd him. They must not visit him unasked, nor stay longer than necessary, nor attempt to make light conversation with him, nor leave until dismissed. His wives must be shielded from public view, and he was exempt from the rule that there be no more than four of them. Such noise as a raucous demonstration by some Banu Tamim women seeking the release of their husbands (although entirely traditional among Arabs to this day) was irksome to him because no voice must be raised in his presence.

In later life, he paid as much as nineteen camels for a single cloak, eight gold pieces for a mantle. He drank from a crystal goblet inlaid with silver, bathed in a copper basin, and burned camphor for its sweet smell. He had, said A'isha, three delights: women, scents and food. He had become a connoisseur of fine Arab foods, with a particular passion for goat shoulder. (He once, in fact, devoured two shoulders and demanded a third. A rattled servant reminded him that a goat only had two shoulders.) In the end, he was painting his eyes with antimony,

Muhammad's eldest daughter, the pregnant Zaynab, flees Mecca (above) for the safety of Medina. Pursued by hostile Meccans, it is said the terrified woman miscarried before eventually being reunited with her father.

8. The huts that housed Muhammad's wives were finally torn down at the turn of the next century by the caliph Malik. People wept to see the destruction of these monuments to the frugality of their Prophet.

stored in a collyrium box. It made them piercing, he explained, and caused his hair to grow. A servant, Abdallah ibn Mas'ud[9] was valet and butler to him—tending to his sandals and clothing, doing his wash, setting out his indispensable toothpicks, holding a screen over him when he bathed, and carrying his staff before him on ceremonial occasions.

As for actual power, as distinct from mere pomp, Muhammad by the end of his life was the equal of almost any potentate. His word commanded instant obedience. All disputes were referred to him. The armies marched only at his command, under commanders appointed solely by him. The democracy of desert tribal life had vanished with the idols.

He did not achieve such stature, of course, without firm qualities of human leadership. Aside from his gift of prophecy, he was preeminently the politician, courteous to all comers and reluctant to say no. He grabbed state visitors delightedly by the hand, and would laugh so uproariously at jokes that he had to hold his sides. Yet he possessed such a commanding mien as to inspire in strangers an awe that frequently became reverent love. And while he remorselessly hunted down his enemies, upon their capitulation he often totally forgave them.

Vengeance, so dear to the Arabs, he employed as a device—sometimes using it, more often not. In battle he was never in the forefront; rather, he was inclined

By the end, the Prophet's power equaled almost any potentate. The armies marched only at his command, under commanders appointed by him. Tribal democracy vanished with the idols.

to lead from behind with the maximum of personal protection. Nevertheless, he inspired his men to such unimaginable feats that the sheer momentum was to carry them across much of the known world.

His dealings with individuals inspired scores of stories, some obviously fictional, but many convincing in their simplicity. One such concerns a young girl whom he carried to Khaybar on his saddle. At one halt, she suddenly fled from him and hid her face. She had begun to menstruate for the first time, he discovered, and her blood lay on the leather. Patiently, he explained what was happening, told her to wash herself and the saddle with salt water, and gave her a necklace to assure her that she had in no way lost his respect. She lived to be an old woman, and throughout her life washed herself and nearly everything else with salt water, and was buried wearing the necklace.

There is also the story of Jabir, a poor soldier returning from Second Badr on a camel so wretched that it lagged far behind. Muhammad struck up a conversation with him. Jabir said his father had been killed at Badr, leaving him, the only son, and seven daughters. He must therefore now marry a woman of experience to raise his sisters, rather than a young damsel of his preference. Muhammad said he wanted to buy the camel. Jabir offered to give it to him. No, said Muhammad, he would buy it, and would take delivery of

9. Muhammad's servant Abdallah ibn Mas'ud ought not to be confused with another servant, Abdallah ibn Abu Sah. The latter, a foster brother of Uthman and once Muhammad's secretary, lost faith in him and departed. When Muhammad was dictating a *sura*, Abdallah ibn Abu Sah had inserted into the text a line he himself had invented—and Muhammad failed to detect the interpolation.

it in Medina, where Jabir's wife could lay out the cushions and they could have dinner together.

"O Prophet," responded the distraught Jabir, "I have no cushions."

Muhammad said he would provide them, which he did. He also paid Jabir for the camel, but then returned the beast to the young man. Jabir, we are told, later became very wealthy. This story made the rounds of the admiring troops, as it does to this day.

Only once is Muhammad recorded as losing his temper with his men, in the fevered aftermath of the Battle of Honein. When the angry faithful were bitterly upbraiding him for giving lavish gifts to his Meccan relatives who had so long opposed him, he hit a man's foot with his whip. Immediately repentant, he gave the fellow eighty she-camels in compensation.

Muhammad was not without quirks, however. One such was an irrational loathing of silk. Another was an intense concern about offensive breath, which he said would be an intolerable handicap in his conversations with Gabriel. Convinced that bad breath was chiefly caused by food remaining in the mouth, he used an elaborate assortment of toothpicks, and washed out his mouth after every meal. This of course inspired devout Muslims to do likewise. (For fear of bad breath he also refused to eat garlic or onions.)

The lifestyle of the early converts to Islam was one of stark poverty, probably very much like this group of poor Bedouin at al-Hasa, Saudi Arabia (below). According to Muhammad, "Nothing will eat up the wealth of a believer more than buildings."

Among many other things, he had strong opinions about the ancient remedy of blood letting, insisting that it must take place an odd (not even) number of times, and on the seventeenth day of any month when it fell on a Tuesday. And he had an extraordinary fear of wind. In windy weather, he would run back and forth, in and out of the house, or to and fro outside, praying for deliverance. During rainstorms, however, he would sometimes go outside and bare his head and chest to the torrent.

There has been considerable argument as to whether and how he dyed his hair. Some sources say that apart from a few white strands his hair remained jet black all his life. On his physical appearance, there is wide concurrence that he was slightly above middle size, with a large head, big bones and broad chest. He walked abruptly as though descending a steep hill, and so quickly that people almost had to run to keep up. When he looked around, he turned his whole body, not just his head.

Much attention has been paid to Muhammad's face, particularly his eyes. Beneath long lashes, they reportedly were large, intensely black and piercing, and so restless as to seldom dwell more than a moment on any one object. His

'The great heterodox Muslim mystics,' says biographer Rodinson, 'tended to look down on the Prophet as being simply a robot . . . a loudspeaker for transmitting God's messages.'

expression was often pensive. When he became angry, he would avert his gaze, a vein on his forehead would swell, and his brow would furrow into a scowl that often foreshadowed someone's execution. When joyful, he would bend his head down, it was said, and normally his face beamed with intelligence. His features were somewhat sensuous, his skin soft and clear, his countenance ruddy, his brow wide, his eyebrows arched and joined, his nose large and hooked.

His bushy beard reportedly reached his chest. The famous "seal" that allegedly lay between his shoulders is so mystically referred to that accurate description is impossible. Most sources agree that it was about the size of a pigeon egg, though one describes it as almost the size of a man's fist. It may possibly have been a very large mole.

There is also disagreement over how the Prophet spoke, some describing his delivery as slow and deliberate, others as rapid. When he preached, his eyes would redden, his voice rise high and loud, and his whole frame become agitated. He is said to have stood so long at prayers sometimes that his legs would swell, and he is reputed never to have yawned in the mosque. Sensitive always to the hazards of bad breath, he covered his face when he sneezed, and his followers naturally did the same.

The twentieth century saw much effort to "explain" Muhammad in terms of psychology. For example, he has been viewed by some as shame ridden because he had no male heir, a condition despised by the Arabs as *abtar* or "mutilated." The 108th sura is cited in support of this contention: "Yes, we have given you abundance. So pray your Lord and sacrifice; it is your enemy who is the abtar."

Some others regard him as a highly spiritual man who nevertheless stopped short of the mystical experience of total union with God, and thereby exposed himself to the temptations of self-love, pride and covetousness. "The great heterodox Muslim mystics," says his atheist biographer Maxime Rodinson, "have tended to look down on the Prophet as being simply a robot, a kind of primitive recording machine or gramophone, a loudspeaker for transmitting God's messages." This whole process of "psychoanalyzing" Muhammad is as offensive to Muslims, of course, as the same process when applied to Christ is offensive to Christians.

But whatever his psychology, Muhammad in the tenth year after the hijra could regard his work as nearly complete. Worship at the Ka'ba had been cleansed of all idolatry, and the time had come to adapt its ancient pilgrimage as a ritual of the new religion. He therefore announced plans to lead the event himself, taking with him all nine wives still alive.[10] The response was stupendous. Some forty thousand believers decided to join him. Since it was the Prophet's last, it has subsequently been known to Islam as the "Farewell Pilgrimage." It has furthermore been precisely and dutifully emulated by Muslims ever since, each of Muhammad's movements and words becoming a sacred precedent to be repeated with all possible fidelity.

Every stop along his route is now the site of one of the historic mosques of Islam. Wearing the pilgrim garb, with Bilal carrying a screen to shield him from the sun, he proceeded down Mecca's main street and pronounced God's blessing on the Ka'ba. His first stop was atop the hill known as Mount Arafat (not to be confused with Mount Ararat near the Armenian-Turkish border, traditional beaching site of Noah's Ark). Here he said certain prayers and pronounced certain blessings. In bright moonlight, he reached Muzdalifa in the valley of that name, which became the second station of the pilgrimage. Here he said the sunset and evening prayers together.

10. Muhammad married at least thirteen women. Khadeja and the first Zaynab died before the pilgrimage of 632. He divorced two others because they refused to consummate the marriage.

There is a wide measure of agreement on Muhammad's physical appearance, but in most Islamic depictions of the Prophet—such as this sixteenth-century Turkish painting (left) showing him receiving details of the Qur'an's eighth sura from the angel Gabriel—he is shown with his face veiled.

Some traditions say that while Muhammad sought to destroy the hair shorn from his head in the Farewell Pilgrimage, to prevent its superstitious collection as a relic, some of his followers begged and received strands of it, Khalid ibn al-Walid being given a whole shock.

In the final rite of the Hajj, hundreds of thousands of Muslim pilgrims gather at Devil's Corner (right), near Mina on the Plain of Arafat, to reenact Muhammad's "stoning of the devil." A cannon sounds at sunset, and the pilgrims throw pebbles at one of three stone pillars representing Satan (below). Each pilgrim then buys a camel, sheep, or goat for sacrifice, and the excess meat is distributed to the poor. The sacrifice is duplicated by Muslims the world over, who celebrate the day as Id al-Adha (the feast of sacrifice), a major holiday of the Muslim year.

The day following, he proceeded in a torrential downpour to Mina on the road to al-Taif, stopping to "stone the devil," a pre-Islamic custom in which the pilgrims throw pebbles at the Devil's Corner, three stone pillars with diabolical associations. At this third station of the pilgrimage, Muhammad's hair was shaved; he ordered it burned to prevent it being superstitiously preserved as relics.[11] Here, too, the sacrificial camels were slain, the meat being dedicated to feed the poor, and Muhammad rode his camel seven times between the two hills of Safa and Merwa without dismounting. After pilgrim garb was exchanged for ordinary clothing, a great feast was held, where a ritual dialogue took place between Prophet and believers:

Question: "What day is this?" Answer: "The day of sacrifice."
Q: "What place is this?" A: "The holy place."
Q: "What month is this?" A: "The holy month."
Q: "This is the day of the great pilgrimage. Your lifeblood, property and honor are sacred, as is this place on this day of the month. Have I made my message clear?" A: "Yes. O God, be my witness."

Muhammad then summed up certain teachings. Muslims must abandon the old vendettas for murder of a relative. They must give up adultery; males must be stoned if convicted of it, and women thrashed (though not severely) and kept alone until they repent. Muslims must not loan money at interest, and must treat their slaves well, clothing them as well as they do themselves.

One version of this speech quotes him as proclaiming all Muslims equal under God: "O people, your Lord is

one, and your ancestor is one. You are all descended from Adam, and Adam is of the earth." Though some historians view this as a later addition, defenders of its authenticity point out that it is consistent with a passage in the Qur'an (Sura 49:13). To the Christian it suggests St. Paul's assertion that in Christ "there is neither Jew nor Greek; there is neither bond nor free; there is neither male nor female. For you are all one in Christ Jesus" (Galatians 3:28).

Then, say his biographers, Muhammad declared his mission to mankind accomplished, and prayed: "O Lord, I have delivered my message and discharged my ministry. O Lord, I beseech thee, bear thou witness unto it." After three more days in Mecca, he paused at the Ka'ba, again made the seven circuits, entered the building for final prayers, paused at Zam Zam to drink and rinse his mouth, refreshed himself with sweet date water from a cup that many others had drunk from, and returned to Medina.

As he was clearly aware, he had established the ritual for the sacred pilgrimage, and regretted only one aspect of it. He should not, he later said, have entered the Ka'ba, because the tiny building was far too small to accommodate the thousands who would wish to follow his example precisely. Those unable to enter might feel, he feared, that their pilgrimage was thereby incomplete.[12]

Two months after this, he decided that another expedition north was necessary to more fully avenge the defeat at Mu'ta. The Tebuk foray, while technically successful, had not actually confronted the strength of the tribes allied to Rome, which therefore remained a threat, and must be taught a lesson.

12. The pilgrimage to Mecca, known as the *Hajj*, is compulsory, once in a lifetime, for Muslims of good health and sufficient funds to journey to the center of their world, where the Prophet received the divine revelations collected in the Holy Qur'an. Less than ten percent manage to make this highest of all Muslim observances, but this currently amounts to an estimated two million yearly. Saudi authorities now set national quotas; would-be pilgrims must apply, and many are turned down.

The impressive development of Mecca's Sacred Mosque, from a 1721 engraving (top), which shows the shrine little changed from medieval times, to the more substantial structure built in the nineteenth century (middle), and the vast modern mosque (above), which can hold up to one million worshipers. At the heart of the mosque's central court is the ancient Ka'ba, about forty feet in height, built of the common gray stone of the district, and covered in black silk. It contains a black stone believed to have been given to Abraham by the angel Gabriel, according to some sources, and by others to be a meteorite that was part of the original, pagan shrine. The photo above (center-right), shows world heavyweight boxing champion, Muhammad Ali, a convert to Islam, kissing the Black Stone during a 1972 pilgrimage to Mecca.

In the footsteps of Muhammad

For fourteen centuries millions of Muslims have flocked to the birthplace of the Prophet

Every year, millions of Muslims gather in Mecca, Saudi Arabia, for the annual pilgrimage to the birthplace of Muhammad, which has been performed for the past fourteen centuries. The largest religious gathering on earth, the pilgrimage, or Hajj, is one of the "five pillars" of Islam. The devout are called upon to make the trip at least once. In earlier times, this was literally the journey of a lifetime, arduous and difficult, often taking months or even years on horseback or on foot. The number of pilgrims annually was less than one hundred thousand—until the middle of the twentieth century, when air travel began to make the journey a real possibility for millions of ordinary Muslims. By 1983, the number of foreign pilgrims exceeded one million, and in 1988, the Organization of the Islamic Conference established a pilgrim quota for each country according to its population. Nowadays, pilgrims are met by air-conditioned buses, escorted by experienced guides and stay in modern hotels and hostels.

The Hajj has profound political significance for the Saudi monarchy, which claims the title Khadim al-Haramayn, or "custodian of the two holy mosques." To prove themselves worthy of the title, Saudi monarchs must show that they are capable of defending the interests of Arabian Muslims and of administering the holy sites for the benefit of worldwide Islam. The Saudis have invested heavily in new airport buildings, roads, water supplies, and public health facilities. The government also distributes bottled water, juices, and boxed lunches, stations ambulances and

paramedics in strategic locations, and relieves pilgrims of the task of having to slaughter the traditional sacrificial animal. (The Islamic Development Bank now sells vouchers for sacrificial animals, which are chosen by the pilgrim and then slaughtered, processed, and frozen for distribution and sale.) ∎

For many centuries the Muslim pilgrimage, or Hajj, involved a long and often hazardous journey across Arabia, and pilgrims usually banded together in protective caravans (like the one, at left, in a nineteenth-century painting by Leon Belly from Paris's Musée d'Orsay). On arrival, the pilgrim's accommodations were usually nothing more than a tented encampment on the dusty plain outside Mecca (top). Today, by contrast, a vast city of air-conditioned tents near Mina, on the outskirts of Mecca, provide shelter for as many as two million pilgrims during the final days of the annual Hajj.

To head the campaign he appointed Osama, son of his foster son, Zayd, by an Ethiopian slave woman. This was a controversial decision, for the young man was not yet twenty.

Next day, Muhammad was stricken with a violent headache and fever, symptoms of pleurisy, a diagnosis that deeply offended him. Apostles of God, he insistently proclaimed, do not get pleurisy—it must be the lingering effects of the poisoning at Khaybar. The symptoms rapidly grew worse, his complexion turning so gray that Abu Bakr burst into tears at the sight of him. A'isha tried to cheer him, but he was beyond humoring. He lay in her room, rising only for prayers. At length, resolved to make a final address to his people, he had his wives draw water from seven wells around Medina and pour it over him. Then, supported by Ali and Abbas, he made his way to the pulpit, stood beside it, and voiced a faltering appeal for an end to the controversy over his appointment of Osama.

As people wept at the sight of him, he returned to his bed. He was soon unable to rise even for prayers, all public access to him was cut off, and the busy babble in the courtyard of the mosque gave way to hushed whispers. He directed that Abu Bakr lead the prayers in the mosque. A'isha objected. She wanted her father to be spared this task because she feared people would never like a man who occupied the Apostle's place, and would blame him for every misfortune that occurred. Finally Muhammad became exasperated, "Give command forthwith as I desire," he ordered, and Abu Bakr began leading the prayers.

By the fourteenth day of his illness, Muhammad was racked with pain. "If a man's faith be strong," he told the alarmed Umar, "so are his sufferings." At Abbas's suggestion, Um Salema prepared an Ethiopian medicine used on pleurisy, a concoction of Indian wood, certain seeds and olive oil. Opening his mouth, his wives forced it down his throat. "What's this that you've done to me?" he spluttered. "Out upon you. This is a remedy for pleurisy." He became furious with them. "Now shall all of you within this chamber partake of the same. Let not one remain without taking it, except only my uncle, Abbas." An astonishing scene followed, in which all his wives had to pour the concoction down each other's throats while their scowling husband looked on. One objected that she couldn't take it because she was fasting. She was ordered to take it anyway.

Another angry scene followed when he overheard two wives describing the

At Muhammad's death, on June 8, 632, few would have predicted the impact of Islam on the world. Yet in the years following, millions would be converted to the Prophet's militant message, and turn towards Mecca in the ritual of prayer he established—as in this painting by the artist Gustave Guillaumet of evening prayer in the Sahara Desert.

beautiful murals in St. Mary's Cathedral in Ethiopia. "Silence!" he commanded, and deplored the Christian habit of making pictures of their saints. In another tirade, he ordered all religions but Islam banished from Arabia. Since this was not done until years later, however, it was either never said or was dismissed at the time as delirium.

He demanded writing materials, to dictate "a command that shall hinder you from going astray forever," but by the time they were produced, he had forgotten all about it. Next, he ordered A'isha to find a few gold coins she had put away, and to give them to the poor immediately. She did so. He was now pulling the bedclothes over his face, then tearing them off again. Finally, he seemed to accept the fact that death was near upon him, and to yield to it. "O my soul," he said, "Why do you not seek refuge in God alone?" With this, a great calm came upon him.

The next day, he seemed amazingly recovered. At prayers, some in the congregation noticed that the curtain over A'isha's doorway was moving. Then Muhammad appeared, pale and haggard, but beatifically smiling. Slowly he moved among them to the front of the mosque. Abu Bakr as prayer leader was standing with his back to the congregation, but he knew by the murmurs behind him that the Prophet was there. Muhammad told him to finish the prayers, and sat down on the floor beside him. When the service ended, people pressed in upon him, although from this scene there survives no quotation from the Prophet.

On his return to A'isha's chamber, however, his strength fast deserted him. A servant brought him a toothpick, and A'isha chewed it to soften it for him. He took it and rubbed his teeth vigorously, then lay with his head cushioned on her lap as she bathed his head with water. "O Lord," he said, "assist me in the agonies of death. Gabriel come close to me."[13]

Faint words now escaped his lips. "Take your hand from off me. It cannot help me now." A'isha removed her hand. "Lord grant me pardon and join me in the companionship on high," Muhammad prayed. He stretched himself, seemed to gaze fixedly upward, and died. A'isha moved his head from her lap and rested it on a pillow, then joined her sister wives in wailing lamentation, beating her breast and hitting her head. It was early in the afternoon of Monday June 8, 632. ■

13. In one tradition, Gabriel at Muhammad's deathbed replies to Muhammad's prayer: "Peace be unto thee, O Prophet of the Lord. This is the last time I shall tread the earth. With this world I have now concern no longer."

This detail from Piero della Francesco's Legend of the True Cross: Battle of Heraclius and Khosrow *captures the ferocity of the last battles between the Roman emperor and the ancient enemy, Persia. This detail is part of a huge fresco created by the Renaissance master for the Church of San Francesco in Arezzo, Italy.*

CHAPTER 5

Unaware of their peril, two ancient enemies battle to exhaustion

Persia and Byzantium, seventh century superpowers, are drawn into a final and mutually calamitous war

As the great Muslim tactician Khalid ibn al-Walid turned his eyes northward from Mecca across the Arabian sands, two ancient and seemingly invincible empires stood squarely before him. Directly north lay mighty Byzantium, still calling itself "Roman," with all that this name implied. To the northeast lay Rome's historic foe, ancient Persia, whose "King of Kings" had claimed world dominion since Darius's assault on Greece, twelve hundred years earlier.

Khalid, soon to prove himself one of history's great generals, knew that these unimaginably wealthy superpowers boasted the world's largest and mightiest armies. The notion that his motley, fractious camel-soldiers might challenge either was preposterous, even though he fervently believed Allah was with him. What Khalid probably did not know, however, was that at this very moment, both empires lay exhausted. Byzantium and Persia, striving for the last half-century to beat each other to death, had both very nearly succeeded, a fact that rendered Khalid's preposterous aspiration not nearly so preposterous.

This death-struggle had not been inevitable. At times one of the contestants, or even both, recognized the need for détente. But Rome's ancient assumption that it represented the highest expression of human civilization, reinforced by two centuries of Christian certitude, rendered unthinkable any permanent acceptance

1. Historian Martin J. Higgins (*International Relations at the Close of the Sixth Century*) observes that Byzantium's reluctance to pay thirty thousand solidi to the Persians arose more from national pride than economic stress. It had paid quadruple that to keep the barbarous Avars at bay. What grated was Persia's insistence that the payment was no longer a subsidy between equals—ostensibly for defending the Caucasus passes against northern barbarians—but a tribute paid by a client state to its overlord. This alone made stable peace impossible.

of Persia. Meanwhile, Persia's rulers apparently believed that to sustain their prestige among their subjects, they must repeatedly demonstrate their might by vanquishing all challengers.

The Byzantine Empire was inherently far stronger, but through the mid-sixth century, in the three decades immediately prior to the birth of Muhammad, the emperor Justinian had striven to restore Rome's ancient glory in the west by reconquering barbarian-dominated Italy, Sicily, North Africa and Spain. (See earlier volume *Darkness Descends*, chapter 10.) His campaigns, although successful in part, had been ruinously costly, and meanwhile he had to purchase peace in the east by agreeing to pay Persia an annual subsidy of thirty thousand gold *solidi*.[1]

This subsidy was inherited by Justinian's hapless successors. Between his death in 565 and the Muslim attack on the Roman frontier in 632, five emperors would rule at Constantinople. Only the first was related by blood to his predecessor, and all five were radically different. In the same period, the Persian throne was mostly occupied by a grandfather and grandson, both named Chosroes. The grandfather was deliberate, cautious, calculating, and it seemed, ultimately well intentioned. The grandson was dashing, brilliant, unpredictable, increasingly vicious, and by the time of his death, probably insane.

Justinian was succeeded by his nephew, Justin, a willful, volcanic ruler distressingly dominated by his wife Sophia, the clumsily devious niece of

Justinian was succeeded by his nephew, a willful, volcanic ruler distressingly dominated by his wife, the devious Sophia. Justin never visited a frontier or planned a campaign.

Justinian's formidable spouse Theodora. Early one morning in November 565, this pair was awakened by a party of senators, pounding at their gate to tell them Justinian had just died. Through the deserted streets, wrote the court poet Corripus, as dawn crept upon the sleeping city to a fanfare of roosters, they hastened to the palace.

The distraught Justin threw himself upon his uncle's body, protesting his unworthiness to replace him. Even Constantinople's numerous cynics admitted that his humility might not be entirely feigned, for Justin idolized his conquering uncle. Moreover, although he was likely in his early forties (his precise birth date is nowhere recorded), Justin had never visited a frontier, let alone planned a campaign. He nevertheless managed to convince himself of one thing: sheer strength of will could overcome all obstacles. Too late, he would discover that it would not.

Sophia, a realist, was remarkably well prepared for this somber occasion. As the sun rose, rumor spread, and a crowd gathered outside, she appeared beside the bier in a luxurious purple funeral robe sewn with gold and set with precious gems. Justin crossed himself and besought God: "If you command me to hold the Roman scepter . . . if it please you that the people believe in me, make me able to do your will. You subject enemies and bend the necks and break the hearts of the proud; you make kings serve. Let me do your will, that I may do what is pleasing to you."

It was Justin's neck that seemingly needed bending, however. Seven days after his accession an embassy from the predatory Avars, kinsmen of the Huns, came to collect their annual subsidy for "protecting" the Balkans from their Slav subsidiaries. "My gift is to let you off with your lives," Justin sneered, and when they protested, he jailed them. The Avar response was to pillage the cities of Thrace for the next five years, until Justin finally agreed to another expensive treaty with the Avar's *khagan* ("Khan of khans").

Similarly misguided was his cancellation of Justinian's payments to certain Persia-allied Arab tribes in Syria, causing them to resume raids against Byzantium's southern borderlands and the friendly Banu Ghassan. The Monophysite Christian Ghassanids at length prevailed, and Harith ibn Jabala, their most formidable chief (introduced in chapter 1), politely requested his own peacekeeping subsidy. Justin replied with a conciliatory letter, but simultaneously dispatched to his eastern commander another letter ordering Harith's assassination.

Somehow, the two letters were catastrophically switched. A flabbergasted Harith, beholding his own death warrant, fumed "So this is my dessert!" and switched sides. Then, further alienating the Ghassanids and many others, Justin unleashed a virulent anti-Monophysite persecution in Syria, Palestine and Egypt. Monks and nuns were scattered "like birds before the hawk," writes the Monophysite bishop John of Ephesus, in his detailed and contemptuous account of Justin's reign.

Justin apparently saw himself as the fearless and resolute Roman of ancient legend. He scoffed at Byzantium's populist political parties, the Blues and the Greens. Proudly antiquarian, he favored the old and dangerously independent aristocracy, whose private armies now notoriously "defended" the provinces by looting them. "The sin is on my head," languidly yawned one governor of Palestine when accused of this, a reply that apparently satisfied the emperor.

He was alert to the slightest hint of sedition, however. He beheaded two senators for treason, without trial. On suspicion of conspiracy he fired

The strategic fortress of Golubac (below), situated at the Iron Gates gorge on the River Danube—the ancient frontier between Roman civilization and the barbarian hordes. Nearby was the provincial capital of Viminacium, where the emperor Maurice held back the Avars in 601.

In his account of the Persian offensive, John of Ephesus records a notable incident. From the mass of enslaved Christian prisoners, the Persian king ordered that two thousand beautiful virgins be selected as gifts to placate the fearsome Turks, lately settled on Persia's northern frontier. Having some notion of how the Turks used women, the Christian girls decided on mass suicide. When their guards gave them permission to bathe privately in a river, they plunged into the swift current; the guards suspected nothing until their drowned bodies floated past.

This is one of the first appearances in Christian history of the dreaded Turks.

his cousin, military commander on the Danube, and banished him to Alexandria. There he was assassinated, reportedly on Sophia's orders. This lady, a daunting piece of work in her own right, had all Theodora's ambition and little of her intelligence, but she was clever enough to manipulate Justin.

Thus Sophia became the first empress whose image appeared on Byzantine coins, and first to be included in the *diptychs*, the state prayers. There are unsettling reports of her viciousness if not depravity, however. She was said, for example, to have kicked the head of Justin's murdered cousin around the royal apartments like a football. And so implacably did she attack the aging eunuch Narses, Justinian's great general, that Narses prudently exiled himself to Italy.

Her husband, meanwhile, determined to accomplish a feat worthy of a Roman emperor, resolved to rid Byzantium of the detestable Persian levy. This would require a war, he knew, and in 572 a pretext was provided by Christian Armenia, the tough little buffer state squashed between Persia and Byzantium, over which the armies of east and west had marched since the dawn of history. (See sidebar, page 260.) Persia currently controlled Armenia but had guaranteed Armenians freedom to practice their religion. Hence, after Persia's king Chosroes I ordered a Zoroastrian fire-worship temple built in the capital of Dvin, Armenia had risen in rebellion. The revolt failed, and the leaders fled to Constantinople. When the Persian envoy next arrived for the annual levy, Justin not only refused to pay it, but loftily asserted his right to shelter his fellow Christians.

Thus began yet another Persian-Roman war, with Persia everywhere triumphant as its armies sliced through Armenia into Syria. The affronted Christian Banu Ghassan stepped aside while the Persians laid waste the whole area of Antioch, torched Apamea, and returned to Persia, herding a reported 292,000 Roman subjects into slavery.[2] In a counterattack, a Byzantine general laid siege to the linchpin Persian fortress of Nisibis. For reasons unknown, Justin suddenly ordered this commander's arrest, provoking the Roman army into panicked flight. With Nisibis safe, the Persians pounced on neighboring Daras,

Once-beautiful Apamea (below) was home to half a million residents and a bustling center of philosophy and the arts—until its decline under repeated invasions by the Persians, followed by the Muslim conquest. This columned street gives some indication of its past grandeur.

Rome's eastern bastion, and the refuge of a thousand aristocratic fortunes. Using Roman siege engines abandoned at Nisibis, they took Daras. The booty was immense, and Persia now held both great Mesopotamian fortresses.

The loss of Daras precipitated Justin into suicidal madness. He was kept like a caged animal behind barred windows, on occasion biting his chamberlains in frenzy. "Gabolo's son is coming to get you!" they would shout, and the name of the Arab chieftain would make him cower in his bed. Or they would amuse him by pulling him about the palace in a little wagon, barking like a dog or meowing like a cat. To Sophia, however, this represented opportunity. For one disastrous year she ruled supreme, negotiating a more humiliating and expensive truce with Persia (forty-five thousand solidi), while barbarian tribes rampaged in the Balkans and Italy. By late 574, the exasperated Senate decided that a firmer hand was needed.

It was evident whose hand this would be: Tiberius, commander of the household troops, who had become what John of Ephesus calls "Justin's keeper." A handsome man in his early thirties, with the easy camaraderie of the army camp, he was already close enough to the center of power to begin exercising it. Justin, in one of his rare lucid moments, was persuaded to adopt him as his son and

The loss of Daras precipitated the emperor into suicidal madness. Justin was kept like a caged animal behind barred windows, on occasion barking, meowing and biting his chamberlains.

appoint him Caesar, appearing at his coronation as a devastated penitent. "Do not return evil for evil," the hollow-eyed emperor advised his new co-ruler, "lest you become like me. I have been called to account as a man, for I fell and received according to my sins. . . . Let not this imperial garb elate you as it elated me." As he spoke, says John of Ephesus, thousands wept.

However, Tiberius's immediate problem was neither the Persians nor the barbarians. It was Sophia, who kept the keys to the treasury and put Tiberius on an allowance. She would not allow his wife in the palace, so that the courtiers prudently ignored this new queen, and Tiberius had to slip out at night to see her. It was rumored that Sophia wanted to marry Tiberius. When spurned, she plotted his assassination, but was caught, which enabled him to put her under house arrest.

In grand strategy, Tiberius proved altogether adequate. He quickly made peace in a man-to-man confrontation with Harith of the Ghassanids. Next he began seeking a truce with Persia, emphasizing the common interests and common problems of the two empires. Persia was threatened by the Turks, Byzantium by the Avars. Why not cooperate and suppress both? When Persia temporized, Tiberius struck hard, invading Armenia and compelling Persian forces in the west to retreat across the Euphrates, where half of them drowned.

Peace was now possible if only Persia would return Daras, but still Persia stalled, hoping for a break. This soon came. The Byzantine army in Armenia, reports John of Ephesus, whether under orders or spontaneously, launched another savage persecution of Monophysites. Soldiers impaled infants on their spears, nuns were raped, monks tortured. Unsurprisingly, twenty thousand Armenians joined the Persians and a Persian victory followed. Then Chosroes died and was succeeded by a son, Ormizd, for whom peace with Byzantium was unthinkable. "Why should I send gifts to slaves?" he demanded.

By now, Justin was also dead. After appointing Tiberius, he had lingered in the palace for four more years, until, pain-racked by bladder stones, he went down in agony, but also in penitence. "Just are thy judgments, O God, for all the sins I committed with my body," he cried. He summoned Tiberius to take the crown as augustus. Death freed the emperor Justin from earthly woes a week later, on October 4, 578. In far off Mecca, Muhammad was now about eight years old.

Medallions of the emperor Maurice (below), which were likely given as a gift upon his accession to the throne or as a reward for services. Mounted in this girdle (held by the Metropolitan Museum of Art, New York), it allowed the owner to carry his wealth with him. The emperor is depicted in military dress in a chariot drawn by four horses.

Tiberius, meanwhile, was developing agonies of his own. Indifferent to civil affairs, he rewarded his troops generously and often remitted taxes, and lavishly subsidized lawyers, doctors, churchmen, bankers—anything to keep domestic peace. Within three years the treasury was destitute, and he was dipping into emergency funds established by Anastasius seventy years earlier. In mid-582, he fell suddenly ill after eating a dish of mulberries. The disease was thought to be dysentery, and death seemed imminent.

But Tiberius had provided for the succession. His son-in-law Maurice was a Cappadocian in his early forties, who rose through the ranks to become Count of the Guards. As commander of the army in the east (there was scarcely any army in the west by now), he had driven deep into Persian territory—not deep enough to shake the obstinacy of Ormizd, but enough to control the front. Upon Maurice the stricken Tiberius conferred the succession.

On August 12, 582, borne on a litter, Tiberius appeared before his clergy and nobles. Too weak to be clearly heard, he had his quaestor, John, read his speech: "May you, Maurice, make your reign our best epitaph; adorn my grave with your virtue." Then, before the weeping court, Tiberius lifted the crown from his head and the robe of purple from his shoulders, and Maurice donned them, while Tiberius fell back exhausted. By next morning, he was dead.

Maurice would rule for twenty years, and be commemorated by the church as a martyred saint. Popular, however, he was not. For one thing, writes John of Ephesus, he inherited a treasury as empty "as if swept clean by a broom," and earned a reputation for niggardliness—especially by contrast to his predecessor.

But Maurice was personally courageous. When the Avars raged right up to the Long Walls of Constantinople, he himself directed the defense that drove them off. In the east, his generals kept the Persians on the defensive, even when the troops mutinied because their pay had to be cut. And then the Persians fortuitously encountered very serious trouble of their own, notably a civil war.

Baram, governor of Persian Media, had repelled a massive Turkish attack in the north. But then he suffered a minor defeat, and Ormizd saw fit to send him a taunting gift: a lady's dress and a knitting kit. "He certainly is his father's daughter," retorted Baram, whereupon Ormizd dispatched a new satrap with orders to send Baram back in chains. Instead, Baram had his intended successor ceremoniously trampled to death by an elephant, and led all northern Persia in a

rebellion on behalf of Ormizd's eldest son. This young man, named Chosroes after his grandfather, prudently departed from his father's court.

The key fortress of Nisibis declared for Baram; the army wavered, then joined him. As the rebels advanced upon Ctesiphon, the Persian capital, Ormizd named his second son as his heir. That did it. His court too opted for Baram, stripped Ormizd of his jewel-studded raiment, dragged him from his throne, butchered his designated heir before his eyes, then blinded him with hot needles, and later cudgeled him to death in his cell. The eldest son returned to the palace and became Chosroes II.

But then came an event astonishing even for Sassanid Persia's turbulent court. Baram, camped with his army outside Ctesiphon, was not satisfied. Declaring the new King of Kings to be "defective and of minimal intelligence," he launched an unexpected night assault. Chosroes II, none too sure of the loyalty of his own troops, fled with a minimum retinue—a mere three dozen nobles, his harem, and their retainers. His destination: the Roman frontier.[3]

He was recognized and received with honor by Roman troops at Circesium on the Euphrates, and from there appealed to Emperor Maurice. "God has so arranged things that the whole world should be illumined from the very beginning by two eyes," Chosroes wrote, "the most powerful kingdom of the Romans and the most prudent scepter of the Persians. For by these greatest powers, the disobedient and bellicose tribes are winnowed."

He offered to return Daras and Armenia, and maintain perpetual peace, in exchange for aid in recovering his throne.

3. Fleeing from his own capital, the young Persian King of Kings, Chosroes II, crossed the Tigris, not knowing whether to turn north to the Turks or west to the Romans. So, "after looking up to heaven and turning his thoughts to the Creator," says the Byzantine historian Theophylact, he released the reins on his mare to let her decide. The animal headed west.

Saint, soldier and student of war

How could a faith dedicated to peace embrace the realities of the battlefield? The pious emperor Maurice writes the book on Christian military practice

It was said of Emperor Maurice that he slept but four hours a night and spent twice as long at prayer each day. Indeed, the parsimonious, red-haired Cappadocian was undoubtedly one of the most devout of Byzantine emperors, and the only one canonized by the Orthodox Church apart from Constantine himself. Yet he was also a soldier, the architect of a military revival in the eastern empire, and widely acknowledged as the author of one of the most effective manuals of warfare ever written.

Maurice is often credited with bringing together the collective military wisdom of his predecessors and their generals into a single, ruthlessly pragmatic document, the *Strategikon* (Handbook of Strategy), which instructed the officers of what was by now a Christian army on the most effective way to combat, and if need be slaughter, their enemies.

But how could a faith that endorses turning the other cheek embrace the realities of the battlefield? Wasn't the very idea of a Christian soldier a contradiction? The early church had frowned on military service, and at the end of the second century, the ethicist Tertullian stated, "The Lord, in disarming Peter, disarmed every soldier." (See *A Pinch of Incense*, chapter 6.) A few decades later the theologian Origen had argued that Christians should be exempt from imperial military service. Yet paradoxically, Origen also imposed upon the armed forces of the empire the moral duty to take up arms in a righteous cause. (See *A Pinch of Incense*, chapter 7.)

A doctrine that recognized a general duty to promote peace and security seemed incompatible with one that encouraged Christians to exempt themselves from that responsibility. The issue was complicated by the fact that early Christian history is replete with military martyrs. Indeed, in 286 the emperor Maximian martyred an entire legion of Coptic Christian soldiers—sixty-six hundred of them—for refusing to swear a pagan oath. (See *By This Sign*, chapter 4.)

Towards the end of the fourth century, Basil the Great, in the thirteenth canon of his first epistle to Amphilochius, bishop of Iconium, offered a solution, though hardly a congenial one. "Our fathers," he wrote, "did not reckon killing in war as murders, but granted pardon, it seems to me, to those fighting in defense of virtue and piety. Perhaps, however, it is advisable that, since their hands are not clean, they should abstain from communion for a period of three years." That soldiers, whose lives were often at immediate risk, should in effect excommunicate themselves during the perils of frontline duty might not, to them at least, seem an

Two Byzantine warriors (from a bas relief at the Museum of Macedonia, Skopje) crudely depict military dress of the seventh century. The chain mail tunic offered limited protection, hence the shield. A large felt cloak provided defense against the weather.

altogether satisfactory solution.

Unsurprisingly, therefore, Basil's suggested prohibition was never observed, and a generation later, Augustine articulated what many, particularly in the military, had probably worked out for themselves: that in a world increasingly marked by savagery, lawlessness and chaos, an empire that represented stability and order was worth fighting for.

This recognition came at a time when warfare, as practiced in the Roman world, was undergoing dramatic changes, not unlike those prompted by the use of gunpowder a millennium later. The legions of Rome had been transformed from the mainly infantry formations that had withstood the ferocious charges of Celts and Germans into more mobile armies of lancers and mounted archers.

The transformation traced its origins to a famous disaster. In 378, Gothic cavalry played a major role in the defeat of a Roman army at the battle of Adrianople, 140 miles west of Constantinople, where forty thousand legionaries were slaughtered. (See *Darkness Descends*, chapter 3.) It was, according to contemporary historian Ammianus Marcellinus, the worst defeat suffered by a Roman army in five hundred years.

Thereafter, successive waves of mounted barbarian invaders had reinforced that lesson. By the reign of Justinian (527–565), the court historian Procopius describes a new imperial legionary.

He is typically a cavalryman, armed with a bow and sword (and sometimes also a spear), loosing rapid-fire volleys of arrows as he thunders over the battlefield. Traditionalists "who reverence and worship the ancient times, and give no credit to modern improvements," were worthy only of contempt.

It fell to the pious Maurice to codify these improvements and turn them into a state-of-the-art manual of warfare that would form the basis of military instruction for more than three hundred years. Whether Maurice himself wrote the *Strategikon*, or as was common, commissioned its production, is not known. The emperor's experience on the Persian front, however, was considered both extensive and brilliant, so his own authorship is altogether possible.

Whoever wrote it, the *Strategikon* employs the simple and direct language of the practical soldier, and demonstrates a clear understanding of command and the stark realities of the battlefield. The book covers everything a commander might want to know, from training and drilling routines to the order of battle and the care of horses. It deals with sieges, ambush and provision of supplies, and advises on specific tactics designed to combat Persians, Franks, Lombards, and the latest horror to arrive from the central Asian steppes, the Avars and the Slavs.

But the *Strategikon* is by no means devoid of Maurice's faith. Officers are instructed on behavior before, during, and after combat. "First," writes the author, "we urge upon the general that his most important concern be the love of God and justice . . . without which it is impossible to carry out any plan, however well devised it may seem, or to overcome any enemy, however weak he may be thought." Prayers are called for prior to every engagement, and the commander should be in good standing with his Maker, so that in the heat of battle he can pray to God as to a friend.

Finally, after combat, "a general should give prompt attention to the wounded and see to burying the dead. Not only is this a religious duty, but it greatly helps the morale of the living." To this end, the Byzantine army was the first to employ medical corpsmen who accompanied units into battle. "In courage," writes the historian Charles Orman (*The Art of War in the Middle Ages*), the revitalized imperial military "were equal to their enemies; in discipline, organization and armament, far superior."

Maurice's overthrow and gruesome execution in 602 was an ignominious end for a military reformer whose reign, according to historian George Ostrogorsky (*History of the Byzantine State*), "marked an important step forward in the transformation of the worn-out late Roman Empire into the new and vigorous organization of the medieval Byzantine Empire."

The contradictions inherent in the concept of the Christian soldier would be debated for centuries. That Christians could fight "the just war" was by now widely accepted, but the precise definition of such a war would remain elusive.

The West would come to fervently endorse the concept of a "crusade" (literally, a war of the cross) to recover what Islam had conquered. While in the East, on the frontiers of Islam, war remained a matter of survival. "The crusading movement, as the West conceived it, was something entirely foreign," writes Ostrogorsky. "There was nothing new in war against the infidel, but to the Byzantines, this was the outcome of hard political necessity."

Four centuries after Maurice, when Emperor Nikephoros Phocas suggested that Byzantine soldiers killed in battle, especially against Islam, should be considered martyrs, he would be vigorously and successfully opposed by the patriarch of Constantinople, Polyeuktos. The patriarch recalled the ancient canon of St. Basil that when a man kills, even in battle, "his hands are not clean." ∎

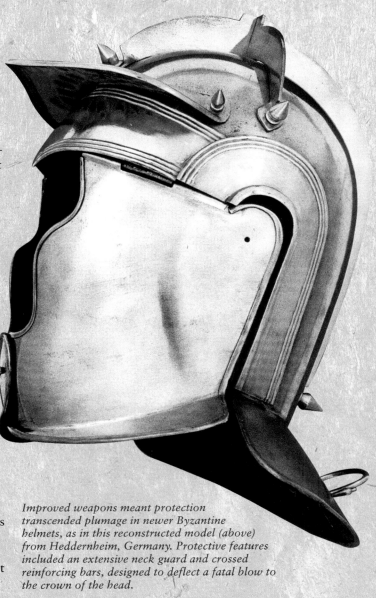

Improved weapons meant protection transcended plumage in newer Byzantine helmets, as in this reconstructed model (above) from Heddernheim, Germany. Protective features included an extensive neck guard and crossed reinforcing bars, designed to deflect a fatal blow to the crown of the head.

The unprecedented offer threw Constantinople into a dilemma. The Senate wanted to reject it. It was not in Rome's interest, they contended, to resolve Persia's internal problems—quite the contrary. But Maurice shared Tiberius's dream of a Roman–Persian entente, which now seemed within reach. He accepted.

Persian troops loyal to Chosroes II now joined the Roman army in Armenia as it moved upon their homeland. Another Roman army advanced into Mesopotamia. Daras went over to Chosroes. Finally, the combined Byzantine forces met Baram at Ganzaca, capital of the Persian province of Azerbaijan, crushed his army and put him to flight. Baram was assassinated, Chosroes returned home in triumph, and Rome and Persia were finally at peace.

Young Chosroes II certainly seemed a promising partner. John of Ephesus calls him a "prudent and wise man," who studied the beliefs of all religions and concluded that the Christian scriptures were "true and wise above those of any other." Before the decisive battle, he prayed to the Arab Christian martyr St. Sergius, though the prayer John records sounds more like a bargain with some idol than a petition to the One God. In any event, Chosroes later sent a thank-you note

Before the battle, the Persian prince prayed to an Arab martyr named St. Sergius . . . hope stirred among Christian optimists that Persia's monarchy might move toward the faith.

and a jewel-encrusted cross to Sergius's shrine. He appointed Nestorian Christian courtiers as his physician, astrologer, and as attorney general for Mesopotamia.

While a refugee in Roman territory, the young man apparently formed a close friendship with Maurice, who called him his son, and a Persian myth even claimed that Chosroes married a daughter of Maurice named Marian. History records no such person or marriage, but later Chosroes did marry a strong-willed Armenian Monophysite Christian named Shirin. Though he was Zoroastrian, he said, he considered her his legitimate wife, and the mother of his heir. For the rest of his life, Shirin had an extraordinary influence over him, and remained with him to his ignominious end.[4]

All these things stirred hope among Christian optimists that Persia's ancient monarchy, so long their enemy, might finally be moving towards the faith. Cynics, on the other hand, read them as mere opportunistic maneuvers by a calculating and persistent enemy. Whatever Chosroes's motives, however, the treaty at last enabled Maurice to confront the Avars, who had been running wild all over the Danube country, laying siege to the towns of Moesia, Thrace and Illyricum, once prime recruiting ground for the Roman army.

In 589, the Avars stormed Anchialus, on the Black Sea just one hundred miles from Constantinople, where they found in its cathedral some ceremonial robes of Maurice's wife, the empress Constantina. The khagan mockingly donned them, and made an offer to the cities of Thrace: "Pay your imperial taxes to me instead, and I'll give you real protection." It cost Maurice eight hundred pounds

4. Chosroes II would best be remembered in the Islamic world for his love affair with the Armenian Christian princess Shirin, much embellished and preserved for future generations by Persian poets and artists. The most famous rendition of the story is the work of the twelfth-century poet Nizami Ganjavi, whose *Khusraw and Shirin* details the competition for her affection between Chosroes and a determined young architect called Farhad. The architect tunnels through a mountain to get to his beloved. Alas, the king persuades him that Shirin has died in the meantime, and the distraught young man plunges to his death. The story is pure fiction, but Shirin and Farhad remain among the most popular names for Iranian children.

of gold to persuade the khagan to head back to his Hungarian pastures.

But in 590, the emperor's temporizing came to an end. He ordered the army of the east to move north. The Romans spent the next decade restoring the Danube frontier, while plague sometimes felled more Avars than they did (including at one point, six of the khagan's sons in a single day). By 601, Maurice achieved peace in both the north and the east, a peace unknown to Byzantium since the days of Justinian.

Was this emperor therefore hailed by all his subjects as the hero of his age? Emphatically not. He was in fact despised. The army loathed him because he not only cut their pay, he cut off their equipment allowance (on the seemingly reasonable grounds that they spent most of it on drink). The aristocrats were hostile because he had replaced so many of them in the provinces with imperial appointees, thus depriving them of their customary graft. The clergy resented him for reducing ecclesiastical tax exemptions. Orthodox Christians condemned him for stopping the persecution of Monophysites and decreeing empire-wide toleration. The people despised him because he spent so little on spectacles and games.

These measures made Maurice "one of the most outstanding of Byzantine emperors," declares Russian historian George Ostrogorsky. But they also made him hated, and he does seem to have had at least two genuine weaknesses. One was for his hometown, tiny Arabissus in Cappadocia, upon which he bestowed a lavish building program, and then, when an earthquake leveled the new buildings, started all over again. "He had a curious love for this insignificant place," remarks British historian John Bagnell Bury (*A History of the Later Roman Empire*). His other weakness was for his family. His father Paul became president of the Senate, his brother Peter a major general.

Had Maurice been cruel, he would no doubt have been feared—but he was merely severe, and therefore was scorned. In the bitter winter of 601–602, popular resentment became menacingly physical. Storms delayed the Egyptian

This surreal landscape, found in Cappadocia, Turkey (below), was used as the planet Tattoine in the original Star Wars *films, and was also the birthplace of the emperor Maurice. These mountains became a natural refuge for the hermit and those seeking asylum, with cave dwellings, rock-cut churches, monasteries, and even entire towns carved from the porous volcanic rock.*

grain ships, causing food shortages that were attributed to the emperor's frugality. In February, the mob stoned the imperial party in procession to Hagia Sophia cathedral. Then they dressed a drunk in a supposedly imperial robe, crowned him with a wreath of garlic, and paraded him through the streets, singing ribald songs.

This incident was only a symptom of what was to come. Fearing a new onslaught of Avars, Maurice ordered the army to winter on the Danube rather than bivouac closer to the city as was usual. This ignited another military mutiny, in which the troops raised on their shields one of their centurions, Phocas by name,[5] and declared him their commander. They marched on Constantinople, determined to proclaim Maurice's eldest son Theodosius as emperor. Another possibility was Germanus, a much-respected senator, and Theodosius's father-in-law.

Maurice, now sixty-three, could have saved his life if he had simply abdicated in favor of his son, suggests Andreas N. Stratos (*Byzantium in the Seventh Century*), "but with an old man's cantankerousness" he resolved to fight it out. Again he mustered the demes to man the walls against the mutinous army, but

Maurice was stoic at the execution of his five remaining sons, quoting from Psalm 119 as they died: 'Righteous art thou, O my Lord, and thy judgment is upright.'

riots against him soon broke out in the city. When both the Blues and the Greens joined in, and with the city aflame, he fled with his family to a shrine across the Bosporus. Crippled by gout, he could travel no farther. His son Theodosius, steadfastly loyal to his father, left to find help from the man whom Maurice had rescued in precisely similar circumstances: Chosroes II.

But it was too late. In the absence of Theodosius, the rebel Phocas invited to his camp the senators, the patriarch, and representatives of the Blues and Greens, for what was expected to be Germanus's coronation. At the crucial moment, however, the army and the Greens raised a great cheer instead for Phocas himself. An unprepossessing man of fifty-five with thick red hair, eyebrows and beard, and a scar across his cheek that darkened in his frequent rages, the centurion was also a sly, sadistic lecher and a drunk. The Senate nevertheless swiftly elected him, and the patriarch agreed to crown him on condition he "confess the orthodox faith." To this he readily agreed, and on November 25, 602, the new emperor entered Constantinople by its Golden Gate on a royal chariot drawn by four white horses, throwing "a continuous rain of gold" to the cheering populace.

Phocas knew he was not secure, however, as long as Maurice lived, so he sent one of his lieutenants across the Bosporus to perform a deed that would long survive in the annals of infamy. Maurice and his five remaining sons—Tiberius, Peter, Paul, Justin and Justinian—were taken to Chalcedon's Eutropius Harbor, where a hideous scene took place. One by one, the former emperor's sons were

5. Chronicler John of Antioch (not to be confused with John of Ephesus, another contemporary historian) notes that the centurion Phocas, who would later become emperor, was one of the legionary representatives to the imperial court in the monthlong argument over wintering the army in Slav territory. John recounts that Phocas was so insolent that one aged patrician negotiator pulled his beard—for which that patrician later paid with his life.

slaughtered before his eyes. Contemporary accounts agree that the nursemaid of one youngster offered to have her own child put to death rather than the prince. But Maurice himself stoically shook his head, and as each boy died, he pronounced the same line from Psalm 119 (verse 137): "Righteous art thou, O my Lord, and thy judgment is upright." Finally he himself was run through. The six bodies were thrown into the sea, the heads arrayed at an army base outside Constantinople, where crowds lined up to view them.

Phocas proceeded to distribute lavish gifts to his troops, order races in the Hippodrome to please the crowds, and have his wife Leontia crowned Augusta. He also executed every senior official and commander who had served Maurice. The empress Constantina and her three younger daughters were imprisoned for the time being in a monastery. The fate of the young Theodosius is simply not known. The two most convincing accounts of these events say he was very soon captured and killed. A less-convincing tale claims he reached the Persian court and played some further role. Another says he was poisoned by Chosroes II, who twenty years later would still claim to be battling Constantinople on his behalf. Yet another has him taking refuge in a Jerusalem monastery.

Such tales, some say, visited upon Phocas throughout his terrible eight-year reign an enduring fear that the prince he had failed to kill would return to destroy him. Equally strange, writes historian Stratos, is the fact "that Maurice, who was loved by no one during his life, was sanctified very soon after his death." Both the Chalcedonians and the Monophysites recognize him as a saint. But perhaps this is not so strange. Maurice's chroniclers, who describe him as spending seven hours daily at liturgies, prayer or scripture study, may exaggerate his piety, but pious he assuredly was. He was also a conscientious Christian, and a man determined however misguidedly to do his duty, and—at his tragic end—a pitiful but noble figure.

Maurice's failures left the empire fragmented, and it never did unite behind Phocas. Faction fights broke out unceasingly in Asia Minor, Palestine, Illyricum and Thrace. Armenians agitated for Theodosius, whom they presumed to be alive. Phocas declared for Christian orthodoxy and repudiated Maurice's policy of toleration, igniting more widespread and bloody campaigns against Monophysitism, and further alienating Syria, Palestine and Egypt. In fear of renewed hostile moves from Persia, Phocas concluded a treaty with the Avars and stripped the Balkans of troops, laying open the Danube basin. First Dalmatia and Illyricum, then Macedonia and Thrace, were flooded with Slavs and Avars. But as Phocas expected all along, his worst trouble came from Persia.

Any interest Chosroes II might have had in Christianity proved short-lived as

Chariot races were a traditional crowd-pleaser in Constantinople's Hippodrome, an enormous arena that seated 100,000 people. Rival teams, the Blues and the Greens, commanded fierce loyalty, often resulting in riots. The ivory above (held in the Museo Civico dell'Eta Cristiana in Brescia, Italy) depicts the Lampadi family, commissioners of the carving, at a chariot race.

he strayed ever deeper into vanity, sensuality, morbid cruelty, ruthless ambition, and magic. In addition to his ample harem, he reportedly was accustomed to travel with a corps of three hundred and sixty astrologers, soothsayers and magicians. Increasingly, he chafed under what he saw as the burden of the treaty he had accepted with Byzantium to regain his throne. How could he break it? The murder of his friend Maurice gave him a satisfactory pretext.

Chosroes was said to have reacted to the killing of the Byzantine emperor with rage, whether real or theatrical no one knows, although historian Bury opts for the latter. However, when Phocas's emissary arrived in Persia—none other than the executioner of Maurice and his sons—Chosroes ordered the man starved to death. He then launched the most devastating assault on the empire since the days of Darius the Great. He seized Daras after obliterating a Roman army sent to relieve it, and subsequently annihilated two more in Armenia.

Syria was next. Edessa was taken and Antioch pillaged, with Christian Monophysites aiding the Zoroastrian Persians at every opportunity. Orthodox

A short-lived Jewish restoration

In the wake of the Persian invasion, a Jewish administration returns to Jerusalem, but with it came the massacre and slavery of the city's Christian population

The conflict between Christians and Jews, bitter and occasionally violent from the first Christian century onward, produced a series of bloodbaths in the seventh century when the Persian invasion of Palestine enabled the Jews to repossess, for three years, their holy city of Jerusalem.

Persia held a mystical charm for the Jews because it was Cyrus the Great of Persia who restored them to Jerusalem in 538 B.C., ending what is known as "the Babylonian Captivity."[1] Now, nearly twelve centuries later, the Persians were on the march again. Could history be repeating itself? Would they again restore Jerusalem to the Jewish people? Was Chosroes another Cyrus?

For this reason, thousands of young Jews volunteered for the Persian army as it moved massively into Syria at the turn of the seventh century. This, however, made them enemies of the Christians who were fighting the Persian advance.

But not all the Christians: Most Syrian Christians were Monophysites, and under vigorous persecution by the orthodox Christian emperor Phocas. When the Monophysites announced plans for a council in Antioch, the imperial authorities forbade it, and issued demands that the Monophysites conform to imperial religious policy and that all Jews become Christians.

"The consequence of this policy was a great revolt of the Jews in Antioch," writes the British historian J. B. Bury (*History of the Later Roman Empire*). "Christians were massacred, and a cruel and indecent punishment was inflicted on the patriarch Anastasius." The eighth-century historian Theophanes furnishes details of the aged cleric's castration: "They hurled his genitals into his face, then dragged him into the *mese* (i.e., the main street), and murdered him and many landowners. Then they burned their bodies."

Phocas retaliated by sending in two generals to quell the rebellion. Bury says they "drove the Jews out of Antioch." Historian Alfred J. Butler, in *The Arab Conquest of Egypt*, describes their "wholesale massacre by hanging, drowning, burning, torturing and casting to wild beasts." The following year, however, as the Persians advanced, the Christians fled the city, the roads were clogged with refugees, and the Jews surrendered Antioch to the invaders—then Damascus, then Caesarea.

In 614, the Persian army arrived before the walls of Jerusalem. A new Christian patriarch, realizing that a defense against the enormous Persian host must ultimately fail, urged immediate surrender on the good terms offered. But the populace, represented by the local wings of the Byzantine Blue and Green political parties, rejected his advice, declared him a traitor, and manned the defenses. It took the Persian army

clergy were killed or deposed, and replaced by Monophysites. In 609, Persia invaded Asia Minor, writes the eighth-century historian Theophanes, "showing mercy on their march to neither age nor sex," and reached Chalcedon, scene of Maurice's execution. In terror and indignation, the citizens of Constantinople watched fire rage through buildings on the opposite shore. Then the Persians left; the fear of them did not.

Phocas vented upon his own subjects his rage at these frightful reversals, and constantly feared for his life—possibly with justification. Between 607 and 609, he uncovered two plots against him and retaliated, according to Theophanes, by commanding the mutilation and beheading of "many" governors, senators and court officials, and even of the betrayers' betrayers. Both Germanus and Maurice's widow Constantina were implicated in a second scheme, and Constantina was tortured into naming other conspirators. Then she and her three younger daughters were slaughtered on the same breakwater at Eutropius that had been soaked with the blood of her husband and sons.

twenty-one days to breach the walls. The historian Andreas Stratos (*Byzantium in the Seventh Century*) describes what followed:

"Jerusalem suffered the fate of a city taken by assault. The savagery of the Persians and particularly the Jews was inconceivable. Slaughter and looting went on for three days. All the great churches were set on fire." He says the estimates of the numbers of Christians killed (based on ancient records, often drastically inflated) range from thirty-four thousand to ninety thousand. Many others were taken as slaves, herded to the Mount of Olives, offered for sale, and then marched off to Persia—the patriarch among them. Jews purchased some of the prisoners, says one early account, in order to put them to death.

As a reward for their help in the conquest, the Persian commander turned Jerusalem over to Jewish administration. In the next three years, however, Persian policy abruptly changed. A broad tolerance for Christians was instituted, particularly for the Monophysites. At the same time, all Jews were ordered banished from the city. What caused this Persian–Jewish rupture is not clear. Some attribute it to the Persian king's influential Armenian Christian wife, Shirin. In any event, these new Persian overlords proved far less benevolent to the Jews than the ancient ones had. ∎

1. Babylon conquered Jerusalem in 586 B.C., destroyed the Temple, and herded thousands of Jews to Mesopotamia. After Cyrus the Great conquered Babylon, he restored the Jews to their homeland, and authorized the construction of a new Temple. The new building was opened in 516, exactly seventy years after the Babylonian conquest, thus fulfilling Jeremiah's prophecy: "And this whole shall be a desolation, and an astonishment; and these nations shall serve the king of Babylon seventy years" (Jer. 25:11).

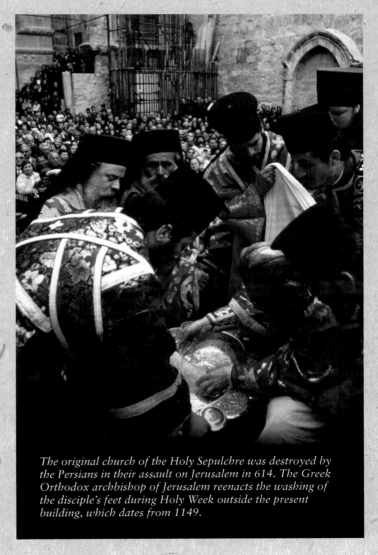

The original church of the Holy Sepulchre was destroyed by the Persians in their assault on Jerusalem in 614. The Greek Orthodox archbishop of Jerusalem reenacts the washing of the disciple's feet during Holy Week outside the present building, which dates from 1149.

Heraclius meets with ambassadors in this illustration from a fifteenth-century manuscript, the Radziwill Chronicle *(above)*. The emperor was forced to negotiate peace treaties involving crippling tributes to the aggressive Avars. In the bottom half of the page, Slav prisoners pull a cart for an Avar master.

Chaos continued in the capital, where Phocas's efforts to ingratiate himself with the Blue faction caused ceaseless fighting between Blues and Greens. When the Greens torched central Constantinople, a Blue district, Phocas had their leader burned alive. In Antioch, the authorities tried to block a Monophysite ecumenical council, civil war resulted, and thousands were slain when imperial forces moved in to suppress it. By now, the emperor was bitterly and universally hated, but also greatly feared.

In distant Carthage, however, one of Maurice's generals had survived all Phocas's purges. His name was Heraclius, and in 608, he struck shrewdly and hard, simply by cutting off the supply of North African grain to Constantinople. This would cause rebellion against Phocas, he knew, just as it had against Maurice when storms blocked the grain fleet. Heraclius, a man of sixty-five, further commissioned his son, also named Heraclius, to assemble a fleet. Meanwhile his nephew, Niketas, marched across northern Africa to Egypt, recruiting as he went. Niketas handily took Alexandria (whereupon the citizens slaughtered the orthodox patriarch), and trapped the imperial fleet up the Nile. At that point, all Egypt went over to him.

In Constantinople, Phocas's situation grew daily more precarious. When he arrived late for the games one day in 609, the crowd greeted him with shouts of "You're drunk! You've lost your senses!" The enraged emperor had his troops lay into the crowd, mutilating many of his subjects, stuffing some in sacks and throwing them into the sea, and hanging others. The mob retaliated by burning government buildings and opening the prisons.

Early that summer, the younger Heraclius sailed his fleet into the Golden Horn, an icon of the Virgin on the topmast of his flagship. Phocas seized as hostages his mother and his fiancée Flavia, who happened to be visiting the city, but pro-Heraclius rioters rescued them. Then the mob, led by a city administrator whose wife reportedly had been raped by Phocas, dragged the emperor from his palace and presented him to Heraclius, in chains, in the Church of St. Thomas the Apostle.

Heraclius confronted him: "Did you govern the state in this miserable fashion?" he demanded. "Will you govern it better?" Phocas sneered. With that he was hideously executed. According to one account, his limbs were one by one hacked from his body, until finally he was beheaded. His three senior commanders were burned in the Hippodrome. The next day, Heraclius was crowned emperor. He also married Flavia, who changed her name to Eudocia.

Thirty-six years old, blond, blue-eyed, and a superb athlete, Heraclius was godly, sincere and courageous. He was so passionately devoted to his people and to his Lord, Jesus Christ, that later chroniclers, especially in the west, would call him the

"First Knight and First Crusader." But he had another side. He was edgy, easily stressed, prone to depression, and eventually developed an uncontrollable fear of water. He would reign for thirty-one years, and was destined to preside over the worst reversal ever to befall Christendom. His reign divides into three distinct phases, the first catastrophic, the second astonishingly triumphant, and the third calamitous beyond anything that he or anyone else in his era could have envisioned.

By 610, the empire left behind by the wretched Phocas was arguably at the lowest state in its entire eleven-hundred-year history. "It seemed that nothing short of a divine miracle could restore it to well-being," writes Bury. To the north the Avar situation was worse than ever. To the south the

Heraclius, defying the Church, married his own niece, Martina. The first child of their incestuous union, a boy, was born with a deformed neck, the second deaf and dumb.

Monophysite conflict had reached a complete impasse. To the east, the Persians had taken Damascus and Antioch, and were threatening Jerusalem itself, Christianity's Holy City.

The treasury was bankrupt, and the troops he brought from northern Africa constituted almost Heraclius's entire army. Most of the Byzantine forces opposing the Persians appeared more loyal to local commanders than to the emperor.[6] Everywhere self-interest seemed to have long since replaced duty and loyalty; depression and despair overhung the whole realm, particularly the capital.

Reversal followed upon reversal. Jerusalem opened its gates to Chosroes's army, and the precious true cross, discovered nearly three centuries earlier by the empress Helena, was carried off to Persia. It seemed that God had indeed abandoned his people. Then the Persians seized Egypt, a Roman possession for six hundred years, cutting off Constantinople's grain supply. Famine resulted, followed by plague among the malnourished populace, and when Heraclius sent a peace embassy to Chosroes, it was contemptuously rejected.

Disaster also darkened his personal life. After two years of marriage and two children (one of them an heir, Constantine), the empress Eudocia died.[7] The following year, Heraclius made a move that would long haunt him. In defiance of a very explicit church rule, he married his niece, Martina, a union forbidden as incestuous. Martina's first child, a boy, was born with a deformed neck; her second son was born deaf and dumb. This was seen by the devout as a divine judgment, and she was referred to thereafter as "the accursed thing."

In 616, Chosroes's army reappeared at Chalcedon. While his soldiers looted city and countryside, their general crossed the Bosporus and arranged with Heraclius to conduct two Byzantine peace envoys to the King of Kings. It was a doomed mission. The enraged Chosroes had the two Byzantines imprisoned, and his general flayed alive (and a bag made of his skin, writes the Greek historian Nicephorus), for failing to assassinate Heraclius when he had

6. Heraclius eventually gained control of this army by inviting its commander to Constantinople, arresting him, and ordering him tonsured as a monk. The emperor then formally visited the troops, and informed them that whereas they had previously been fighting for their general, they were now fighting for the empire. The soldiers accepted this.

7. As the funeral procession bearing Eudocia's body moved through the streets of the capital, a servant girl—whether accidentally or deliberately is not known—spat out a window, and the spittle landed on the gowned body of the empress as the cortege passed by. Heraclius made a human sacrifice of the girl on his wife's tomb, and her mistress barely escaped with her life. It seemed the overreaction of a man near his wit's end.

the chance. As for peace, his haughty reply to Heraclius included the following inflammatory passage:

> Refusing to submit to our rule, you call yourself a lord and sovereign. Having gathered together a troop of brigands, you ceaselessly annoy us. . . . You say you have trust in God. Why then has he not delivered out of my hand Caesarea, Jerusalem, Alexandria? And could I not destroy Constantinople? But not so. I will pardon all your faults if you will come hither with your wife and children. I will give you lands, vines and olive groves. . . . Do not deceive yourself with a vain hope in Christ, who was not able to save himself from the Jews that killed him by nailing him to a cross. If you descend to the depths of the sea, I will stretch out my hand and seize you.

To counter this doom-laden ultimatum, Heraclius had no army, no money and no support from his church. His capital, moreover, was threatened by the Avars as well as the Persians, so he decided on a desperate strategy. He would abandon Constantinople to its fate. He would move his government to his hometown of Carthage—far from Persia, loyal to his family, and well situated for the recovery of Egypt and Italy. He shipped the treasures of the imperial household in advance, doubtless asking God's blessing on this audacious expedient.

God's answer soon came, when the ships bearing the treasure sank in a storm, and Constantinople discovered the emperor's intention. The reaction of its people bordered on the miraculous. "The possibility of losing the emperor brought suddenly home to Constantinople the realities of its situation," writes Bury. "It awakened the city from the false dream of a spoiled child," and "to this awakening we may ascribe the salvation of the empire."

Salvation also came from the church. The reigning patriarch, Sergius, was a born leader with a signal ability to stir the consciences and resolve of his people, and of his emperor. He demanded that Heraclius swear he would never abandon Constantinople, and Heraclius so swore. Now, incestuous marriage notwithstanding, the emperor had in the patriarch a powerful ally.

Equally important, the current crisis was no longer merely one more hopeless struggle for survival; that message from Chosroes had unintentionally transformed it into a crusade to save Christianity. On this favorable tide, Heraclius moved swiftly. Using the loss of Egypt as sufficient pretext, he ended the welfare dole, the automatic daily ration of government flour that so long had grievously burdened the imperial treasury. This alone had three instantly beneficial effects. It drastically cut the cost of government. It furnished a new supply of labor, since idleness was now impossible. And it strengthened the army, because idlers who would not produce were promptly conscripted.

The churches, as directed by Sergius, melted down golden vessels and ornaments to produce coinage that would finance a new army.

A rare gold cross (below) from the fifth century that escaped the meltdown to finance Heraclius's army. It exemplifies the artistry of the Byzantine goldsmiths. The precious metal was greatly valued for jewelry and for lavish decoration of churches and icons with gold leaf.

Almost overnight, a new spirit took hold of the Christian capital. But Heraclius did not move precipitously. He took five years to equip and train an army, and not until 622 was he ready to put it to full use.

Before that, however, the Avars experienced the effects of the new resolve animating Constantinople. In 619, in a plan he doubtless regarded as a knockout blow, the khagan began demonstrating a new amiability towards Byzantine envoys. He wanted to make peace, he told them, to put an end to all this waste and war. Could he meet the emperor personally outside the Long Walls of the city? Heraclius, hoping not to have the Avars at his back when he attacked Persia, readily agreed.

A magnificent reception was arranged for the khagan in the suburbs of the city, where tens of thousands of spectators waited to greet him. At the very last moment, however, Heraclius was warned that he was walking into a trap. Swiftly seizing a poor man's cloak, he threw it over his shoulders, hid the crown beneath it, and bolted back within the walls. While he speedily organized a defense, a screaming Avar horde was already pouring into the suburbs, rounding up by some accounts more than two hundred thousand civilian prisoners.

To their surprise, however, they were shortly stopped dead by an unwontedly resilient civilian and military force, and had to withdraw. In the following week, Heraclius ransomed all the civilian captives, and the Avars signed a treaty that would keep them at bay for seven vital years. Moreover, the Byzantine exarch in Italy made a treaty with the barbarian Lombards, spurring them to attack the Avars from behind, and divert their attention from Constantinople.

Next came Persia. Heraclius spent the winter of 621–622 in seclusion—some said in prayer, others in conference. Probably it was both. By Easter all was ready, and he had his son Constantine, aged ten, made regent under Patriarch Sergius: "Into the hands of God and his mother, and into yours, I commend this city and my son," he told the patriarch. Then he and his army, more than one hundred and twenty thousand strong, entrusting Constantinople to God and its own defenses, set sail under the icon of the Virgin. In this same season of the year 622, possibly the same month of June, Muhammad's Muslims moved from Mecca to Medina in the hijra.

For years to come, Heraclius's counteroffensive against the ancient enemy in the east would provide material for Christian storybooks. How he realized that if his fleet controlled the Bosporus, the Persian army there could not attack the capital.

Heraclius's brilliant campaign against Persia captured the imagination of generations of storytellers. In this medieval manuscript from the encyclopedic history Le Miroir Historial *of* Vincent de Beauvais *(above), the coronation of Heraclius appears as the central image.*

How for the first time in two hundred years, a Roman emperor led his troops in battle. How he outwitted the Persians by taking his army in an end run right around Asia Minor and unexpectedly landing in Cilicia, St. Paul's home province. How he further confused them by moving his army back and forth. How he defeated one army in the Persian province of Azerbaijan, then quickly turned and drove Chosroes out of the north. How he became a hero to the Persian troops by freeing fifty thousand enemy prisoners and sending them home (which meant he needn't feed them over the winter). How the worst of all possible perils arose when the Persians finally made a treaty with the Avars for a combined assault on Constantinople, now hundreds of miles behind him. And finally, how he recruited thousands of good soldiers in Christian Armenia so that he could split his army three ways, sending one unit back to defend the capital, one to take on the Persian army still in Cilicia, and one to pursue the offensive in the Persian heartland.

It reads like romantic fiction, yet is nevertheless true, and the great crisis came with that final combined attack on the Christian capital in 626. Some eighty thousand Avars and their allies struck at the city's walls, where twenty thousand of Heraclius's crack troops awaited them. All through July, the Avars labored with their siege engines but could make no headway, and at month's end, the khagan offered peace, at a conference in his tent of three uniformed Byzantine officers and three Persian envoys clad in silk. The Romans were forced to stand while the Persians sat, a deliberate affront, and the meeting failed because the Romans seemed no longer interested in making peace. Instead, they intercepted the vessel carrying the Persian negotiators back to Chalcedon, killed one of them right in front of the Persian army, threw another into the sea, and sent the body of the third to the Avars as a gift for the khagan.

A few days later, there was worse news yet for the khagan. Slav sailors in rowboats and other small vessels, on the shore of the Golden Horn opposite the capital, awaited a signal by night that the Persian army was ready to simultaneously attack across the Bosporus in a tiny fleet that they, too, had managed to assemble. But the Romans discovered the plan, sent them a premature fake signal, and sank all their boats as they attempted the crossing. Then they doubled back and sank the Persian force as well. That same night, the Avars were also assailing the walls of the city, and both defenders and attackers reported seeing the figure of a woman on the ramparts, encouraging the Byzantine soldiers. Unquestionably, the Christians agreed, it was the Blessed Virgin. That was enough for the khagan. The next day, he burned his siege engines and withdrew his army. The city had been saved.

Heraclius's second army had meanwhile defeated the Persians in Cilicia. Now his third army, reinforced by veterans from the other two, moved steadily through Persia towards Ctesiphon, to a decisive battle at the ancient city of Nineveh. There, Chosroes gave his commanding general an ultimatum—victory or death—and the desperate man, with nothing to lose, challenged Heraclius to personal combat. Heraclius accepted and swiftly killed him. When devastating defeat for the Persian army followed, Chosroes had the corpse of his unfortunate general thrashed, affirming what many had already suspected—that he was losing his mind.

Heraclius then proceeded to Dastagerd, site of the palace where Chosroes II liked to live in unparalleled luxury, with his host of servants and a harem, by now said to number three thousand women. The King of Kings consequently fled to Ctesiphon, where he had not set foot for twenty-four years. If you ever return there, the Zoroastrian magi had warned him, you will be destroyed.

And so it was. The Persian nobility rose against him. They seized him and ordered him starved to death, while his children were one by one executed before his dimming eyes. They spared only Seroes, his eldest son, who reputedly watched with satisfaction the demise of his brothers, sisters and father. The fate of his mother, Shirin, is not recorded. The Persian army at Chalcedon made immediate peace with Constantinople. Seroes signed a treaty returning all Roman territorial possessions, and to crown all, the true cross was returned with much ceremony and rejoicing to Jerusalem, now once more in Christian hands. It was by now 628. In four years, Muhammad would be dead, and Khalid ibn al-Walid would be ready to launch his preposterous endeavor.

Meanwhile, with Heraclius's life's work complete, or so he must have supposed, he returned to Constantinople to enjoy in relative tranquility the fruits of his victories. But his empire, although alive, was destitute. It was as religiously divided as ever, and it was exhausted by internal strife and constant warfare. The condition of Persia, its longtime enemy, was worse. Seroes reigned a mere eight months, and repeated regicide and rebellion thereafter rapidly enthroned and deposed one Persian king after another. Such, then, was the state of the world's two superpowers in what, unbeknownst to them both, would be their darkest hour. ■

The high price of doctrinal clarity

Byzantium's seesaw efforts to woo or suppress the empire's Monophysites cause some to view the Muslim invasion as liberation from cruel oppression

I t is one of the ironies of history that when the Muslim armies arrived at the frontiers of Egypt, many Christian Egyptians warmly welcomed them. The descendants of those Christians would have the next fifteen centuries to regret this hospitality, for from that time forward they were destined to live as an impaired class, subject to a special tax not levied on Muslims, eventually denied access to senior public office, often compelled to wear distinctive clothing, prohibited on pain of death from spreading their faith to Muslims, and periodically suffering deadly persecution. Even so, their mistreatment by the Byzantine Empire immediately prior to the Arab conquest goes a long way to explaining why they saw the Muslims as their deliverers.

Behind the Byzantine mishandling of their Egyptian prefecture lay a political premise few in the seventh century would have seriously challenged: that if the empire were to remain united, all its subjects must embrace a single religion. That religion was Christianity, and five church councils had carefully defined its beliefs.[1]

Disastrously, however, two of those councils had alienated large factions within the faith that did not accept their conclusions. The Council of Ephesus in 431 had seen the followers of Nestorius break away and eventually concentrate in neighboring Persia. There, despite persecution, Nestorian

Christianity (which was understood to deny the unity of Jesus Christ, the God-man) flowered and spread into central Asia. The Council of Chalcedon, held twenty years later in part to reconcile the Nestorians, instead set off an equally contagious movement on the other theological extreme. Known as the Monophysites, these were understood to deny the real distinction between the humanity and deity of Jesus Christ, as declared at Chalcedon. They held sway in Syria, Palestine and Armenia, and with particular fervor in rural Egypt— where there soon came to be both a Coptic and a Melkite patriarch.[2]

To regain the Monophysites, the emperor Zeno, in 482, had proposed the compromise doctrinal statement known as the Henoticon, and the emperor Justinian, sixty-two years later, had advanced another instrument, known as the Three Chapters. Both were rejected by the Monophysites and by Rome. At one point, Justinian kidnapped and imprisoned the pope Vigilius in an attempt to coerce western acceptance (described in chapter 10 of *Darkness Descends*, a previous volume in this series).

Since the Monophysites wouldn't compromise, Justinian took strenuous efforts against them, deposing and often imprisoning their clergy, while issuing pleas for Christian unity. However, he did so with a distinct reluctance.

1. The first five ecumenical councils were the Council of Nicea (325), the First Council of Constantinople (381), the Council of Ephesus (431), the Council of Chalcedon (451), and the Second Council of Constantinople (553). The Council of Nicea is covered in a previous volume, *By This Sign*; the Councils of Ephesus and Chalcedon, and the two Councils of Constantinople, in the volume *Darkness Descends*.

2. The term *Melkite* (sometimes spelled "Melchite") comes from the rendering in Greek of the Syriac word meaning "imperial." The Melkites were those Christians in Egypt and Syria who, in accepting the Council of Chalcedon, concurred with imperial policy.

For one thing, his beloved empress, Theodora, was a born-again Christian, rescued by a Monophysite convent from a dissolute life and thereafter a Monophysite sympathizer. For another, the Monophysite bishop, John of Ephesus, his close friend for more than thirty years, had conducted successful missions to the remaining pagans in the Ephesus area, all of whom became Monophysites. Also, the famous Arab tribe, the Banu Ghassan, so essential to the empire's defense on the Persian frontier, was Monophysite. Finally, Justinian knew that to seriously crack down on the non-conformists in Egypt would risk real trouble there. So in Egypt and among the Arabs, he largely ignored Monophysitism.

His nephew and successor, Justin II, knew no such caution. Justin assembled the Monophysite clergy in the capital, presented them with a proposed doctrinal edict, and urged them to amend it in such a way as to make it acceptable to themselves. Their proposed amendments, however, outraged those who accepted Chalcedon, and who replied with a series of sub-amendments, equally unacceptable to the other side. Finally exasperated, Justin proclaimed the edict anyway, replete with the offensive sub-amendments, and instructed the patriarch of Constantinople to enforce it on the recalcitrant Monophysites.

That patriarch, John Scholasticus, did so with a vengeance, all grimly documented by Justinian's old friend, the missionary John of Ephesus, who denounces Scholasticus with lurid accounts of his ferocious assault on the Monophysites. Nuns are portrayed as being dragged shrieking before Chalcedonian clergy, communion bread forced down their throats. Monophysite priests and nuns are turned over to the Praetorian Guard for punishment. Two noblewomen are shorn of their hair and made to clean toilets in a monastery. Monophysite clergy are jailed and stripped to discourage their escape.

Scholasticus's painful death after thirteen years in office is welcomed by John with undisguised satisfaction. The patriarch suffered "a deadly fire in his bowels and in his heart," writes John, and even turned against his own supporters, cursing them for bringing this judgment upon him.

Unfortunately, the new patriarch, Eutychius, maintained the persecution, and this time John of Ephesus himself was imprisoned—in a leaky jail (he writes) that flooded every time it rained—and he was forced to sleep in blankets previously used to wrap dead bodies.

Centuries of isolation and persecution have made the Coptic people of Egypt proud and insular. Copts are descendants of the ancient Egyptians and divided from Eastern Orthodoxy by their long-held Monophysite stance. This Coptic girl displays a tattoo of a cross on her right wrist, a common distinguishing feature among Copts.

3. There are numerous variations in the name of Jacob Baradaeus. In various early medieval records the name appears as Al-Baradai, Burdoho, Burdeono and Burdeaya, all derived from the Syriac word for the ragged garment worn by beggars, the disguise he wore throughout much of his ministry to prevent his arrest.

4. The conflict that divided the Monophysites deeply grieved John of Ephesus in his dying years. He tells, for instance, how three Alexandrian bishops, determined to consecrate an alternative to Paul of Antioch, stole into his episcopal city, bribed a caretaker to leave a church door unlocked, and hid in a nearby house, waiting to consecrate the alternative patriarch at night. They were betrayed; however, the house was surrounded, and they escaped through a basement latrine—less ashamed (writes John) of their foiled plot "than of their dress, all covered with filth and ordure."

Under the next emperor, Maurice, the Monophysites were left alone. They could not, however, be described as "at peace," for a fierce conflict broke out between their two foremost champions. One was Jacob Baradaeus, the missionary bishop of Edessa, whose fervid evangelism during Justin's persecutions fired up the Monophysite movement all over Syria, much of Asia Minor, and among the Arab tribes—so fervid, in fact, that many Monophysites became known as "Jacobites."[3] John of Ephesus says that Jacob, in his astonishing twenty-five-year mission, ordained a hundred thousand clergy and consecrated eighty-nine bishops, one of them John himself. (Though the numbers are certainly exaggerated, the success of Jacob's work is undoubted.)

Jacob, often disguised in beggar's rags, could certainly spellbind, but he had no talent for administration, and his converts soon shattered into assorted sub-denominations. One such convert was the revered Paul, whom Jacob made Monophysite patriarch of Antioch. Seized by imperial authorities, Paul was imprisoned at Constantinople, accepted communion from the Chalcedonian patriarch, but later escaped and returned to Syria. There he was

The Annunciation and the Visitation of Mary and Elizabeth are portrayed side-by-side on this sixth-century Coptic textile (left), from the Victoria and Albert Museum in London. It is typical of the Coptic style, featuring bold colors and ornamental features, such as stylized trees and a decorative border.

denounced by Jacob as an apostate, but when Paul recanted and rejoined the movement, Jacob forgave him.

The Monophysites in Egypt did not, and in a painful attempt to reach Alexandria and reconcile that conflict, the aged Jacob died in the summer of 578, his achievements in chaos. John of Ephesus died some five years later, at the age of about eighty. He, too, saw his lifelong work reduced to an internecine brawl.[4]

During the reign of Heraclius, which began in 602, Patriarch Sergius of Constantinople came up with another doctrinal panacea. The Monophysites were viewed by their opponents at Constantinople and Rome as effectively denying that Jesus Christ had any human nature whatever (a charge the Monophysites denied). Sergius saw an acceptable compromise in the concept of the *thelesis*, which translates into English as "the will."

In a letter to Pope Honorius at Rome, Sergius propounded a new doctrine that came to be called Monothelitism. It held that although Jesus Christ had two natures, one divine and one human, he had but one will; always an expression of the one divine *thelesis* (or will) of God—because Jesus' will and God's were one and the same. In effect, Monothelitism represented a doctrinal saw-off. If the Monophysites would concede the two natures of Christ (as defined at Chalcedon), their opponents would concede that Jesus and God were of one will.

This compromise quickly gained a significant supporter. Astonishingly (and as it later turned out, unwisely), Pope Honorius wrote to Sergius in support of it, thereby implying that

Rome and Constantinople were united. They were not, however, because Honorius's letter could not be considered doctrinally conclusive. Nevertheless, the formula was proclaimed as the "Ecthesis," and presented to the Monophysites for approval. The reaction at Alexandria was grievously disappointing. The Melkites rejected it because, they said, it amounted to the total rejection of Chalcedon. The Copts rejected it because it did *not* reject Chalcedon.

Heraclius, meanwhile, had made two key appointments, both disastrous. To the patriarchate of Jerusalem he named the Palestinian monk, Sophronius, a militant and saintly man, gifted in theology. Heraclius apparently hoped that the appointment, if it did not convince the monk to support the Ecthesis, might at least muzzle his criticism of it. It did neither. More calamitously, he named as Melkite patriarch of Alexandria a certain Bishop Cyrus, who was a Nestorian, and therefore militantly opposed to the Monophysites. Cyrus undertook the imposition of the Ecthesis in Egypt with a ferocity that lasted ten years, and left tens of thousands of Egyptians with a deep hatred of everything Constantinople stood for.

In *The Arab Conquest of Egypt*, the historian Alfred J. Butler gives a gripping account of Cyrus's onslaught— how the Coptic clergy fled for their lives when he arrived; how the Coptic faithful were lashed, tortured, imprisoned and executed; how torches were held against the flesh of the Coptic patriarch's brother "until the fat dropped down from both his sides"; how a community of monks plotted Cyrus's assassination, were betrayed by one of their own number, and were killed, maimed or had their hands cut off as punishment; how, when confronted with recalcitrant monks in one monastery, Cyrus flew into an insane rage, ordering one old monk beaten "until his blood ran like water"; and how, though thousands capitulated, tens of thousands more kept the faith and conceived an implacable hatred of Byzantine Christianity.

Besides his ecclesiastical powers, Cyrus was also made prefect of Egypt, putting him in control of the government and the army, in addition to the Melkite church. It was in the capacity of prefect that he would later surrender Egypt to the Muslims.[5]

Meanwhile, Sophronius proved to be what historian Butler calls "a similarly ruinous miscalculation." Rather than supporting Monothelitism, Sophronius championed its rejection, turning Palestinian Christians vehemently against it. Thus, all hope vanished for a settlement with the Monophysites. Heraclius reacted in fury, at one point issuing an edict that all who continued to reject Chalcedon should have their ears and noses cut off. They never were. Too many tens of thousands of ears still listened to the Monophysite message, and too many noses turned up at Heraclius's ill-starred Ecthesis.

Still, Pope Honorius had approved the single-will concept advanced in

> Heraclius decreed all who denied Chalcedon have their ears and noses cut off.

5. Coptic history attributes Egypt's surrender to the Muslims to a certain al-Mukaukis. Since he is not otherwise identified, he remained for centuries in Coptic history a darkly mysterious figure of loathing and execration. Most historians agree it could refer only to the despised patriarch Cyrus.

Sergius's original letter. But in Rome, too, support for the Ecthesis began to evaporate. Rome's theologians reasoned that, to be fully human, Jesus must have had a human will, but no human being could in any sense accommodate a divine will. So there must have been two wills, not one, and Pope Honorius must have erred when he wrote in approval of Sergius's Monothelite theory.

Honorius died before he saw the actual Ecthesis document, but his two successors denounced it—Pope Severinus (who served two months and died), and Pope John IV, who held a synod at Rome that condemned it. John IV then formally apologized for the

Fourteen centuries after the disastrous final war between Byzantium and Persia, there remain around two million Christians in Syria. About half belong to the Syrian Orthodox Church (like these two members of the Syrian Orthodox clergy, left, celebrating Ascension Day). There are also significant numbers of Catholic, Syrian, Nestorian and Armenian Christians, and a small number of Protestants. All still face restrictions in the predominantly Muslim country.

Ecthesis on behalf of Honorius. On his deathbed, even the emperor Heraclius himself disowned it.

By the end of Heraclius's reign, so many bishops had been deposed and others persecuted for refusing to accept the Ecthesis, that to suddenly renounce it would have made its advocates look foolish, criminally irresponsible if not actively evil. Unsurprisingly, then, the new patriarch of Constantinople, Pyrrhus, held a council that affirmed the Ecthesis, thereby cementing it as a major theological issue between east and west. Confusingly, Pyrrhus then had second thoughts, traveled to Rome, submitted himself to the new pope, Theodore, and recanted.

But the Ecthesis was far from dead at Constantinople. Out of the bedlam that attended the death of Heraclius (see chapter 10), the emperor Constans, aged seventeen, emerged victorious, and announced himself in support of the Ecthesis. He appointed a new patriarch named Paul—whom Pope Theodore promptly deposed.

To resolve the conflict, Constans came up with another idea. He would sweep the whole issue under the rug. By imperial edict, all talk of the one or two wills in Jesus Christ was forbidden. Called "the Type of Constans," the edict was proclaimed throughout what was left of the empire. Any bishop caught speaking of Christ's will, whether one or two, would be deposed, any monk excommunicated, any government official fired, any army officer cashiered, any person of senatorial rank stripped of his property—and anybody else whipped or deported. The Type met with almost instant rejection at Rome, because it forbade discussion of "two wills"—which by now had become church doctrine in the west.

The Type appeared in 649, the year that Pope Theodore died. His successor, destined to become the last martyred pope, was Martin I, a big man with firm convictions on the universal authority of the bishop of Rome. He began his papacy with a council in Rome that condemned the Ecthesis, Cyrus, Sergius, Pyrrhus, Paul and the Type, in a sweeping denunciation of the entire Constantinople theological endeavor. One figure strongly in support of Martin in this initiative was Maximus the Confessor, whose tongue and one hand would be cut off by imperial authorities for his obstinacy. (See page 220.) Following the council, Martin commissioned a bishop to go east and clean house, deposing the Monothelite clergy in Alexandria, Jerusalem and Antioch—all lands now held by the Muslims.

This was too much for Constantinople. Rome's rule in the west, while resented, had to be accepted. But Rome, as Constantinople saw it, was not merely meeting a crisis occasioned by Monothelitism and the Muslim takeover, but rather trying to extend its power to appoint and depose bishops in the east as well. Olympus, the imperial exarch at Rome, was ordered to have Martin assassinated, but through grace or blind luck, Martin was never where the assassin expected him. This so spooked Olympus that he confessed the plot to the pope, and then led an abortive rebellion in Italy against the emperor Constans. Olympus died within the year.

Constans dispatched another, less sensitive exarch. He made the pope captive, spirited him to a waiting vessel, and told him he must face trial at Constantinople for aiding in the failed rebellion. The charge was treason.

Martin was imprisoned on the Aegean island of Naxos, then conveyed as a captured criminal to the capital. He was left all day on the deck of the vessel at dockside, so that the

> *The exarch captured the pope and told him that he would face trial for treason.*

Martin, described by his biographer Theodore as "of noble birth, a great student, of commanding intelligence, of profound learning, and of great charity to the poor," is brought to life by Giambattista Tiepolo, the great Venetian artist.

hew him to pieces," said the prefect of the city, passing sentence.

He was thrown into a jail cell, but he was not executed. As Martin was being tried, Patriarch Paul lay dying. Constans visited him to give the triumphant news of the pope's conviction—but Paul was far from jubilant. "Woe to me," he said. "I now have this to answer for, as well." He pleaded with Constans to stop mistreating Martin, and to spare his life. Constans met him halfway. He let Martin live, but banished him to Chersonesos on the Crimean Peninsula of the Black Sea. There, on September 16, 655, Martin I, pope and martyr, died. Three years later, Constans himself came to a miserable end.

So did Heraclius's venture into theology. The next emperor, known as Constantine IV Pogonatus, resolved to reunite east and west. He deposed the Monothelite patriarch of Constantinople, and called a major church council there in 680, presiding over it himself with two legates from Rome beside him in positions of honor. It ratified the decisions of Martin's council held at Rome, and condemned as heretical Pope Honorius. The next pope, Leo II, declared the council of 680 the Sixth Ecumenical Council of Christianity.

Early in the eighth century, a move to discredit the Sixth Council and revive Monothelitism failed. That was the end of it, but the Christians had paid a fearful price for the experiment. Indeed, the whole prefecture of Egypt may be said to have been lost to the Muslims because of it. ∎

waterfront rabble could jeer him. To break his spirit, he was locked up for ninety-three days in the prison at Prandearia. It didn't work. Tried by a panel headed by Constans' financial adviser, Martin denied all suggestion of insurrectional conspiracy and hit back sharply at the "ignorant malevolence" of his accusers. Constans, following the trial from an adjoining room, sent him a message: "You have abandoned God, and God has abandoned you." Whereupon, the pope was formally stripped to the waist, and chains were hung about his neck. "Take him and

In the middle of the seventh century, the lightly armed and mobile Arab armies erupted out of Arabia to attack the soft underbelly of the two greatest powers in the world, Christian Byzantium and the empire of the Sassanian Persians. In this nineteenth-century engraving, Arab cavalry flood into the plain of Syria's Orontes River to attack the provincial capital of Antioch.

CHAPTER 6

Persia, Syria, Palestine and Egypt fall before Islam's slashing swords

As the great empire of the Sassanids disintegrates, the Muslims turn West, destroy Byzantium's armies, and biblical Antioch and Jerusalem bow to the Qur'an

Muhammad would speak no more. No longer would Arabia's affairs turn on every new revelation uttered by its Prophet, conqueror and heaven-appointed master. The Prophet's body, still warm, lay in A'isha's quarters, where his wives beat their faces in wild lamentation. Grief and confusion also convulsed the crowd milling outside in the courtyard, as through the throng shouldered the towering figure of Umar ibn al-Khattab, one of the earliest stalwarts of the faith. Approaching the pallet–bier, this impulsive warrior gazed intently upon the beloved face, serene and seemingly lifelike. Exultation mounting within his loyal heart, Umar cried, "The Prophet is not dead! He has only swooned away!"

Al-Mughira ibn Shu'ba, the man who had hewn down the great Arabic idol al-Lat two years earlier, tried to convince him that Muhammad was indeed dead. "You lie!" Umar thundered, ". . . the Apostle of God is not dead. Your own treacherous spirit has suggested that imagination. The Prophet of the Lord will not die until he has rooted out every hypocrite and unbeliever." Haranguing the crowd, Umar insisted that Muhammad was just visiting the Creator; he would return in due course, and would surely chop off the hands and feet of any faint hearts who prematurely accepted his demise.

Many onlookers began to waver. Their leader had indeed appeared cheerful at prayers that very morning, looking so much stronger that Abu Bakr had sought permission to visit an oasis outside Medina. Now he raced back to the sun-dried mud complex that was mosque and home to the Prophet. A slight, stooped, unassuming man, Abu Bakr slipped through the multitude listening to the nearly delirious Umar. Inside the living quarters, the devout disciple raised the striped sheet that covered the recumbent body, and kissed his master's face. "Sweet were you in life and sweet you are in death," he murmured. Closely examining the rigid features, Abu Bakr recognized the truth.

Outside, he called for silence from the confused assembly and most obeyed, for the Prophet himself had designated him their prayer leader. Although Umar continued to rant, Abu Bakr proclaimed, "Let anyone who worships Muhammad

On June 8, 632, in a meeting hall at Medina belonging to the Banu Saida clan, Muslim leaders congregate to heatedly debate the issue of a successor to Muhammad. Despite his initial reluctance, the diminutive Abu Bakr (center left, below) becomes the first of the Prophet's Companions to be named caliph or "successor."

know that Muhammad indeed is dead. But whoever worships God, let him know that the Lord lives and does not die." Those sobering words—a well-known warning from Muhammad himself—once more reduced the audience to weeping, while even Umar collapsed, trembling in horrified acceptance.

The news had not paralyzed everyone in Medina, however. A messenger hurried up to inform Abu Bakr that crowds of citizens were already congregating in a hall belonging to the Banu Saida clan, to select a new leader from among themselves. Quickly Abu Bakr and Umar led their followers to that meeting, paramount in their minds the need to maintain unity within the whole community of Islam.

Arabs had always been deeply divided by tribe and clan, personal bloodlines being a matter of indelible pride. Medina's dominant tribes, the Aus and the Khazraj, had willingly accepted Muhammad as a refugee, and possibly as a peacemaker for faction-riven Medina, but had soon begun to resent this imperious outsider and his Quraysh clansmen from Mecca. With the Prophet dead, they could regain their autonomy. "Let the Muslims have their own chief. As for us, we will have a leader from ourselves," cried supporters of Saad ibn Abada, a Khazraji sheikh.

Against this Medinian pride, Abu Bakr, about sixty years old and one of Muhammad's first converts, pitted his characteristically humble diplomacy. There was no question, he said, that Medina aristocrats deserved high renown, but other Arab tribes would in fact follow only the Quraysh, the traditional keepers of Mecca's holy places. "We are the noblest of the Arabs," Abu Bakr gently asserted—but personal aggrandizement was not his aim. Let the people choose between two other Quraysh: Umar and Abu Ubaida ibn al-Jarrah (selected by Muhammad to lead the Muslims into Mecca).

Umar proved equally self-abnegating. "Did not the Apostle of God choose you to lead the prayers when he was ill?" he demanded of Abu Bakr. "We swear allegiance to you!" Gigantic Umar then seized his diminutive colleague by the hand in token of his submission. Deeply moved, Meccans and Medinians followed his example, filing by to swear fealty to the Prophet's devoted Companion. Thus on June 8, 632, these customarily fractious Arabs managed to maintain their unity, a crucial victory for the Muslim faith. As title, Abu Bakr chose "caliph," simply meaning "successor."

This unity was nevertheless frail; the Quraysh themselves were far from perfectly united, a fact that Muslims would come to rue. Abu Bakr was of the Banu Taim, a relatively minor clan, while Muhammad and Ali were of the Banu Hashem, longtime rivals to the Banu Umayya in Mecca. Their squabbling, quiescent under the Prophet's rule, now reemerged. When Abu Bakr was selected, Ali was preparing his foster father's body for burial beneath A'isha's chambers. Not for six months would he accept the new caliph; some hold that he himself coveted the succession. In any case, the clash between his clan, the Hashemites, and the Umayyads would later convulse Islam—and thereby help save a beleaguered Christianity.

Medina was secure, but at the news of the Prophet's death another revolt blazed through Arabia, whose tribes Muhammad had subdued, but in no sense tamed. For him, the nomads and oasis-dwellers had mouthed submission to God, and even grudgingly paid a tax, but now the Bedouin gladly resumed their ancient cycle of raiding and feasting, celebrated with poetry (much of it excellent) in praise of daring heroes and luscious women. Amid this rebellion—labeled "the Apostasy" by Muslim historians—only a few lucky tax collectors escaped with their lives. The less fortunate were buried alive, burned, stoned, thrown over cliffs or used for target practice.

But Abu Bakr was undeviating in his fidelity to the Prophet's wishes. For example, Muhammad had planned an expedition against Syria, to revenge his previous defeat by Byzantine forces at Mu'ta in Palestine. His grandson, Osama ibn Zayd, was to command it, and Abu Bakr's determination to proceed with it seemed imprudent to practically everyone. With a full-scale Arab revolt in progress, how could he leave the heart of Islam wide open, while sending the cream of his forces far away under an untested twenty-year-old youth? But Abu Bakr was adamant. "Even if wild dogs rove around the feet of the wives of the Messenger of Allah," insisted the caliph, pale yet resolute, "I would still dispatch the army of Osama as ordered by the Prophet."

Very soon, with Arab rebels at Medina's very gates, two northern Bedouin tribes offered to continue in adherence to Islam, provided the much-hated tax be withdrawn. Again Abu Bakr refused to temporize. Never would their taxes be reduced, he bluntly informed the insurgents—not by the value of "an old piece of rope." Within days, a Muslim force was scratched together to back him up. The undisciplined rebels, taken by surprise in a dawn attack, were utterly routed.

Two months later, the Syrian expedition returned, rich with plundered herds. Moreover, the inexperienced leader had managed to avoid Byzantine regulars, perhaps by wisely heeding the advice of the shrewd Khalid ibn al-Walid, who had quietly served as a volunteer in his ranks. Now Abu Bakr commissioned this redoubtable officer to recover all rebellious Arabia for the faith. His first task: to deal with the Banu Asad, headed by one Tulaiha, a self-proclaimed prophet and Muhammad imitator. Little is known about the Battle of Buzakha that followed, except that

Khalid's sparse force of four thousand captured the would-be prophet and scattered his followers. Then Abu Bakr freely pardoned the streams of surrendering rebels, executing only individuals known to have killed Muslim tax collectors.[1]

Khalid next turned east toward the Persian Gulf. With heavy reinforcements he entered the territory of yet another self-styled prophet, Musailama, who had once offered to split the world with Muhammad. Retorting that the Creator disposes of his creation as he sees fit, Muhammad had branded Musailama "the liar." But Musailama had acquired a following among the Banu Bakr federation, whose grazing lands extended to the Euphrates River, border of the mighty Persian Empire. The Battle of Yemama against this formidable foe was the fiercest yet. With a wild charge across a sandy plain, the Banu Bakr almost shattered Khalid's force, even plundering his own tent. But Zayd ibn al-Khattab, Umar's brother, bore forward with the banner of Mecca's Emigrants, while

At Yemama, with a wild charge across a sandy plain, the Banu Bakr almost shattered Khalid's force, even plundering the commander's own tent.

another general advanced with the revered emblem of the Helpers from Medina. Both died in a maelstrom of slashing swords and hot-blowing sand that went on for hours, but finally the Banu Bakr broke and retreated to a nearby oasis, taking shelter within a walled enclosure of date palms.

Onto that wall the Muslims hoisted two men, according to the tradition, who leaped down among their adversaries. One died almost instantly. The other, fighting with the blade Muhammad had used at Uhud, reached and opened the gate. His comrades poured into the compound, later aptly renamed the Garden of Death. Amid the palm trunks, the trapped warriors of the Banu Bakr fought to the last man. One javelin thrust permanently ended the prophetic career of Musailama.[2] The Muslim account puts the total dead and wounded at Yemama at ten thousand. This may be an exaggeration, but so many Companions of Muhammad died there that Abu Bakr reportedly feared the Qur'an could not survive much longer as an oral tradition. He therefore ordered that the testimony of witnesses still alive be recorded. (See page 63.)

Admiration for Khalid was not universal, however, in part because of one ugly incident. Surrender was such a bitter pill for the proud Bedouin that some clans just drifted away into the desert, although if challenged they would profess Allah. Khalid sent out patrols to round up such fugitives, one of which netted Malik ibn Nuweira, a renowned chief and poet of the Banu Tamim. Malik and some supporters, under guard in Khalid's camp, were put to death that same night, and within twenty-four hours Khalid took possession of Malik's exceedingly beautiful widow. Scandalized gossip spread. Malik had seemingly not merited execution, and Umar, suspecting the obvious, demanded justice, but Abu Bakr accepted Khalid's story that the guards had misinterpreted his orders.

1. The "prophet" Tulaiha escaped from the Battle of Buzakha toward Syria, and Muslim clemency was extended to him when he later embraced Islam. Tulaiha had the good humor for which the Bedouin are so justly famous. After his conversion, the pretender remarked that his prophetic gift had been but "a puff or two, like a bellows."

2. Musailama was slain by a javelin specialist named Wahshi. This famous spearman had also stalked and killed Hamza, Muhammad's uncle, at the Battle of Uhud. (See chapter 2.) A drunkard to the end of his life, Wahshi would tell visitors: "With this weapon, I killed Hamza and Musailama, the best and worst of men."

"I will not sheathe a sword which God has drawn for his service," the caliph ruled.

Muslim ambition meanwhile shifted southward, and with every victory, fresh tribal levies rallied to the cause. In the southeast, Oman yielded after just one significant battle. Thence Islamic warriors thrust west along the coast of the Arabian Sea into Yemen, while another offensive drove south from Mecca. The disunited Yemenis put up little resistance, except for a determined stand by the largely Christian Kinda tribe, in its fortress at Najran, which ended in the massacre of almost the entire garrison.

By mid-633, the Muslims had completely suppressed the Apostasy throughout Arabia, imposing unity on a people never previously united. But Arab culture remained as warlike as ever, a characteristic they fully shared—as had the Prophet himself, for that matter. The eyes of the faithful, ever searching for worthy prizes, now turned toward the wealthy empires of Byzantium and Persia.

Few Islamic leaders could read. They kept no treasury records. Abu Bakr, head of government, found time to milk the family goats. The caliph's counselors, seated on rough rugs or the dusty ground of Medina, understood almost nothing about

Islam's first leaders were simple men. Few could read. They kept no treasury records. The caliph Abu Bakr found time to milk the family goats. His counselors sat on rugs, or the dusty ground.

these two great powers. They surely knew, however, that population alone must pose a gargantuan obstacle to the propagation through war of their new faith. Historian Pringle Kennedy (*Arabian Society at the Time of Mohammed*) estimates Arabia's population at six million in Muhammad's lifetime. Persia's dominions, stretching three thousand miles from the Euphrates River to India, encompassed at least fifty million souls, and the Byzantine Empire roughly thirty million.

Geographically, Persia and Byzantium shared the same vulnerable under-belly—a single sweep of nomad-haunted desert—but in more than a millennium neither empire had been seriously threatened from this direction. The military thinking of the desert tribes was primitive in the extreme: rob, rape, then run before imperial troopers showed up. The Bedouin had no more notion of actually farming the rich neighboring plow lands than a coyote aspires to owner-ship of a favorite chicken coop.

Byzantine and Persian commanders, accustomed to sneering at the Arab rabble, initially had little fear of rising Islam—and no wonder. The typical nomad bore an inferior sword and possessed little or no armor. Superbly equipped Persian soldiers, clad in steel from helmet to leg greaves, had spears, swords, axes or iron maces, bows, and thirty arrows. Trained in both infantry and cavalry maneuver, they made short and bloody work of any desert foe in head-to-head combat.

The Arabs were similarly primitive in military organization. Their chief battle tactic was a headlong charge; supplies were pirated along the campaign route.

The Byzantines, by contrast, had books on military science that taught officers to contend with different types of foe and terrain. Armored cavalry with lances constituted the Greek-speaking empire's most powerful punch, supported by massed archers on foot and horseback. A cart carrying a flourmill, trenching gear, and other equipment accompanied each platoon. Ships could bring supplies and reinforcements to the fighting brigades.

Additionally, the two frequently warring empires subsidized neighboring Arab dynasties to help protect their respective frontiers. The Christian Arabs of the Banu Ghassan tribe, allies of Byzantium, had long screened the approaches to Syria and Palestine. Their great rivals were the Lakhmid federation (including the partially Christian Banu Bakr), which protected the Persian borderland along the Euphrates. However, both emperors had contemptuously jettisoned their Arab satellites a generation before the Muslim onslaught.

During the Byzantine orthodox suppression of the Monophysites in 581, imperial troops had seized the ruling chieftain of the Banu Ghassan, and quelled an armed rebellion by his sons. The region nonetheless remained in political turmoil, and soon the Persian frontier also began seething with Arab aggression. In 605, the Persians reacted by executing the Lakhmid sovereign and trying to exert direct rule over the Lakhmid confederacy.

For a generation, the Banu Bakr continued their usual hit-and-run hostilities against Persia, easily fended off by Persian troops, but impossible to permanently eliminate. John Bagot Glubb, British general and historian, compares the Bedouin to Viking fleets. Their camel herds, numbering in the thousands, traveled the desert like ships on the sea, and because the imperial cavalry could not penetrate deeply into the sands, the nomads always could count on a safe retreat.

In early 633, however, the Banu Bakr faced disaster. Khalid's Muslim army had appeared in their rear and annihilated a sizable portion of their manpower at the Battle of Yemama. Muthanna ibn Haritha, an important Banu Bakr chief and possibly already a convert to the new religion, realized that his people were now caught between the Persians and the Muslims. The desert, Muthanna recognized, was no protection from Islam's ferocity. On the other hand, an alliance with these fellow Arabs would strengthen his tribe's hand against the detested Persians. Khalid, short of troops, readily agreed.

So did Abu Bakr. After all, the caliph no doubt reasoned, the Persians could hardly launch an assault across the Arabian Peninsula against Medina itself. He and his colleagues were more interested in tackling the familiar realm of Byzantine Syria, long traversed by Mecca's caravans. But what harm in also testing Allah's will against the Zoroastrian fire worshipers? Thus did the Muslim campaign to subdue Arabia evolve haphazardly into an unforeseen attack on the Persian colossus.

The Persians, as it happened, were then extremely vulnerable. Not since 628,

A sixth-century Persian silver plate (above), richly decorated with a scene from a royal lion hunt. The Persian nobility considered the desert Arabs no match for their more sophisticated weapons and military tactics.

when they slaughtered Chosroes II, their King of Kings, along with eighteen of his sons, had they enjoyed stable rule. Chosroes's one remaining son disposed of every other royal claimant he could, but he himself lasted only eight months. In the next four years, no fewer than nine individuals were enthroned and summarily disposed of, until finally one surviving royal scion, a sixteen-year-old boy named Yazdegerd, was discovered and crowned. He would enjoy a somewhat longer reign, about six years.

Meanwhile, local government carried on as usual under regional administrators called satraps, among whom none ranked higher than the thoroughly hated Hormuz, governor of the Persian Gulf coastal region. A virtual monarch in terms

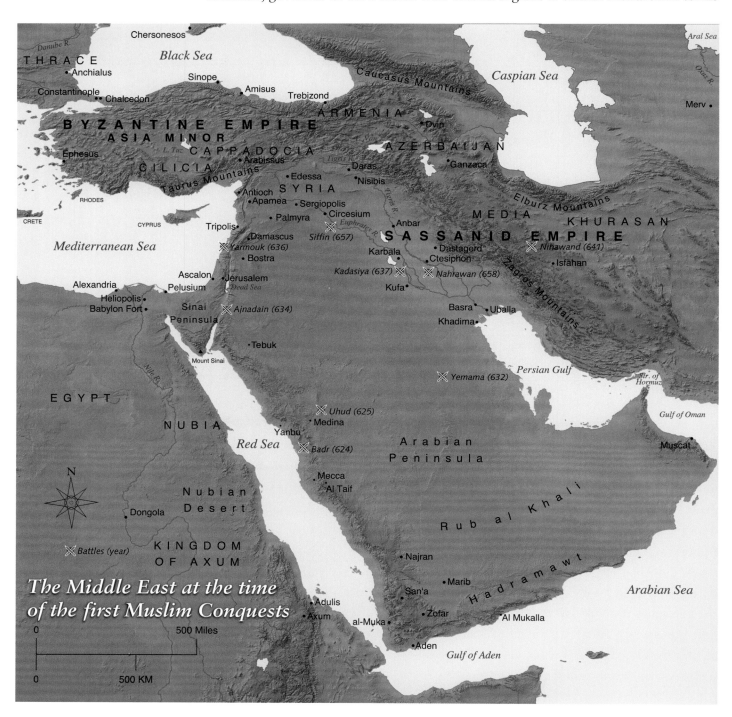

The Middle East at the time of the first Muslim Conquests

of personal authority, he wore a headpiece studded with diamonds and pearls worth one hundred thousand *dirhams* (the *dirham* being a silver coin roughly equal to the annual tax of an average family).

To Hormuz, tribesmen like Khalid and Muthanna were vermin best known for running away, but in his first encounter with upstart Islam the vermin outmaneuvered him, luring him into a strenuous round of march and countermarch through desert terrain. Muslim tradition says the heavily equipped Persian forces were exhausted by the time Khalid confronted them at Kadima, near the head of the gulf. But Hormuz had a trick up his own sleeve. Arabs liked to open a formal battle with an individual combat between champions from either side. The satrap, a skilled swordsman, decided to challenge Khalid to personal combat, and then have several Persians rush forward and murder him.

Fighting blade to blade, neither gained the advantage. Hormuz therefore proposed that they wrestle, and Khalid agreed. Dropping their swords, the pair seized each other. Immediately, as planned, three Persian soldiers rushed upon

The Muslims unquestionably pulverized their enemy at Kadima and speedily advanced, exacting tribute at the port of Uballa and laying waste the lush countryside.

the now weaponless Khalid, but he—in mortal peril—picked up Hormuz and swung his body around in a great circle. In the brief respite thus gained, a Banu Tamim sheikh galloped up and beheaded the Persian troopers, while Khalid sank his dagger into the treacherous Hormuz.[3]

Whatever the veracity of this well-loved story, the Muslims unquestionably pulverized their enemy at Kadima and speedily advanced, exacting tribute from the key port city of Uballa and laying waste the lush countryside. After victory in a second battle, at Walaja, they cautiously retreated to the desert's edge, but these triumphs must have further shaken the chaotic Persian court.

At the Euphrates River, Khalid met a geographic fact that would dominate the entire Persian war. On its easterly bank were irrigation ditches, plowed fields, and peasant villages. Arab light cavalry, if trapped by a superior Persian force among such obstacles, might be destroyed before it could retreat across the broad Euphrates to the desert. But on the open plains of sand and gravel along the western bank, the rapidly moving Arabs could maneuver effectively against armored Persian formations.

Muslim strength always lay in speed. Tens of thousands of men could be concentrated for a key battle, or dispersed in far-ranging sweeps to wreak brief havoc among the villages east of the river. Khalid and Muthanna proved masters at inflicting maximum pain with their highly flexible forces. As their nomad army moved northward, however, it encountered a mighty alliance of thoroughly alarmed Persians and Christian Arabs from the Syrian Desert.

A desperately fought clash took place at Ullais, on desert terrain. Muslim

3. The jewel-encrusted headpiece worn by Hormuz—virtually a crown—was sent to Medina after the battle. Abu Bakr decided that this bit of plunder, fruit of a personal duel, should belong wholly to Khalid. The Arab commander, who could not possibly wear the satrap's extravagant hat, reportedly sold the precious stones for cash.

historians claim the tide turned for Islam only after Khalid lifted his arms and vowed to Allah: "If you give us victory, I shall see that no enemy warrior is left alive, until their river runs with their blood!" Caught on the inhospitable west side of the Euphrates, they say, thousands of the defeated Persians were beheaded in fulfillment of that grim pledge.

'Chastity had become too hard'

Despite attempts to prevent intermingling, Arab armies acquired a flood of females, breeding away the raw aggression of the desert and generating a new, less vigorous people

Muhammad himself confirmed Muslim rules of conduct towards captured females, in 626, during a campaign against several Bedouin tribes. In a raid against the Banu al-Mustalik, the spoils of victory had been substantial: two thousand camels, five thousand sheep and goats—and two hundred women. One warrior later recalled: "We were lusting after women, and chastity had become too hard for us." How would Islam's founder react to his followers' proposed rape en masse of their helpless prisoners?

The Prophet ruled that his men could force immediate intercourse upon the captive females. When asked by the soldiers if they should practice coitus interruptus to help prevent pregnancy of women who might later be ransomed back to their tribe, Muhammad said the precaution was not necessary.[1] It is debatable whether even Muhammad could have imposed restraint on a menfolk long accustomed to copulating with females who fell into their hands. Rabbi Nathan, a Talmudic writer of the time, complained in exasperated exaggeration, "Nowhere in the world is there such a propensity towards fornication as among the Arabs," adding, "If all the sexual license in the world were divided into ten parts, then nine would be distributed among the Arabs and the tenth would be enough for all the other races."

Hyperbole aside, Byzantine soldiers may well have raped captives on occasion. Generation upon generation of men in the Roman world continued to own concubines. But Christians behaving this way were clearly in disobedience to both their religion and their civil law. The Justinian Code, adopted in the sixth century, deemed rape a capital offense, prohibited forced prostitution, and enabled women to inherit property. The Church vigorously condemned concubinage. Within Christendom, loose sexual conduct became increasingly shrouded by shame.

Very different laws evolved across the realm of Islam. Following instruction from the angel Gabriel, the Prophet decreed that Muslims could have as many as four wives. The Qur'an's Sura 4:3, for example, states that men may "marry such women as seem good to you, two and three and four; but if you fear that you will not do justice [between them], then [marry] only one or what your right hands possess. . . ." A husband could divorce any wife by simply uttering, "I divorce thee." In that event, a woman had no right to marital property or financial support beyond the return of her family's original dowry.

The Qur'an has explicit rules governing women whom men possess "by their right hands." The phrase traditionally referred to females captured in war or purchased as slaves. A man could marry a female slave if he wished, and could not sell a woman after she bore a child whom he acknowledged as his own. In that case, she would be freed upon his death, and the child enjoyed the same hereditary rights as the child of a wife.

But a female prisoner could be sold, abandoned, given away, or killed at the master's whim. All of her possessions were his, including her body. She did not

A detail from a mural at Isfahan, Iran (left), showing a woman of the royal court writing during a picnic. For a few, the idle life of the harem offered the time and opportunity for education.

Khalid now proceeded to capture Hira, the former Lakhmid capital. Next to fall was Anbar, where the Arabs, lacking siege equipment to breach the powerful fortifications, filled the moat with slaughtered camels and swarmed over the walls. Most of Persia's eastern frontier was now in their hands. Pagan Arabs were hunted down throughout the Syrian Desert and subjected to Muhammad's

count toward the legal limit of four wives. Muslim warriors commonly raped women on the battlefield within view of their husbands and fathers, a compelling display of dominance.[2]

When the Arabs conquered Persia, Syria and Egypt, they began acquiring a flood of females. Huge harems developed. Al-Mutawakkil is said to have had four thousand concubines. Musa ibn Nusair's haul reportedly included three hundred thousand captives from Africa, plus thirty thousand virgins in Spain. Whatever their numbers actually were, slaves living in one of these gigantic harems led, for the most part, an idle existence. Damsels would sing and play music for their master while he and his guests reclined on a *diwan*—a sofa bordering three sides of a room. Elaborate feasts would include the finest quality game, rich sweets and rare fruits, all served on trays of precious metals and wood inlaid with rare ebony and tortoiseshell. Privileged Muslims in this pre-tobacco period smoked perfumed spices while the more dissolute drank prohibited wine.

Despite their impediments, some slave-girls gained impressive educations, as well as significant influence over their masters. The beautiful Tawaddud, for example, impressed the caliph al-Rashid with her knowledge of medicine, law, astronomy, philosophy, music, mathematics, grammar, poetry, rhetoric, history, and the Qur'an. On occasion, a woman held by the right hand used feminine wiles and graceful wit to acquire wealth in her own right. Others gratefully accepted a legitimate marriage with a poor man who might lack the financial resources to otherwise obtain a wife.

Following the earliest conquests, Arab leaders initially attempted to prevent intermingling between their people and conquered races. For this reason, the caliphs established exclusively Arab garrison cities in Iraq (Kufa, Basra), Egypt (Fustat), and North Africa (Qayrawan). But infidel women, imported into the garrison communities, produced thousands of mixed-heritage children, virtually all recognized as legitimate under generous Muslim precepts toward progeny. In

A wealthy Muslim and his harem (above) in a rare photograph taken in Cairo, Egypt, in 1880. The harems of some of the early Muslim conquerors were said to have numbered in the thousands.

744, Yazid III became the first caliph born of a slave mother, soon followed by others of similar antecedents. Thus the raw aggression of the desert almost immediately diluted itself, generating the new, less vigorous civilization of Islam. ∎

1. The following Hadith is cited by the Muslim historian Bukhari (volume 9, book 93, number 506), quoting the eyewitness Abu Said al-Khudri: That during the battle with Banu al-Mustalik, they (Muslims) captured some females and intended to have sexual relations with them without impregnating them. So they asked the Prophet about coitus interruptus. The Prophet said, "It is better that you should not do it, for Allah has written whom he is going to create till the Day of Resurrection."

2. In his *Annals of the Early Caliphate*, William Muir writes of how "Persian ladies, both maids and matrons, 'taken captive by the right hand,' were forthwith, without stint of number, lawful to the conqueror's embrace; and in the enjoyment of this privilege, they were nothing loath to execute upon the heathen 'the judgment written.'" The historian recounts how the well-known Muslim leader Muthanna once captured a Persian princess and left his brother Moanna to "besiege her" in the middle of the battle. The great Arab general Khalid, Muir says, once forced himself upon a young maiden as another battle wore to a close, ordering her father: "Man, give me your daughter!"

terrorist choice: Islam or death.

What transformed flight-prone Arabs into warriors of such astonishing persistence? Two explanations seem obvious: They had always lived through their wits and raw courage at the edge of starvation, which breeds tough individuals, but now to this native hardihood were welded the assurances of Islam. Soldiers recounted visions of heaven opening before their eyes on the battlefield itself, with celestial virgins wiping the brows of dying heroes. And running away was no longer acceptable; any Muslim who fled from the infidel would suffer in hell's eternal fires.[4]

To the riches of paradise were now added the riches of Mesopotamia, specifically the immensely productive belt of good soil between the Tigris and Euphrates Rivers. The Prophet had spelled out how the booty of war must be divided (one-fifth to the Muslim treasury, originally administered by himself; the remainder divided among the victorious warriors), and any community that resisted was subject to unrestricted pillage. Mesopotamia, a cradle of human civilization, yielded extraordinary hauls of precious metals, weapons and tools, luxurious clothing and carpets, horses and other livestock, delicious foods, and women of dazzling beauty—all theirs for the taking.

The average Bedouin, having spent his life wearing a single coarse woolen garment, and munching a few dates on a good day, now found himself enriched beyond his wildest speculation. Islam, which promised sensuality and luxury in the world to come, was also delivering staggering quantities of those same blessings in this world. Such a win-win prospect drew swarms of warriors from the sands, where most adult males—slaves included—were potential soldiers. Entire clans migrated toward the front, families in train.

For the conquered, however, the arrival of Muhammad's followers was an excellent approximation of hell on earth. The men were frequently slaughtered outright, their chiefs sometimes singled out for the grotesque agonies of crucifixion. Adult male survivors became slaves. Screaming women and children, dragged from homes and hiding places, were assessed, inventoried, and like everything else, parceled out among the victors. The majority probably ended up in slave markets, but first the prettier women and girls were often forced to copulate with the Islamic warriors who had just slaughtered their fathers, husbands, brothers and sons. Muslims for many generations interpreted the Qur'an as specifically sanctioning the rape of women captured in battle.[5] Equally relevant, the holy book limits Muslims to four wives, but puts no numerical restriction on female slaves.

To be fair, no vanquished people in the Middle East (or anywhere else, for

Despite the conversion of the Persian Empire to Islam, some held to the ancient Zoroastrian religion. To this day, their descendants gather annually in the southern Iranian village of Chak Chak to worship around a traditional Zoroastrian fire altar (as in the photograph, above, taken in 2001).

4. In *The Moslem Doctrine of God*, Samuel Zwemer draws on the Qur'an and Muslim Hadith (officially sanctioned traditions) to present Muhammad's picture of the fate suffered by the damned: "Hell shall be a place of snares, the home of transgressors, to abide therein for ages. No coolness shall they taste nor any drink, save boiling water and liquid pus. Meet recompense!" Zwemer, a Reformed Church of America missionary to the Arab world at the turn of the twentieth century, notes: "The word *Jehannum* (Gehanna) occurs thirty times; fire (*nar*) is still more frequently used; there are six other words used for the place of torment."

5. Sura 23 (verses 5 and 6) of the Qur'an describes as "successful" those men "who guard their private parts, except before their mates, or before those whom their right hands possess (i.e., slaves captured in war), for they surely are not blamable." Early Muslims interpreted this as authorization to copulate at will with female slaves captured in battle. Many modern Muslims keenly dispute the interpretation.

that matter) then expected gentle treatment from conquerors, whoever they might be. Furthermore, Muslim leaders carefully balanced their terror policies. The agricultural peasantry, as well as any towns that voluntarily submitted, were generally spared pillage and rape. Instead, they received written guarantees of protection, in exchange for specified annual tributes—subjugation contracts that Islamic courts would faithfully honor for hundreds of years.

Such leniency exploited the social cracks running deep through both empires. Mesopotamia was governed by Persians, but the workers who tilled its fertile soil were descendents of the ancient Sumerians and Babylonians. The choice Islam presented them was: Resist and face terrible treatment, or submit to Islamic rule and be treated better than by the Persians. Nor were the Persian Zoroastrians forced to choose conversion or death, like the animistic polytheists of Arabia. (This distinction was arguably reasonable. The dualist Persian prophet Zarathustra—Zoroaster to the Greeks—taught that Ahura Mazda will

The 'Sword of God' loses his edge

Khalid ibn al-Walid's military genius carried the Muslim armies to astonishing success, but the general's extravagance and excess caught the critical eye of the caliph Umar

As the military genius whose historic achievements had enriched the rapidly expanding Muslim world, Khalid ibn al-Walid's share of the plundered empires made him wealthy beyond measure. Many friends flocked to his residence in northern Syria seeking the customary largesse. In about 638, one delighted Bedouin chieftain of the Kinda tribe received the princely sum of one thousand gold pieces. Scandalously, Khalid also indulged on occasion with a bath in water mixed with wine, a prohibited practice.[1] Unfortunately, stricter Muslims sniffed the fragrance of the forbidden grape clinging to Islam's foremost warrior.

Word of these extravagances filtered back to the imperious caliph Umar in Medina, a man alert to the corrupting tendency of riches, who also feared the rise of potential military aspirants to political power. So Umar decided to act. He ordered his governor in Syria to summon the great general to the mosque at Hims, where an Arab assembly had gathered. Before it stood the black Bilal, tall and gaunt, who had served as muezzin to the Prophet himself. As Umar's emissary, Bilal posed Khalid with a direct question: Where did the one thousand gold pieces come from?

The accused Khalid, unprepared, stood silent— not necessarily implying guilt, considering the state of accountancy among the desert conquerors. But as the assembly looked on, hushed, embarrassed and shocked, Bilal stepped forward and removed the helmet and cloth headpiece of Islam's most renowned military hero. He then used that kerchief to bind his

wrists. In his stentorian voice, Bilal again demanded an answer, citing the caliph's authority. "The money was my own," Khalid finally answered. With relief, the Syrian governor came down from the pulpit and released the esteemed veteran's hands.

Summoned by Umar to Medina, Khalid obeyed promptly. The caliph stripped away twenty thousand gold pieces from his general's fortune of eighty thousand, and deposed him from any role in government. However, an announcement sent to all provinces of the Arab Empire proclaimed that the "Sword of God," as Khalid was known, was still held in high official esteem. His removal from power, Umar explained, merely illustrated the spiritual principle that Muslims should trust in Allah, rather than in any human "arm of flesh," no matter how talented.

Khalid retired in Syria, where his manner of life appears to have been lavish. During a period of serious plague, the Arab paladin reportedly lost forty sons. Even his financial fortunes later ebbed, reports British historian William Muir (*The Caliphate: Its Rise, Decline, and Fall*). "The hero who had borne Islam aloft to the crest of victory and glory ended his days in penury and neglect." Khalid died in the eighth year of Umar's caliphate, his fate a testimony to the fleeting nature of this world's rewards. ∎

1. The custom of bathing in water, dear to the classical world, diminished across much of barbarian Europe, but was retained by the Muslims. Arabs also had a traditional passion for both alcohol and scents, later inventing the process of distilling them into liquor and perfumes.

ultimately subdue all evil and achieve universal harmony.)

With Yemen subdued and Persia on the defensive, the Islamic leaders turned toward Syria, long the prized possession of Rome, and now of Byzantium. One military column, led by Amr ibn al-Aasi, journeyed past the Gulf of Aqaba at the head of the Red Sea to destroy a Byzantine force at Dathin in southern Palestine. A second approached Syria via eastern Palestine, where it drove back troops led by the Byzantine governor Sergius, killing Sergius himself.

After that, however, both Muslim armies bogged down in rugged terrain. A worried Abu Bakr called on Khalid, who developed a daring plan. He would lead half of his army from Persia to the Byzantine front. Then, in an unprecedented military maneuver, he would drive north through the waterless desert east of Palestine and Lebanon, to capture the city of Palmyra. He could then slash into Syria, forcing the Byzantines to fall back from Palestine in order to defend Damascus and Antioch.

But how could thousands of men and beasts be fed and watered along that forbidding desert route? Why, by butchering ten of the best camels daily for every hundred lances. Water and milk drawn from their carcasses were mixed and fed to the cavalry horses. After five days, however, that supply was exhausted, and the chief guide still could not locate a certain crucial well, a tiny life-giving pinpoint in the burning plain. At the brink of total catastrophe, however, the well was found, the expedition saved and Palmyra fell, although Khalid failed to sustain his thrust toward Damascus.

The emperor Heraclius, now wholly alerted to the Muslim menace, replied with a sudden attack on the force devastating southern Palestine. Although this stratagem nearly succeeded, the Muslim leaders dispatched thousands of camel troops on a desperate dash toward the threatened region. Given free passage by the inhabitants of the mountains of Moab (almost certainly Monophysite), they reinforced the Muslims in Palestine just in time to thoroughly maul the imperial forces at the Battle of Ajnadain.

In August 634, Abu Bakr fell sick with a fever that would not break. After consulting with other Companions of the Prophet, he made a crucial announcement to the assembled faithful: The next caliph was to be Umar ibn al-Khattab. "We will obey, we will obey!" they promised in chorus. Before he died, Abu Bakr advised the passionate Umar to be more gentle and patient with people. How quickly Umar absorbed this advice is debatable, but the succession proceeded smoothly, and the new caliph took the additional title "Commander of the Faithful."

He also developed a character that could forward plans of unprecedented dimensions while retaining much of his simple humanity. During a drought, tradition says, Umar carried flour to poor families at night, even helping one old woman cook her supper. The impetuous young warrior had been learning self-discipline and compassion, and Bedouin simplicity became his trademark as a ruler. The ninth-century Muslim historian al-Tabari describes him attending a festival barefooted. One dignitary encountered him herding camels, clad only in a loincloth, with a short cloak wrapping his head. He is said to have berated victorious generals for wearing bright cloaks over their chain mail, fearing that pride and luxury might destroy the Arab fighting spirit.

After Ajnadain, the demoralized Byzantines beat a general retreat. Damascus fell in 635; Muslim accounts hold that a Monophysite bishop and monks helped them scale the wall by night. In 636, however, the Byzantines counterattacked with their largest army to date. The Arabs retreated to the desert, and Theodorus, the Byzantine commander and brother to Heraclius, fortified a key pass along the Yarmouk River, barring them from Syria. Or so he hoped.

But Theodorus was at a disadvantage. Medina sent reinforcements, and Arab infiltrators wove through ridges and lava fields to the Byzantine rear. Furthermore, notes Princeton University historian Philip Hitti, the Yarmouk district is "one of the most torrid spots on earth," highly uncongenial to the northerners among the Christian troops. Theodorus's army also suffered internal disaffection, due to its high proportion of Monophysite Christian Arabs and Armenians. And to cap all, most of the local population was also Monophysite. No one knows how much his recruiting was hampered, nor to what degree intelligence efforts were thwarted, on account of Byzantium's long, bitter, and futile campaign to enforce Christian unity.

The standoff on the Yarmouk continued four months until, on August 20, 636, Islam attacked, in an assault reportedly intensified by the confusion of a sudden sandstorm. Historical details are sparse, as always, but the traditions have a ring of truth. Amid a blizzard of hard-driven grit, the best-trained troops can become blind and deaf, and coordinated maneuvers impossible, but the Arabs were well accustomed to such maelstroms, and they had the wind at their backs. Out of searing clouds of sand erupted wave upon wave of shrieking fanatics, flooding every defense. The entire imperial force was annihilated, and

After the Battle of Yarmouk in 636, the new caliph himself, Umar ibn al-Khattab, left Medina to visit the newly conquered lands. This nineteenth-century engraving (below) shows him outside the walls of Jerusalem.

FIKENSHER

Yarmouk would be recognized as one of history's decisive battles.

Heraclius, learning at Antioch of the disaster, rode sadly over the Taurus Mountains toward Byzantium, crying out as he left: "Peace be with you, holy and blessed land! Syria, farewell. There is for me no more returning to you; nor shall any Roman visit you forever, but in fear and trembling, until the accursed Antichrist shall come." Christians would long mourn their loss of the holy places: of Bethlehem, birthplace of Jesus; of Nazareth, home to Mary and Joseph; of Jerusalem, where the Word of God perished and then rose triumphant over death; of the Damascus road where Paul was blinded that he might see; and of Antioch where the word "Christian" came into being. All was now lost to Christendom, just as Jerusalem had once been lost to Jewry. Not for some 450 years would Christians return there—as crusaders fighting to recover their loss.

Christian communities were offered similar terms to the Zoroastrians. They must pay a special tax. There must be no ringing of bells, no processions with crosses and other emblems. The Christian gospel must not be preached to Muslims, upon penalty of death. Death was also the penalty for any Muslim who became Christian. No new churches might be built, and existing ones sometimes were preempted as mosques. Islam must, in every public sense, visibly

The Christian gospel must not be preached to Muslims, upon penalty of death. Death was also the penalty for any Muslim who became a Christian.

predominate over Christianity and Judaism. (See sidebar, page 176.)

When Umar himself visited Jerusalem following its conquest, its patriarch, Sophronius, conducted him around the Church of the Holy Sepulchre. Gazing at the rough clothing of his new Arab master, the sophisticated bishop whispered in Greek to a companion: "Surely this is the abomination of desolation spoken of by Daniel the Prophet standing in the holy place!" But the visitor was not entirely abominable. When the time for midday prayer arrived, Umar's servant started to spread the caliph's prayer mat on the church floor. The conqueror stopped him, preferring to go outside to worship. "Otherwise," he explained, "the Muslims would want to seize this church as a mosque."

While the Byzantines were being driven back into what is now Turkey, other Islamic armies met in climactic battle with the Persians. Khalid had been transferred to Palestine and Muthanna, the Banu Bakr chief who had brilliantly seconded him, doubtless felt a claim to replace him on the Persian front. But Medina's leadership, townsfolk all, felt the age-old distrust of their kind for the desert-dwelling Bedouin. Instead, Umar artlessly assigned command to Abu Ubayd ibn Masud, a young man with just one distinction: He was first to volunteer for Persia when most fighters preferred Syria.

That Muthanna, a proud sheikh in his own right, agreed to serve under this unknown neophyte demonstrates the power of Islam over men's minds in its first flowering. In this case, however, faith proved misplaced. The inexperienced Abu Ubayd equated caution with lack of faith in Allah. Ignoring Muthanna's contrary advice, he had a makeshift bridge constructed over the Euphrates and led the army into battle on Persian ground. When the Persian general broke the Arab formations with squads of elephants, a Muslim chief died slashing at one of the great beasts.

Abu Ubayd's entire army would indeed have been lost at this Battle of the Bridge had not Muthanna managed to repair, and hold, that crucial structure during the headlong retreat. Following the debacle, Umar put the Banu Bakr chief back in charge. He also reinstated tribes previously forbidden to fight because of their rebellion during the Apostasy. Now they filled up the ranks, as did Christian Arabs (mostly Nestorian or Monophysite) who volunteered to fight the Persians alongside their Muslim Arab brethren.

The Persian commander was Rustem, a respected veteran who had engineered the crowning of young Yazdegerd. He boldly risked his forces across the Euphrates, and at the ensuing Battle of al-Buwaib, the Persians advanced in three columns, spearheaded by elephants. Muthanna pulled his beard in anxiety as the Arab line gave way, but it steadied up and he led a ferocious counterattack of Christian Arabs against the Persian center. At that point, a stripling soldier killed the field commander, Mihran, and the Persians broke and ran—but the Muslims had secured the bridge. Again Islamic forces obliterated a whole army.

Dying of wounds he had sustained earlier at the Battle of the Bridge, Muthanna now asked to be replaced, and this time Umar chose shrewdly. Saad ibn Abu Waqqas had reputedly been the first to draw blood for the Prophet, who was his close relative. Saad's large, shaggy-haired head would prove capable of both caution and well-calculated daring. Short, stocky, and about forty years old, he first led perhaps four thousand reinforcements towards Persia.

The emperor Yazdegerd yearned for a decisive blow against the Arabs, but Rustem resisted court pressure and delayed month after month. Perhaps the Arabs would start fighting among themselves, he hoped, as so often before, but they did not. Instead, Saad used that rain-rich winter to collect and train troops in the tens of thousands.

By spring 637, Rustem could no longer resist his sovereign's direct order. The King of Kings in turn may have been influenced by the agony of his people, so long subjected to large-scale Arab foraging raids. Once again, the Persians crossed the river to fight, this time onto a field known as Kadasiya. So important was the outcome of this battle that the royal banner of the Sassanid dynasty accompanied the army, as did Rustem himself.

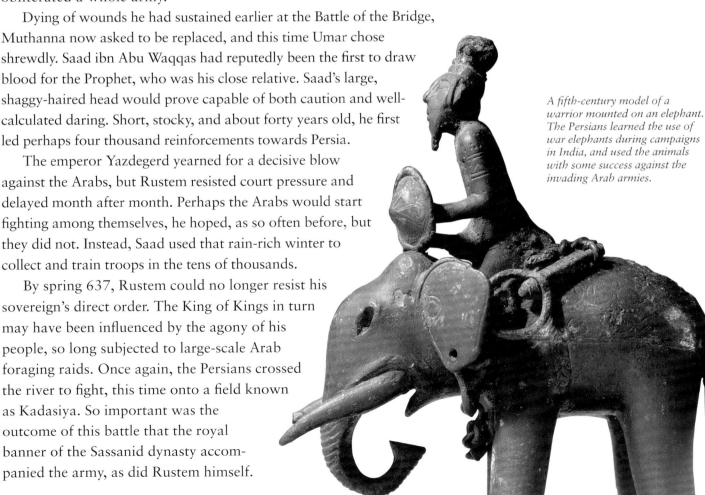

A fifth-century model of a warrior mounted on an elephant. The Persians learned the use of war elephants during campaigns in India, and used the animals with some success against the invading Arab armies.

The arch of the great audience hall and part of the ornate façade (above) are all that remain of Chosroes' great palace at Ctesiphon, on the Tigris River at present-day Taq-i-Kisra, Iraq. The Persian capital fell to the invading Muslims in 637.

On its eve, Saad became ill. Rather than plunge personally into the thick of the fight, he had to observe and direct it from the roof of a nearby building, causing deep suspicion among his officers. Even Muthanna's widow, remarried to Saad, jeered him for lack of courage. "Oh, for an hour of Muthanna! Alas, there is now no Muthanna!" she reportedly wailed over and over, until the exasperated Saad slapped her.

Again the Persians initiated battle, their infantry formations led by thirty-three elephants. Arab swordsmen tried to rush under the huge animals and stab upward with their swords, but still they came on. For two days, the momentum seesawed back and forth; on the third, massive Muslim reinforcements arrived from Syria. One of their leaders dismounted, charged at an elephant on foot, and stuck a lance directly in its eye. The beast stampeded, and so did a second wounded elephant, wreaking havoc among the Persian formations, but still both sides held strongly.

That night, the frustration of the Bedouin boiled over, and they launched a surprise night attack. Town-bred leaders never employed this risky tactic, but the desert tribesmen, weaned under the stars, were as familiar as wolves with nighttime raiding in packs. The Persians, caught unaware, failed to organize effectively in the dark, and in Islamic lore, this became the "Night of Fury." By the following day, the exhausted Persian center gave way, enabling an Arab warrior to kill Rustem himself.

Terrible disaster again followed for the Persians. Several regiments escaped across the river, but most died fighting or fleeing. Kadasiya proved as decisive in the east as Yarmouk in the west. Rustem was the last leader with sufficient stature to rally all Persia's empire, which now began to fall piecemeal. Ctesiphon, the capital, bisected by the Tigris River, was first. The western portion of the city yielded with little fight; the remainder surrendered when Muslim forces found a downriver ford and traversed the Tigris.

In Syria, Heraclius used Byzantium's control of the sea to suddenly reoccupy Antioch, rallying Christian Arabs to the cause, but on land, Islam seemed invincible. Antioch was soon lost again. In Persia too, the young King of Kings himself mounted a counteroffensive, but was defeated in a one-day battle. Late in 638, Yazdegerd escaped over the Zagros Mountains into northern Persia, where he organized yet another defense. It too failed, and with three more victories, the Muslim tide rolled relentlessly eastward, Yazdegerd fleeing before it.

His enemies painted the emperor as irredeemably and stupidly arrogant, alleging for example that when he took refuge with the satrap of distant Khurasan, south of the Caspian Sea, he was visited by the Khakan of the Turks, who asked for his daughter in marriage. The emperor coldly replied that no Turk ranked higher than a slave. The Turkish response was an immediate attack, forcing Yazdegerd to further flight. Finally, the last Sassanian sovereign was butchered near the city of Merv, and his naked corpse flung into a river.

The Persian Empire, dating back to the sixth century before Christ, had been annihilated, Zoroastrianism too all but disappeared,[6] and for almost a thousand years, no native dynasty would govern Persia. Its Muslim conquerors would face sporadic regional rebellions, although never on a scale to threaten their overall grip. By mid-century, their war banners were on the Oxus River in central Asia, whence Islam would march eastward into China. Within half a century of Muhammad's

The Persian Empire, dating back to the sixth century B.C., had been annihilated. For almost a thousand years no native dynasty would govern Persia.

death, the cry of "Allahu Akbar!"—"God is great!"—was shouted by Islamic warriors in the Indus River delta, source of India's Hindu civilization.

The next Islamic target was obvious, at least so far as Amr ibn al-Aasi was concerned. One of the victors in Syria and Palestine, Amr now resolved to invade Egypt, although the caliph Umar had grave doubts. Umar, knowing that the bountiful Nile Valley and Delta was Byzantium's main source of grain, likely assumed that this economically crucial province, home to about nine million Christians, would be fiercely defended. How could Amr's miniscule army of thirty-five hundred men possibly take the place? They would be annihilated.

Umar did reluctantly assent, however, perhaps because Amr cited two strategic advantages. Outside the fertile valley of the Nile itself, Egypt consisted mostly of desert, congenial territory for his nomads and inhospitable to Byzantine troops, and as with the Euphrates, so with the Nile. He could strike and withdraw, and wear down the enemy.[7] Moreover, Alexandria and other cities were primarily inhabited by Greek-speaking orthodox Christians, but the bulk of the rural population were Coptic peasants, Monosphysite in faith, speaking the ancient tongue of the pharaohs, and resentful of the Greek overlords and their orthodox clergy. His Muslims would perhaps appear as their champions.

Amr led his camel-mounted horde against the fortified town of Pelusium at the easternmost point of the Nile Delta. He had no siege equipment, but a sortie by its garrison failed, and his hard-charging Muslims followed the retreating Christians through their gates. The town fell, and Islam had its Egyptian foothold, but seemingly insurmountable obstacles remained. Chief among them was Alexandria, with its million inhabitants, so easily reinforced from the sea as to appear impregnable to any attack. Further, the soggy ground of the Nile Delta's perimeter, all 120 miles of it, was tough terrain for Muslim cavalry. Finally, a fortress called Babylon,

6. After the Muslims conquered Persia in the seventh century, the Zoroastrian faith virtually died there. A small number of Zoroastrians fled to India, where most are concentrated today and known as the Parsees. Those who remained behind have survived centuries of persecution, systematic slaughter, forced conversion and heavy taxes. They number about eighteen thousand, residing chiefly in Yazd, Kernan, and Tehran, in what is now Iran. The Persian Zoroaster, also known as Zarathustra, is thought to have founded this faith in the seventh century B.C., though some scholars believe it may have originated as early as 3000 B.C.

7. Muslim hit-and-run strategy, so successful against both the Persians and Byzantines, bears some resemblance to the military strategy being used by Muslim zealots against Israel and much of the Western world when this volume was written. Through it, small teams can harass and wear down a much more powerful enemy, often turning his technological superiority against him.

at the strategic point where the Nile broadens into the Delta, possessed formidable walls eight feet thick and sixty feet high.[8]

These disadvantages were offset, however, by the Byzantines' staggeringly incompetent defense. After winning an open battle at Bilbeis, Amr managed to bottle them up inside the Babylon fortress and hold them there. The defenders assumed that time was on their side, but it was not. Umar, encouraged by the astounding success of this small expeditionary force, dispatched an army of twelve thousand. Astonishingly, only after this did Babylon's commander decide to come out and fight. At the Battle of Heliopolis in the open desert his regulars were cut to pieces; only a desperate fraction regained the safety of the fortress.

The fate of Byzantium in Egypt now lay in the hands of a man so inept as to be later suspected of outright treason against the emperor. Cyrus, patriarch of Egypt, had visited upon Egyptian Monophysites such brutal crackdowns that many of them

The fate of Byzantium in Egypt now lay in the hands of a man so inept he would later be suspected of outright treason to the emperor.

would see the Muslims as much the lesser of two evils. (See sidebar page 144.) Cyrus now took it upon himself to negotiate with Amr for the surrender of Babylon, long before its garrison of five thousand had depleted its resources. Agreement in hand, he then hastened to Constantinople to seek imperial ratification.

The Arabs, Cyrus told the emperor Heraclius, were so willing to die and so indifferent to physical hardship as to be invincible. Heraclius, who did not believe him, had him arrested, tortured and exiled, and hostilities resumed at Babylon. But the emperor's indomitable spirit was ebbing fast; he seemed to be having some sort of breakdown. Then one night, a Muslim assault party gained a foothold on the wall. The Byzantine garrison, rather than strongly parrying this modest incursion, capitulated on condition they be allowed to leave in safety.

Thereafter, Amr skillfully continued to present himself to the Copts as the docile champion of an essentially irenic religion. One widely circulated story told of a dove found nesting on his tent when it was about to be dismantled. Citing Bedouin rules of hospitality, the general allegedly abandoned the tent rather than disturb the bird. Moreover, Muslims could truthfully cite an injunction from Muhammad, whose Coptic concubine had borne him a son: "When you conquer Egypt, be kind to the Copts, for they are your protégés and kith and kin." All this proved very persuasive.

Before advancing against Alexandria, says Islamic tradition, Amr taught the locals another lesson. He entertained a delegation of Copts at two successive suppers. The first evening, the diners sat down to a dish of camel meat boiled in salt water. The Arabs ate heartily; the Egyptians could scarcely choke the stuff down.[9] At the second meal, Egyptian delicacies were served, which the guests eagerly ate. Amr then suggested that the tougher fiber of the Arabs enabled them to conquer their more delicately bred enemies.

8. Babylon occupied the strategic site at which the Muslims would later construct Cairo. Its name, the same as that of the great city of ancient Mesopotamia, appears curiously out of place in the Nile Valley. It may have originated when the Babylonian monarch Nebuchadnezzar invaded in 567 B.C., or was possibly conferred on the place by Babylonian prisoners of war.

9. Camel meat is said to be an acquired taste. The Bedouin thrive on it. Most non-Arabs regard it as tough, disgusting, and essentially inedible, although some few hardy Westerners express a fondness for it, likening it to beef. At Amr's celebrated banquet, however, the Muslims may have served their guests flesh from a male camel in rut, said to be invariably rank.

The Copts got the message. Not many individuals initially converted to Islam, but many communities tamely surrendered. For any towns that resisted, terror was not neglected. At Nikiou, between Babylon and Alexandria, the Byzantine defenders finally panicked and fled, and the Muslims mass-slaughtered Copts throughout the city and environs. The imperial army lost several more rounds of heavy fighting before withdrawing into Alexandria.

The great city sprawled between the Nile Delta and the edge of the desert, which facilitated the Muslim approach, but victory was far from assured. Alexandria's mighty fortifications were bounded by the Mediterranean, a lake, and a network of canals, leaving only a strip of dry land for an assault, and Constantinople could reinforce at will the already large garrison. Orthodox Christians dominated the population of Greeks, Italians, Jews, black Africans and many others. When Amr failed in his first assault, and sustained heavy losses, the Christian determination to resist grew stronger.

But Constantinople at that crucial time was roiling in political confusion (described in chapter 10). In the turmoil, the honey-tongued Cyrus, supposedly in disgrace, nevertheless managed to get reappointed as patriarch of Alexandria—and as its secular governor as well. He then pursued the policy that earned him a lasting reputation for what looks very like treason: He persuaded Constantinople that Alexandria should be surrendered immediately.

Egypt's Coptic Christians, at that time a majority of the country's population, reached an uneasy accommodation with the invading Arabs. They would survive and, like Shenouda, patriarch of the Coptic Church (pictured above in 1992), remain staunch followers of Christ, despite fourteen centuries of Muslim domination.

The Arab army had by then actually lifted its siege of the great port, and most of its soldiers had returned to Babylon. Morale within the Christian capital was high. Cheering orthodox crowds greeted the new governor's ship when it docked in Alexandria on September 14, 641. Cyrus, without informing anyone, immediately initiated a personal parley with Amr. "God has given this country to you," was this ecclesiastical bureaucrat's pliant greeting to the Muslim commander.

Amr may have been startled, even dumbfounded, but he did not neglect to impose the usual humiliating terms of surrender. Riots broke out all over the city, the furious populace storming through the streets, but gradually the suave Cyrus made his case, persuading both the military commander and civic officials that submission was only sensible. With tears, he assured the Alexandrians that his work would save them, their children, and their churches from utter destruction. The disillusioned citizens, with no hope of succor, eventually accepted this rationale.

Why did Cyrus betray his religion, his empire, and common sense? Some argue that he was a frail and sentimental old man, a view difficult to reconcile with his unrelenting violence against the Monophysite Copts. The classic notion that bullies are usually cowards also suggests itself. But whatever the explanation, it was Cyrus's final act. He happened to die even before the Arabs could occupy the city.

Five years later, a Byzantine fleet recaptured Alexandria and put its thousand-member Muslim garrison to the sword. A nine-month campaign then raged between imperial and Muslim armies, climaxing at Nikiou, from which Amr emerged victorious. He turned again to Alexandria, and for reasons never satisfactorily explained, this time the metropolis failed to withstand his siege. Reports of treachery from within remain unproven but plausible. When the Muslims did burst in, they vengefully destroyed half of the buildings and ripped down the landward portion of the massive walls.

Alexandria, founded a millennium earlier by Alexander the Great, was the most wondrous city they had yet captured, its palaces and statuary rivaling

The faith would survive in Egypt. The Copts, with a record of endurance through fourteen centuries of hostility, would prove to be among the toughest Christians.

Constantinople itself. When it fell, the wide liberties enjoyed by its artists, and enthusiastically supported by the city's affluent Byzantine citizens, withered.[10] Although writers still wrote, Islam would be little inclined to idealize any concept of intellectual freedom. More positively, Hellenism's remarkable scientific accomplishments (as when the Alexandrian philosopher Eratosthenes accurately measured the size of the earth, for example) would survive Muslim governance.

Under Islam also, Alexandria's oft-heard voice within Christendom would be stilled. The city where the Septuagint translators first opened the Old Testament to the Gentiles, where Origen laid much of the foundation of Christian theology, and where Athanasius defied the world in his stubborn defense of the divinity of Christ, now became a city where the first concern of Christians was the very survival of their faith. The new Arab capital of Cairo was meanwhile becoming Islam's most sophisticated center of theology and religious jurisprudence.

Christianity was not entirely wiped out. For centuries the Muslims would need educated Copts to administer the country, nor do they seem to have been particularly eager to convert the peasantry to Islam. But gradually Christianity was eroded by Muslim "soft persecution"—such measures as penalizing taxes, humiliating dress codes, and prohibition of any Christian preaching. Judaism faced the same curtailment, of course. Later, when Muhammad's followers had become a majority, Muslim rulers and mobs would periodically instigate savage persecution of Christians, a pattern that still continues.

The faith would nevertheless survive in Egypt. The Copts, with a record of stalwart endurance through fourteen centuries of hostility, have proved

10. The Greek-speaking culture known as Hellenism swept the lands conquered by Alexander, later migrating to and permeating Rome itself. Where classical Greeks had subordinated the individual personality to the needs of the *polis* (city), Hellenistic artists crafted the world's first powerful expressions of human individuality. From them came the realistic personal portrait, precursors of the romance novel, and other forms of individualism. Hellenistic humanism was reinforced by the intensely personal nature of Christianity, which stresses that God loves every individual and helps each person to identify right from wrong in his own life. (The modern philosophy that right and wrong are purely subjective opinions on the part of the individual, however, would repel Hellenes, as it does Christians.)

themselves among the world's toughest Christians. Trustworthy statistics regarding non-Muslim Christians cannot be obtained from its present government, but many Copts believe their numbers total roughly ten million within the country (approximately fifteen percent of the population), plus an emigrant community totaling some two million. If so, they are more numerous today than when Amr ibn al-Aasi's nomad army first conquered them.

As for the Muslim steamroller, soon after the conquest of Egypt it would encounter its first serious setback, coming not from outside Islam but within. The emerging empire, largely lacking written accounts and other administrative tools, relied heavily on the faith, insight, and integrity of its leaders, and was not disappointed. Umar's personal integrity was typically legendary.

Another strength was the direct contact between the early caliphs and their subjects. Supplicants seeking an audience with Umar would be told "Just talk to him in the street or at the mosque." The Commander of the Faithful strode among the mud buildings of his capital with no pomp whatever, and even slaves made appeals directly to him. This of course carried danger, too. One such supplicant was Abu Lulu, a Persian captive who told the caliph that his master demanded too much of his pay when he rented him out as a carpenter. Umar listened carefully, did the mathematics, and shrugged. The deal seemed fair enough to him, he said, drawing a surly grumble from Abu Lulu.

But Abu Lulu did more than grumble. On November 3, 644, Umar made his way through the ranks of assembled Muslims to the front of the mosque in Medina to lead the prayers. With his back to the congregation, he lifted his hands in worship—and Abu Lulu, presumably in a demented frenzy, darted forward and stabbed him. Then the slave hurled himself into the crowd, slashing several more men before sinking his fatal blade into his own body.

Most Muslim historians view this murder as marking the end of their first truly golden age. "The good fortune of Islam was shrouded in the grave clothes of Umar," declared the scholar Ibn Khallikan five centuries later, which morally and militarily makes excellent sense. Umar ibn al-Khattab rivaled Alexander the Great as the top single conqueror of all time, his armies overcoming two of the world's most powerful civilizations during a caliphate that spanned less than ten years.[11] In all history, only Genghis Khan would seize and hold more territory, and the Mongol chieftain's

11. The simultaneous Muslim victory over Persia and Byzantium would be the equivalent, in terms of proportionate populations today, to Canada's conquering all of the United States along with more than half of Russia. Furthermore, a reasonable comparison would require that Canada begin as a nation of warring tribes, poorly armed and economically impoverished. Such a prospect would be rightly regarded as preposterous. It is this very improbability that bolsters the faith of the Muslim.

In this painting by Luigi Mayer (below), Muslim soldiers relax outside Alexandria's Canopic Gate, amid the ruins of the Gymnasium. The ancient capital of Cleopatra finally fell to the armies of the caliph in 646, and many of its buildings were laid waste.

thirteenth-century empire would be culturally sterile and short-lived, while Islam would move beyond mere force of arms to forge an enduring civilization.

From a non-Muslim perspective, Muhammad's initial two successors actually surpassed the Prophet himself in terms of character. Abu Bakr and Umar apparently took fewer wives and concubines. There is no record of their "marrying" captive women or making them concubines. They reportedly indulged in even

Submission and survival

The Muslim empire's treatment of Christians and Jews was far from consistently bad, but discrimination and taxation were invariably the lot of the 'People of the Book'

Muslims believe that their Prophet specified a place of the highest honor for Jesus, whom they call *Isa*. Christ, according to the Qur'an, was born of a virgin. He healed the sick and raised the dead. As the true Messiah, Isa will return one day to rule all of humanity. In contrast, one traditional *Hadith* (saying) portrays Muhammad as humbly uncertain even of securing a place in heaven. The Arab Prophet exalted the Jewish Isa as the breath of God, the spirit of God, and the Word of God. But he also fiercely condemned the central doctrine of Christianity: that Jesus is God incarnate who died to redeem mankind.

The Creator, Muhammad insisted, is too august ever to procreate. Sura 4:171 states, ". . . Allah is only one God; far be it from his glory that he should have a Son, whatever is in the heavens and whatever is in the earth is his, and Allah is sufficient for a Protector." Furthermore, Jesus did not die on a cross, nor did he die at all. The Qur'an maintains that God took Jesus directly to himself (Sura 4:157–158) without death. By mistake, the Jews crucified a scapegoat—a common Muslim speculation holds that the executed substitute may have been the arch-traitor Judas—rather than the Messiah.

Equally alien to Muhammad was the core of Christ's ethical teaching and behavior. Where Jesus preached love even toward enemies, Muhammad taught that anyone dying in battle against the human foes of Islam would gain eternal bliss. Where Christ insisted that salvation comes through belief in him, the Arab Prophet said every man's sins will be weighed against his virtuous acts.[1] While Jesus personally rejected earthly power and his followers have debated deeply about its usage, the words and deeds of Islam's founder constitute an outright instruction to grasp earthly power.

The Prophet's attitude toward Christ's followers evolved over the course of his life. Initially, he hoped for ready acceptance. Sura 5:83 states: "And when they [i.e., Christians] hear what has been revealed to the apostle [i.e., Muhammad] you will see their eyes overflowing with tears on account of the truth that they recognize. . . ." But disappointingly, few Christians accepted Muhammad's message willingly. So the new faith resorted to force. Sura 9:29, for instance, admonishes: "Fight those who do not believe in Allah, nor in the latter day, nor do they prohibit what Allah and his apostle have prohibited, nor follow the religion of truth. . . ." No limit is placed on this battle until victory is achieved. To Christians and Jews who submitted to Islamic rule, Islam granted the right to live as second-class citizens. These fellow "Peoples of the Book" had to pay a special head tax, known as a *jizya*, "in acknowledgment of superiority and they are in a state of subjection" (Sura 9:29). (To be fair, Christians faced with the practical pressures and temptations of government have often adopted discriminatory policies.)

Believers within Islam are consistently enjoined to do battle against infidels. The concept of *jihad*—a word meaning "struggle"—has two interpretations: the outward fight against unbelievers, and in a tradition that developed much later, the inner struggle with one's own human nature. The Prophet himself habitually waged holy war, to the point of ordering the secret assassinations of several people who had mocked him.

Muslims who maintain that their religion is not committed to incessant war with all non-Muslim nations can make several points based on their scripture. Muhammad usually couched his discussions of war in terms of defense. Also, the Prophet's directives were forged within the context of the Arabian Peninsula, the only place that he knew well. Take, for instance, the order that all polytheists must be exterminated unless they immediately accept Islam.[2] That sura was practicable regarding Bedouin tribes who still worshiped their traditional gods. But no Muslim leader aspired to a universal slaughter of the Hindus, conquered later by the tens of millions.

On the basis of the Qur'an, early Muslim theolo-

fewer luxuries. Leadership was clearly conferred upon them, not seized, and neither man exalted himself as an oracle. Their personal example of self-abnegation was crucial to the foundation of Islam, and to this day, millions upon millions of men and women tread faithfully in the footsteps of the first two caliphs. The same would not always be true of their successors, however, as the Muslim world was about to discover. ■

gians divided the world into the Dar al-Islam (the House of Submission) and the Dar al-Harb (the House of War). Within the Islamic realm, harmony should prevail as long as the *dhimmis*[3] behaved submissively. Muslim rulers dealing with the war realm controlled by non-Muslims are permitted to make temporary truces, as Muhammad did himself when he had no practical alternative. Nonetheless, the ultimate goal remains conquest of the entire Dar al-Harb.

The Qur'anic requirement that dhimmis remain visibly humbled would take many forms in centuries to come. Dhimmi orphans were routinely conscripted into Islam. Dhimmi testimony was unacceptable in a Muslim court. On occasion, government regulations required Christians and Jews to be officially slapped in public when paying their annual inferiority tax, to wear a neck tag indicating that the tax had been paid, to ride no animal more noble than a donkey, to keep their houses and shops lower in height than their Muslim neighbors, to remain unemployed if a suitable Muslim could be found, to always pass a Muslim on the inferior left side rather than the right, and much more.

Perhaps the most onerous curtailment on Christians, however, was the prohibition on the preaching of the gospel. Any attempt to influence Muslims towards Christianity was punishable by death. Even church bells could not be rung. Any Muslim who converted to Christianity was subject to execution. And while Muslim tourists have been welcome to visit St. Peter's in Rome or any other Christian holy place, the penalty for a Christian found in Mecca or Medina remains execution. However, some Christians see in these draconian rules an implicit acknowledgement of the power of the cross, the New Testament, and Christian witness. These instruments are so feared that Muslim authorities still commonly feel constrained to ban them on pain of death.

Yet Islam's treatment of Christians was far from consistently bad. Upon conquering new territory, Arabic and later Turkish rulers sometimes lowered taxes on their new Christian subjects, an obvious way to reduce the impulse toward revolt. Skilled dhimmis populated the upper ranks of Muslim administrations for centuries in Cairo, Baghdad and elsewhere. Cash-strapped Muslim regimes often discouraged dhimmis from converting because their treasuries would lose

A Coptic textile from the time of the Muslim conquest (right). Skilled artisans and administrators who shunned Islam might still prosper, but under the rule of the caliphs Christians and Jews were clearly second-class citizens.

significant revenue from the head tax imposed on infidels.

But thanks to taxation and social discrimination, punctuated by outbreaks of stunning violence, the overall condition of dhimmitude remained thoroughly unpleasant. "With the passing centuries, Christian populations that formerly constituted majorities dwindled to minorities—even disappearing from certain regions," the Egyptian-born Jewish sociologist Bat Ye'or reminded an academic conference at Jerusalem's Hebrew University in 1996. During the twentieth century, Muslims continued slaughtering large numbers of dhimmis. The toll from jihad and dhimmitude has continued until the present day, claiming victims from Indonesia to New York City and Washington, D.C. ■

1. The role of divine grace versus human works in individual salvation has long generated passionate discussion within Christianity. Islam's perspective on this subtle question is illustrated by Sura 8:29: "O you who believe! If you are careful of (your duty to) Allah, he will grant you a distinction and do away with your evils and forgive you; and Allah is the Lord of mighty grace."

2. Sura 9:5: "So when the sacred months have passed away, then slay the idolaters [i.e., polytheists] wherever you find them, and take them captives and besiege them and lie in wait for them in every ambush, then if they repent and keep up prayer and pay the poor-rate, leave their way free to them; surely Allah is forgiving, merciful."

3. An Arabic word meaning "protected" which was applied by the Arab–Muslim conquerors to indigenous non-Muslim populations who surrendered by a treaty (dhimma) to Muslim domination.

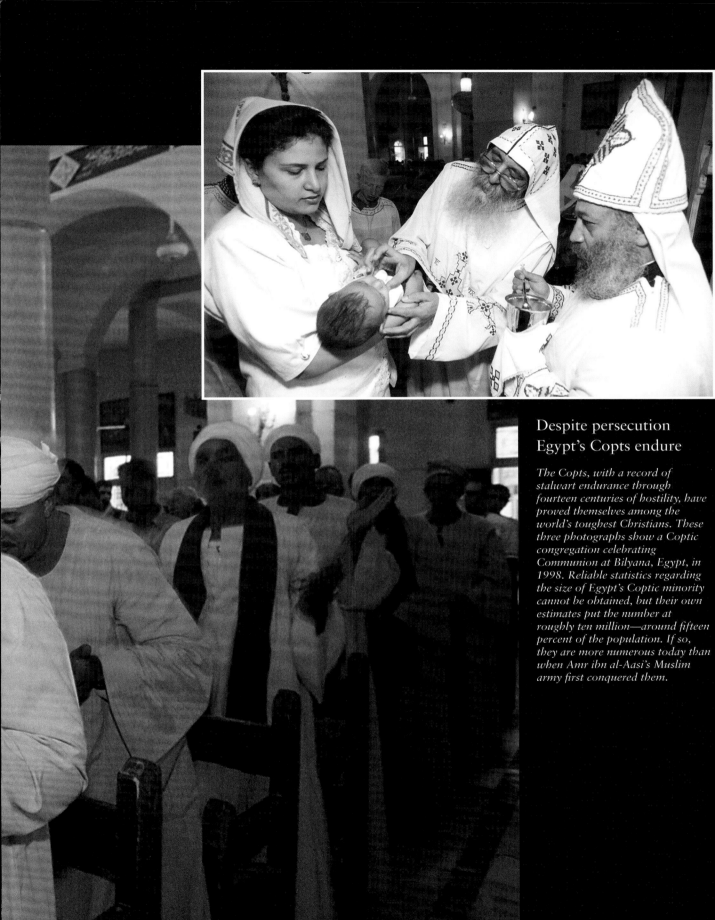

Despite persecution Egypt's Copts endure

The Copts, with a record of stalwart endurance through fourteen centuries of hostility, have proved themselves among the world's toughest Christians. These three photographs show a Coptic congregation celebrating Communion at Bilyana, Egypt, in 1998. Reliable statistics regarding the size of Egypt's Coptic minority cannot be obtained, but their own estimates put the number at roughly ten million—around fifteen percent of the population. If so, they are more numerous today than when Amr ibn al-Aasi's Muslim army first conquered them.

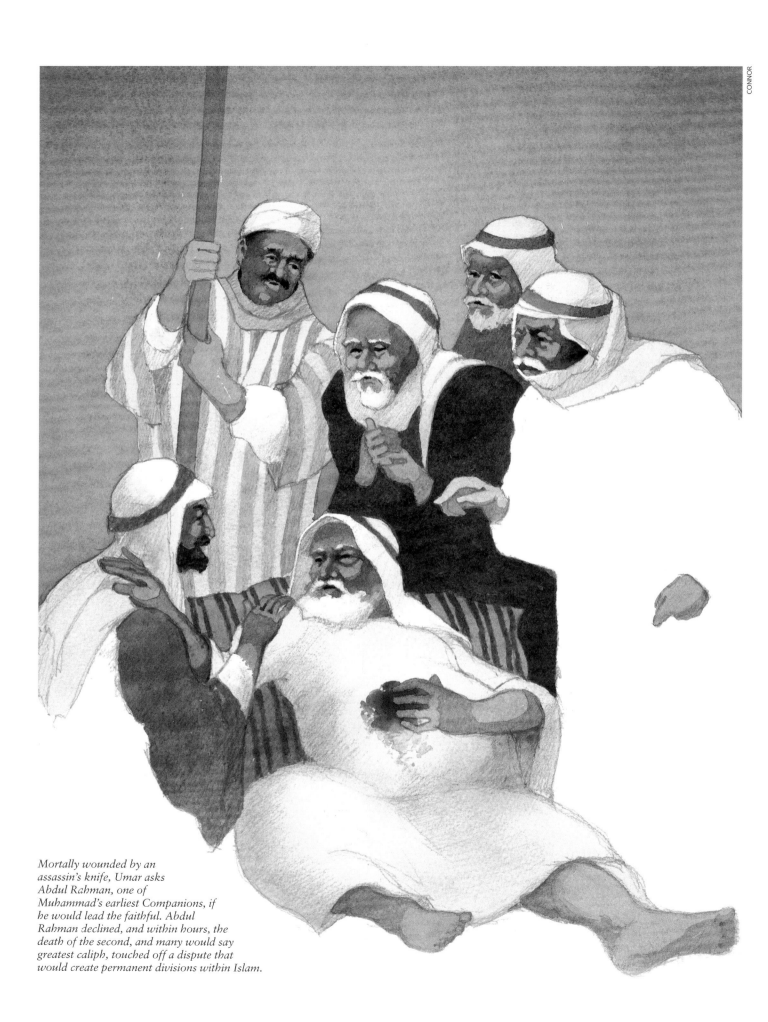

Mortally wounded by an assassin's knife, Umar asks Abdul Rahman, one of Muhammad's earliest Companions, if he would lead the faithful. Abdul Rahman declined, and within hours, the death of the second, and many would say greatest caliph, touched off a dispute that would create permanent divisions within Islam.

CHAPTER 7

Violence and schism shatter Islam's unity

A bitter war of succession creates a permanent rift with repercussions which will echo down the ages

Caliph Umar did not die immediately, although the knife wound in his back was so severe that when he took a drink of milk, it gushed out of his stomach, and he remained clear in mind. His thoughts concentrated on that all-important question, the succession. He first inquired of Abdul Rahman, one of the Prophet's earliest Companions, whether he would serve as Commander of the Faithful. But Abdul Rahman declined the honor of ruling an empire, so the dying warrior appointed a committee of five men to determine who would succeed him.

The five power brokers met immediately, and immediately launched into loud wrangling. Surely they could keep their voices down, Umar's son protested—they were disturbing his father—but the racket continued until the stricken caliph himself intervened. Would they please, he politely requested, postpone the debate until he died? Several hours later Islam's second and, many would say, greatest, caliph was gone.

Among the quarrelsome quintet, tempers and arguments continued at boiling point. In fact, the confrontation that emerged during those tense negotiations in November 644 would forever divide Islam. Besides Abdul Rahman, the electors assigned to this extraordinary task force included Ali, Muhammad's cousin, son-in-law and adopted son. Equally prominent was Uthman, married to two of the Prophet's daughters in succession.[1]

Umar wanted his successor chosen by acclamation, as he and his predecessor Abu Bakr had been, but he clearly sensed that rivalry had become inevitable. Therefore, he laid out a unique selection procedure. The committee of five must determine the succession within three days. Further, if they failed to reach unanimity, any losing candidate was to be beheaded to prevent future strife. During the next two days of heated argument, Ali and Uthman each pushed his own claim, but neither was willing to risk execution.

Both were members of the same tribe, the princely Quraysh of Mecca. Ali, however, represented the Banu Hashem, Muhammad's own clan, while Uthman hailed from the far more prestigious Banu Umayya, Mecca's hereditary war leaders. Muhammad had detested tribalism, the basic organizational form of

At first Uthman's generosity, leniency and affability came as a relief after the stern values of Umar. Particularly his decision to raise allowances.

Arabic society. Clan squabbling, he taught, should be replaced by a unifying devotion to Allah, an ideal he strove for most of his life with only marginal success.

On the third day, the electors agreed to abide by the personal choice of Abdul Rahman, the man whom Umar had first approached. This arbiter chose to make his announcement before the assembled faithful in Medina's mosque, where partisans of the two major candidates were on the brink of blows. As he rose to address the assembled faithful, Abdul Rahman assuredly realized that the Ali–Uthman clash—a clan wrangle of the classic Arab type within the Quraysh tribe—might easily destroy Islam.

He therefore strove to establish the authority of the new caliph as unquestionable. Calling Ali to the front of the mosque, he posed a careful query: "Do you bind yourself by the covenant of the Lord to do all according to the Book of the Lord, the example of the Prophet, and the precedent of his successors?" Ali, equivocating slightly, cautiously replied: "I hope that I should do so. I will act according to the best of my knowledge and ability." But Uthman, to the same question, boldly answered: "Yes, I will." And with that, Abdul Rahman decreed Uthman the new caliph.

It was an ironic victory. While Ali had repeatedly risked his life for Islam, the Umayyads (the faction led by the Banu Umayya) had not only rejected the new religion, but become its arch-foes. Only after Muhammad had conquered their power center of Mecca did the patrician clan embrace Islam. But Muhammad, practicing what he preached, did not discriminate against them. He promoted many of his former adversaries to high posts, and now the entire Arab empire had fallen into their hands.

The dynasty initiated by Uthman, known to history as the Umayyads, would

1. The remaining two members of the five-man committee assigned to choose a successor for the caliph Umar were Zubayr ibn al-Awwam, a senior commander who had led the Muslim assault party over the wall of the fortress Babylon in Egypt, and Saad ibn Abu Waqqas, conqueror of Iraq.

largely ignore the Prophet's precept of the
equality of all Muslims. Instead, they would
impose the old Arab order: Arabs over all
other peoples, Quraysh over all other Arabs,
and Umayyads over all other Quraysh.
Uthman went so far as to criticize his two
predecessor caliphs. Why, he wondered, had
they not enhanced the fortunes of their
kinsfolk, as good Arabs should?

*Uthman, the third caliph of Islam,
reading the Qur'an (above), from
an eighteenth-century Indian
painting held by the Victoria and
Albert Museum, London.*

Nevertheless, the seventy-year-old Uthman
was plainly devout, and had broken ranks
with the rest of the Banu Umayya to become
Muhammad's fourth convert, undiscouraged
by a brutal beating from an angry uncle. He
had endured exile to Ethiopia, and poured
much of his comfortable fortune into the
fledgling cause, once personally providing the
Muslim force with a thousand camels and
horses. After the deaths of Muhammad's daughters, he had other wives, one of
whom, Naila, a former Christian whom he married five years after he became
caliph, would stand valiantly beside him to his violent death.

At first, Uthman's generosity, leniency and affability came as a relief to the
faithful after the stern virtues of Umar. His early decision to raise the allowance
of all Muslim chiefs was certainly popular, among the chiefs anyway. Early on,
however, the new caliph faced an especially delicate judicial decision. Umar's
son, hearing that a Persian nobleman had been seen with the dagger that
murdered his father, promptly killed the man. But the slain aristocrat was
posthumously proven innocent; furthermore, he was a Muslim. Islamic law
called for the death penalty—but should Umar's family, having just lost its father,
also lose a son? The public seemed horrified at the prospect. Thus, where Abu
Bakr or Umar would almost certainly have enforced the law, however harsh,
Uthman commuted the sentence to a fine, then paid the fine himself. So the killer
suffered no penalty whatever. People noted that.

They also noted Uthman's blatant favoritism towards his family. Egypt's
conqueror, Amr ibn al-Aasi, was replaced by the caliph's half brother, an
apostate who had barely escaped alive from Muhammad's wrath. Uthman's
cousin, Mu'awiya, fastened a steely grip upon Syria. Iraq was handed over to a
half brother, who would later be removed from office and scourged for leading
the Friday prayers while drunk. (Muhammad reputedly had executed this man's
father as a prisoner of war, prophesying that his children were destined for
hellfire.) The military bases at Kufa and Basra in Iraq were commanded by
younger Umayyads. The governor of Kufa, whose father had died fighting
against Islam, generated ferocious resentment when he publicly stated that the
whole Fertile Crescent was now a "Garden of the Quraysh."

Ever congenial, the new caliph seemed to court universal affection by neglecting to discipline the errant, whether friend or foe. He smiled amiably as Umayyad grandees commandeered unearned estates in Iraq and cultivated their taste for marble palaces, extensive harems, luxuriant clothing and rich foods. All this infuriated the Bedouin and other less-fortunate participants in the new Islamic imperium. Equally offensive, when a rabble rebelled against the governor

Price of a drink: eighty lashes

Ask each accused whether wine is lawful or forbidden, ordered the caliph Umar. If he answers forbidden, give him eighty stripes. If he answers lawful, behead him

During Muhammad's mystic overnight journey to Jerusalem, as described by the Prophet, Gabriel brought him two cups—one of milk, the other of wine. Muhammad chose the milk and drank it. The angel congratulated him. Selecting the wine, Gabriel said, would have led his congregation astray.

So goes the story. It meant that Muslims should be prohibited from consuming alcohol altogether, the Prophet decided.[1] But if Muslims expected this decree to be easily enforceable, it was in for a most unpleasant disappointment.

Wine and gambling, says Philip K. Hitti, in his *History of the Arabs*, were "the two indulgences dearest to the Arabian heart"—next, of course, "to women." Both were abolished by one verse of the Qur'an (Sura 2:219). According to the legal system inspired by the Qur'an, the use of alcohol merits forty to eighty strokes of the lash.

However infallible the Qur'anic prohibition, there is ample evidence that it was not enthusiastically received by the faithful. When Muhammad died, drinking became a major enforcement problem for the caliphate. The records, observes historian William Muir (*Annals of the Early Caliphate*), are "significantly marked by the frequent notice of punishment for drunkenness."

Stern as always, the caliph Umar did not shrink from exacting the prescribed punishment. Even so, the drinking problem worsened, particularly at Damascus, where offenses grew so numerous and the penalty was so onerous that the governor was reluctant to impose it. Umar was not so squeamish. Ask each accused whether wine is lawful or forbidden, he ordered. If he answers "forbidden," give him eighty stripes. If he answers "lawful," behead him.

Umar did not stop there. A number of governors were themselves fired for drinking, and when one Muslim was discovered bootlegging, the caliph ordered his house set ablaze with the bootlegger

locked inside. Another perpetrator was exiled, but escaped and fled into Byzantine territory, where he apostatized from Islam and joined the wine-drinking Christians. When Umar's own son was accused, the caliph had only one response: eighty lashes.

It was all to no avail. The disorder persisted, particularly in Islam's foreign postings. Impressionable Muslim youths routinely traveled in the major fleshpots of the new Islamic Empire. There, says Muir, "intemperance and libertinism were rife." They often succumbed and returned home with a newfound fancy for "voluptuous living."

Nor was the problem restricted to the young. Khalid, greatest of Islamic generals, was removed from command due to his indulgence in luxury and wine. (See sidebar, page 165.) Again, the caliph Uthman had to deal with his drinking brother. As governor of Kufa, his brother had appalled the faithful by conducting the morning prayers so drunk that he went right on into the noon prayers without realizing it. "The scandal was great," writes Muir. "The majesty of Islam must be vindicated." It was. The brother was called home, lashed, and deposed.

With the advent of Yazid in 680, drinking officially became a crisis within the caliphate itself. He reportedly drank daily, sometimes competing with a trained monkey, and was known widely as Yazid of wines. Improvement came slowly. The caliph Malik (685–705) drank only once a month, but then so heavily that he suffered severe bouts of vomiting. His successor, Walid, drank just every second day, and Hisam (724–743) only once every Friday.

But the pattern of slow progress took a turn for the worst in Walid II, caliph for one year after the death of Hisam. The historian Philip Hitti describes Walid II as "an incorrigible libertine, who is said to have gone swimming habitually in a pool of wine, of which he would gulp enough to lower the surface appreciably." One day, Walid supposedly opened the

at Kufa, Uthman did not have the ringleaders executed, but tamely sent a new governor. He is also said to have pliantly allowed a Jewish convert to wander through Iraq, Syria and Egypt proclaiming that Muhammad would return in messianic fashion, that Ali was the Prophet's legitimate representative on earth, and that the Umayyads were evil.

When Caliph Uthman did crack the whip, it sometimes evidenced weakness,

Qur'an and his eyes fell upon the verse, "And every disobedient ruler will be brought to naught." Walid disagreed, and shot the sacred book to pieces with a bow and arrow. His reign was an unpopular one, and lasted only a year before he was killed in battle.

There were other problems, not the least of them a kind of theological inconsistency. Muslim martyrs were promised a heaven, not only of eminently seductive black-eyed *houris*, but also of "generous wine from the springs," notes Oswald Charles Wood in his *History of the Assassins*. Skeptics might ask: If wine is so evil, how come they drink it in heaven? Because, counter the Muslims, the wine of heaven does not cause drunkenness, which is the fault of wine on earth.

Fifteen hundred years after Umar and Uthman, the enforcement problem remains. Today, alcohol consumption is illegal in Saudi Arabia, Iran, Sudan, and several other Islamic countries. Yet large quantities of liquor are regularly seized by authorities there every year. Lucrative black markets persist, providing bottles of whiskey, for example, at roughly one hundred dollars each.

The spirit of Umar likewise remains. Islamic governments periodically impose an awesome severity. In 2002, a Saudi Arabian court sentenced Gary O'Nison, a London businessman, to eight hundred lashes and eight years in jail for running an illegal drinking club. The following year, in Iran, a man known only as Davoud, who had been twice arrested and once whipped for drinking, was sentenced to death. According to Robert E. Burns (*The Wrath of Allah*), Muslims convicted of drinking for the third time can be beheaded in Saudi Arabia, despite Muhammad's proscription that Muslims be executed only for adultery, murdering a fellow Muslim, or deserting Islam.

Finally, there is the problem of Qur'anic literalism. The great book specifically prohibits only a drink called *khamr*, probably date wine. On the

grounds that this was the only kind of alcoholic beverage most Arabs had ever heard of, the prohibition was expanded to include all spirits.[2] Backsliding Muslims in Western countries find solace in this. "I resolutely never touch khamr," says one, "I avoid it like the plague. But I will take the odd Old Crow." ■

1. Despite the ban of alcohol, notes Desmond Stewart in *Early Islam*, Muhammad himself had consumed *nabidh*, a mild fermented drink made from raisins or dates mixed with water.

2. The word "alcohol" is thought to be derived from the Arabic "al-kuhul," which is defined as "powdered antimony." However, a number of Arab scholars claim the word's origin is "al-kol," used to describe a spirit or *jinn* that took one's mind away. The word "alcohol" may have entered western languages via Sicily, where Christian, Islamic and Byzantine cultures met.

Although Muhammad had forbidden the consumption of alcohol, taverns—like this one (above) illustrated in Baghdad in 1237—remained a common hangout for Muslim men. A slave, bottom right, is pictured crushing raisins or dates, which when mixed with water made a mildly fermented drink called nabidh. *Legal nabidh was no more than two days old. Illegal nabidh was older, and much stronger.*

Women mourn the death of their men in combat during Islam's great seventh-century schism, in this detail from a fresco at the Imam Zadeh Shah Zaid Mosque, Isfahan, Iran.

2. How Uthman lost the Prophet's ring is described by the historian William Muir (*The Caliphate: Its Rise, Decline and Fall*): "It was a favorite and meritorious occupation of Uthman to deepen the old wells, and to sink new ones, in the neighborhood of Medina. He was thus engaged when, directing the laborers with his pointed finger, the ring slipped and fell into a well. Every effort was made to recover the priceless relic. The well was emptied, the mud cleared out, and a great reward offered; but no trace of the ring appeared. Uthman grieved over the loss. The omen weighed heavily on his mind; and it was some time before he consented to supply the lost signet by another of like fashion."

not resolve. His crackdown on gambling was seemingly aimed at the young, who resented it, more than at the privileged, who ignored it. Minor additions to the ritual of the annual pilgrimage to Mecca aroused heated controversy. Then came an evil omen. He lost Muhammad's silver signet ring down a well, and frantic efforts to recover it proved futile.[2] Eventually, even commoners did not fear to scorn their ruler to his face as the old man walked the streets of Medina.

In 655, the Umayyad provincial governors convened in Mecca, and noted that a spirit of seething revolt clearly was envenoming much of the Arab community. But what should he do, the old caliph, now eighty-one, pleadingly asked his own appointees. No solutions were forthcoming, however, and rebel conspirators were meanwhile coordinating a full-scale insurrection. Military expeditions from Basra, Kufa and Fustat (an Arab army cantonment in Egypt) converged on Medina in early 656. The Medinians donned armor and manned their walls, however, and Uthman's one concession was to agree to appoint a new governor of Egypt.

The dissidents left, and the Medinians relaxed their guard—but six days later, the revolutionaries suddenly reappeared. The Egyptian group claimed to have caught a black slave carrying a letter instructing the Umayyad governor of Egypt to arrest and execute their leaders. The messenger allegedly belonged to the caliph's household, they charged, and the letter bore his seal. Just then, whether by coincidence or design, the Iraqi contingents also reappeared, and the mutineers managed to talk their way through the city gates.

Uthman calmly denied sending the letter, and firmly rejected demands that he abdicate. He was either a liar or a fool, shouted his implacable adversaries—and a tyrant, too—and that Friday in the mosque, stones rained upon the Commander of the Faithful. He was taken unconscious to his home, which his enemies blockaded while Medina's residents, although their sympathy for Uthman was rapidly increasing, nevertheless cowered in their dwellings. Only a small band of young Quraysh guarded their tribal leader against the large, primarily Bedouin mob. Ali refused to intervene effectively, thus posing a disturbing possibility: Was the Prophet's son-in-law the secret author of this rebellion? Uthman certainly thought so, and said so.

An impasse of several weeks' duration ensued, during which Mu'awiya set out from Syria with a powerful Umayyad force, already assembled in the event of trouble. Hearing this, the insurgents refused to allow any water into the caliph's palace. Uthman's defenders, and Ali, too, remonstrated with them that the caliph and his household were being treated worse than prisoners on a battlefield, but were ignored. The besieged family signaled its deepening desperation from the roof. A'isha, Muhammad's favorite wife, tried to penetrate the cordon with a mule carrying water, but the desert warriors roughly turned her back.

As the Syrian troops drew nearer, the rebels realized that their time was running short, and on June 17, 656, they attacked the palace, hammering down its stout gate and simultaneously pouring over the rooftops. They found Uthman seated with the Qur'an spread open on his knees. Abu Bakr's son, a leading rebel, seized him by the beard, but could not bring himself to slit the throat of Islam's chief. Three other individuals also shrank from such a deed. But some, less squeamish, drove their swords into the old man's body, while

The less squeamish drove their swords into the old man, while Naila loyally threw herself across her husband in a hopeless attempt to protect him.

Naila loyally threw herself across her husband in a hopeless attempt to protect him, and the sweep of a blade sliced off her fingers. The regicides started to remove the head from Uthman's corpse, but were stopped by the shrieks and sobs of his women.

For three days, no outsider ventured to enter the house. Silence reigned over it—a silence that marked the end of Islam's original idyll. For an amazing quarter-century the Quraysh had led all Arabia in triumph after triumph, but now Muslim unity had been shattered by the war cries of Quraysh slaughtering Quraysh. Henceforth, the Umayyads would be the dedicated enemies of Ali, whose partisans would be called Alyites.

Six days after Uthman's murder, however, Ali accepted the caliphate. Short, full-bearded and stout in middle age, he unquestionably had a strong claim, as one of Muhammad's first converts, his cousin, the husband of his daughter Fatima, and an energetic lifelong supporter. The historical records are factually shaky as usual, since all accounts originate a century or more later, and are written by Islamic scholars with partisan axes to grind. However, it seems that Medinians and mutineers alike felt that Ali would bring more vigor to the helm of the Arab Empire than Muhammad's aging contemporaries.

The rebels dispersed to their bases in Iraq and Egypt. The Umayyad soldiers marching to relieve Uthman halted and returned to Syria. Throughout the new empire, devout and battle-hardened veterans waited to see how their new chieftain would deal with the killers of Muhammad's third successor. Islam might have been healed at this crucial point, suggests British historian John Bagot Glubb (*The Arab Conquests*), by the spectacle of a Hashemite caliph wreaking vengeance on behalf of the Umayyads. Virtually the whole Arab aristocracy, he surmises, would have rallied behind Ali against the Bedouin mutineers.

But Ali did nothing to avenge Uthman, contending that he lacked sufficient armed strength to punish the regicides. Further, he dismissed all Umayyad governors and appointed Alyites in their place, many of them his cousins. From Syria, Mu'awiya viewed his own dismissal by Ali as tantamount to a declaration of war. In defiance, he nailed Uthman's blood-soaked shirt and Naila's amputated fingers to the pulpit of his great mosque in Damascus, a grisly and visible demand for vengeance.

Mu'awiya had reason for confidence. Syrian Muslims were the most disciplined of any provincial garrison, and Syria's Monophysite Christians were apparently content with their governor's relatively benign administration. As one twelfth-century Monophysite patriarch of Antioch would comment, "It was no light advantage for us to be delivered from the cruelty of the Romans . . ." (*Chronique de Michel le Syrien*). Mu'awiya, therefore, secured his northern border by paying a peace tribute to the Byzantines, and waited upon events.

Another rival Quraysh group was meanwhile emerging in Mecca; A'isha and two close Companions of the Prophet (each with his own aspirations to the

Nailing Uthman's blood-soaked shirt and Naila's amputated fingers to the pulpit in Damascus, Mu'awiya demanded vengeance. Soon two Muslim armies stood face-to-face in open warfare.

caliphate) also raised the standard of revolt. Muhammad's youngest bride, now his most-respected widow, exhorted all the faithful to fulfill their holy duty by avenging her husband's slain successor. Now in her forties, the tireless A'isha accompanied a punitive expedition from Mecca to Basra, Iraq, and street fighting broke out within that military cantonment. The Meccan faction, emerging triumphant, promptly identified and executed hundreds of participants in Uthman's killing, write professors Sayed Abdul Qadir and Mohammad Shuja-ud-Din in *History of Islam, Part I*.

Ali was in a tight spot. Medina had no standing army, a vulnerability that had unquestionably contributed to his predecessor's death. The Bedouin tribes were as likely to sack the town as to fight for him, and Egypt had fallen into faction-ridden confusion. His best hope was the military cantonment at Kufa in Iraq, twice as large as the Basra garrison, and still harboring many of Uthman's adversaries. Ali sent his son Hassan to woo these troops by promising to transfer his capital to Kufa. The ploy succeeded.

Marshalling Kufans and tribesmen, Ali marched against Basra in December 656, and for the first time, two Muslim armies stood face-to-face in open warfare. But the caliph, a patient and persuasive man, managed from his position of numerical superiority to induce his foes to negotiate. This stratagem nearly worked, as Ali assured his opponents that he would avenge Uthman just as soon as circumstances permitted. But this commitment inevitably leaked back to his own troops—who were by no means all of one mind.

Many Bedouin, along with others offended by post-Muhammad developments, saw themselves as inevitably exploited by the Qurayshite aristocracy, whether of the Alyite or Umayyad variety, and this category included the regicides. They had acted not as champions of Ali, but as opponents of Quraysh elitism. Now they believed that their best policy was to encourage war between the Quraysh clans, since rapprochement among the Quraysh would mean continued exploitation, and very possibly death, for them. So they hatched a counterplot, gambling their lives on an attempt to trigger full-scale fighting between the Alyites and the Umayyads.

Their plan played out brilliantly. In the gray light of dawn, their lancers charged full-tilt into the Basra lines, ending any hope of a treaty, while yells of "Treachery!" arose from both sides. Ali, watching as thousands of warriors leaped into combat with instinctive efficiency, shouted in vain that it was all a false alarm. The Muslims, undefeated for a generation, proceeded to inflict terrible casualties upon each other in this encounter, known as the Battle of the Camel, after the animal that carried A'isha amidst the carnage. Her litter, initially positioned behind the lines, had become engulfed in the battle, taking so many arrows that it resembled a hedgehog. Seventy dauntless soldiers died defending her, and her two fellow conspirators both perished in the fighting.

Ali took possession of Basra, which remained unsacked, and the vanquished troops accepted pardon. The fallen of both sides were buried with identical honors, side by side in common graves. A'isha, unharmed, received a courteous visit from Ali, who greeted her with a rebuke, that under the circumstances, seems rather mild: "The Lord pardon you for what has passed, and have mercy upon you." "And upon you also!" the lady briskly responded. But thereafter, the thoroughly shaken A'isha became affectionately reconciled to Ali, dismissing their earlier feud over her imputed infidelity to the Prophet as a mere family squabble. Nor did she ever again meddle directly in affairs of state. Instead, the sharp-tongued lady, like other contemporaries of the Prophet, became a voluble and valuable source of stories and sayings attributed to Muhammad.[3] A'isha died at age sixty-six, having spent forty-seven years in widowhood.

With Basra beaten, Ali next sought peace with Mu'awiya, but the Syrian governor vigorously rejected any truce until all Uthman's murderers were punished. Unfortunately, whether he wanted to or not, Ali could not have complied. The conspiracy that began at Kufa,

3. The remembered sayings and deeds of Muhammad, and of things done in his presence and therefore with his tacit approval, eventually numbered in the thousands. Later they were rigorously categorized in collections known as *hadith*, often viewed as second only to the Qur'an in authority. From these are drawn rules known as *sunna* (meaning the practice of the community, specifically the Prophet's original community), which provide the foundation for much of Islamic Law, known as the *Shari'a*.

A gruesome depiction (below) of the bloody civil war that wracked Islam in the mid-seventh century, from a fresco at Isfahan, Iran. Female prisoners are carried away on the back of a camel (the small, veiled figures), while their captor flaunts the head of an enemy.

and thwarted the projected truce at Basra, was still energetically growing into Islam's first breakaway sect: the Kharijite movement, made up of devout Muslims, mostly from the humbler classes, many of them able to recite the entire Qur'an by memory. Populist and puritanical, the Kharijites had no love for the Umayyads, and their loyalty to Ali was shaky, too.

Kharijite translates as "dissenter." Its Arabic root (*khraja*) also means "to purge" or "to throw out," denoting their determination to rid Islam of human impurities. They yearned for a world governed by the will of God rather than the debased dictates of sinful mankind, and true to their Bedouin heritage, they evinced egalitarian impulses suggestive of a primitive democratic socialism. Their

The Kharijites believed that all deviants from true Islam were fit targets for their violence. Had not the Prophet himself set clear precedents in this regard?

preachers taught that even a slave could become caliph if Allah so willed, that all Muslims should be treated as brothers, that extreme wealth and luxuries are sinful, and that Islamic rule should be based on Qur'anic principles and not aristocratic faction. Their urge to reduce the social disparities and injustices of their times represented a sentiment that would echo and re-echo in later events, both eastern and western.

But the Kharijites developed another and less benign urge, based on a conviction that their beliefs should be backed by individually initiated violence. Others deemed them fanatics. Not so, they countered; didn't the Qur'an instruct believers to "command the good and prohibit evil?" (Sura 9:71). Hadn't the Prophet himself set clear precedents in this regard? Therefore all deviants from the real, true Islam were fit targets for their violence. Sociologists Fuad Baali and Ali Wardi observe that the sectarians "did not hesitate to kill the women and children of their enemies and to plunder their property," on the grounds that Umayyads and Alyites were both "the worst of infidels" (*Ibn Khaldun and Islamic Thought Styles: A Social Perspective*). Assassination was not just permissible, it was mandatory.

The immediate Kharijite controversy, however, also stemmed from a different cause, namely Muhammad's failure to clearly spell out a method of selecting his successors as political and theological leader of Islam.[4] With no such specific provision, Ali had no way of establishing the legitimacy of his caliphate. Thus, when he became dependent on the Kufa garrison, the Kharijites—driven by their hatred of Quraysh greed under Uthman—were able to block any compromise with Mu'awiya, arch-advocate of vengeance for that murdered caliph.

The inevitable military showdown between Mu'awiya and Ali took place in the early summer of 657, in gravel-strewn desert far up the Euphrates River near Siffin. The commanders, both notably deliberate men, tried again to reach a compromise—but failed. Warriors from the same tribes, even the same families,

4. Sheikh Mohammad Iqbal, a twentieth-century historian from India, reports: "There is a tradition that the old Amir, son of Tufail, came to the Prophet and said, 'If I embrace Islam what would my rank be? Wilt thou give me the command after thee?' 'It does not belong to me,' said the Prophet, 'to dispose of the command after me.'" Muhammad apparently favored the Arab tribal custom of selecting a new sheikh by tribal consensus, a model that could not be translated directly into a more complex society (*Political Thought in Islam*, compiled by Asif Iqbal).

now had to attack each other; since few were enthusiastic about such a prospect, the opening rounds amounted to little more than light skirmishing. After two months, however, the Battle of Siffin erupted in earnest.

Constantly foremost in the bloodshed were the Kharijites. One headlong charge by four hundred Bedouin "readers" (devotees who memorized long passages of scripture) almost reached Mu'awiya himself. Equally fierce was an aged Companion of the Prophet who died embattled at Siffin, while crying out that paradise was near. Muhammad himself had predicted, it was said, that this man would be killed by "a cruel and unjust people," which now was naturally taken to mean the Syrians, who had indeed killed him. The Iraqi troops, their cause apparently vindicated on the highest spiritual authority, redoubled their attack on the correspondingly downcast Syrians.

Such morale-destroying discouragement could indeed have been fatal, but for one individual. Amr, twice conqueror of Egypt and now a field commander in Mu'awiya's army, rallied his disheartened troops. What, he demanded, is this fight about anyhow? Isn't it simply about Ali's wicked refusal to punish the killers of a holy caliph? Isn't this the only real cause of all these unnecessary deaths? Amr's rationale restored the Umayyad spirit, and after another indecisive day, he further demonstrated his sure grasp of Bedouin psychology. Next morning, pierced on the spear tip of every Umayyad cavalryman was a page from the Qur'an. "The word of God!" they

A Muslim shrine towers over the medieval walls of Kufa, Iraq (left), with the remains of the Umayyad cantonment in the foreground. The city became the center of the violent Kharijites, Islam's first breakaway sect.

shouted as they tore into the Alyite ranks. "Let the word of God decide!"

"Ignore this trickery!" shouted Ali, backed by a Kharijite leader yelling, "Victory is near! Keep fighting," but the Bedouin warriors refused to assault the Qur'an. Ali had no choice but to parley, and also to acquiesce in a notably disadvantageous proposition. The question of the caliphate was to be arbitrated by two umpires, one appointed by each side, both sworn to act in the spirit of the Qur'an. Worse yet for Ali, his troops insisted on nominating as his arbitrator a former governor of Kufa, whose heart was more neutral than Alyite. Mu'awiya nominated the cunning Amr.

When negotiations got underway, Amr proposed that both Mu'awiya and Ali forego the caliphate in favor of a third candidate, to be selected by the citizens of Medina. Ali's man agreed to this proposition, in effect acknowledging before this multitude of Muslims that the reigning caliph ought to abdicate. But Amr, stepping forward in his turn, treacherously and clearly proclaimed his support for Mu'awiya. On that basis, the Umayyads claimed the caliphate.

Followers of Imam Ali who fell in the battles during Islam's seventh-century schism continue to be regarded as martyrs by the faith's Shi'ite minority. This Persian fresco (above) from the Imam Zadeh Shah Zaid Mosque, Isfahan, Iran, depicts four such, covered with arrows.

The enraged Ali refused to acknowledge the result of this mischievous procedure, but he could not renew his attack against Syria. First, he had to deal with an armed revolt by four thousand Kharijites who, true to their violent creed, began massacring even children and pregnant women in Allah's name. When other Alyite supporters brought these diehards to bay at the Battle of Nahrawan in 658, eighteen hundred of them mounted a suicidal charge directly onto their enemies' spears and virtually all died, although their movement was by no means extinguished. After that, Ali had to eradicate an armed flare-up in Basra in favor of Mu'awiya. After Siffin, the luckless fourth caliph was consistently victorious, but he was to enjoy neither peace nor prestige. He was even deserted by one of his own brothers, who went over to his Syrian rival.

The Umayyads, by contrast, prospered mightily. Amr invaded Egypt for the third time in 658, and Abu Bakr's son, the Alyite governor, mounted only a feeble resistance. (Because this man allegedly had laid violent hands on Uthman, his captors burned his corpse inside a donkey skin.) Backed by Egypt's vast revenues, Amr acknowledged Mu'awiya, not Ali, as caliph. Now there were two caliphs, one in Kufa and one in Damascus. Two years later, Umayyad forces took

Mecca and Medina, extracting oaths of allegiance to Mu'awiya at sword-point before returning to Syria. The Alyites counterinvaded the holy cities from Iraq. When the competing caliphs finally tired of the pointless destruction and arranged a truce, the border between their realms replicated the former Byzantine–Persian frontier.

Both parties, if not content, were now at least resigned. But a third party— the Kharijite movement—was neither, and three Kharijite warriors in Mecca, lamenting the division of Islam, resolved on a solution. This unholy schism, they

So little regarded was Ali at the time that the location of his grave is unknown. Perhaps he was too patient to be the ruler of such a turbulent people.

decided, was obviously the fault of three Quraysh: Ali, Mu'awiya and Amr. The solution was equally obvious: They must assassinate all three. Each conspirator chose one target, swearing to slay him during Friday prayers on the fourteenth day of Ramadan, and their astonishingly audacious plot might easily have succeeded. But in Egypt, the Kharijite killer, having murdered the Friday prayer leader, discovered afterward that he was not Amr.[5] The attacker assigned to Mu'awiya wounded him, but not fatally. In Kufa, however, the third assassin gashed Ali's skull and side with a poisoned sword, and he died the next day. Islam's fourth caliph had reigned less than five years.

So little regarded was Ali at the time that the location of his grave is unknown. Perhaps he was too patient to rule a turbulent people. The horrific events of his caliphate echo through Islam to this day, however, commemorated in two Islamic denominations: the Shi'ites, as the Alyites would later be known, and the spiritual descendants of the Kharijites. The latter, on account of their anarchic philosophy, fractured into many groups, sometimes, but not always, displaying the original blend of slaughter and religion. One famous manifestation of their violent side resurfaced in Persia and Syria during the eleventh century, in a sect popularly known as the Assassins. The name derives from hashish, a drug given to these thoroughly trained fanatics who terrorized both other Muslims and the Christian Crusaders.[6]

Organizationally, no Kharijite group survived the medieval period, but theologically, their modern spiritual heirs, at least in part, were the so-called "Islamists," who in later centuries would instigate bloody revolt against corrupt governance and infidel influence. In 1981, Islamists assassinated Egyptian President Anwar Sadat. Al-Qaeda, the terrorist organization formed and led by Osama bin Laden of Saudi Arabia, also breathes the Kharijite spirit of bloodshed initiated by suicidally devout individuals. Most prominent among its many deeds was the destruction of the World Trade Center in New York City on September 11, 2001. Equally consistent with the Kharijite tradition were the Palestinian suicide bombers who killed and injured thousands of Israeli civilians, by no means excluding children.

5. Amr was sick at home on the day chosen for his assassination. Under questioning, the unrepentant Kharijite who unwittingly killed the man taking his place at the prayers admitted that Amr himself had been the designated victim. "You intended to kill me," Amr replied, "but Allah intended to kill you." Then he ordered that the assassin be executed.

6. The medieval sect called the Assassins, properly the Nizari branch of the Ismaili Muslims, was the spiritual descendant of the seventh-century Kharijites. In later centuries, it took a curious turn away from externally directed violence. Instead, this stream of "seceders" refocused its strong tendency toward individualism into a peaceable inward piety. Today the group, led by the Aga Khan, may have up to twenty million adherents. In North Africa and South Arabia, another moderate Kharijite movement, called the Ibadites, established itself as a separate state during the seventh century. Its adherents did not feel impelled to exterminate their theological adversaries either. Today, the Arabian sheikhdom of Oman remains officially Ibadite.

After fourteen centuries emotions still smolder

The impact of Islam's seventh-century schism still reverberates throughout the Muslim world. After the overthrow of Saddam Hussein in 2003, members of Iraq's Shia community stand in front of a huge mural (1) commemorating two assassinated clerics. A popular uprising by Iraqi Shi'ites at the end of the 1991 Gulf War was suppressed with brutal force, leaving cities such as Karbala (6) in ruins. After the arrival of American forces in 2003, Shi'ites searched for relatives missing since the uprising. Outside the town of Hilla (2), some three thousand bodies were discovered in a mass grave, but for the first time in a quarter-century, Iraqi Shi'ites were also free to visit shrines in Najaf and Karbala—and to commemorate the death of Imam Hussein with traditional displays of grief and self-flagellation in a celebration known as Ashoura. In this photograph (4), men carrying a blood-soaked banner make their way to Karbala through a sandstorm. In many parts of the Islamic world, the bloodier aspects of Ashoura are restricted, but in the Persian Gulf state of Bahrain, thousands of men still flock to local mosques to receive a ritual head wound (5), symbolic of Hussein's death. Islam's Sunni majority officially regards such behavior with reservation, but Sunni, too, has its extremists—such as these members of the militant group Sipah-e-Sahaba (3), demonstrating in Karachi, Pakistan, in support of the September 11, 2001, attacks against the United States. ■

Persia and Iraq, whose non-Arab populations so heartily resented consistent Umayyad favoritism for Arabs, provided a multitude of ears sympathetic to the claims of Ali and his descendants. Today, the Shi'ites constitute the majority of Muslims in Iran (the modern name for Persia) and Iraq. Elsewhere within Islam, they form significant minorities, often articulating the concerns of the poorer classes. They constitute perhaps ten percent of the world's Muslims, and over the centuries have evolved a distinct theology and legal system, while continuing to share the Qur'an with the rest of Islam.

Following Ali's assassination, the Kufa troops rallied to his son Hassan. In a society where the familial connection was so important, Hassan was an appealing candidate, for his mother Fatima had been Muhammad's favorite daughter, and the Prophet had delighted in playing with Hassan and his younger brother Hussein as children. Pious and grave in manner, Hassan was temperamentally even more pacific than his father. After six months he agreed to abdicate in favor of Mu'awiya, on condition he be granted a royal revenue for life. (Thereafter, Hassan reportedly lived in Mecca, married and divorced scores of wives, and was fatally poisoned by an embittered wife eight years after his "retirement.")

Mu'awiya, enabled by Hassan's resignation to reign over a relatively united empire, proceeded to use the imperial treasury to buy loyalty among the Arab tribes. Although personally devout, he governed politically. One particularly skillful coup involved his half brother Zayyad, sired by their father during a brief encounter with a slattern. Despite his unacknowledged paternity, Zayyad had achieved high office under Ali, entirely due to his own competence; after Ali's death, Mu'awiya declared his half brother to be a legitimate scion of the Banu Umayya. A scandal ensued among the class-conscious Arabs, but Zayyad governed Persia and Iraq with outstanding ability and loyalty, his performance equaling that of Amr in Egypt.

When he grew old, Mu'awiya persuaded Muslims—and where necessary forced them—to swear loyalty to his son as his heir apparent, something no

The slain Imam Ali ibn Abu Talib, Islam's fourth caliph, lies in the arms of his adopted father, Muhammad, in this seventeenth-century fresco (above), from Isfahan, Iran. Ali, assassinated in 661, is revered by Shi'ite Muslims, Islam's second-largest sect.

A young Shi'ite (above) wears a picture of Ali and his son Hussein, grandson of Muhammad, as he prays inside the Imam Ali Mosque at Karbala, Iraq. Hussein and many members of Ali's family died in fighting at Karbala in 680.

previous caliph had attempted. Islam's rulers in centuries to come would prefer a hereditary system to popular acclamation, but at this time, the novelty infuriated rival claimants to the caliphate. When Mu'awiya died in 680, the ever-restless Kufans deluged Ali's surviving son, Hussein, with invitations to revolt, a proposition to which Hussein finally and fatally agreed.

From Medina, the Alyite prince set off across the desert with his family, accompanied by only a few dozen warriors. But before he reached Iraq, the Umayyad governor, having decisively quelled sedition in Kufa, dispatched an armed force that pinned down the little expedition from Medina at a place called Karbala, near the Euphrates. Hussein, despite his hopeless position, refused to surrender his claim to the caliphate. In the same spirit, his womenfolk rejected the opportunity to leave his side.

All parleying over, arrows showered into the huddle of tents in the desert. The Kufa troops, attacking in overwhelming numbers, practically annihilated Ali's nephews, grandsons and other relations. Hussein's severed head—whose lips had been kissed by Muhammad himself—was displayed in the mosque at Kufa. This courageous man, although imprudent by any worldly standard, has impressed many Muslims as an admirable model of Islamic virtue. Every year, Shi'ite millions attend highly emotional ceremonies in remembrance of the brutal fate of Ali's family.

Just four of Hussein's children and one of his sisters survived the massacre. Treated courteously by the Umayyad court, they were permitted to reside in Medina, where many pilgrims heard their recollections of Karbala, and carried the Alyite message homeward. To these poignant memories soon were added other causes of dissatisfaction. Mu'awiya's successor, for example, was subjected to a torrent of vituperation for leading a dissolute life unworthy of a Muslim.

In Mecca, a Quraysh claimant to the caliphate successfully raised the unruly tribes of Arabia against Damascus, and the Kharijite threat exploded again. But the rebel factions, far from uniting, fought each other. After the Meccans defeated the Kharijites in a series of battles, their own forces fell as relatively easy prey to the Umayyad army. Medina itself was sacked for three days by Muslim troops.

Although triumphant in war and astute in politics, the Umayyad dynasty never could staunch the startling torrent of moral denunciation attracted by its caliphs, and was further damaged by recurrent rebellions on behalf of one or another Alyite descendant. Over time, moreover, a shrewder crew worked its way to the forefront: a numerous clan descended from Muhammad's Uncle Abbas, the man who so consistently supported his nephew, while so long delaying actual commitment to Islam.

With devious skill, this Abbasid faction gradually grew until its strength matured—then openly challenged the Umayyads. The Abbasids seized power in 750, amid a welter of Umayyad blood, subsequently forsaking Damascus to create Baghdad as the capital of what would be Islam's Golden Century, in terms of culture. Their caliphs were deliberate and reverent in their public pronouncements, and they championed the development of the *Sunna* movement. The Sunnis describe themselves as followers of a "middle path," based on the practice of the Islamic community as defined by the *hadith*, the collected sayings and deeds of the Prophet, and by the twentieth century would account for close to ninety percent of Muslims.

The duration of the Abbasid dynasty was shorter—scarcely two centuries—but glorious. With Sunni advice, they crafted a workable administration for their increasingly complex empire, and their Christian subjects were helpful, too. Until the ninth century, notes British historian Laurence Browne in *The Eclipse of Christianity in Asia*, all the doctors,

A U.S. Abrams tank (bottom) patrols the streets of Karbala, Iraq, in April 2003, with the Imam Ali Mosque in the background. The arrival of American troops meant that, for the first time in decades, Iraqi Shi'ites were able to make their traditional pilgrimage to the mosque—which they consider to be among Islam's holiest sites. These women (below) were among the hundreds of thousands of Shi'ites who made the emotional journey to Karbala.

7. In the tenth century, three centuries before it came into use by Europeans, Arabs imported the mathematical concept of zero from India. Beyond the fusion of Greek and Indian mathematical concepts, the Arab Empire's numeric work centered on the decimal, algebra and trigonometry, which in turn provided the foundation for the modern mathematics developed by western civilization.

September 2001: Demonstrators in Islamabad, Pakistan (below), march in support of Islamic militant Osama bin Laden. A few days earlier followers of bin Laden had hijacked American aircraft and flown them into the twin towers of New York's World Trade Center and the Pentagon in Washington, D.C. The roots of bin Laden's violent brand of Islam can be traced directly to the bloody schism of the seventh century.

astrologers and philosophers appointed by these caliphs were Christian, and so were their all-important tax accountants. (The welcome later turned sour when Muslims became educated, and resented the influence and prosperity of the infidels.)

To this Iraqi metropolis on the Tigris, traders brought silk, gold, rare woods, perfumes and a host of other treasures. Palaces and gardens worth millions of gold pieces graced its riverbanks; beautiful shrines and mosques, public baths and luxuriant gardens abounded. Out of Baghdad came such folkloric tales as the *Arabian Nights*, with heroes like Sinbad the Sailor and Ali Baba. Its scholars assimilated Greek science and philosophy, and made significant contributions to mathematics.[7] In the meantime, dynastic quarrels sometimes slowed, but never halted the spectacular military success that carried Islam both eastward and westward, generally on the razor edge of Muslim swords.

But a parallel phenomenon was by now observable amidst the barbarian chaos of western Europe: the Christian church, which in the darkest hours of the Dark Ages became a unifying force strong enough to stop dead the Muslim advance. Its crucial unification was largely the accomplishment of one man, a contemporary of Muhammad, and his work, too, would play a lasting role in human history. ■

An insider challenges Islam

Raised in the caliph's household, and the Muslims' senior Syrian administrator, John of Damascus mounts Christianity's first theological opposition to Muhammad

The last father of the eastern church, its greatest poet, and the first Christian writer to challenge Muhammad as a false prophet, grew up in the new Muslim capital of Damascus as an intimate of Caliph al-Walid's family, and served as a senior bureaucrat of the new order. But he was fiercely denounced, not by the Muslims, but by the imperial authorities in Constantinople, who, by one account, tricked the caliph into ordering the amputation of one of his hands.

This was John of Damascus, who was despised by Constantinople in his own time as a notorious traitor and "wronger of Jesus Christ."

He was born about forty years after the Muslim conquest of Syria. While details of his life are sketchy, his grandfather, Mansur, may have been instrumental in delivering Damascus into the hands of the invading Arabs.[1] As a result, the family's name became cursed in Constantinople (where it was sometimes officially rendered in Greek as *Manzeros*, or bastard). The Mansur clan clearly prospered under the new regime, with John's father becoming the caliph's chief administrator.

The family was, however, acknowledged to be devoutly Christian. Tradition holds that John's father spent much of the wealth earned in the service of the caliph in buying the freedom of numerous slaves brought to the capital as a result of Muslim raids around the eastern Mediterranean. One such was the monk Cosmas, who became tutor to the Mansur children, including the precocious John. In addition to algebra, geometry and music, as an intimate of the caliph's own family, John seems to have learned a great deal about the new religion of Islam, which was little understood by most Christians. Like his father before him, John became the caliph's chief administrator, a role in which he, too, seems to have excelled and prospered.

The cause of John's estrangement from his Arab masters is not certain, but his biographer (a tenth-century patriarch of Jerusalem) says that his forceful opposition to attempts by Emperor Leo III to ban the veneration of religious images (a conflict to be dealt with in the next volume) led to an imperial plot to discredit him in the eyes of the Muslims. A letter bearing John's forged signature and offering to deliver Damascus to Byzantine forces found its way to the

1. The historians Eutychius and Ibn al-Amid both record that Mansur was a Christian leader who helped negotiate the surrender of Damascus in 635, although others refer to an unidentified "bishop" and "a friend of the bishop" as the negotiators.

JOHN ON THE INCARNATION

Being perfect God he became perfectly human and accomplished the newest of all new things, the only new thing under the sun.

caliph—who condemned his bureaucrat and ordered that his hand be amputated.

Whether this is legend or fact, the by now middle-aged John left the caliph's service and entered the monastery of St. Sabas, near Jerusalem. He eventually became a priest, and his considerable intellectual gifts were put at the disposal of the church. John's most famous work is *The Fountain of Wisdom*, a comprehensive survey of the theology of the early church, and a landmark in Christian antiquity. Written in three parts, the third book is titled *Concerning Heresy*, and contains Christianity's first detailed analysis of "the deceptive superstition of the Ishmaelites,"[2] which John recognized lay at the heart of the Muslim onslaught.

JOHN ON CHRIST'S SACRIFICE

Through nothing else has death been abolished, ancestral sin loosed, hell despoiled, resurrection bestowed, the way back to pristine blessedness made straight, the gates of paradise opened, our nature set down at the right hand of God, and we become children of God and heirs, save through the cross of our Lord Jesus Christ.

John's intimate knowledge of Islam's origins and practices, and his familiarity with the Qur'an (no doubt gained during his years in Damascus) is unique in his time, and led him to conclude that Islam was, in fact, a Christian heresy. Aware of the Arabs' idolatrous past (then very recent), he gave Muhammad credit for leading his branch of the family of Abraham back to monotheism—but says the Prophet then got it all terribly wrong.

"Jews, Arians and Nestorians, from each one of these Muhammad acquired a particular teaching, and thus he formed his own heresy: from the Jews, absolute monotheism; from the Arians, the affirmation that the Word and the Spirit are creatures [and thereby not divine]; and from the Nestorians . . . that Christ was simply a human being."

John was aware that Islam acknowledged Jesus as a prophet, who had been superseded by Muhammad—through whom God's will had finally and perfectly been communicated in the form of the Qur'an. But where, beyond the word of Muhammad, is the evidence to support any of this, asked John? He found the whole idea preposterous.

"Muhammad, the founder of Islam, is a false prophet who, by chance, came across the Old and New Testament, and who . . . thus devised his own heresy." John also criticized many of Muhammad's laws as faulty and erroneous, and was particularly skeptical of those related to marriage and divorce, which he suspected were merely self-serving. Or, as the *Catholic*

Encyclopedia puts it: John "vigorously assails the immoral practices of Muhammad and the corrupt teachings inserted in the Qur'an to legalize the delinquencies of the Prophet."

John continued to be a prolific writer until the end of his life (around 749), and his analysis of Islam remained the basis of Christian theological opposition to Muhammad's creed for many centuries. In addition, his adaptations of music for liturgical use is often credited with doing for the eastern church what Gregory the Great accomplished for the West. Some of his hymns are still in use today. Best known among them are two Easter hymns: "The day of Resurrection, earth tell it out abroad," and "Come, ye faithful, raise the strain of triumphant gladness," both translated by the nineteenth-century British scholar and clergyman John Mason Neale.

Once, a fellow monk, grief-stricken by the death of his brother, convinced John to write a hymn about death. Having been charged never to do anything simply because he wanted to do it, John was ordered to do penance. The penance, devised by his elder at the monastery, was to return to Damascus, where John had once been a distinguished official, and sell baskets at an outrageously high price—so that he could suffer scorn and rejection. John did as he was told. But, says the monastic tradition, the Virgin appeared in a vision and said that John must be allowed to write again because Christ desired it. So the elder withdrew the restriction, and the hymn became part of the funeral liturgy of the eastern church. It freely translates like this:

What earthly sweetness remains unmixed with grief?

What glory stands forever on earth?

All things are but feeble shadows or deluding dreams–

In only one moment, Death shall take their place.

But in the light of Thy countenance, O Christ,

And in the sweetness of Thy beauty,

Give rest to him whom Thou has chosen,

For Thou alone lovest mankind. ∎

JOHN ON THE POWER OF REASON

Man's reason unites him to incorporeal and intelligent natures, for he applies his reason and mind and judgment to everything, and pursues after virtues, and eagerly follows after piety, which is the crown of the virtues.

A youthful-looking Pope Gregory the Great, from an illustration by Antonello da Messina in the Galleria Nazionale della Sicilia, Palermo, Italy. Gregory was, in fact, already middle aged when he assumed the leadership of the western church.

CHAPTER 8

The man who laid the foundational unity of the Christian West

Out of chaos and anguish, Pope Gregory the Great rekindles united faith and purpose – in the nick of time

Had the Muslims vanquished the Christian countries of North Africa a half-century sooner, the results of their subsequent assault upon western Europe would unquestionably have been very different. Gazing across the Mediterranean toward Italy, France and Spain, they would have beheld a civilization still pulverized by barbarian invasions, religiously fragmented, and deep in a state of squalid savagery—a harvest ripe for the Muslim sickle.

But in those dark years, more than two decades before Muhammad began his war for the unity of the Arab peoples, a very different man of God had been diligently forging the unity of the Christian West. He seemed the epitome of paradox: implacable yet pliable; harsh yet merciful; pragmatic yet romantic; condemned by some nineteenth-century liberal scholars as unintellectual, yet his name is linked to a musical form that is arguably the greatest Christian cultural accomplishment of the era; and his spiritual works guided Christians through the entire Middle Ages.

Born to wealth and influence, this man renounced great possessions to become a monk, but was then yanked back to become bishop of Rome, and therefore, in the eyes of the faithful, successor to the apostle Peter. He would be known to later centuries as Pope Gregory the Great. As such, he was destined to play a key role in the preservation of the West against the Islamic onrush, although Islam was a term he never would have heard.

Two attributes in particular made Gregory great. One, that most indispensable yet unglamorous of gifts, was his superb talent for administration. With this skill he would provide Western Europe with what it would need most in the crisis that was coming, namely a respected authority and central leadership. He set the Christian church at the undisputed core of medieval western society.

The second vital attribute was his ability to discern and address the central anguish of his people. In a Europe where danger, disease, slavery, exhaustion, anxiety, agony and death lay on every side, he addressed the deep fear that can haunt believers in such times: How could a good God create such a world? Their experience seemed to say that either there was no God, or God was indifferent to the pains of his creatures, or God was himself evil. This was the terrible question raised by what some regard as the most remarkable work of ancient man, the Book of Job. In his commentary on that Old Testament work, Gregory faced it head-on, and provided the kind of reassurance that defeats despair.

Gregory became pope in the year 590. Western Europe was a chaos of barbarian kingdoms. Italy in particular had been reduced by nearly two centuries

Two attributes made Gregory great. His talent for administration gave Europe both respected authority and central leadership, and he set the church at the core of medieval western society.

of invasion and counterinvasion to a state of seemingly terminal devastation. Its latest attackers were the Lombards, a small but ferocious barbarian conglomerate that had streamed across the Alps twenty-two years earlier, and driven the forces of Byzantium out of much of the territory painfully regained under the emperor Justinian two decades before that. Now, as Lombard chieftains skirmished against the remaining imperial enclaves, and against each other, famine stalked the devastated countryside. City dwellers went hungry too. Plague followed close behind, and to these afflictions were added such disasters as storms and floods of unusual severity.

Two years prior to the Lombard incursion, for example, a pestilence notable for causing boils, fever, and swift death almost depopulated Italy's northeastern region of Liguria, writes the reputed "father of Italian history," Paul the Deacon, in his *Historia Langobardum*. Corpses lay unburied and "dread silence" covered the land. Famine struck in the year 570, and the year 589 brought down upon the countryside "a deluge of water . . . such as is believed not to have existed since the time of Noah," which washed out whole farms, carried off corpses of men and cattle, and obliterated highways.

At Rome, the waters of the Tiber crept up the city's walls, broke over them, and crashed into the low-lying sectors as people ran screaming ahead of them. It was said that "a great multitude of serpents, and a dragon of astonishing size, passed by the city and descended to the sea." This was straightway followed by "a very grievous pestilence called inguinal" (i.e., of the groin). In its train came another scourge chillingly described by Paul as "a scab disease of such a kind that no one could recognize his own dead on account of the great swelling and inflammation."

Gregory was meanwhile diligently pursuing his chosen vocation in St. Andrew's Monastery at Rome. Always frail of body, rendered faint by fasting, and afflicted by gout and bouts of malaria, he had decided as a young man to leave the life of public service that his family characteristically followed. Instead, he believed, his vocation was to serve God as a monk, through prayer, meditation and contemplation of the divine light within that gives clarity to the mind and peace to the soul. Twice before he had been summoned from his monastic life to serve the church in the world, but now in the year 589, at the age of almost fifty, he was finally at peace.

And so he might have continued, except that God apparently had other ideas. To Gregory's heartfelt chagrin, an urgent summons arrived from Pope Pelagius II, and the need was undeniable and immediate. With famine and plague simultaneously besetting Rome, said Pelagius, the citizens were panicking. Where could

Rome's Castel Sant' Angelo by night (below). The one time papal fortress on the banks of the Tiber was originally the mausoleum of Emperor Hadrian. It is now topped by a statue of an angel sheathing a sword, in memory of Gregory's vision in 590, promising the end of a deadly outbreak of plague.

they turn? Government itself seemed to have disappeared; the church must bear the whole burden, and he needed help. So Gregory agreed to become Pelagius's assistant, but worse was to follow. Early in 590, Pelagius himself died of plague; dread and despair now truly gripped the populace.

What could Gregory do, he must have wondered—he, a mere monk and papal secretary? The answer was clear. He must call the people to repentance, reassuring them of God's ultimate mercy. So he organized processions throughout the city that converged upon the Church of the Blessed Virgin. "We beseech thee, O Lord, in all thy mercy," the people chanted, "that thy wrath and thine anger may be removed from this city, and from thy holy house." Yet

Above Hadrian's mausoleum, Gregory beheld a fearsome vision. It was the archangel Michael, God's warrior, sword in hand. But he was sheathing the sword, not brandishing it!

1. After Gregory's fearful and hopeful vision of the warrior archangel Michael sheathing his sword above Hadrian's second-century mausoleum, the great building was renamed Castel Sant'Angelo (Holy Angel Castle). In the third century, although it remained the tomb of Hadrian and his family, the emperor Aurelian had converted it into a fortress. A fortress it would remain. In the thirteenth century, a fortified corridor was added to connect it to the Vatican, through which more than one pope would flee for his life.

2. Whitby, in Yorkshire, England, was perhaps the most famous example of a double monastery for both monks and nuns. The *Life of Gregory* was written anonymously by a monk there, probably between 710 and 730, a century after Gregory's death. A Northumbrian, and considered a poor writer, he drew his material largely from oral tradition centered in Canterbury.

heaven seemed deaf to their pleas. During one of these processions, writes Paul the Deacon, eighty people fell dead in a single hour. Was this God's answer?

Then, glowing above the massive mausoleum of the emperor Hadrian, Gregory beheld a fearsome vision. It was the archangel Michael, he said, God's warrior, sword in hand. But look! There was something else. The great angel was sheathing his sword, not brandishing it! The plague had been halted, Gregory declared. And so it had.[1] Meanwhile, the citizenry had reached an unshakable decision. Gregory must become their next bishop. His horror at such a prospect became the stuff of legend. An occasional summons to meet some crisis was one thing. But bishop of Rome? From such an office there could be no escape—it was a lifetime sentence.

He sought to flee the city, says the document called *The Earliest Life of Gregory the Great*, written by "an Anonymous Monk of Whitby."[2] Finding all the city gates guarded to prevent his escape, he had himself smuggled out in a barrel and then hid in a nearby wood, but the people, guided by a heavenly vision, found him and brought him back. Less dramatic testimony to his reluctance also exists. He wrote a letter begging the emperor Maurice not to confirm his election, but city officials intercepted it, and substituted a contrary plea of their own. The imperial imprimatur arrived late that summer.

Thus it was that on September 3, 590, before the high altar of the old St. Peter's Basilica built by Constantine, amidst heartfelt psalms of praise, this would-be contemplative monk was consecrated bishop of Rome, sole apostolic see in all the west. Gregory himself did not rejoice. "Under the color of the episcopate," he wrote to a friend, "I have been brought back into the world; I am enslaved to greater earthly cares than I ever remember to have been subjected to as a layman." Filled with foreboding, he added: "I fear greatly for those who have been committed to me."

Certainly, he faced an intimidating prospect. Around him lay the crumbling city of Rome, once the capital of the world, and now the shabby capital of one small and impoverished region, whose abandoned agricultural lands were reverting to wilderness. Beyond Italy, things were little better. Recurrent plagues after 542 had killed an estimated one-third of the empire's population. People scarcely wept anymore, wrote the historian John of Ephesus. "They were stunned as if giddy with wine. They were smitten in their hearts and had become numb." Gregory concurred. "All is destroyed, bones and flesh alike, all the glories and lawful institutions of the world," he wrote. "What is left to the few who survive?"

Gregory's most hideously pressing problem was security—primarily security against the Lombards. In 568, three years after the death of Justinian, they had come over the Alps as ostensible allies of the Byzantines. Soon, the allies became invaders and rampaged through the whole northern peninsula so ferociously that most cities surrendered without resistance, thereby reducing their peoples to Lombard slavery.

In the ensuing two decades, the Lombards had established a collection of feuding duchies in the north, and two large ones southward: Benevento and Spoleto, both ravenously eyeing what was left of Rome. Neither of these ever actually attacked the city, but constantly threatened it, and periodically tried to starve it through blockades. Between the northern and southern Lombard duchies, the Byzantines maintained control of a corridor running from Rome in the west to Ravenna in the east—roughly the area that a century and a half later would become the papal states.

Soon after Gregory's consecration, Spoleto began a new offensive against the city, directed by its duke Ariulf. Gregory persistently describes this chieftain as the "unspeakable Ariulf," since his wanton cruelty was considered remarkable even by Lombard standards. How ironic it would be, the pope lamented, if the once-great city of Rome should fall not even to a king, but to "a mere duke." With Ariulf's troops very near, "killing and mutilating," he appealed to the Byzantine exarch in Ravenna for help. No help was available, the exarch replied.

So the pope opened personal negotiations with the "unspeakable" Ariulf, with notable results.[3] According to Paul the Deacon, when the duke met with Gregory, "his heart was touched by divine grace, and he perceived there was so much force in the pontiff's words that with most humble courtesy he made satisfaction. . . ." A treaty was signed; Gregory agreed to an undisclosed payment of money, and Ariulf's men withdrew. But the treaty failed to keep the peace for long, because of Gregory's second greatest problem: Constantinople, which insisted that it still ruled Italy, though it could now maintain no more than several precarious toeholds.

On this occasion, the current emperor, Maurice, repudiated the treaty, severely reprimanding Gregory for presumption. To Maurice, the Lombards were not a nation, nor even a people, but a collection of renegade robbers with whom no treaty must

3. Aside from his personal impression of Gregory, Duke Ariulf of Spoleto seemingly had another reason to listen to the Christian prelate. While fighting the Byzantines on the Adriatic coast, writes Paul the Deacon, he perceived a mighty warrior guarding his flank. His men denied seeing any such person, but when Ariulf later saw an icon of a local saint, Sabinus, in the nearby basilica, he stopped short, crying: "That is the face and that is the figure of the man who guarded me in the fight!"

GREGORY THE GREAT ON JOY FOR THE CONVERTED SINNER

There is more joy in heaven over a converted sinner than over a righteous person standing firm. A farmer has greater love for land that bears fruitfully after he has cleared it of thorns, than for land which never had thorns but which never yielded a fruitful harvest.

ever be made. Gregory replied that he did what had to be done, adding grimly that he was assuredly not motivated by fondness for Lombards. "For my sins," he once wrote to a friend, "I find myself bishop not of Romans but of Lombards, whose promises stab like swords and whose kindness is bitter punishment." The Byzantines (who often seemed little better) took advantage of Gregory's treaty to recapture seven Lombard-held towns along the corridor—whereupon the Lombards recaptured the towns, and laid siege to Rome as well.

There Gregory had been preaching daily in St. Peter's on the apocalyptic prophecies of Ezekiel: "Where are they who aforetime rejoiced in her magnificence? Where is all their pomp, their pride, their frequently disordered revelry? Lo, she sitteth desolate. . . ." The suffering citizenry needed no reminder of the biblical applicability of this. From the city walls, they could see their fellow citizens, chained together by the neck, being led off for sale as slaves. Starving and mutilated refugees, some with their hands chopped off, crept up to the gates. Gregory tried to ransom as many prisoners as possible, authorizing bishops to sell sacred vessels if necessary.

He even took charge of routine civic needs—raising money, for example, to repair aqueducts. By now, in the estimation of church historian W. H. Hutton (*Cambridge Medieval History*), Gregory was the actual ruler of Rome and central Italy, both spiritually and temporally, although this could not be openly recognized. By 595, five years into his fourteen-year papacy, he worked out the terms of another treaty with Ariulf and other Lombard dukes. If Constantinople didn't want to sign it, he said, he could do so on behalf of the city alone.

These direct negotiations brought down upon him Maurice's full fury, with accusations of lying, disloyalty, and even stupidity. Obviously, the emperor charged, Gregory was Ariulf's dupe. "If the captivity of our land were not daily and hourly increasing," the pope replied with dignity, "I would gladly hold my peace as to the contempt and derision that are poured upon me." But as things stood, he protested, he could not remain silent. And he, too, had complaints. Why had Maurice repudiated his compact with Spoleto? And why were there no imperial troops to defend Rome? How could the emperor criticize the way the city was trying to defend itself, when the empire was doing so little in this regard?

The emperor, being himself thoroughly Christian (and soon to be martyred, along with his family, and one day canonized by the Eastern Church), went directly into theology. He threatened Gregory with "the terrible judgment of Almighty God." Retorted the pope: "We do not yet know how each man will appear on that day. . . . I will say this, however, that as an unworthy sinner I have more hope from the mercy of Jesus when he comes than I have from the justice of your piety. . . . Perchance the things which you praise he will blame, and those which you blame he will praise."

Such language struck the historian Thomas Hodgkin (*Italy and her Invaders*) as "bold almost to insolence." Nevertheless, a two-year truce was forged in 599 between the Lombards and Constantinople. Italy's imperial authorities had finally realized that the Lombards were there to stay, and must be recognized. This truce was soon broken by the Byzantines, replaced by another that was broken by the Lombards, and again replaced. But at least a peace process was under way. When Muslim raiders—always the harbingers of Muslim conquest—arrived in southern Italy a century and a half later, they would meet with a united resistance centered upon Rome and its bishop.

Small concern for Italy's well-being could even now be expected from Constantinople, however, a fact that Gregory had learned long since. A public servant born and bred, he was the son of a Roman senator, and a scion of the powerful and pious Anicii family. (Some scholars say Pope Felix III, 483–492, was an ancester.) Schooled in both law and humanities, he had been appointed prefect of Rome at thirty-three, presiding at Senate meetings, and responsible for police matters and certain courts of law.

His chief early biographer, a ninth-century monk called John the Deacon, (not to be confused with the eighth-century Lombard historian, Paul), provides a physical description of Gregory in middle life, based on a fresco portrait still preserved in John's time at St. Andrew's Monastery. It showed a man of medium height and sturdy build, John says, with a bald head fringed by dark hair, dark eyes, somewhat aquiline nose, full lips, swarthy complexion and prominent chin. Wearing the formal dress of his day, he gazed out mildly from the picture.

His portrait notwithstanding, neither formality nor mildness figured prominently in Gregory's reputation.

GREGORY THE GREAT ON SEEING CHRIST IN EVERYONE

When you see any abject persons in this world, even if their deeds seem blameworthy do not look down upon them. Then their vices bring about an increase of holiness in you. But we see many people of whose merits we are unaware. Therefore we must honor them all, and you must humble yourself before everyone, inasmuch as you do not know who among them may be Christ.

GREGORY THE GREAT ON DENIAL OF SELF

It may not be difficult for a man to abandon his possessions, but it is very difficult for him to abandon himself. Renouncing what one has is not so much, but renouncing what one is amounts to a great deal. The Lord commands those of us who are coming to him to deny ourselves because we who are coming to the public contest of the faith are taking up a struggle against evil spirits.

Decisiveness, determination and dedication were more his style, as typified by the fact that upon the death of his father, he had immediately sold the family estate, and spent the proceeds on relief for the poor and the endowment of seven Benedictine monasteries. One of them was St. Andrew's, installed in his ancestral home on Rome's Coelian Hill, where Gregory himself was admitted as a humble lay brother.[4] But he never did succeed in escaping the world.

First, Pope Benedict I insisted upon ordaining him one of the "deacons of Rome," in charge of distributing alms in one of the city's seven divisions. Then Pelagius II dispatched him to the court of the emperor Maurice to plead (in vain) for military and other assistance. This firsthand experience of eastern politics thoroughly soured him on Constantinople—and afforded an early glimpse of his future. Except for certain good friends, he seemingly disliked the city, the court, and the emperor Maurice, too. He also became convinced Rome could only be saved by a man on the spot, and independent of Constantinople—not realizing that one day he would become that man.

That Constantinople should consistently obstruct his efforts to restore the failing western empire must therefore have come as no real surprise, and the same would apply to his efforts at unifying the church. Upon his consecration, for example, he wrote to reassure the eastern bishops regarding his stand on the emperor Justinian's unsuccessful attempt to resolve the Monophysite controversy thirty-seven years earlier. (See earlier volume, *Darkness Descends*, pages 277 and 280.) Vigilius, bishop of Rome at that time, had vigorously opposed Justinian's formula, but Gregory, like other popes since, now fully accepted it.

This effort at amity unexpectedly backfired, however, when the bishops of Italy's whole northern region, the Lombard area, stubbornly reiterated their rejection of the Justinian compromise. Moreover, when Gregory tried to discipline them, they appealed to Maurice, and he backed them. "Afflict them no further in the present troubled state of Italy," the emperor ordered. Gregory argued long and eloquently, but obeyed.

Maurice's unwelcome theological endeavors underlined the inescapable central problem. Did the emperor run the church, or did the pope? "Give unto Caesar that which is Caesar's, and unto God that which is God's," Jesus had said (Matt. 22:21, Mk. 12:17, Lk. 20:25). Theoretically, the two should complement each other, and Gregory considered himself an entirely loyal subject. But the line between, always difficult, was made worse by the rooted assumption that imperial authority always trumped episcopal. This arrangement, later deplored by its critics as "Caesaropapism," would continue to cause serious problems throughout history whenever Christianity became the state religion.

In this respect, Italy, for all its tribulations, enjoyed an important advantage. With the emperor so far away, the western church had a degree of freedom not

4. Gregory drew his spiritual strength, his biographers say, from a personal monastic regime of prayer, meditation, reading and fasting, which he observed all his life as best he could. His household at the Lateran Palace was run in almost monastic style, its staff of clerics sharing an austere common life. Entertaining was not high on the agenda. As Gregory told one bishop accused of excessive banqueting, such lavish living was likely to lead to "gossip, slander and idle stories."

enjoyed by the eastern patriarchs. It was a freedom Gregory would exploit to engender in the new western monarchies a confidence in the papacy they would assuredly need in the coming clash with Islam. Even so, Gregory never did refuse a direct imperial order. He boldly argued, remonstrated and equivocated—but when push came to shove, he obeyed his emperor.

On some matters, of course, Gregory fully concurred with Constantinople. He agreed, for instance, that the unity of the West depended on general adherence to basic Christian belief as defined in 325 at the Council of Nicea, which decisively rejected Arianism. All the barbarian peoples, except the Franks, had come into the West as Arians, including "the despicable Lombards," as Gregory acidly referred to them. But even Lombards, he believed, could and should be saved. The true faith might enable God to amend their lives, "or if they should happen to die, as is more desirable, they might pass absolved from their crimes."

In the critical years preceding the Muslim invasions, all the tribes one by one did accept the Nicene view of Jesus. So too did the Lombards, through socialization, intermarriage and the efforts of the Italian clergy, constantly encouraged by Gregory. Notably contributing to this process was a remarkable Christian woman, Theodelinda. Born an orthodox Christian, she was married to a Lombard king, and upon his death, a strange succession took place. So respected was Theodelinda that the Lombard dukes agreed to accept as their sovereign whomever she now chose to marry. She chose Duke Angiluf, who proved satisfactory to the Lombards, and quite a strong ally of Gregory. Angiluf himself did not forsake Arianism, but agreed for example that his son be baptized a Nicene Christian. Gregory sent warm congratulations to Theodelinda, and gifts to the baby prince.

Meanwhile, his enthusiasm for missions bore lasting fruit. He sent Augustine to Canterbury, England, leading sixty years later to the unification of the church in Britain. (See subchapter that follows.) All over western Europe, he used the monks as powerful transmitters of divine grace, through lives dedicated wholly to God, often appointing them as bishops. He urged monasteries to operate according to rule, preferably the rule of St. Benedict, whom he greatly admired, and to whom he dedicated the entire second book of his four-volume *Dialogues*. The monk's service to God must be twofold, Gregory believed. He must seek God in the contemplative life, while also working out the Christian's duty to his fellow men. Those who aspire to "the citadel of contemplation" should first prove themselves in action among God's people in the world.

Gregory's liturgical and musical accomplishments exhibit the same theme: service to God and man. He wanted the best physical expression attainable of this duality, and his contribution to the Roman liturgy and sacred music is impressive. He established the Roman

GREGORY THE GREAT ON GOOD WILL

Nothing can be offered to God more precious than good will. Good will means to experience fear for the adversities of another as if they were our own, to give thanks for a neighbor's prosperity as for our own advancement, to believe another's loss is our own, to count another's gain our own, to choose to help a neighbor in need not only to the extent of your ability but even to assist him beyond your means.

Schola Cantorum (school of singers) at the Lateran, for instance, and his name is closely linked with the plainsong style of liturgical singing commonly known as "Gregorian chant."

As bishop of Rome, of course, he had wide ecclesiastical power. Among other prerogatives, he could grant or withhold confirmation of the election of most western bishops, and often did withhold it. In his hundreds of letters to prelates in Gaul, Spain and Africa, many of which survive, he freely advised, exhorted

A fourteen hundred-year-old hit

With its roots in the papal chapel, and sung by Roman orphans, Gregorian chant forms the basis of Western music and its popularity survives to the present day

In 1994, Spanish monks from Santo Domingo de Silos recorded their own Gregorian chant, a modest project with no grand aspirations. Unexpectedly, the disc racked up more than four million sales in forty-two countries. Their success stunned the producers, marketers, and no doubt the Benedictine monks themselves. For twenty-three weeks, fourteen hundred-year-old music competed among the top ten hits of the American pop chart with the likes of gangsta rapper Snoop Dogg and MTV's Beavis and Butthead. In Spain, fans began mobbing the cloistered monastery in disruptive numbers. "The irony of all this," producer Rafael Gil told *Billboard* magazine, "is that the music, which clearly relieves stress for most people, has brought the monks more stress than they'd ever known."

Guido's music staff in a twelfth-century manuscript of the Gloria in excelsis Deo *(left), held by the British Library, London. The number of lines in a staff was not yet standardized (here four are used). Groups of notes called* neumes *represent pitch; symbols for rhythm came later.*

Gregorian chant, ancient itself, has still more ancient roots. Early Christians adopted the familiar Jewish psalmody, which in turn was highly influenced by pagan music in Egypt. Evidence of antiphonal singing (i.e., two sides of a congregation taking turns) can be traced back to ancient Babylon and Sumeria. The Celtic tradition provides one tantalizing example of how music traveled in the ancient world; the psalmody still found in some remote Gaelic communities bears a striking resemblance to that practiced by the desert monks of Egypt.

During the second to fourth centuries, hymns were increasingly used as vehicles for theological instruction, intercessions and seasonal celebrations, as well as for praise and thanksgiving. In the second century, Melito of Sardis's "Homily" magnificently greets the Easter feast:[1]

> Born as a Son,
> Led like a lamb,
> Sacrificed like a sheep,
> Buried as a man,
> He rises from the dead as God,
> Being by nature both God and man.
> He is all things;
> When he judges, he is Law,
> When he teaches, Word,
> When he saves, grace,
> When he begets, father,
> When he is begotten, son,
> When he suffers, lamb,
> When he is buried, man,
> When he rises, God.
> It is I, says Christ,
> I who have destroyed death,
> And triumphed over the enemy
> And trodden hell under foot,
> And chained the strong men,
> And brought man to the heights of heaven.
> It is I! says Christ.

and rebuked, always with the clear underlying assumption that ultimate authority over them resided in the Apostolic See of Peter. His *Liber Regulae Pastoralis* became the veritable textbook of the medieval episcopate, and continues in use today as a manual guiding Catholic bishops. England's future King Alfred reputedly translated it into Old English, and it circulated widely in Gaul. In the ninth century, Hincmar, archbishop of Rheims, reported that every bishop at his consecration was given a copy.

Less formal is another ninth-century Easter hymn by the Irishman Sedulius Scotus, addressed to Archbishop Tado of Milan and delighting in images of the Resurrection found in nature. Here is John McGuckin's translation:

> Christ, our True Sun,
> last night from darkness rose,
> And in the Lord's fields,
> the mystic harvest now is springing up.
> The wandering clan of bees,
> happy in their chores,
> Murmur far through scarlet flowers,
> gathering their honey about.
> How many birds now soften the air with melody,
> And as dusk falls the nightingale
> modulates her song,
> While in the church
> the choir chants hymns of Sion,
> And in its various modes
> sing Alleluias hundredfold.
> Tado, father of your people,
> the joys of this celestial Pasch,
> the threshold of the light,
> Are rightly yours. All Hail.

Hymns reflected both the temporal and the eternal, as in this intensely personal hymn written by St. Gregory Nazianzen in the fourth century:

> All thanks to you, the King of All,
> And Maker of all things.
> All thanks to you who by your Word,
> Commanded spiritual and material forms,
> And summoned into being
> What was not there before...
> And yet, I too shall make my prayer:
> Immortal Father,
> Before you I shall bend the knee,
> To signify my heart;
> Immortal Father,
> In your presence, I lay down
> My inmost mind prostrate.
> I rest my brow upon the ground,
> To make my prayer to you.
> And so I lie, a suppliant.

Early hymns were frequently composed for the purpose of private devotions. As observed by Ian Bradley in *Celtic Christian Communities*, the prayers and hymns of the earliest Celtic tradition "are for reciting in the kitchen, the bedroom, the milking parlor and the fishing boat rather than in the pew." Hymns were personal, earthy, humble and intimate, as these verses demonstrate:[2]

> God, and Spirit, and Jesus,
> From the crown of my head
> To the soles of my feet;
> Come I with my reputation,
> Come I with my testimony,
> Come I to Thee, Jesu –
> Jesu, shelter me.
>
> God, bless Thou Thyself my reaping
> Each ridge, and plain, and field,
> Each sickle curved, shapely, hard,
> Each ear and handful in the sheaf,
> Each ear and handful in the sheaf.
>
> Come, Mary, and milk my cow,
> Come, Bridget, and encompass her,
> Come, Columba the benign,
> And twine thine arms around my cow.
> Ho my heifer, ho my gentle heifer,
> Ho my heifer, ho my gentle heifer,
> Ho my heifer, ho my gentle heifer,
> My heifer dear, generous and kind,
> For the sake of the High King take to thy calf.
>
> Bless, O Chief of generous chiefs,
> My loom and everything a-near me,
> Bless me in my every action,
> Make Thou me safe while I live.
>
> I will cast down my hook,
> The first fish which I bring up
> In the name of Christ, King of the elements,
> The poor shall have it at his wish.

There were, of course, formal composers of hymns for ceremonial occasions, generally monastics and bishops. Venantius Fortunatus, a sixth-century poet from northern Italy, whose influence lasted well into the Middle Ages, was considered to be the major literary figure of his time in Gaul. Two of his hymns are still well known today: *Pange Lingua* (Sing, my tongue, the glorious battle) and *Vexilla Regis* (The royal banners forward go).

The early church fathers condemned the use of musical instruments during worship. The flute,

While striving always for the unity of the West, Gregory was not insistent on complete uniformity of practice. "When there is one faith," he wrote to his Spanish friend, Bishop Leander of Seville, "difference of usage does no harm to the church." Therefore, he backed Leander in allowing the formerly Arian Spaniards to continue using single-immersion baptism, rather than the three immersions required in the Roman rite. Similarly, when Augustine of Canterbury asked what liturgical rite to use in Britain, Gregory did not simply order him to use the Roman or Gallic mass. He advised Augustine to ascertain

tambourine and cymbal had strong associations with pagan ritual, while the disreputable circus and theater employed the hydraulus (ancestor of the modern organ). The *Canons of Basil* (373) decree that: "If a lector learns to play the guitar, he shall also be taught to confess it. If he does not return to it he shall suffer his penance for seven weeks. If he keeps at it he shall be excommunicated and put out of the church."

To this day, the Eastern Orthodox churches sing *a capella* (unaccompanied). But other traditions follow the Old Testament, which sanctions the use of instruments in sacred music. Among the Copts, cymbals and triangles accompany the liturgy. Ethiopians use drums, as well as hand-clapping and rhythmic dancing. In the West, the hydraulus was rehabilitated as early as the seventh century, to train and accompany singers.

Gregorian chant, another characteristic western musical expression, began in the papal chapel.[3] In the fifth century, a *schola cantorum* (choir school) was created in Rome, possibly doubling as an orphanage. The chants are simple, generally staying within the range of an octave, with melodic lines that followed the natural stresses of the text. (Earlier, church chant likely consisted of lines sung in monotone, with a change up or down only on the final word.) An envoy from Gaul brought the innovation to the attention of his king. A Gallic schola cantorum, established in Metz, disseminated Gregorian chant across western Europe.

By the eleventh century, the repertoire of chants had become too large to memorize. Rudimentary musical symbols first consisted of markings to indicate inflection, accent and length of notes. A crucial breakthrough was achieved by an eleventh-century monk, Guido d'Arezzo. Thanks to this Italian Benedictine's invention of the staff, which enables pitch

to be recorded accurately, the western world acquired its first method of music notation. On that foundation, virtually all of modern music has been erected. ∎

1. The greatest translator of ancient hymns is undisputedly the English Victorian John Mason Neale, whose carefully crafted and poetic translations, still appearing in new hymn books, are familiar to Western churches. His *Hymns of the Eastern Church* introduced to the West this previously unavailable resource, some of which existed only in fragments. Ancient Greek hymns pose particular problems in translation, as their prose/free verse form is difficult to convert to rhymed meters while still retaining the original meaning.

2. These verses are from the collection *Carmina Gadelica*, collected by Alexander Carmichael in the mid-nineteenth century. Carmichael was a customs and excise inspector who traveled the Scottish Highlands and islands on foot and by sea in the course of his work. His passion for recording the ancient hymns and poems resulted in six volumes of collected material, and an honorary degree from Edinburgh University.

3. Pope Gregory's role in helping to popularize the music named after him is not clear. This doctor of the church did not compose music nor did he refer to it in his writing, but he assuredly encouraged its development.

Gregory the Great teaching a group of boys to sing (above), from a nineteenth-century illustration by John Rogers Herbert. The style of music we know as Gregorian chant began in the papal chapel during Gregory's lifetime. There was already a well-established choir school in Rome, which may also have doubled as a home for children orphaned by the plague or the rampaging Lombards.

which one would best please God and the English converts.[5]

So too with the Jews, whose position within the empire was restricted by imperial legislation. Gregory approved this restrictive legislation, and urged the Visigothic monarchy in Spain to duplicate it, but within its limits he insisted that the rights of Jews as Roman citizens be rigorously observed, and that they be treated with scrupulous fairness. He saw the Jewish people as sadly blind in not recognizing that the great messianic promise of their own scriptures had in fact been fulfilled. But he forbade attempts to forcibly convert them, "lest those whom the sweetness of preaching and the fear of future judgment might have invited to believe be repelled by threats and terrors." Besides, he argued, conversions by force were never sincere. On the other hand, however, some gentle encouragement, such as a lower rent or tax, would not be amiss.

But quite another side of his personality is evidenced by six years of vehement correspondence with state and church officials in Africa, urging punitive action

Gregory urged the Visigoths to duplicate laws restricting Jews, but insisted their rights as citizens be rigorously observed, and that they be treated with scrupulous fairness.

against both the Donatists and the remaining pagan peoples there. Donatism had emerged after the imperial persecutions of the third century. (See earlier volume, *By This Sign*, chapter 6.) Strictly speaking, Donatism began as a schism, not a heresy, but over time had become both heretical and extremely violent, resorting to what a later generation would call terrorism. Against the Donatists, Gregory demanded stern measures, including beating and torture.

Probably the best portrait of the man comes not from his biographers, but from himself. Of his voluminous correspondence, some eight hundred letters survive, encompassing personal, ecclesiastical, governmental, diplomatic and administrative activity, many of them written by a man too sick to rise from his bed.[6] Many involve real estate. By the end of the eighth century, writes Prosper Boissonnade in his *Life and Work in Medieval Europe*, fully one-third of the soil of Western Europe would belong to the church. Eighteen hundred square miles of it belonged to the see of Rome. Known as the "Patrimony of St. Peter," it consisted of more than four hundred rural estates, most of them in Sicily, which produced wealth to support the church, its monasteries and convents, and its numerous charities.

Management was delegated to local officials called "rectors (rulers) of the patrimony." One was a subdeacon named Peter, responsible for the Sicilian estates, and Gregory's instructions to him are exhaustive. Peter must ensure that all dealings are scrupulously honest (fair prices, no false measures, loans when necessary, respect for boundaries, no harboring of runaway slaves). But would Peter also please keep in mind that the purpose of the patrimony was to produce revenue? What, for instance, was the point in maintaining all these stud horses, while receiving hardly

5. The missionary monk Columbanus wanted Pope Gregory to arbitrarily command the Irish to celebrate Easter on the same date as the rest of the West. Gregory demurred, mildly replying that the deviant Irish dating was of long standing, and seemingly had done little harm. Columbanus, also a stubborn man, kept on arguing; Gregory just didn't answer. Columbanus, it is said, blamed Satan for misdirecting his correspondence.

6. It is noteworthy that Gregory maintained his mammoth workload despite constant illness. "It is now all but two years that I have been confined to my bed," he wrote to the patriarch of Alexandria in 599, "and so tortured with the pains of gout that scarcely on festival days have I been able to rise for the space of three hours to celebrate the rites of the Mass."

GREGORY THE GREAT ON LOVE
The commands of the Lord are many, and yet one—many in the different things to be done, one in the root of love.

7. In one letter to Peter, the steward in charge of administering the vast Sicilian estates under Rome's direct control, Pope Gregory berates him for sending him "one miserable horse and five good donkeys" to use as transport in Rome. He can't ride the horse, he complains, because it is miserable, and he can't ride the donkeys because they are donkeys.

8. Still another of Gregory's epistles informs an elderly bishop (whom Gregory apparently considers "simple," perhaps on account of extreme age) that he will not punish him for certain unacceptable behavior. However, he issues a stern warning: "Since we still spare your gray hairs, we exhort you, wretched old man, to think ahead, and restrain from such levity of manners and perversity of deeds."

any stud fees? "It is a very hard thing that we should be paying sixty *solidi* a year to our stud-grooms, and not receiving one eighteenth as much back."[7]

Peter had also to represent the pope in weightier matters. He must recommend suitable candidates for the priesthood and for vacant bishoprics. He was to tactfully persuade a certain bishop to be less severe. He was to mediate a dispute between another bishop and a neighboring aristocrat. He was to depose an unsatisfactory abbot. Peter, it appears, lasted eighteen months on the job and quit.

Gregory made tough demands on his clergy as well. "Bad priests are the cause of people's ruin, and what is only a fault in a layman is a crime in a clergyman." Offsetting his demands, however, are flashes of wit and humor. How fortuitously God has arranged things, he observes. We no sooner congratulate ourselves on some great gift we possess, for example, than we are humbled by the unpleasant discovery of one we lack.

Then, too, there are endless letters meeting the concerns of individual people: arrangements for the care of the orphaned daughters of the great poet Venantius Fortunatus; instructions to a rector to pay the debts of a Syrian merchant whose creditors will otherwise seize his son;[8] and an appeal to his old friend, Bishop Marinianus of Ravenna, who is ill and vomiting blood, to come to Rome and be cured. Failing a cure, Gregory tells Marinianus, "whichever of us God calls first" could die in the other's arms.

Not a few letters are extremely severe, of course, such as the one summoning to Rome a certain Bishop Maximus, newly elected in what is now Croatia. Although his consecration had been approved by the emperor, Gregory charged that Maximus had lived an evil life, and had purchased his episcopal votes. Maximus not only defied the summons, but countered with a false allegation that Gregory himself had murdered another bishop. This wrangle continued for several years, but Gregory prevailed. Maximus wound up lying prostrate on a church pavement and declaiming, "I have sinned against God and the most blessed pope Gregory." After that, Gregory allowed him to assume his episcopacy.

Not that he won all his battles. One lost cause was his virulent campaign against the continuing use of the term "ecumenical bishop" (i.e., "universal bishop") by the patriarchs of Constantinople. Rome had long been mildly annoyed by this and in 595, when the patriarch John repeated the title over and over again in one routine document Gregory blew up. No bishop should be subjected to the headship of anyone but Jesus Christ himself, he insisted. To address anyone—emphatically including himself—as "universal bishop" was a profane and wicked idea. (Gregory referred to himself as the "servant of the servants of God.")

When John refused to back down, and the emperor approved the use of the offending title, and the patriarchs of Antioch and Alexandria seemed indifferent, Gregory angrily broke off communion with Constantinople. Succeeding patriarchs nevertheless continued to use the title, and a century later Rome itself would begin to apply it to the pope. But at the time, writes J. B. Bury (*A History of the Later Roman Empire*), the "ecumenical bishop" fight was one of many irritants that arguably justify dating Christendom's final east–west schism to the reign of Maurice and the pontificate of Gregory I.

Undoubtedly Gregory's greatest miscall, however, was the panegyric he dispatched to the new emperor Phocas after the death of Maurice. This effusion begins like a liturgy: "Let the heavens rejoice and the earth be glad!" It continues in the same tone: "By your benign actions may all the citizens of our Republic, until now so grievously afflicted, regain their cheerfulness of soul. . . . I delight to think, with a grateful heart, what praise is due to Almighty God for removing the yoke of our sadness. . . ." And more of the same.

Did Gregory not know that Maurice and his sons were butchered by Phocas, and Maurice died a very Christian death? (See page 134.) Did he not foresee that Maurice's widow and children would soon be murdered as well, and that from Phocas's record, it was altogether clear what kind of emperor he would be? Whatever his personal feelings, say his defenders, Gregory was naturally obliged to acknowledge the new ruler or perhaps, he really did not know the frightful details of Maurice's death. Whatever the explanation, his encomium to one of the worst of all emperors stands as a stain on an otherwise exemplary life.

Other than this, the chief accusations historians bring against Gregory are that he never did learn Greek, scorned the Roman classics as heathen, and lacked literary polish. His nineteenth-century translator, James Barmby (writing in Britain's great liberal era), accuses him of naiveté. His accounts of the Latin saints are tales of marvels, Barmby writes, childish, grotesque, and not "edifying to readers of the present day," and his biblical scholarship is "utterly incompetent." Bury faults Gregory's language as lacking in academic polish, and Gregory himself for having "launched the church into the waters of ignorance and barbarism."

In the twentieth century, however, Bishop Gregory has fared better than his critics. Some today regard Barmby's translation as almost unintelligible, while the erudite Bury is seen as having failed to appreciate the horrors being endured by Gregory's flock, the people to whom his biblical and spiritual writings are primarily addressed. Gregory was not writing for academic, literary or artistic approval, but

GREGORY THE GREAT ON THE TRANSIENCE OF THIS WORLD

Every day the earth is visited by fresh calamities. You see how few remain of the ancient population: each day sees us chastened by new afflictions, and unforeseen blows strike us to the ground. The world grows old and hoary, and through a sea of troubles hastens to approaching death. Therefore, my friends, do not love what you see cannot long exist.

9. Practical man that he was, Gregory was no anti-academic, but he had strong opinions on dishonest scholarship, false reason and aberrant literary style, too. "The wisdom of this world is concealing the heart with stratagems," he wrote, "veiling meaning with verbiage, proving the false to be right and the true to be false. . . . This perversity of mind is called urbanity . . . while the wisdom of the just is scoffed at, because the virtue of purity is reckoned by the wise of this world to be fatuity."

for the benefit of people facing death, destitution and despair.[9] He clearly understood the fragility of civilized order in what Augustine called "the City of Man," writes the late twentieth-century historian R. A. Markus (*Gregory the Great and his World*). Nothing evidences this better than his most ambitious literary work, the *Magna Moralia*, an extensive allegory based on Job, a biblical subject that few ancient commentators, and not many modern ones, hasten to tackle.

In this thirty-five-volume work, totaling more than five-hundred-thousand words, Gregory, a man for whom pain had become a way of life, sought to bring meaning and purpose to the suffering that much of his flock was day by day enduring. In the Old Testament, Job is portrayed as a God-fearing and prosperous individual whose faith, says the devil, will evaporate if his riches are removed, and he will curse God. So God permits Satan to take them away, one by one, until Job is utterly destitute and stricken with disease, trying through dialogues with three friends to fathom what has befallen him. But though dumbfounded by his fate, Job does not yield to despair. He declares his faith in words like those which Handel would make memorable in one of the great arias of his oratorio, *The Messiah*: "I

Gregory's response was not to promise that suffering would cease, because he knew it would not, but rather to give it purpose. 'Unless [the soul] sighs, it does not eat,' he writes.

know that my Redeemer liveth, and that he shall stand at the latter day upon the earth" (Job 19:25). In the end, God restores Job and doubles his wealth.

What did this have to teach the Christians who clung to their faith through famine, disease, war and death? Gregory's response was not to promise that the suffering would cease, because he knew it would not, but rather to give it purpose. "Unless [the soul] sighs, it does not eat," he writes. "The prophet sighed and ate when he said, 'My tears were bread to me.'" God takes satisfaction in driving his saints toward repentance and reconciliation, a process that can be learned from example: "Virtue acts quietly, but the recognition of virtue is stirred up by the whip. Left alone, Job kept what he was to himself; beset by troubles, he brought the sweet odor of his fortitude to the notice of all. It is that way with ointments that do not spread their scent abroad unless they are stirred up, and with incenses that do not give off their aroma unless they are burned."

So what is the fundamental purpose of pain? Willingly accepted, says Gregory, it wards off the danger of eternal damnation. Accompanied by intense longing for God, pain can open a door through which floods God's exquisite light. He knew from his own painful experience that this was the peace, which, as Paul said, "passes all human understanding." In short, pain can foster virtue and end in triumph. To western European and North American Christians of the late-twentieth century, this would seem a harsh and strident message. To sixth-century Christians in Italy under the Lombards, or twenty-first-century Christians in Sudan, living under the Muslims, it would evoke a very different response. It transformed personal hardship, a trigger for despair for the natural man, into a powerful signal of hope for the Christian.

Unlike Job, however, Gregory the Great did not die with all his problems solved. When he went to his grave at the east end of the Basilica of St. Peter, beneath the altar to St. Andrew on or about March 12, 604, the Lombard problem, though easing, was far from over. Rome was again in the grip of a famine, and most no doubt expected further and more horrible plagues.

When his successor as bishop of Rome, Sabinianus, cut off free rations in the city, riots followed. Some actually complained that Gregory had caused the shortage by his many lavish expenditures—the very largesse from which they themselves had so often benefited. A furious mob sought to burn his books, but a courageous assistant calmed the crowd by convincing them that he had often seen the Holy Spirit, in the form of a dove, hovering near Pope Gregory when he was writing those very books. The books were saved, and very soon afterward, their author was canonized by popular acclamation.

Though the problems of Western Europe remained unsolved, where to look for solutions had been clearly established. The critical James Barmby provides an admirable summation: "It is impossible to conceive," he writes, "what would have been the confusion, the lawlessness, the chaotic state of the Middle Ages without the medieval papacy; and of the medieval papacy, the real father is Gregory the Great." The ultimate authority in the former empire was no longer in any doubt. It had once resided in a Roman emperor. Henceforth, it would reside in a Roman bishop, and it would be he, more than any king, who would stir the spirit that stopped, and kept stopped, the Muslim onslaught in the west. ■

This seventeenth-century painting by Rutilio Manetti (below), as in so many later depictions of Gregory the Great, shows him with a dove at his shoulder. At Gregory's death, an assistant prevented an angry mob from destroying the pope's writings by insisting that he had often seen the Holy Spirit, in the form of a dove, hovering over Gregory as he worked.

Bright lights in a dark world

In turbulent and dangerous times, six saints personify the enduring faith and piety of Christians who through their accomplishments and example illuminate the world

A master coin maker who despised wealth

Eloy of Noyon, senior counselor to the seventh-century Frankish king Dagobert, and master of minting his coinage, had an unusual home life. Beggars and cripples constantly surrounded his stately house in Marseilles. Every day, Eloy would personally tend to this miserable flock, washing their feet and distributing charity. Such behavior by the equivalent of a modern cabinet secretary amazed people just as much then as it would today.

Eloy was born in Gaul in 590. His father, recognizing exceptional talent in his boy, sent him to apprentice with Abbo, master of the mint at Limoges. Clotar II, the Franks' monarch at that time, later commissioned the young craftsman to design and construct a throne. The resulting creation so impressed the king that he took Eloy into his palace, and appointed him master of the main mint at Marseilles.

Despite his new position, Eloy came to despise worldly wealth. First, he devoted his income to almsgiving and ransoming prisoners from the slave markets. When his funds were finally exhausted, the zealous bureaucrat gave away his furniture and clothing.

Eloy quickly won the confidence of Clotar's successor, Dagobert I, who came to the throne in 629. The Christian counselor used his influence to found monasteries and convents at Solignac and Paris, assuring the king, "These are the ladders by which we will both be able to climb up to heaven." He also helped reestablish peace between the Franks and Bretons, improved the law of the kingdom, and convinced Dagobert that those who had been executed should be given a Christian burial.

In 639, Eloy was consecrated a priest, and made bishop of Noyon in Flanders, part of France, in the same year. He traveled and preached throughout his mostly pagan diocese, often risking his life. Much of Flanders embraced Christ as a result. This holy man, later canonized by the church, died in 660. According to the pious tradition, when his tomb was opened a year later, the body was found unspoiled and exuding a pleasing scent.

This patriarch served 7,500 masters

John the Almoner (550–611), upon his consecration as the orthodox patriarch of Alexandria in 608, ordered his staff to draw up a list of his "masters." His assistants reacted with astonishment. Who, they asked, might these masters be? "Those whom you call paupers and beggars," John replied, "I call lords and helpers, for they truly help us, and grant us the kingdom of heaven." He became known as the Almoner (almsgiver) for his generosity, and was soon doling out a generous ration of daily benefits to the astonishing number of seventy-five-hundred poor people.

John was born to noble parents in Cyprus. After disease killed his wife and children, he had entered religious life, distributing all of his wealth to the poor. Well beyond age fifty, his reputation for piety had earned him the patriarchate. But his large-scale charity drew envious eyes. The Byzantine governor Nicetas approached him one day, demanding church money for the state. "What is offered to the heavenly King must not be given to an earthly," came the answer. Nonetheless, John revealed the whereabouts of the cash (it was under his bed), leaving the decision to Nicetas. The governor seized the money. Unperturbed and still kindly, John subsequently sent a personal gift to the royal official. Nicetas, conscience smitten, returned the original money, adding a substantial bonus from his own funds.

A horde of refugees fled to Alexandria when the Persians conquered Palestine with great cruelty. (See page 136.) The patriarch John, whose own diet and furnishings were exceedingly austere, had almshouses and hospitals built for the sick and wounded, and sent a huge supply of necessities to aid in the rebuilding of Jerusalem. On becoming aware that his death was imminent, the patriarch returned to his Cypriot birthplace, and left this world in 611 with great peace.

The stubborn witness got his tongue torn out

Maximus the Confessor (580–662) was a Christian of sharp and remarkably stubborn mind. In 662, the imperial court at Constantinople publicly ordered the eighty-two-year-old churchman to accept the Monothelite precept that Christ possessed only one divine will. But Maximus refused. The emperor Constans II, knowing that neither an earlier exile nor previous bribery attempts had moved the man, ordered him flogged, his right arm cut off, and his tongue torn out. The mutilated offender was then paraded through the streets as an example, and sent into exile, where he soon died.

Born of noble family, this native of Constantinople had become the highly valued secretary to Emperor

Heraclius. Seeking the contemplative life, he moved to Chrysopolis, a monastery outside the capital. Fleeing the Persian siege, Maximus later spent time in Rome, where Pope Martin had become the focal point of resistance to Monothelitism. In fact, the Greek-speaking Maximus strongly advocated papal primacy, arguing that "from the coming down of the incarnate Word amongst us, all the churches in every part of the world have held that greatest church alone [i.e., Rome] as their base and foundation. . . ."

After his arrest in Rome on imperial order for rejecting Monothelitism, Maximus endured six years of exile in Thrace, where he suffered from the intense cold and from hunger. Assuming he had by now had enough, Byzantine clergy were sent by the court to secure his recantation. They found him not only defiant, but also so persuasive in his views that they themselves began agreeing with the rebel. From Thrace, Maximus went to his trial and death in Constantinople. His many writings, still honored in both the Roman and Orthodox traditions, stress the complementary union of man with God as adopted sons of God through baptism and other sacraments, leading ultimately to holy living and contemplation.

Dozing deacon awakes as a superb poet

Romanus the Melodist, a sixth-century deacon from Syria, visited Constantinople's Church of the Theotokos for the first time on a Christmas Eve. Tradition tells how, despite the elaborate ceremonial, he fell asleep. In a dream, the Virgin Mary appeared, gave him a roll of paper, and told him to eat it. Romanus obeyed. On awakening, he discovered he had received the divine gift of sacred poetry.

Thereafter, Romanus wrote about one thousand hymns, and probably invented the *kontakion*, a hymn of the Eastern Liturgy. (The Greek word kontakion means "from a pole" and refers to the hymns that were published as a scroll of text wrapped around a wooden stick). Karl Krumbacher, a nineteenth-century German scholar of Byzantine poetry, says: "In poetic talent, fire of inspiration, depth of feeling, and elevation of language, Romanus surpasses all the other composers."

The following verse, whose startling finale survives the dilution inflicted by translation, comes from a hymn Romanus wrote for Good Friday:

> Heaven, tremble and be amazed.
> Earth, sink down in chaos.
> Sun, do not dare to look on your Master
> Willingly hanged upon the tree.
> Let rocks be shattered, for the Rock of life
> Is now being wounded by the nails.
> Let the veil of the Temple be rent in two,
> As the Master's body is pierced
> With a lance by the lawless.
> In short, let all creation tremble,
> Groaning at the passion of the Creator.
> Only Adam dances.

The mysterious man in the cell

Renowned for his prophecies and spiritual discernment, a monk named Barsanuphius lived in strict isolation at a monastery in Gaza, Palestine. Little is known of his pre-monastic life, but he seemed to have been born an Egyptian sometime around the year 540. Only the abbot Seridus ever saw him, when delivering the monk's rations of bread and water. Although Barsanuphius received many letters from correspondents across Christendom requesting his counsel, his fellow monks began to suspect that he was no more than an invention of the abbot. To prove his existence, the recluse emerged, washed the feet of his colleagues, and reentered his cell. Barsanuphius believed there were "three men perfect before God," whose prayers, by God's grace, protected the entire world: John of Rome, Elias of Corinth, and "another in the diocese of Jerusalem," i.e., himself. After his death, a blast of fire supposedly surged from the doorway of his cell.

The bishop stood barefoot in the snow

Lambert, the beloved and widely revered bishop of Maastricht (in modern Netherlands), fled from his diocese and retired as a simple monk to the monastery of Stabulaus (Stavelo). Awaking from his sleep late one night for prayer, he accidentally disturbed the monastic silence. The abbot yelled out a punishment without bothering to look at the guilty party. The renowned bishop, accepting the punishment, stood barefoot in the snow for the rest of the night. In the morning, the abbot recognized the miscreant and apologized profusely. But Lambert cheerfully replied that it had been an honor to serve God.

Born to local nobility in 635, the dedicated priest was elected to the post of his mentor, Bishop Theodard, after the latter was murdered in 671. Childeric II, the king who confirmed Lambert's appointment, was assassinated himself four years later. Lambert then retreated to Stabulaus, where he suffered his night in the snow.

But Pepin, king of the Franks in all but title, insisted that the ascetic monk take up his bishopric again in 681. The Frankish flock grew rapidly under his care, but much savagery persisted, even among his disciples. In 708, Lambert's followers killed two robbers who were plundering their church. An armed band, either bent on vengeance, or (some said) recruited by the court because Lambert had criticized the king's second marriage, attacked Lambert at Liege. A lance impaled the bishop as he stood in prayer with his arms extended in the form of a cross. Many Belgians are named for this martyr, who died in 708 at the age of seventy-three. ∎

A mission to the 'angels'

Touched by the sight of a group of tall, fair-haired captives in Rome's slave market, Pope Gregory dispatches Augustine to bring the light of God to the heathen English

In the early summer of 597, a lumbering Frankish merchant vessel coasted along the towering chalk cliffs that mark the shores of southeast England. Entering the broad reach of Sandwich Bay, it negotiated its way through treacherous sandbars and into a mile-wide arm of muddy water separating the island of Thanet from the mainland. In the prow of the vessel stood a tall, broad-shouldered cleric in a russet-colored robe, and behind him crowded a hushed and somber group of more than thirty similarly garbed monks. The silence was broken only by the cries of circling gulls and the shouts of crewmen as they eased the ship alongside a crude mooring. After an absence of more than a century and a half, the Romans had returned to Britain.

The man leading this mission was no general and his troops were armed with nothing more than hope and conviction, yet they were destined to have a more lasting impact than the legions disembarked not far away by Julius Caesar in 54 B.C. In charge of this new Roman invasion was Augustine, prior of St. Andrew's Monastery in Rome. He had led his company of monks more than eleven hundred miles across Europe, through potentially hostile lands, with a mandate from his mentor, Pope Gregory, to bring the light of God to the heathen English. It was no small undertaking, but Augustine shared at least one trait with the conquering Julius: a powerful determination to succeed.

Augustine landed in what is now the county of Kent, and was then the kingdom of the same name (in the local language, it was called Cantware). It had been the first area of Britain conquered and settled by the pagan north German invaders after the departure of the Roman legions in the early fifth century. Among the first to land had been a party led by the warrior brothers Horst and Hengest, who initially were welcomed by the local Britons, and given Thanet in payment for their aid in holding off later arrivals. Yet nothing had delayed for long the onslaught of the Saxons, their cousins the Jutes, and the even more ferocious Angles (after whom the conquered lands would eventually be named).

The process of conquest had been slow but unrelenting, and by the time of Augustine's arrival, the Saxons and Jutes were in possession of most of southern and central England, while the Angles ruled the eastern half of the island. After 150 years of intermittent warfare, the Celtic Britons had been pushed into the rugged southwest peninsula of Cornwall, the mountains of Wales, and western England from the estuary of the river Severn to southern Scotland.

In the late-sixth century, the outside world knew little about Britain or its people. There was some trade between the island and the nearby European mainland, but to all intents and purposes, it had become a land of myth and legend.[1] So, with the Lombards at the gates of Rome, the Frankish kings mangling Gaul with endless, bloody civil wars, and Christianity fighting for its very survival in so many parts of the former western empire, why did Gregory choose this moment to send a party of monks on a mission to a distant and almost forgotten corner of the old empire? After all, the conversion of the invaders, up to this point, had been of concern only to Irish missionaries based on the island of Iona on the west coast of Scotland. (See *Darkness Descends*, chapter 9.)

Perhaps because Gregory was one of the few in Rome who had not forgotten it. There is a story, possibly legendary, but known to generations of English schoolchildren, which tells of Gregory walking through the slave market in the Roman Forum and noticing a group of tall, fair-haired captives. When informed that they were Angles from Britain, he noted that this seemed appropriate, "for they have angel faces, and it becomes such to be coheirs with the angels in heaven." The incident is said to have made such an impression on Gregory, then an abbot, that he asked for and was granted permission to lead a mission to these people. That mission was aborted (with Gregory being recalled after three days on the road), but it seems likely that he never quite forgot about his barbarian angels.

So, seven years after being conse-crated bishop of Rome, Gregory called upon the energetic and reliable Augustine, a veteran church administrator and monk much like himself, to reestab-lish a Roman presence in Britain. The middle-aged Augustine was prior of the monastery Gregory had founded on the site of his family's estate in Rome, and as such, was bound to Gregory as his abbot as well as his pope. It was this man who was tasked to lead a group of monks to convert the English, who Gregory imagined "placed in the corner of the world, and until this time worshiping sticks and stones."

Augustine's original destination was the eastern part of the island populated by Gregory's Angles, but by the time the party had reached southern Gaul, the monks were stricken with serious second thoughts about the whole mission. It is not known whether this change of heart was caused by news of strife between the Franks, who were embroiled in yet another civil war, or a clearer picture of the barbarous English gained from merchants who had been to Britain, but Augustine traveled back to Rome to report to Gregory on a serious crisis of confidence among his followers.

Gregory gave Augustine a letter to

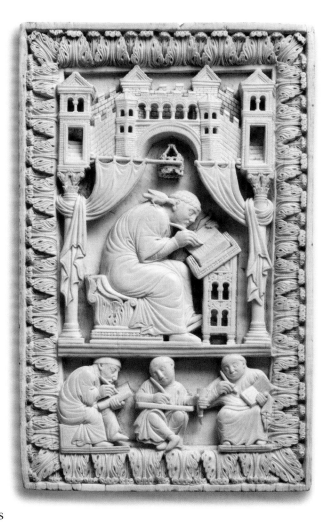

A tenth-century German ivory (above), from Vienna's Kunsthistorisches Museum, showing Gregory the Great and three scribes busy writing. A prolific letter writer, Gregory wrote a number of introductions to ease the passage of Augustine's mission through Frankish kingdoms often embroiled in civil war.

1. The sixth-century Byzantine historian Procopius repeats a commonly held view that myste-rious Britain was a land of perpetual mist and darkness in which no human being could possibly survive. Historian Arthur J. Mason (*The Mission of St. Augustine To England*) notes that the fishermen of the Frankish coast described "Brittia" as "a land of ghosts, whither the spirits of the departed were ferried at night by unseen pilots." The twentieth-century Christian essayist Dorothy L. Sayers suggests another reason Britain has so rarely been conquered: Once they experienced the weather, would-be invaders lost all interest in the job.

BEDE ON THE LESSONS OF HISTORY

If history records good things of good men, the thoughtful hearer is encouraged to imitate what is good; or if it records evil of wicked men, the good, religious reader or listener is encouraged to avoid all that is sinful and perverse, and to follow what he knows to be good and pleasing to God.

the monks, urging them to stiffen their resolve, and strengthened Augustine's authority by making him their abbot. In his letter, the pope urged, "Let not the toil of the journey nor the tongues of men predicting evil deter you; but with all earnestness and zeal finish what, by God's direction, you have begun, knowing that a great labor is followed by a greater glory of eternal reward."

The mission's destination was also changed. It would now proceed to Kent and the kingdom of Ethelbert, who some thirty years earlier had married Bertha, a Christian Frankish princess and daughter of a king of Paris. Augustine had undoubtedly learned that Kent was the oldest and currently most powerful of the English kingdoms, and that Ethelbert had allowed his queen to practice her religion, and even to bring with her a Frankish bishop, Luidhard. So there were some Christians in Kent, and Augustine might reasonably have surmised that the chances of a friendly reception would be greater. In that fateful decision lay both the success and limitations of Augustine's mission.

Ethelbert, in his little capital of Durovernum (Canterbury), was probably unaware that he was the target of a Roman mission, but converting a king was the surest way of converting his people. Yet why would a pagan king, already well into middle age, consider changing his beliefs? If he were at all inclined to Christianity (a reasonable possibility after three decades of marriage to a Christian queen), why had Bishop Luidhard not convinced Ethelbert?

The most likely answer is politics. Ethelbert's marriage suggests good connections to the powerful Franks, but conversion by his wife's bishop might have suggested too much foreign influence.

Augustine's arrival in Kent is recorded in detail by the most gifted chronicler of the early history of the English church, the Venerable Bede, in his *Ecclesiastical History of the English People*. Written around 731, the Northumbrian monk's meticulously researched history has been recognized as a monument of scholarship for over twelve centuries.

Bede says that Augustine and his party were asked to wait at Thanet while the king considered what to do about them. They did not have to wait long. After a few days, Ethelbert and his court arrived and the monks were summoned to an audience with the king. An ancient oak tree in a clearing on the island was for centuries believed by locals to mark the place of the encounter. Bede says it took place in the open because of Ethelbert's superstitious reluctance to meet the Romans indoors "if they had any witchcraft, they might on their entrance get the better of him."

It must have been a striking scene. The grizzled warrior Ethelbert, fully armed and in his kingly regalia, seated with Queen Bertha and surrounded by sharp-eyed nobles, ready to defend their king from these peculiar newcomers. Bede tells us that the monks entered the clearing behind a tall cross and bearing a painting of Christ. They sang a litany as they walked towards the king, praying for the salvation of his people. The tall and dignified Augustine was invited to sit while he spoke to Ethelbert of the purpose of his mission.

Ethelbert's response to this overture was canny. According to Bede, the king told Augustine, "Your words and promises are plausible, but since they are new and doubtful, I cannot at once assent to them, and leave the customs which I have long observed with the whole English race." In other words, "I'll think about it." But he welcomed the Romans to his capital at Canterbury, and allowed them to begin their missionary work.

For Ethelbert, conversion by an emissary of fabled Rome would, no doubt, have seemed flattering, and perhaps more politically advantageous than conversion by a Frankish bishop. He would also have been aware of the success in battle of the Christian Frankish kings, and no doubt been impressed by it. Success on the battlefield was a Saxon king's major responsibility (and only guarantee of longevity), and the idea of having Christ in his corner would have had a practical appeal.

The exact timing of Ethelbert's conversion is not known, but he may have been baptized before the end of 597, and thousands of the king's subjects were baptized during the mission's first Christmas in England. For Augustine, this was a crucial first step. Ethelbert was the overlord (in Saxon, the *bretwalda*), of a large piece of southeast and central England, extending from the Channel coast northwards to the river Humber. The patronage of this powerful chieftain allowed Augustine to quickly establish churches in the old Roman town of Durobrevis (Rochester), twenty-five miles northwest of Canterbury, and then in London. In 601, a second party of monks arrived from Rome to reinforce Augustine's mission, which was busy building a monastery at Canterbury.

But having secured the conversion of Ethelbert and much of southeast England, Augustine was now faced with the challenge of extending his mission northwards and westwards. To the west of the Saxon lands were the original inhabitants of the island, the Celtic Britons, who presented Augustine with an interesting problem. Many were already Christian.

The Celtic church in mainland Britain, reinforced by the Celtic Irish missions from Iona, had survived during the Saxon onslaught and a century and a half of, at best, sporadic contact with Rome. It is clear from Gregory's instructions to Augustine, which gave him authority over "all the bishops of Britain," that he was aware of the existence of Celtic bishops, but in Rome, little was known of the state of Celtic Christianity; which may help explain Augustine's behavior when he attempted to reestablish Roman authority over these little-known provincials.

There was no central church government among

BEDE ON PRAYING FOR ENEMIES

Imitate your Lord, intercede for your enemies; and if you cannot do that, at least beware lest you presume to pray against them. For thus progressing daily, you will reach that stage when, with the Lord's help, you can also intercede for them.

the Celts, and Bede informs us that "Augustine, using the help of King Ethelbert, summoned to a conference the bishops and doctors of the nearest province of the Britons." It took place somewhere on the western borders of English territory, likely a few miles from the Severn estuary. According to Bede, this first meeting was cordial, with a disagreement over the dating of Easter the only significant issue.

It is not, however, difficult to imagine Celtic misgivings. It was not that they failed to recognize the prestige of Rome. They always had, in theory at least. As historian Margaret Deanesly (*Augustine of Canterbury*) puts it: "Rome was very distant, but certainly very holy." The problem was that these Roman newcomers had arrived under the protection of enemies with whom the Celts had been locked in a life and death struggle for a century and a half. In fact, only thirty years earlier, one of the few Celtic ecclesiastical documents of the period to survive (the *Synod of Lucus Victoriae*) imposed a heavy penance on any Christian who acted as a guide to the English "barbarians," or in any way aided them.

It is also likely that the Celtic bishops felt deserving of a certain amount of respect for keeping Christianity alive in Britain in the face of invasion and slaughter. The Anglo-Saxon tribes were, in the opinion of many historians, more fearsome than the Goths or Franks, yet the Celtic Britons had withstood them for generations, while at the

same time successfully preserving their faith. In fact, the sixth century had produced a number of very holy Celtic fathers who had done much to strengthen the church, among them the saintly Dewy or David (patron saint of the Welsh). Now along came this Roman demanding to know why they had not been busy converting the invaders!

By the time of a second meeting with Augustine, Bede says the Celtic bishops had taken the advice of a wise hermit on how they should respond to the emissary of Rome. The hermit suggested that if Augustine were "meek and lowly of heart" they ought to listen to him. If, however, "he is not meek, but proud, it is clear that he is not of God, nor should you give heed to his word." The hermit suggested a disarmingly simple test of Augustine's humility: If he stood to greet the Britons, they should listen to him. If he remained seated, "Let him in turn be scorned by you."

Augustine, of course, knew nothing of this, and his demeanor at the second conference was beyond unfortunate. He remained seated, and when the Celts did not quickly fall into line, Augustine resorted to threats. He warned the Celts "that if they would not receive peace with their brethren, they would get war from their enemies, and that if they would not preach the way of life to the English people, they would in revenge find death at their hands."[2]

As Britain's preeminent twentieth-century leader, Winston Churchill

When the Celts did not fall into line Augustine resorted to threats.

2. Bede (who considered himself English) recounts with some satisfaction that Augustine proved to be correct. In 616, the pagan Northumbrian king Ethelfrith, slaughtered a combined British (Celtic) army near Chester. His rampaging troops went on to massacre twelve hundred unarmed monks, many from the great Celtic monastery at Bangor in north Wales that had undoubtedly supplied a number of delegates to the second meeting with Augustine.

notes, in his *History Of The English-Speaking Peoples*, an opportunity had been lost for "a general and lasting peace for both races, reconciled in the name of Christ." Churchill identifies two reasons for this historic lapse: "First, the sullen and jealous temper of the British bishops, and secondly, the tactless arrogance of Augustine."

The sad failure to make any inroads with the Celtic British Christians effectively marked the limit of Augustine's mission. He consolidated the foothold made in Kent, but was unable to spread the gospel much beyond Ethelbert's sphere of influence. He died in Canterbury in 604, and was later buried in the monastery church of St. Peter and St. Paul. The Roman mission continued, but it remained dependent upon royal support and developed into a stop-and-go affair of conversion and relapse—even in Kent.

Old King Ethelbert died in 616 and was succeeded by his impetuous and pagan son Eadbald. Despite the protests of Lawrence, Augustine's successor as bishop of Canterbury, Eadbald married his stepmother (Ethelbert's much younger, second wife). Farther north, in the kingdom of the Middle Saxons, it was much the same story. The Christian chieftain Sabert died, and his three pagan sons demanded the sacrament from Augustine's appointee as bishop of London, Mellitus. When Mellitus refused, they ran him out of town, and he fled to his fellow bishop, Justus, in Rochester. Seriously unnerved, the pair then decided to retreat to Christian Gaul, and urged Lawrence to join them.

Augustine's foothold in England stood in peril of complete collapse, but Lawrence was made of sterner stuff than his colleagues. He had his bed moved into the church of the monastery at Canterbury in search of divine inspiration. It is said that as he slept, St. Peter appeared to him, and scourged him for daring to think of abandoning his flock. In the morning, Lawrence, his courage restored, showed the welts on his back to Eadbald, who was suitably impressed, and shortly renounced both his paganism and his new wife.

Mellitus and Justus eventually returned to England, and both, in turn, served as bishop in Canterbury. It would be forty years before London had another bishop, but Justus was able to take advantage of a favorable political development and extend the Christian mission to northern England, to the distant kingdom of Northumbria.

Edwin, Northumbria's energetic young ruler, had become the new overlord of the English, and had married the Kentish princess Ethelberga (Eadbald's sister). Like her mother, Bertha, she was a Christian who insisted on practicing her religion and bringing with her as spiritual adviser the monk Paulinus. In 625, Paulinus, ordained a bishop, was given the critical task of converting Edwin.

The Northumbrian king dragged his feet for two years, but eventually called a meeting of his nobles and advisers to decide the issue. In one of

BEDE ON DEATH
We all have a common ending of temporal life in the certitude of one and the same hope, as we close our eyes in death, we trust that we shall be found immediately in the true life and shall remain in this forever.

the most evocative passages in Bede's history, he recounts a story told at this council by one of Edwin's warriors:

> Man's present life on earth seems to me, compared with that time beyond which we know nothing, to be as if, when you are sitting at supper with your aldermen and nobles in the winter time, and a fire is lighted in the middle and the hall is warmed, while outside storms of wintry rain and snow are raging, some sparrow were to fly very quickly through the house, in at one door and out another. During the time that he is inside, he is untouched by the storm, but when that little moment of calm has run out, he passes again from the warmth into the winter, and you lose sight of him. So this life of men appears for a little while, but what follows it, and what went before it, we do not know at all. So if this new teaching has brought us

anything sure, we should do well, I think, to follow it.

Edwin's head priest, Coifi, also admitted the futility of his paganism. "I saw long ago that what we worshiped was nothing at all; because the more carefully I sought the truth in that worship, the less I found it." He even volunteered to tear down the kingdom's pagan altars. This was enough for Edwin, who was baptized at York, and began construction of a church there.

Sadly, after half a dozen years, a pagan revival swept away most of what Paulinus had achieved, but Christianity stubbornly retained its foothold in Northumbria. The Christian prince Oswald prevented what might have become the complete extinction of the faith in northern England, and as king built a perma-

The site of the monastery first established by Aidan in 635, on the island of Lindisfarne (below), off the coast of Northumbria, England. Now known as Holy Island, it is also home to the ruins of a thirteenth-century priory.

nent Northumbrian base for the Celtic monks of Iona, the western Scottish island where Columcille had established a mission in 564.[3]

The monk Aidan arrived as bishop to Oswald's kingdom, and he proved to be as influential in the conversion of the English as had Augustine. The monastery Aidan founded at Lindisfarne (an island a short distance off the northeast coast of England, near Oswald's stronghold of Bamburgh) became the spiritual center of the north. Around the same time, Felix, a Burgundian monk from Canterbury, converted many in eastern England, and by 634, the monk Birinus had begun a successful mission in the central area of the island. By the time of Aidan's death in 651, Christianity appeared firmly established from Northumbria to Kent.

But the patchwork of conversion—Irish monks in the north and midlands, sporadic missions on the east coast—left Canterbury with clear influence only over Kent and part of eastern England. The result was an English church that still lacked the central authority envisaged by Gregory, and in which the Celtic monks of Iona had great influence. Rome undoubtedly saw this as a challenge, for as Margaret Deanesly put it, the Celts held dear "the rugged tradition of monastic holiness that had come to them ultimately from Egypt." The Celtic calendar and liturgy were from Gaul rather than Rome, and isolation had left Celtic Christianity essentially tribal and rural in nature.

To the Romans, there was probably a dangerous whiff of Pelagianism about the independent-minded Celts. (See *Darkness Descends*, chapter 5.) Celtic monks even cut their hair differently. The monks of Rome shaved only the tops of their heads, while the Celts are thought to have imitated an earlier form of tonsure borrowed from the pagan Druids that left only a fringe of hair on the forehead. It was, says Churchill, "a choice of the grotesque."

These issues were resolved at the Synod of Whitby in 664, when Oswald's son, Oswy, called together Celtic and Roman clerics from around his kingdom to reconcile their differences.[4] Whitby traditionally was seen as a "high noon" showdown between Celtic and Roman Christianity, but in recent years, historians have increasingly accepted that the divisions were less pronounced than once thought. There had been notable cooperation between the monks of Iona and Canterbury, and the Celtic church had never seriously disputed the prestige of Rome, viewing its bishop as Peter's successor. In the view of historian D. J. V. Fisher (*The Anglo-Saxon Age*), "The divergent practices of the Celtic church were the result not of opposition to Rome, but isolation from it."

The central dispute, over the dating of Easter, was an ancient one revolving around the method used in calculating the Paschal full moon in relation to the spring equinox. It had once divided Rome from Alexandria and the eastern churches, and more recently had been a point of contention between Columbanus, the Irish missionary to the

> To the Romans, there was probably a whiff of Pelagianism about the Celts.

3. Oswald had been educated in Ireland and Iona, and in 635, it was to Iona that he appealed for help in converting his pagan realm. The first monk dispatched to aid him, Corman, was apparently a dismal failure, and returned to Iona after two years. Aidan, Corman's replacement, was much more successful. As abbot–bishop in Northumbria, he created with Oswald a union of church and monarchy that would become a model for all of Saxon England. Aidan's monastery at Lindisfarne would train generations of monks in the business of conversion, and would have such a profound impact on English Christianity that it would become known simply as Holy Island.

4. The little north Yorkshire fishing village of Streaneshalch, a place better-known by its later Viking (Danish) name of Whitby, was likely chosen as the site of the synod because it was home to a large double monastery, housing both monks and nuns, and governed by the Abbess Hilda (614–680).

The snow-covered ruins of a Benedictine abbey (above) built in 1078, at Whitby, England, on the site of the earlier Saxon monastery founded by Saint Hilda that served as the venue for the Synod of Whitby. The abbey flourished until the dissolution of monastic communities by King Henry VIII in the mid-sixteenth century.

5. In the late-twentieth century, there developed in Britain a new interest in the history of England before the Norman Conquest (1066), with an explosion of popular histories and novels dealing with events such as the Anglo-Saxon invasion and the Synod of Whitby. The best fictional depiction of Whitby and the clash between Celtic and Roman observances (soundly based on historical fact) is contained in British author and broadcaster Melvyn Bragg's best-selling *Credo*.

Burgundians, and Rome. (See *Darkness Descends*, chapter 9.) In fact, until 525, the Celtic and Roman churches had used the same method to fix Easter, but in that year, most of the Christian world adopted the eastern system. The isolated Celts, who may not even have been aware of the change, continued to date Easter in the manner of their respected saints and church fathers.

At Whitby, Colman, the abbot of Lindisfarne, put the case for the traditional Celtic dating of Easter, while the young cleric Wilfrid, destined to become a major figure in the English Church, argued the Roman cause. King Oswy took little time in deciding in favor of Wilfrid, who had become a close spiritual adviser. For Oswy, governing a kingdom in which some celebrated Easter at one time and some another, Whitby may have seemed nothing more than a sensible housekeeping measure. He was clearly

the driving force behind the synod, and it was his authority that now backed the adoption of Roman observances throughout northern and central England.[5]

Colman relinquished Lindisfarne and took many of its monks back to Iona (and then to Ireland where he founded a monastery at Mayo), but the general impact of Whitby was to further the consolidation of the English church and bind it to the wider Roman world. Within five years of the synod, that process would find a powerful champion in a new archbishop of Canterbury: Theodore, a sixty-seven-year-old Greek monk from St. Paul's home town of Tarsus in Asia Minor.

Theodore was a controversial choice. Rome was suspicious of Greek clergy, and Pope Vitalian (657–672) was originally reluctant to appoint a Greek to Canterbury. Theodore was also far from youthful, yet during his twenty-one-year episcopate, he did much to transform the English church. He held the first national councils of English bishops, to promote unity, define the limits of jurisdiction, and place some authority over the wandering monks who were still at work in the remaining pockets of paganism. He traveled the length and breadth of England, consecrating bishops and organizing dioceses. Historian Fisher calls Theodore "one of the greatest, if not the greatest of all medieval bishops of Canterbury."[6] Most importantly, Bede says, he was the first archbishop whom the whole of the English church willingly followed.

In nine decades, the mission begun by Augustine had made enormous strides, and the vision of Gregory had to a large extent been realized. The island that had drifted into myth and legend had rejoined the wider world, and the foundations of Anglo-Saxon Christianity had been soundly laid. Bede, writing about forty years after Theodore, was able to describe a Christian England with strong cultural links to the outside world: a country in which paganism was already a fading memory.

"Nor were there ever happier times since the English first came to Britain," wrote Bede. "For they had strong and Christian kings who were a terror to barbarian peoples; the desires of all were bent on the joys of the heavenly kingdom about which they had recently heard; and whoever wanted to study sacred learning had masters ready to teach him." ■

6. Pope Vitalian had originally chosen Hadrian, an African monk and abbot of a monastery near Naples, as the new bishop of Canterbury, but Hadrian asked to be excused, and suggested instead the Greek Theodore. Vitalian reluctantly agreed, on the condition that Hadrian accompany Theodore to England, and stay with him for a time to ensure that he introduced nothing "after the manner of the Greeks, contrary to the true faith, into the church now subject to him."

The interior of St. Paul's Church, Jarrow, England (left). Still in use, much of the church survives from the seventh century, when it served as a chapel in the monastery where the Venerable Bede spent most of his life. It is now part of an extensive site dedicated to preserving Northumbria's Saxon heritage.

Frankish warriors burst into a Muslim camp at Poitiers, in what is today south-central France (depicted in this nineteenth-century engraving from Guizot's History of France*). After the conquest of North Africa and Spain, the seemingly invincible Arab-led armies probed northwards into Frankish territory, and for the first time encountered the fearsome, ax-wielding Franks.*

CHAPTER 9

The fearsome Franks halt the Muslim tide

Across North Africa and Spain, Islam seems unstoppable, until Charles Martel and his men of the north block the way

Muslim tradition preserves and cherishes the triumphant story of Uqba ibn Nafi, the daring cavalry commander who led his little Arab force west from Egypt along the three-thousand-mile coast of North Africa, defying all the perils of the Byzantine-held ports and highly untrustworthy Berber tribesmen, until finally he reached the waters of the Atlantic Ocean. There, urging his horse into the surf and scanning the boundless waters, Uqba cried out in triumph and frustration: "*Allahu Akbar*! [God is great!] But were it not for this sea, I would still ride on to the unknown kingdoms of the west, preaching the unity of Allah, and putting to the sword the rebellious nations who worship any other god but him!"

The year was 683, but Uqba's shout would resonate in the fears of twenty-first-century Americans. Thirteen hundred and eighteen years later, on the opposite side of that same ocean, other Muslims, having hijacked three airliners, would issue the same cry, "Allahu Akbar!" as they tried to make good on Uqba's vision.[1]

His declaration was in fact the high point of an endeavor that began forty-one years earlier, when the Muslims, looking west from Egypt, decided that their conquests had scarcely begun. Egypt was certainly a prize, but if the whole world was to be conquered for Islam, as the Prophet was taken to intend, it was merely one step.

1. Sixteen days after the Muslim attack on the World Trade Center in New York, the man whose organization took "credit" for the attack, Osama bin Laden, issued a statement linking it to the "tragedy of Andalusia." This is the Muslim name for Spain, whose conquest by Muslim armies is described in this chapter. Andalusia became a Muslim "tragedy" when Christian forces pushed the Muslims out of Spain after a war that lasted more than seven hundred years.

So they pushed tentatively along the Mediterranean's south shore in pursuit of the next great prize: Christian Carthage, home of Tertullian, Cyprian and the mighty Augustine, all of whom had played such pivotal roles in the growth of Christianity, and the bounteous prefecture of North Africa.

By the seventh century, however, Christianity in North Africa had fallen on bad times. The mixed population of Carthaginians, Romans, Vandals and Byzantines was rent by dissension, both political and religious. The mountains and deserts of the interior, little touched by any invader, were the domain of the Berbers, also known as Moors from their presumed original homeland in Mauritania. The Berbers may be descendants of the biblical Canaanites, or the Phoenicians, and as John Bagot Glubb observes in *The Great Arab Conquests*, they are a stubborn people who even today resolutely preserve their distinctive race and their Hamitic-derived languages.

Although the Christian faith was vibrant in the Roman-dominated cities, it was also afflicted by various schisms and heresies. Its bishops were particularly suspicious of Byzantine theological ultimatums, and most of them had little use for those issued by Rome either. In the sixth century, African bishops fought so bitterly against Justinian's "Three Chapters" edict that the emperor finally arrested and

Once subjugated by Islam, the fighting skills of the North African Berber people made them invaluable assets in Muslim armies. Present-day Berbers (like this woman and child, below) maintain a strong culture incorporating language, customs and music. Roving entertainers (at bottom) preserve Berber music, poetry and heroic stories by traveling from village to village.

deported many of them. In the seventh, they vehemently opposed the similar Monothelitist doctrines of Emperor Constans II.

The advent of Islam increased the religious tension, as refugee theologians from Muslim-conquered Alexandria moved to Carthage, bringing with them, says historian Henri Daniel-Rops, "their eternal taste for theological wrangling" (*The Church in the Dark Ages*). However, the most damaging schism in Christian North Africa had been created by the Donatist movement—rigorist, exclusivist and peculiar to North Africa alone. For three hundred years, Donatism had survived ferocious efforts to extirpate it, and on the eve of the Arab invasion was as lively as ever.

Inland, a Christian presence of any kind was relatively weak. Some Berbers had adopted Judaism. Many more had become Christian, but were likely to espouse their faith—or to abjure it—more from political convenience than religious conviction. (Under Islam, this tendency would continue, despite frequently grievous consequences. "When the Berbers apostatize," declared one exasperated Muslim historian, "they do it twelve times over!")

Politically, the story was the same. The Roman Empire had never really subdued or gained the allegiance of the Berbers, and Byzantium oscillated between conciliation and ferocious retribution. Late in the sixth century, after the whole region west of Egypt was elevated to the status of a seven-province prefecture, its governors won significant victories over the Berber tribes, controlling their chronic

The Muslim conquests increased religious tension, as refugees from Alexandria moved to Carthage, bringing a taste for theological wrangling.

raiding. But one governor, the praetorian prefect John, characteristically forced two of their chieftains to serve him as slaves. Such humiliating gestures gave the Berbers further cause to hate Byzantium.

For these and other reasons, the Muslims met little resistance in the 660s, as they moved all the way to the city of Barqa, about five hundred miles along the coast. Within a decade, an Arab–Berber army commanded by the above-mentioned Uqba had established a base south of Carthage, which he called Qayrawan, to command the surrounding country and serve as a rallying point for further conquests. However, the offensive bogged down, partly because of supply problems,[2] and partly because Uqba possessed neither taste nor talent for compromise. He treated his Berber allies with what historian C. H. Becker calls "impolitic haughtiness," (*Cambridge Medieval History*, volume 2), and was inclined to summarily execute any who accepted Islam and then recanted.

So Uqba was replaced as North African commander by a freed slave named Dinar Abu al-Muhajir, who clapped Uqba into irons and shipped him east. Dinar, who did understand diplomacy, made an ally of the paramount Berber chief, Kusaila, an erstwhile Christian, and was able to advance to the border

2. The communication and supply problems experienced by the Arabs in their conquest of North Africa would be replicated in the twentieth century as the British army fought the German Afrika Korps, notes John Bagot Glubb in *The Great Arab Conquests*. The British, like Uqba, were based in Egypt and advanced to Barqa, which stretched their supply line too far; they were then driven back. The Germans advanced from their base at Tripoli to Alamein, where they were defeated for much the same reason.

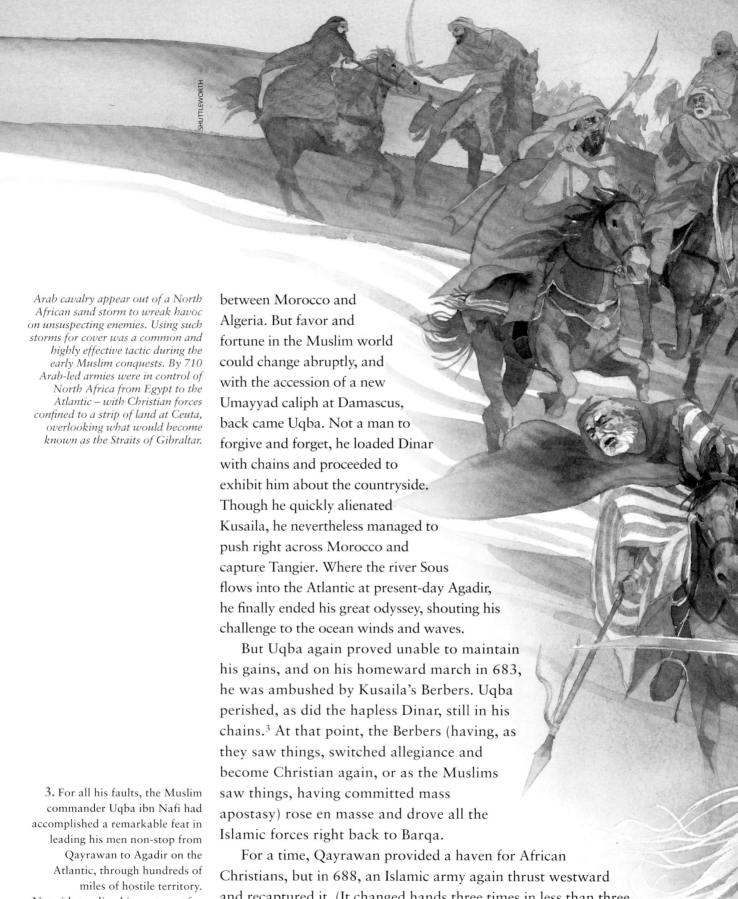

Arab cavalry appear out of a North African sand storm to wreak havoc on unsuspecting enemies. Using such storms for cover was a common and highly effective tactic during the early Muslim conquests. By 710 Arab-led armies were in control of North Africa from Egypt to the Atlantic – with Christian forces confined to a strip of land at Ceuta, overlooking what would become known as the Straits of Gibraltar.

3. For all his faults, the Muslim commander Uqba ibn Nafi had accomplished a remarkable feat in leading his men non-stop from Qayrawan to Agadir on the Atlantic, through hundreds of miles of hostile territory. Notwithstanding his contempt for the Berber inhabitants, his daring and style, and perhaps his consequent death as well, compelled the enduring admiration of the Berbers right up to the twentieth century.

between Morocco and Algeria. But favor and fortune in the Muslim world could change abruptly, and with the accession of a new Umayyad caliph at Damascus, back came Uqba. Not a man to forgive and forget, he loaded Dinar with chains and proceeded to exhibit him about the countryside. Though he quickly alienated Kusaila, he nevertheless managed to push right across Morocco and capture Tangier. Where the river Sous flows into the Atlantic at present-day Agadir, he finally ended his great odyssey, shouting his challenge to the ocean winds and waves.

But Uqba again proved unable to maintain his gains, and on his homeward march in 683, he was ambushed by Kusaila's Berbers. Uqba perished, as did the hapless Dinar, still in his chains.[3] At that point, the Berbers (having, as they saw things, switched allegiance and become Christian again, or as the Muslims saw things, having committed mass apostasy) rose en masse and drove all the Islamic forces right back to Barqa.

For a time, Qayrawan provided a haven for African Christians, but in 688, an Islamic army again thrust westward and recaptured it. (It changed hands three times in less than three decades.) About this time, Chief Kusaila fell in battle, and an extraordinary woman made her spectacular appearance on the stage of events: the legendary Dahia al-Kahina (Dahia the Priestess), known to her opponents as "queen of the Berbers." Reputedly a seer and prophetess, she was an African

of Jewish faith, and her army comprised Berbers, Jews and Christians.

In *Outrageous Women of the Middle Ages*, historian Vicki Leon speculates that al-Kahina headed a Berber tribe of the Atlas Mountains. This turbaned woman, her white robes vividly accentuating her coffee-colored skin and kohl-lined eyes, must have been a compelling figure as she charged with her warriors into battle, silver dagger flashing. Regaining the conquered territory as far east as Tripoli, for some five years she ruled much of North Africa. Her nemesis was a new Muslim commander, Hassan ibn Numan, expert strategist and diplomat.

By getting some of the Berber tribes on side, Hassan defeated the doughty queen in 703 in a battle near Gafsa (Tunisia), in which she herself was killed. Her head, it is said, was sent to the caliph—gruesome recognition of Muslim regard for a notable enemy. She had slowed, although not stopped, the Muslim invaders, but they were equally impeded by another factor.

On land, they could beat Byzantines, Berbers, or even both together, but they could not offset the power of the Byzantine navy that supplied the coastal cities. When Hassan captured Carthage in the summer of 697, the Byzantines regained it the same fall by using their fleet. Now, however, came a reversal that for

Almost all of North Africa was under Islamic control, with every vestige of Latin or Greek civilization quickly disappearing—as were most Christians.

centuries to come would prove decisive: Islam became seaborne, Byzantium's control of the Mediterranean ended, and the tables were turned. (See sidebar, page 251.) In 698, the Muslims once more took Carthage, dispersing a Byzantine fleet with a bigger one of their own, and soon all the African coastal centers were in their hands.

It remained only for their next general, Musa ibn Nusair, backed by Berber allies, to sweep through Morocco, persuading or coercing the indigenous inhabitants to embrace Islam, if only to share in the battles and the booty. By 708, almost all North Africa was under Islamic control, with every vestige of Latin or Greek civilization quickly disappearing. So were most of its Christians—and more completely, historians note, than in any other conquered region. Many died in the conquest itself, many fled to Europe when Umar II made them choose between apostasy and exile, and many accepted Islam. The whole process took only about half a century.

By 710, the holdout Christian area consisted of a strip of land centered on a formidable fortress at Ceuta. Ruled by a governor who was still at least nominally responsible to the Byzantine emperor, it was located on the African side of that narrow gap framed by the promontories known to the ancients as the Pillars of Hercules, where the waters of the Atlantic Ocean mingle with those of the Mediterranean Sea: the Strait of Gibraltar, eight miles across at its narrowest. North of the strait lay a truly fabulous bonanza, the country

soon to be named by the Muslims *al-Andalus* (Andalusia).

The rest of the world now calls it Spain and Portugal; to the Romans, who had conquered most of it by 133 B.C., it was Hispania. With eight million or so loyal Christian inhabitants, and a thriving economy, it had been a bulwark of the old empire. But in 414 came invasion by some two hundred-thousand Visigoths, migrant tribes who had fought their way from eastern Europe via Gaul and Italy, sometimes as an ally of Rome, sometimes as its enemy. Over the next hundred years, the invaders drove out the Roman legions, and took over most of the Iberian Peninsula; they would rule it for the next two centuries.

The early effects of the Visigoth invasion mirrored that of barbarian incursions everywhere: roads and bridges in disrepair; mines and irrigation systems in disuse; cities deteriorating; little trade, and that sustained only by "foreigners." Successive Gothic monarchs gradually adopted and adapted Roman administrative techniques, while blending Roman law with their own legal traditions. Although the Visigoths were Arian heretics in religion, their kings relied heavily on Hispania's strong orthodox Christian ecclesiastical establishment, without which they could hardly have governed the large Hispano-Roman majority.

"Of all the kingdoms of western Europe, the Visigoths gave the best promise of a glorious future in the last years of the sixth century," writes the Oxford historian C. W. C. Oman (*The Mission of St. Augustine to England*). The chief drawback was their Arian religion, which their kings long tried to maintain among the Visigoths, and at times to force upon the whole populace. Before the end of the sixth century, however, King Reccared, brother of the martyred Hermenegild (see sidebar, page 241), resolved to put an end to this chronic religious dissension. In 589, he embraced orthodox

The city of Toledo (above), located on the Tagus River in Spain, was a thriving capital under the Visigoths. Labyrinthine Arab-style streets, ancient synagogues, and a magnificent Gothic cathedral testify to the vibrant history of a city influenced by Jews, Christians and Muslims.

4. The Third Council of Toledo was summoned in May 589 by the Visigoth king Reccared, to formally renounce the Arian Creed. It began with three days of prayer and fasting, says the Smith and Wace *Dictionary of Christian Biography*. Then the royal *tomus* (declaration) was read, outlining with particular clarity the distinction between Arian unitarianism and the Trinity-based orthodox creed of Nicea and Constantinople. Of the thirty-three Councils of Toledo, which took place between the fifth and sixteenth centuries and became an institute of government unique to Spain, this was arguably the most important.

Christianity, urging his Arian bishops and nobles to do likewise.

Like the Roman emperors, Reccared believed that to safeguard his kingdom—and his throne—all his subjects must share one faith. To further the process, just as the emperor Constantine had summoned the Council of Nicea, so Reccared summoned the Spanish bishops to a solemn gathering in 589, where, again like Constantine, he set the terms. This was the Third Council of Toledo, which formally adopted full Nicene orthodoxy as the official faith of the Visigoth state.[4] Most of his subjects followed their monarch's lead, and he decisively suppressed a rebellion by a group of determined Arians who did not.

Under Reccared, the Visigoth capital of Toledo grew in opulence and influence, while Seville became a center of piety and learning under Bishop Isidore, a man whose life span (560–636) closely matches that of Muhammad (ca. 570–632). Isidore was famed for his sanctity and lavish almsgiving, for defending Trinitarian doctrine against Arianism, for founding schools and convents, but chiefly for his astounding erudition. His monumental *Etymologiae* comprises twenty books treating an immense range of subjects: theology, etymology, the seven liberal arts (grammar, rhetoric, dialectic, arithmetic, geometry, music and astronomy); natural science; political science; and what a later age would call social science. He clearly intended his work as a compendium of knowledge for a new Spain, a vision that would be cut short by the arrival of Islam.

Whatever qualities the Visigoth kingdom might have cherished, however, tolerance was not among them, as was evidenced in its horrific treatment of the Jews. Anti-Jewish policies, writes historian J. M. Wallace-Hadrill in *The Barbarian West*, represent "a grisly feature of seventh-century Visigothic legislation." As one instance, in 616, King Sisebuto ordered that all Jews either be baptized or expelled. Even if they did convert, they were still

"Good" King Wamba (above), a beloved Visigoth ruler, was possibly known more for his sterling personal qualities than for a notable reign. In one extreme incident, he was drugged and tonsured as a monk by a usurper, thus barring him from the throne. With good grace, Wamba cheerfully retired to a monastery. Filippo Ariosto painted this portrait in the sixteenth century.

A rebellious prince and martyr

In defiance of his Arian father, Hermenegild embraces his mother's Nicene faith and pays the ultimate price when he refuses the sacrament from heretical hands

It is one of the ironies of early medieval history that almost all the barbarian tribes who founded Christian Europe, with the notable exception of the Franks, were Arian, not orthodox Christian, when they broke through the Roman frontiers and found themselves confronting orthodox Christian belief. This story played out differently with each nation, but none is more fascinating than the drama of the Visigoths in Spain, centrally featuring the prince and martyr Hermenegild.

Hermenegild's father, the Visigoth king Leovegild, who subdued most of the Iberian Peninsula by the late-sixth century, did his best to make its inhabitants embrace Arianism, sometimes by persuasion, sometimes by force. But Leovegild's first wife, Hermenegild's mother, embraced the Christianity of the Nicene Creed. She greatly influenced her son, although she died when he was a child. Moreover, his father arranged for him a political marriage to a pious and notably steadfast Christian princess named Ingunthis, daughter of King Sigisbert of Austrasia.

Even so, Hermenegild might have kept his religious sympathies to himself except for his stepmother, Goswintha, Leovegild's second wife.[1] This woman, a devout Arian, constantly abused poor Ingunthis both physically and mentally, to make her abjure her faith. At length, the sympathetic king sent the young couple out of Goswintha's reach by assigning Hermenegild to govern his southern territory from Seville.

However, the move placed the prince in a heavily Christian district of Hispano-Romans, and next door to one of the remaining Byzantine possessions in Spain. It also brought him into the orbit of Leander, the brilliant monk and priest, later to be named archbishop. In any event, Hermenegild announced in 579 that he was abandoning Arianism, and was received into the Christian faith by anointing with holy oil.

Unfortunately, this awoke the national aspirations of the region's Hispano-Romans, who proclaimed Hermenegild king and raised a rebellion against his father. When Hermenegild accepted the rebel role—whether through faith, political ambition, or both—a complex and brutal six-year war began. The prince reportedly was deaf to all paternal entreaties, especially after Leovegild began another brutal crackdown on Nicene Christianity. His claim was backed by the Suevi, rival barbarians with aspirations of their own, and he was initially aided by the Byzantines (but later they sold him out to his father).

At length Hermenegild had to capitulate, casting himself upon his father's mercy. Leovegild reportedly entrusted his errant son to one of his dukes, who locked him up and repeatedly demanded that he recant. The final and fatal test, according to an account written a little later by Pope Gregory, occurred on Easter Eve in 585. To Hermenegild's dungeon cell came an Arian bishop who offered him Holy Communion. The prince, strong in his faith, refused to receive the sacrament from heretical hands, and was summarily executed with a battle-ax.[2]

Whether this was Leovegild's intention is far from clear, but death did not end Hermenegild's story. Although most orthodox bishops had not supported his rebellion, the lower clergy probably did. The people assuredly revered him, writes Henri Coppee in *History of the Conquest of Spain by the Arab Moors*, and so the faith in Spain "was watered with Hermenegild's blood." A year later, Leovegild himself, on his deathbed, may have accepted the Nicene Creed; some chroniclers claimed he would have done so long since, but for his implacable wife.

In due time, the martyred prince was recognized as a saint. Meanwhile, his younger brother Reccared, an able ruler and still officially Arian, took over the Visigoth kingdom, and within three years was able to commit himself and the kingdom to Nicene Christianity. Even Reccared could not eliminate endemic Visigothic conflicts over the royal succession, but his fifteen-year reign nevertheless inaugurated a century of relative peace and prosperity in which the Christian faith could grow strong. ■

---

1. The labyrinthine intra-family relations of the Germanic dynasties can severely tax comprehension. Ingunthis, the Frankish princess who was married to the doomed Visigoth prince Hermenegild, was in fact his cousin. Goswintha, the fanatic Arian queen who so cruelly treated the young bride, was both her grandmother and his stepmother. The widow of Hermenegild's uncle, Goswintha had subsequently become the second wife of Hermenegild's father.

2. Most historians agree that the unfortunate Christian princess Ingunthis did not long survive her husband, although her precise fate is unclear. Her Frankish relatives seemingly believed she was dead, but accepted the assurances of her brother-in-law Reccared that he was not responsible. According to one chronicler, she and her infant son took refuge with the Byzantines in southern Spain, but both died at Carthage on the way to Constantinople.

regarded with suspicion and contempt. The Fourth Council of Toledo, in 633, ordered that children of converts be taken from their parents to be properly educated. Later councils wavered between impossibly punitive taxes on Jews, punishments like scourging and the shaving of all their hair, and hunting them down as suspected traitors. More and more fled the country, mostly to Africa.

The precise cause of such concentrated venom is elusive. Spain and North Africa abounded in Jews, refugees over the years from persecution in other places. Intelligent, hard working, and often well educated, they tended to acquire wealth and influence, and probably virulent envy as well. The most odious legislation, however, appears to have been inspired by the Visigothic fear of religious diversity.

Even so, the major weakness of seventh-century Spain did not lie in religious intolerance, but in its monarchical system. Custom decreed that any suitable member of the ruling family, not just a son, could succeed to the throne, a provision that positively encouraged assassination. Eleven of Spain's thirty-three

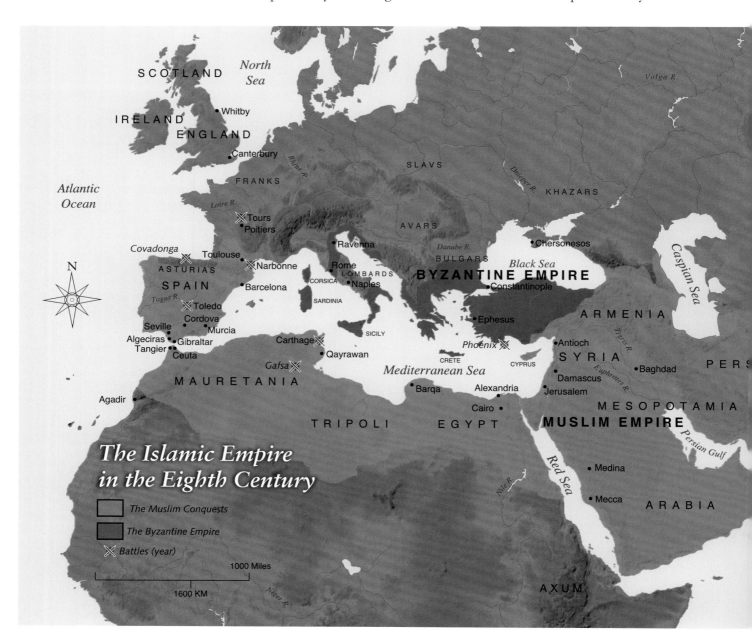

The Islamic Empire in the Eighth Century

- The Muslim Conquests
- The Byzantine Empire
- ✕ Battles (year)

1000 Miles

1600 KM

Visigoth kings were in fact assassinated, and three were deposed; the rest reportedly died unaided. Anyone with royal possibilities was also a likely target; both of Reccared's sons, for example, were killed within two years of his death in 601.

In the century that followed, there were able Visigoth kings and even erudite ones. Sisebuto (612–621) was reputedly an author and poet. Swintila, who ruled for nineteen years, drove the Byzantines from their last stronghold in southern Spain. There were church builders like Recceswinth (649–672), especially remembered for San Juan de Banos at Palencia, one of the few churches to survive Muslim rule. There was even one particular monarch lovingly recalled in Spanish history as "Good King Wamba." But many reigns were undistinguished and venal, and such, according to Visigoth chroniclers, was the second-to-last: that of Witiza, from 701 to 709.

Witiza began well, writes historian Henri Coppee (*History of the Conquest of Spain by the Arab Moors*), but reputedly degenerated into "private vice and

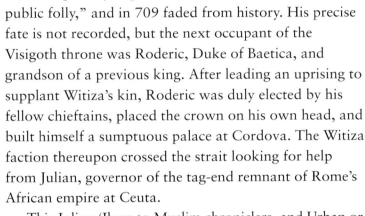

public folly," and in 709 faded from history. His precise fate is not recorded, but the next occupant of the Visigoth throne was Roderic, Duke of Baetica, and grandson of a previous king. After leading an uprising to supplant Witiza's kin, Roderic was duly elected by his fellow chieftains, placed the crown on his own head, and built himself a sumptuous palace at Cordova. The Witiza faction thereupon crossed the strait looking for help from Julian, governor of the tag-end remnant of Rome's African empire at Ceuta.

This Julian (Ilyan to Muslim chroniclers, and Urban or Olban to some later historians) is a figure of some mystery. The eighteenth-century historian Edward Gibbon, in *The Decline and Fall of the Roman Empire*, calls him "Count Julian, the general of the Goths." Arab chronicles variously identify him as a Berber merchant, or chief of a Moroccan tribe. Whoever he was, he apparently ruled Ceuta and environs as a quasi-independent territory, and he is believed to have helped Witiza's sons by sponsoring a two-vessel raid on the Spanish coast.[5]

Such a small raid was scarcely enough to alarm Roderic. But it should have, for this spectacle of Christian fighting Christian did not escape the attention of Tariq ibn Zihad, Muslim governor of Tangier. Jewish traders and refugees would certainly have kept Tariq informed if no one else did. Who had better reason than they to detest the Visigoths? And for him and his commanding general, Musa ibn Nusair, Spain offered lavish plunder to retain the loyalty of their new and easily disillusioned Berber allies. Musa obtained from Caliph al-Walid I permission to

5. Theories vary as to why Count Julian aided Witiza's sons. One is that their father had helped him repel a previous Muslim attack. Another, more popular, is that King Roderic had basely seduced Julian's lovely young daughter, Florinda, while she lived at the Visigoth court as a maid of honor. Captivated by her beauty but frustrated by her virtue, writes historian Henri Coppee, Roderic at last "either overcame her scruples or resorted to violence." When poor Florinda got word to her father, Coppee theorizes, the enraged Julian vowed revenge. Curiously, Spanish tradition denigrates poor Florinda as a wanton; her name in folklore is not Florinda, but "La Cava," a colloquial crudity.

invade, albeit accompanied by a stern warning to proceed with caution. An exploratory raid in 710, which returned with unprecedented booty, greatly augmented the recruiting of a major invasion force to be commanded by Tariq.

Now events moved swiftly. How swiftly and how treacherously can scarcely be imagined, for it was Christian Count Julian who helped the Muslims conquer Christian Spain. Most of what follows is extensively disputed as to detail, and much of it is more legend than history, but the result was entirely real: Muslim domination of Spain for more than seven hundred years. Tariq probably crossed the strait in April 711, with seven thousand men, in merchant ships again supplied by Julian. A contingent of Witiza supporters may have followed, and possibly Julian himself. Tariq is believed to have landed at the great stone massif then known as Mons Calpe, which thereby acquired its modern name: Gibraltar, from *Jabel Tariq* ("Tariq's Mountain"). Within months, he had taken the cities of Carteya and Algeciras, and was marching on Cordova.

King Roderic had been fighting the Franks and Gascons on his northern borders, but a supporter, Count Theodemir, managed to stave off an attack on

Roderic's army confronted the Muslim invaders at Lake Janda. By which time Tariq's soldiers had been joined by five thousand Berbers.

Cordova until July, when Roderic's army arrived to confront the invaders. They probably met at the point where a small river called the Barbate flows into Lake Janda, not far from the town of Medina Sidonia. Arab sources make the unlikely claim that the Goth army numbered a hundred thousand, and the Arab historian al-Kortobi contemptuously describes Roderic as an effete potentate in gold crown and silk robe, riding languidly to battle in a chariot. Gibbon picks up on this, commenting that "Alaric would have blushed at the sight of this unworthy successor . . . reclining on a litter or cart drawn by two white mules."

However that may be, by then Tariq's original seven thousand soldiers had likely been augmented by another five thousand Berber horsemen, and the turbaned Berbers with their pennants, lances, scimitars and flashing cutlasses must have posed a daunting spectacle. But what clearly defeated Roderic was, as usual, the fatal disunity of the Visigoths. According to all reports, whole sections of his army deserted to the invaders as various chieftains decided to deal rather than fight. Some say that among these was Oppas, a brother of the late Witiza. What role was played in the battle by Witiza's sons is uncertain, but they and their recruited forces appear to have been on hand, perhaps waiting to see what would happen.

The consequence for Roderic was complete and ignominious defeat—and possibly death. At a crucial point, according to legend, Tariq spotted a nobly caparisoned warrior he believed to be the Visigoth king, rushed upon him, and split his skull, helmet and all. As rumor flew through both hosts that Roderic was dead, his warriors scattered in panic, and their exultantly pursuing enemies slaughtered them by hundreds. But had Roderic indeed been killed? Credible sources categorically deny that he was the warrior singled out by Tariq. Nor was his body found by Lake Janda—only, according to some tales, a magnificent, riderless warhorse with a ruby-encrusted golden saddle, presumed to be the king's famous steed Orelia, along with a royal crown and a pearl-embroidered sandal.

One credible theory is that Roderic, wounded, was borne along by his retreating army. Spanish sources, writes historian Rafael Altamira (*Cambridge Medieval History*), offer evidence that he rallied his forces at Medina Sidonia, held out another two years while being pushed gradually north, and died in a final battle in Salamanca province in 713. And the ninth-century *Chronicle of Alfonso III* describes a tomb discovered near the town of Viseu in central Portugal, inscribed in Latin "Here lies Rudericus, king of the Goths."

These events surely persuaded the Muslim invaders that Allah was fighting for them. As in Egypt, an apparently powerful nation had simply collapsed before their tiny armies. How else could this be accounted for? Therefore, although Musa had instructed Tariq to secure his landing and await further orders, Tariq was not so inclined. Instead, he dispatched his men in separate brigades to take town after town, and they continued to meet with signal success.

Byzantine inhabitants made no pretense of resistance because they never had much liked the Visigoths, comments historian Gabriel Jackson, in *The Making of Medieval Spain*, and the same was doubly true of any remaining Jews. Both hoped for better things from the newcomers, and in most instances were not disappointed. Tariq's commanders would leave one of the Jews in charge at each town, along with a small garrison, and move on to the next.

Initially, few Visigoths put up a fight either. One exception, Count Theodemir, lost most of his army defending the mountain passes of Murcia, and took refuge in Orihuela. Spanish legend tells how he had all the women there dress as warriors, with helmets and long lance-like rods, and their hair artfully arranged, beard-like, beneath their chins. He posted them on the walls to simulate a hefty garrison, then negotiated with the Muslim commander a surrender on favorable terms. Once official seals and signatures were affixed, of course, and the Muslims entered the town, the ruse was obvious. So impressed was their commander by Theodemir's boldness, however, that he appointed him governor of Murcia, which the Arab conquerors took to calling Tudmir (Theodemir's land).[6]

Meanwhile another Muslim force, assigned to capture Cordova, found a breach in the wall, infiltrated the city by night, and took it with scarcely a fight. Tariq marched on Toledo, where tradition holds that Jews opened the gates to him. There he reportedly met with Julian and some of the Witiza faction, and assigned

A sixth-century Visigoth gold cross (above). Whatever the qualities of the Visigoth kingdom, religious tolerance was not among them.

6. "Where are the soldiers I saw lining your walls?" the Muslim general demanded of Count Theodemir, defender of Orihuela, after the town negotiated favorable terms and surrendered. Theodemir acknowledged his trickery: "Soldiers have I none," he replied; "with these women [disguised in armor] I manned my walls." But the Muslim commander honored the surrender terms; a bargain was a bargain. Such chivalrous attitudes, historian Stanley Lane-Poole observes in *The Berbers in Spain*, greatly impressed the Visigoths, and their descendants as well. For centuries, the Christians would address their Andalusian enemies as "Knights of Granada, Gentlemen albeit Moors."

them official posts, including that of archbishop of Toledo. This went to a man called Oppas, who may or may not have been Witiza's brother. It is quite unlikely, however, that he was a legitimate bishop in communion with Rome, and a traitor to his faith. His name, a common one, does not appear on the official list of Toledo archbishops, and as Warren H. Carroll observes in *The Building of Christendom*, the Muslims preferred to install heretical bishops of their own choosing.

By the end of 711, less than half a year after their landing, they controlled half the Iberian Peninsula, but Musa was less than pleased with Tariq's performance. Not only was Tariq getting most of the glory and of the plunder, he was also bypassing important cities. So Musa followed his lieutenant across the strait with another eighteen thousand men, including cohorts of Arabs as well as Berbers, and attacked Carmona, Seville and Merida. Merida obstinately resisted, not capitulating until June 713, and Seville later rebelled and was subdued by Musa's son Abd al-Aziz. Musa himself proceeded to Toledo to confront Tariq with his disobedience.

In *The Berbers in Spain*, historian Stanley Lane-Poole tells the tale of their encounter. Tariq stepped forward to welcome the supreme governor of North Africa to the conquered Visigoth capital—whereupon Musa lashed at him with his whip, furiously upbraided him for exceeding orders, and put him in chains.

Tariq stepped forward to welcome Musa to Toledo, whereupon Musa lashed at him with his whip, upbraiding him for exceeding his orders.

But Tariq was in favor with the caliph, al-Walid, who now ordered Musa to reinstate him (for "he must not render useless one of the best swords of Islam"). Al-Walid also ordered Musa to come in person to Damascus, which to his very great sorrow he did the following summer.[7]

As Musa departed on the long march to Damascus in 714, the Muslims in Spain were extending their conquest to the Douro River in the northwest, writes Jackson, "more by diplomacy than battle." In the northeast, they captured Saragossa (the old Caesarea Augusta) on the Ebro River, and received the submission of such other cities as Barcelona on the Mediterranean coast. Andalusia began settling down in relative peace under Abd al-Aziz, a process greatly encouraged by consistent application of the policy that had worked so well from the beginning. While resistance was met with utmost severity, submission was always rewarded by what has since been widely recognized as the mildest governance the Muslims ever accorded any country.

The only property confiscated was that of the pro-Roderic faction or the church; other estate owners merely had to pay equitable taxes. Local judges and priests continued to function as before. There were no forced conversions of Christians or Jews; they simply had to pay a poll tax. Conversion was usually discouraged, in fact, since the Andalusian emirs (governors) were reluctant to forego this tax revenue. Even the clergy, perhaps bearing in mind the peninsula's

7. Musa ibn Nusair, Islamic conqueror of the Iberian Peninsula, began his triumphal march from Ceuta to Damascus in 714, trailing hundreds of noble Visigoth captives, vast retinues of slaves, and much treasure. The caliph, al-Walid, although very ill, delightedly received him and his offerings, but forty days later, al-Walid died, and his brother Suleyman became caliph. Accusing Musa of rapacity and self-aggrandizement, Suleyman forced the eighty-year-old warrior to stand all day in the hot sun and to pay an enormous fine, then banished him. Musa's son Abd al-Aziz, first governor of Andalusia, fared even worse. He was murdered on Suleyman's orders, and his head sent to Damascus so the caliph could exhibit it to his exiled father.

long Arian history, made no protest. There seem to have been no martyrs, or even very militant Christians—except, that is, in mountainous Asturias.

In this narrow northern strip on the Bay of Biscay, which even Rome had never penetrated, constant rain and snow had carved countless cirques, sink holes, alpine lakes and huge underground caverns into the great mountains of the Picos de Europa range. Here, at a place called Covadonga, the few stubborn Visigoth nobles who would not submit to the new Islamic overlords took refuge, perhaps finding allies among the independent-minded Iberian and Celtic inhabitants of Asturias. Establishing themselves in a cavern they called Santa Maria, they elected as their king a cousin of Roderic's named Pelayo, who had fled the country about fifteen years earlier to escape death during Witiza's takeover.

In their mountain fastness, they waited for the blow they knew would come: the last Muslim thrust to secure all Spain for the Qur'an. About 722, it came. An army of twenty-five thousand, according to *The Chronicle of Alfonso III*, pushed north to put an end to what the Arab sources call "these despicable barbarians." It was led by a Muslim commander and by Archbishop Oppas of Toledo, two experienced fighters, but the legends say that the hills and the heavens were both against them. An appearance of the Virgin Mary turned back their own arrows on the attackers. Then Pelayo lured them into a narrow defile, where his men loosed great boulders to crush them and block their retreat. Then the Diva River rose in a terrible storm and drowned many of the trapped warriors.[8]

After this, Muslim strategists decided that further effort to subdue the northwest—Galicia, Asturias, Leon, Castile and their mountainous neighbors—just was not worthwhile. Already they possessed, as the first European province of the Islamic Empire, the largest, richest and generally most pleasant part of the peninsula. Moreover, the remaining northeastern region offered far more beguiling possibilities than the stony, inhospitable, cold northwest. It was a

The caves and gorges of Spain's Picos de Europa Mountains provided an effective refuge for the Visigoth remnant holding out against the Muslim invasion. Pelayo and his small army, reputedly encouraged the night before the battle by the Virgin Mary, were victorious in the Battle of Covadonga, securing a sliver of territory for Christianity. This chapel (above), built into a mountain cave at Covadonga, dates from the eighth century.

8. Pelayo, first king of the Christian refugees in Asturias, who in effect launched the reconquest of Spain at the Battle of Covadonga, reigned nineteen years. In later centuries, the craggy battle site would be transformed into a memorial, and the remains of Pelayo and his wife, Gaudiosa, were entombed in the Cave of Santa Maria itself. Made accessible by a marble stairway in place of the original rough ladder, it became a popular shrine. Even in the nineteenth century, writes historian Henri Coppee, the locals liked to point out to visitors the streams that ran with Muslim blood, and the great rocks the defenders hurled down upon them. In 1918, the whole area would become a vast national park.

richer source of booty, and it offered a clear passage into the continent. Although Musa himself probably never crossed the Pyrenees, some chronicles claim that he dreamed of a land link across Europe to the caliph in Damascus.

Though clearly attractive at the time, this strategy was to prove a grave error. Within a generation, Pelayo's son-in-law, Alfonso I, would make the first small moves of the *Reconquista*, the recovery of Spain. To complete the reconquest would take more than seven centuries, but it began with the Battle of Covadonga. An old North American Indian proverb warns: "If you destroy a wasps' nest, do not forget to destroy the wasps." The Muslims neglected to destroy the wasps.

They began instead to raid into Visigoth territory north of the Pyrenees, easily defeating Duke Eudo of Aquitaine in 719, and thereafter pillaging his towns almost at will. They seized Narbonne, which they would hold for forty years, attacked Toulouse and Carcassonne, and in 725, reached into Burgundy to sack Autun. But by now, they were seriously threatening the kingdom of the Franks, the land later known as France, a people the Muslims had not yet encountered, and would not soon forget. The Franks were noted for many things, some outright contradictory: for fervent fidelity to Christian orthodoxy, for saintly monks and nuns, for fearless ferocity in war, for implacable determination, and not infrequently for gross cruelty and licentiousness.

In 732, a year that looms large in Christian history, the armies of Islam came up hard against the Franks. A major raiding force led by Abd al-Rahman ibn Abdullah al-Ghafiqi, the new emir of Andalusia, again defeated Eudo on the Garonne River near Bordeaux, then stormed, plundered and burned the city. Al-Rahman next headed towards Tours on the Loire, the city of Blessed Martin, revered pilgrimage center of the Franks, and therefore an especially promising prospect for more pillage.

But on the old Roman road that led from Poitiers to Tours (and thence to Paris, about another hundred miles distant) the booty-laden raiders encountered a formidable force of Franks. Tall, blond, hefty foot soldiers, they doubtless were veterans of constant conflict with invaders on other fronts: Bavarians, Alamanni, Saxons and Frisians. Moreover, they were commanded by the man who was currently establishing his control over the Merovingian kingdoms of Gaul, and founding in the process a new and powerful dynasty: Charles, a natural son of Pepin II. (See earlier volume, *Darkness Descends*, chapter 8.)

Charles Martel (below) acquired the nickname "the Hammer" after his victory at the Battle of Tours in 732. Charles's fearsome and disciplined warriors, accustomed to the terrain and weather, halted the Muslim invasion in one of the most decisive battles in European and Christian history.

Unnerved by this spectacle, the Muslims drew back and made camp, the chronicles say, and for most of a week, the two armies took each other's measure with light skirmishing. Charles was probably doing some local recruiting. Al-Rahman may have been moving some of his loot to a safer locale, while seeking a way to outflank his opponents. But at length he gave the signal and his mounted Berbers attacked, swooping in with javelin and cutlass on their small, swift horses. According to J. F. C. Fuller (*Decisive Battles of the Western World*), this was the sole Berber battle tactic: a wild, headlong charge continually repeated and "very wasteful of men." (Of defensive tactics, Fuller adds, they possessed none worth mentioning.)

The Franks, clothed in leather and steel, their fair hair streaming below their helmets, were armed with spears, battle-axes and great two-edged swords, and drawn up as a solid phalanx ranged shoulder to shoulder, shield to shield. "The men of the north stood motionless like a wall of ice," writes the awestricken chronicler Isidore of Beja. All day long, as wave after wave of Muslim cavalry

The Franks were clothed in leather and steel, fair hair streaming below their helmets, and drawn up in a solid phalanx.

crashed against them, they hacked and slashed down men and horses until the road and surrounding fields were choked with corpses.

Behind the carnage, the wall of Franks held firm—immovable, silent, awaiting the next charge, its dead propped up by the living—and against it, the Muslim cavalry eventually cracked and broke. By nightfall, so many Berber and Arab bodies were strewn on the battlefield that it became known in Andalusia as the Pavement of Martyrs. One of the martyrs was the commander himself, al-Rahman, leaving his army leaderless, but the Franks had no way of knowing this. They only knew, as they slumped exhausted in their places, that the attacks had ceased.

At dawn, their scouts cautiously approached the silent enemy tents (which were made, admiring Christian chroniclers noted, of crimson, yellow, and purple silk) and discovered—no one at all. The entire Islamic force was gone. They had abandoned the field, their tents, and even plunder and equipment. As for the Frankish leader, he had earned a name that would ring down the centuries: Charles Martel, meaning Charles the Hammer. "As a hammer of iron, of steel, and of every other metal," declared *The Chronicle of Saint Denis*, "even so he dashed and smote in the battle all his enemies."

Gibbon saw the Battle of Tours, sometimes called the Battle of Poitiers,[9] as decisive for the future of Europe. "A victorious line had been prolonged above a thousand miles from the Rock of Gibraltar to the banks of the Loire," he wrote. "The repetition of an equal space would have carried the Saracens to the confines of Poland and the highlands of Scotland . . . and the Arabian fleet might have sailed without a naval combat into the mouth of the Thames. Perhaps the

9. History recognizes three "Battles of Poitiers," the first in 507, when Clovis's Franks defeated the Visigoths of Alaric II; the second in 732, when Charles Martel stopped the Muslim attack into France; and the third in 1356, when England's "Black Prince," son of Edward III, defeated the French in the Hundred Years War.

interpretation of the Qur'an would now be taught in the schools of Oxford, and her pupils might demonstrate to a circumcised people the sanctity and truth of the revelation of Mahomet."

Later historians have scoffed at Gibbon's suggestion, pointing out that al-Rahman's offensive was no more than a large exploratory raid, aimed not at conquest but at plunder, but this contention ignores the fact that every Muslim conquest from Syria to Spain began with just such exploratory raids. When the raiders returned triumphant, loaded with loot and leading their despairing trains of enslaved people, conquest inevitably followed. In this first Muslim encounter with the Franks, however, the pattern was conclusively smashed. Here, the raiders had to abandon their booty, they brought home no slaves, and their leader and most of their comrades were dead.

After several more desultory ventures north of the Pyrenees produced similar results, the Muslims of al-Andalus seemed to lose all serious interest in the land of the Franks. Besides, the Berbers of North Africa now rose in rebellion against the Umayyad caliphate, just as they used to rebel against the Romans. This cut off Andalusia from Damascus, and also blocked the emirs' chief source of fresh warriors.

Fifteen years before the Battle of Tours, however, the Muslims had launched an attack whose long-term implications for Europe would nowhere be disputed. It was a full-scale attack on Constantinople—and it filled with dread that citadel of Christianity in the east. ■

The intensity of the clash between the Franks and Muslims at Tours is captured in this painting by the nineteenth-century artist Carl von Steuben (below). Muslim forces would remain for years in some areas of southern France, but the battle effectively marked the end of Muslim expansion in the west.

'This unfaithful and cruel sea'

The desert Arabs' fear of salt water gives way to practical military considerations, and in half a century Muslim fleets effectively control most of the Mediterranean

Perhaps the greatest Muslim triumph in Islam's century of conquest was not won on land but on water, something of which the desert-born Arabs had a pathological fear. They handily overcame it, however, and in a series of encounters with the Byzantine fleet, scored what some describe as the most decisive victory of them all. They claimed the Mediterranean Sea for Islam.

For more than eight hundred years—from the Roman destruction of Carthage in 146 B.C.—the Mediterranean had been *mare nostrum*, "our sea," to the Romans. Maritime trade was the source of much of the empire's wealth, and the sea was its highway. When Rome became Christian, it became, in effect, a Christian sea.

At the close of the seventh century A.D., however, much of the Mediterranean fell to the Muslims. For the next hundred years, the Byzantines would contest the issue, but in Muslim hands it would largely remain.

For the Muslims, intent on bestowing Islam upon the world, control of the Mediterranean was not a matter of choice, but of necessity. As long as the coastal cities of Syria, Palestine, Egypt and North Africa could be easily supplied by the Byzantine fleet, taking them was difficult and holding them impossible. Alexandria had fallen and been recaptured from the sea. So had Carthage.

However, the whole suggestion of risking his armies on the uncertainties of the sea was unthinkable to the caliph Umar. "Better to hear the flatulence of the camels than the prayers of the fishes," says an old Bedouin proverb. But Umar's provincial officialdom was less timorous. Even before the Muslim armies had extended their reach through North Africa, the Arab governor of Syria, Mu'awiya, had lobbied the caliph for permission to launch an attack on Cyprus, the large and strategically important island a mere fifty miles off the Syrian coast. "The isles of the Levant are so close to the Syrian shore," he wrote, "you might almost hear the barking of the dogs and cackling of the hens. Give me leave to attack them!"

Umar's response was unequivocal: "I will never let any Muslim venture on the sea. . . . How can I permit my soldiers to sail upon this unfaithful and cruel sea! By God, a single Muslim is dearer to me than all the treasures of the Greeks. Do not try and dissuade me now that I have made known my wishes. Remember the fate of al-Ala. . . ."[1]

So when Amr, the Arab governor in Egypt, planned to make the great port city of Alexandria his capital, Umar quickly scotched the idea. "I do not wish any water to lie between me and the Muslims, either in summer or in winter." Amr established a new capital on the Nile, near the desert fortress known as Babylon. It would eventually become Cairo.[2]

Soon, however, necessity dictated policy. Clearly, some form of naval organization was necessary, if only to defend the conquered coastal territories. Therefore, Umar's successor, Uthman, permitted Mu'awiya to carry out naval operations, but with the curious stipulation that commanders take their wives on naval campaigns—presumably to prevent rashness. Thereafter, the Muslim fleet grew rapidly.

In 648, Mu'awiya successfully raided Cyprus, and over the next half-dozen years, Muslim vessels struck across the Mediterranean as far as Sicily (attacked by a fleet of two hundred ships in 652). The important Aegean islands of Cos and Crete were comprehensively pillaged. The Byzantines found an attack on the large island of Rhodes particularly galling. The raiders dismantled what remained of the Colossus of Rhodes, one of the wonders of the ancient world, and sold it for scrap![3]

Conquest soon succeeded raiding. In 653, Mu'awiya landed on Cyprus again, plundered it for forty days, established a garrison of twelve thousand men, and permanently occupied it. The following year, a huge Byzantine fleet (at least seven hundred ships) set out from Constantinople and met a smaller Muslim squadron in battle. It was the first great sea engagement between the upstart Muslims and the dominant sea power of the Mediterranean—and the result was a humiliating defeat for the Christian forces.

Uneasy at first, the Muslim commanders put many of their troops ashore and sailed out to meet the Byzantines with half-manned ships.[4] Since they considered themselves far better soldiers than sailors, they lashed their ships together with chains, creating a floating battlefield, then laid into the Byzantine marines with sword, spear and dagger. A bloody business, it lasted a day and a half, and became known as the Battle of the Masts. Unable to maneuver against the tightly packed mass of Muslim vessels, individual Byzantine ships closed with the enemy and were picked off one by one—until most of their fleet was destroyed. An estimated twenty thousand Christian sailors and marines perished.

For the Christians, it was a calamity, but politics prevented the Muslims from exploiting it. With Mu'awiya's attention focused on the Muslim civil war (see chapter 7) there were no further naval battles for a decade. The Byzantine emperor, Constans II, used the time well. He moved an army and fleet to Sicily, reestablished imperial control of much of southern Italy, and reinforced the Byzantine presence in North Africa and the islands of the western Mediterranean. (This last reunification of Byzantium's far-flung possessions would stand for over thirty years, until the final, decisive Muslim assault on North Africa.)

Meanwhile, in the eastern Mediterranean, the end of the Muslim civil war meant a return to large-scale naval conflict. And from 669 on, the Muslims aimed at nothing less than Mediterranean conquest, says the historian Archibald R. Lewis (*Naval Power and Trade*). Their main interest now was Constantinople itself. Several expeditions were aimed at the imperial capital, including a testing raid that penetrated as far as Chalcedon, a stone's throw away on the Asian side of the Bosporus. A much bigger operation against the islands of the Aegean followed. Crete was attacked and Rhodes overrun,

all as the first necessary stage in a massive assault on the Byzantine capital.

In 673, a vast armada of Egyptian and Syrian naval vessels arrived to initiate what would become a seven-year blockade of Constantinople. The empire was heavily dependent on shipping for essential supplies from other parts of the empire. However, with some difficulty, the capital could be resupplied from the Black Sea, to the north, and via land routes on the European side of the Bosporus. As a result, ultimately the siege was ineffective, and the Muslim fleet withdrew.

Muslim hegemony in the eastern Mediterranean now seemed to be in retreat. After a thirty-year occupation, their garrison left Cyprus and the caliph was forced to accept a peace treaty and an annual tribute to Byzantium of three thousand pounds of gold, fifty captives and fifty horses. But by the century's end a new Muslim initiative gave them undisputed control in both east and west.

The flash point this time was the ancient city of Carthage, taken by a Muslim army in 695, and regained by the Byzantines from the sea the following year. Back came the Muslims in 698, recapturing the city, and this time making their conquest permanent.

Since Carthage was vulnerable to Byzantine sea attack, the conquerors dug a canal connecting the sea to a nearby inland lake. There, with the help of one thousand Coptic shipbuilders sent from Alexandria, the Muslims built a new fleet of one hundred warships. This also gave birth to the city of Tunis, capital of modern day Tunisia.

With that, Carthage was abandoned, and the Muslim fleet, operating from its impregnable new base, gained complete mastery of the western Mediterranean. Never seriously challenged by the Byzantines, the Muslim navy launched massive raids against the strategic island of Sicily, and in the coming decade, they protected the flank of the Muslim armies in their conquest of Spain.

Not once did the Byzantines attack them. ∎

1. Umar's experience of the sea had been all bad. In 638, the Muslim general al-Ala landed troops on the farther coast of the Persian Gulf. Cut off from his ships by an enemy force, he had to be rescued by Umar. Three years later, Umar authorized a naval operation on the Red Sea to ward off attacks on Arab shipping and settlements. This, too, had turned into an unmitigated disaster, with most of the ships destroyed by weather or enemy action.

2. Amr himself was no fan of the sea, writes historian Aly Mohamed Fahmy (*Muslim Sea-Power in the Eastern Mediterranean from the Seventh to the Tenth Century A.D.*). In a letter to Umar, he sums up the traditional Bedouin attitude to salt water. "The sea is like a huge monster upon which innumerable tiny creatures climb; nothing but the sky above and the water beneath; when it is calm, the heart is sad, but when it is tempestuous, the senses reel. One must trust it little and fear it much. Those who sail it, like worms on a splinter, are now engulfed and now scared to death."

3. The Colossus of Rhodes, built in 282 B.C., was a one-hundred-foot-tall bronze statue of the Greek sun god, Helios, standing astride the entrance to the harbor. An earthquake had toppled it in 226 B.C. but its impressive remains drew visitors for eight hundred years—until Mu'awiya's raiders dismantled it and sold it to a Jewish trader, who carried off the scrap on the backs of nine hundred camels. For many years, pieces of it turned up along the Asian caravan routes.

4. The Arabs adopted two main types of naval vessels, common in the eastern Mediterranean at the time. *katenai* were auxiliary transport ships, large and heavy, used mainly for hauling supplies, but which could also carry marines and be used as fighting vessels. The main "battleships" of the Arab fleet were *dromons*; sleek, two-story vessels with long banks of oars to supplement the sail. According to naval historian Admiral W. L. Rogers (*Naval Warfare under Oars*), they had a regular crew of two hundred rowers and forty or more fighting marines. In battle, there would have been a hundred or more troops packed on the dromon's deck.

Once the Muslims had overcome their antipathy for salt water, they became masters of the Mediterranean, a crucial development in their final conquest of the coastal cities of North Africa, and the invasion of Spain. The capture of Carthage, in 698, proved to be the demise of the ancient and once-powerful city, whose ruins are pictured here.

The fabled city of Constantinople, from a medieval German woodcut. By 717, much of the Christian world had been lost to Islam, and the Muslim juggernaut once more turned its attention to the imperial capital. Its fall appeared imminent, a foregone conclusion.

CHAPTER 10

Islam's final goal, the glittering prize of Constantinople

A great Muslim armada blockades the Byzantine capital, but Christian determination and a deadly secret weapon decide one of the most pivotal events in western history

To the Muslims in the ninety-seventh year of hijra (the Christian year 717), the war to conquer the world for Islam was all but won. The vast and ostensibly omnipotent Persian Empire had by now been Islamic for eighty years. Syria was Muslim, as was the government of Egypt. In North Africa, the cries of the muezzin sounded from mosques that had once been churches, and the Berbers were learning to memorize the Qur'an rather than listen to the Bible. The Mediterranean could now be considered a Muslim sea. Muslim troops were hard at work on the conquest of Sicily. Italian ports were under attack, and it seemed certain that southern Italy would be engulfed. Anyone could see that Rome would soon fall. It had never been easily defensible, and it was now little more than a ghost city. Spain, too, was already Muslim, its surviving Christian element driven into the mountain fastnesses of the north. France and the Franks would be next, or so it was assumed. The Muslim conquest of what is now Pakistan was under way. The vast, mysterious empire of China would dependably fall when Allah was ready to move his attention farther east.

Near at hand, the last remaining formidable Muslim objective was Constantinople, seat of the once-great Roman–Byzantine Empire, whose imperial rulers of late had behaved like madmen, and whose government was corrupt to the core. Its imminent demise was a foregone conclusion, the ruling caliph was confident, and this last and greatest conquest would assuredly spell the end of the fading religion known as Christianity.

For eight decades leading up to the fateful year 717, when the overwhelming naval and land forces of Islam would appear before Constantinople to deliver the final blow, one calamity after another had befallen the Christians. Indeed, it seemed to some that Christ himself had finally forsaken his people. The reversals went right back to the 630s and the reign of the emperor Heraclius, the man who lost Christendom to the Persians, and then heroically, even miraculously, snatched it back from them, only to see most of his empire conquered in a few short years by this ominous desert phenomenon, whose adherants called so assuredly and triumphantly on God, whom they named Allah.

From the catastrophic loss of Syria, Jerusalem, Palestine, and the impending fall of Egypt, Heraclius had headed home to his capital, enfeebled in body and mind. At Chalcedon, he could go no farther. Now afflicted by a pathological

Byzantium had found itself in desperate straits before, but the empire now seemed to relapse into lethargy, its neglected cities wasting away.

dread of water, he refused to make the half-mile crossing until a bridge of boats and barges was chained tightly together, piled with tons of soil, and bordered with high artificial hedges, so that he could ride over it without seeing the water. To such an absurdity had the world's greatest empire been reduced. Ensconced in the imperial residence, he fell ill with dropsy, and suffered grievous affliction,[1] while contemplating an empire sick at heart and sicker at soul.

Both Heraclius and Byzantium had been in desperate straits before, of course. Twenty-five years earlier, when he had roused the city to defend itself against the Persians and Avars, he had worked a startling moral reform. But the empire now seemed to have relapsed irretrievably into lethargy. Its neglected cities were wasting away. The ill-trained, ineffective army was often enmeshed in politics. The barbarians ravaged the provinces undeterred, killing, stealing and abducting. Learning was in hopeless decline. Meanwhile, in the provinces and the capital alike, the aristocracy continued to live in luxury described and deplored by the twentieth-century historian Prosper Boissonnade in *Life and Work in Medieval Europe*: "Their dwellings, half palaces and half fortresses, were elegantly decorated, spacious and beautiful. There they displayed all their luxury; their embroidered robes, their gold plate, gems, enamels, and precious silks, their table groaning under abundant foods, their stables full of fine horses and carriages."

The church, too, was becoming steadily more dissolute. The Quinisext Council,[2] held at Heraclius's Trulla Palace a half-century after his death, would paint a detailed portrait of Christians reverting to pagan superstition and licentiousness. Canon 61 issued by that council would forbid soothsaying, the selling

1. The condition called "dropsy" occurs when the body's ability to discharge fluids is impaired and edema or gross swelling results. All of which, the historian Nicephorus piously adds, the emperor had clearly brought upon himself—as "the penalty for his moral transgressions, and the final judgment for marrying his niece."

2. The Quinisext Council of 692 was so called because it was considered the completion of the Fifth Council of 553 (*quintus* means fifth) and the Sixth of 681 (*sextus* means sixth). It is also known as the "Trullan Council," because it took place in the domed room (trullus) of the imperial palace. Although its moral strictures gained wide attention, its principal function was not disciplinary, but rather to reconcile the administrative practices of the eastern and western churches.

of tufts of wild animal hair as amulets, and the working of "enchantments." Canon 63 would ban invocation of the god Dionysius at the grape harvest and other pagan festivities, with lewd dancing and male–female role reversal. The bishops would also find it necessary to forbid their clergy to run taverns, to act as loan sharks, charge for the sacraments, bathe with women, or serve as pimps. (Some historians warn, however, that fulminations heard at church councils do not necessarily reflect general Christian behavior, but unusual moral abuses.)

In the midst of social decline and personal agony, Heraclius died on February 11, 641, at the age of sixty-six. No deathbed description survives. He was "one of those unfortunate heroes who have outlived their glory, and have thereby won the sympathy as well as the admiration of posterity," writes the historian J. B. Bury in his *History of the Later Roman Empire*. But Heraclius fared better in death than in life. "He passed into medieval legend," Bury notes. By the twelfth century, he was celebrated in written romance and in heroic painting and sculpture, including a massive statue at Barletta, Italy.

Though precedents existed, many believed that Heraclius's plan for the succession reflected the final frailty of his mind, and the machinations of his scheming wife, Martina. She was the niece he married after his first wife died, incurring the church's denunciation for incest. He established a triumvirate—his eldest son Constantine III, twenty-nine, who had already ruled with him for seventeen years; Heraclonus, aged fifteen, his eldest son by Martina; and Martina herself. The immediate result was a ten-month feud in which Constantine III died (poisoned, some said, by Martina), in which the army was recalled from the Muslim front in Asia Minor to protect Constantine III's children, and in which three emperors reigned at once. One of the three was banished, his nose slit;[3] another simply disappeared. Martina was exiled by the Senate, after her tongue was silenced by being cut out. Finally Constans II, eldest son of Constantine III, was proclaimed emperor at age eleven.

Child though he was, Constans knew he had to grow up quickly. For his grandfather Heraclius, Islam had been only the nightmare of his final years; it was Constans's principal threat from the start. In 646, when he was sixteen, an immense Byzantine fleet, sent to the relief of Alexandria, was decisively defeated near the harbor entrance. The Muslims then advanced along the African coast, taking first Barqa, then Tripoli. In 646, a Byzantine army striving to drive them

The emperors Heraclius, Constantine IV and Tiberius (above), pictured in a seventh-century mosaic at the Basilica of Saint Apollinaire in Classe, on the outskirts of the important Byzantine city of Ravenna, Italy.

3. The practice of mutilation by the Byzantines, which began with the Heraclian dynasty, originally included the slitting of the tongue or occasionally its outright amputation, as with the empress Martina, or the slitting of the nose, as with her deported son. Nose-slitting was intended to so disfigure the victim that he would become ineligible to rule. The practice of mutilation continued through most of Byzantine history, though the historian J. B. Bury (*History of the Later Roman Empire*) speculates that it eventually consisted of "little more than a severe and indelible brand that did not affect the victim's general well-being."

In 651, an Arab army rampaged through the cities of Asia Minor and returned to Syria with five thousand Christian slaves. The same year Byzantine forces failed to halt an invasion of Armenia, which eventually became subject to the expanding Muslim Empire.

from Syria was wiped out, and in 647, a 120,000-man Byzantine army was obliterated near Carthage. In 649, the Muslims, rapidly gaining naval power, pillaged Cyprus. In 651, they broke through into Asia Minor and returned to Syria with five thousand Christian slaves. That same year, a Byzantine attempt to save Armenia from Islam failed, and three years later, that ancient Christian country became an Islamic tributary state. The rich island of Rhodes fell in 655. Sicily went next. The eastern Mediterranean became a Muslim sea.

By now, Constans was twenty-five. Eager to do more than look on in helpless horror, he took personal command of a newly assembled Byzantine fleet. Although warned in a dream that he was headed for calamity,[4] he ordered an attack on a Muslim squadron at Phoenix, off the southwest coast of Asia Minor. But as each ship came alongside an enemy vessel, the scimitar-swinging Muslims easily bested the Christians, and the decks ran red with their blood.

Changing garments with a sailor, Constans escaped by leaping from one ship to another, while one intrepid Byzantine soldier stood by the man who had donned the emperor's clothes, fighting off the swarm of Muslims who sought to take the biggest

Constans executed a master plan to save the empire. He would move his capital back to Old Rome, or, better still, he would move it to Sicily.

prize of all, an imperial prisoner. Finally, both were slain, and the impersonation discovered—but not the emperor. The destruction of the Byzantine fleet in 655 would have spelled immediate doom for Constantinople if the Muslims had followed it up, but they could not. From 656, they were distracted by civil war, giving Constans a five-year breather, and in 659 the caliph, Mu'awiya, agreed to a treaty.

In those five years, Constans executed his master plan to save the empire. With Egypt, Palestine, Syria and Armenia gone, and with Asia Minor and the eastern Mediterranean threatened, he concluded that Constantinople was doomed. Moreover, he intensely disliked the place. His theological effort to restore the unity of the faith, known as "The Type," had been contemptuously rejected there (see subchapter, page 144), and its people continually demonstrated their disdain for him. He would therefore move his capital back to Old Rome, or better still, to Sicily. From there, he reasoned, he could safeguard Carthage, North Africa and Spain against Islam, recover Egypt, and eventually regain Italy from the Lombards.

His grandfather before him, reasoning likewise, had been persuaded to stay, but nobody pleaded with Constans to stay, and one final act sealed his reputation as a scoundrel. To secure the succession, he named his eldest son co-emperor, as Constantine IV, and probably bestowed the title of Caesar on his two younger sons. Then, to prevent rival claims, he quietly had his own younger brother executed. This, thought the capital, was cold-blooded murder.

Constans left for Italy with an army in 662, briefly occupied Naples, and then became the first eastern emperor in nearly three hundred years to visit Rome.

4. The night before the naval Battle of Phoenix, the emperor Constans dreamed he was in Thessalonica. He awakened and immediately consulted an interpreter of dreams as to what this meant. It means, said the interpreter, "that the victory inclines to your foe." Next day, Constans found good reason to wish he had heeded the warning.

For the defiant, Islam spells misery

To the Christians of Armenia, the Muslim conquest becomes one more ordeal in a long history of pain and suffering which continues into the modern era

That Armenia's Muslim conquerors should want to confer with the nation's former leaders had seemed in all respects understandable. After all, those leaders had long been running the country. So some four hundred Armenian noblemen obliged—along with their retainers, and according to one account, their families. The meeting, they discovered, was to be held in a church. That was odd—yet reasonable, too. Armenia was the oldest Christian nation in the world. So into the church they went, most of them anyway. And they waited.

The scene that ensued can be imagined. A distinct uncertainty settles on the crowd. The women huddle up to the church walls and attempt to soothe their children, who, seemingly aware of peril, whimper fearfully. The men stand. They speak in hushed, uneasy voices. Then, from outside the open doors, comes the audible trot of horses. Then voices. The language is not at all familiar.

Suddenly, there is a crash of activity. The church doors are slammed shut. Locks clank. Windows are barricaded. "That's smoke!" someone shouts. With a piercing cry, the Armenians realize in horror that the church is being set ablaze around them. A stampede ensues. Women scream. Babies cry. Men hopelessly heave themselves against the doors with all their collective might. Soon, people without further strength collapse. Others trip and trample over them.

The screaming turns to convulsive coughing, then to gasping, finally to a strange and eerie silence. The church has become a mass tomb.

The rest is history. The church that night in Nakchivian, an Armenian city close to modern Azerbaijan, was burned to the ground by the Muslims. How many died is unknown. Most of the four hundred Armenian nobility perished. Those few who had decided to wait outside the church were rounded up, tortured and crucified. One question, it seemed, had been answered. Life under the Persians had often been a horror of brutality and bloodshed. Though the Muslims tolerated those who surrendered without resistance, this would never include the Armenians. They always resisted. So for them, under the Muslims, nothing would change.

Suffering was scarcely a novel experience to the Armenians. They had struggled to retain their Christian faith against Persian persecution since their conversion in 301. They had invented an alphabet, forged a written language, translated the scriptures, composed a liturgy, built hundreds of churches, and trained their priests and monks who taught their people to read. Then came an ultimatum. In 450, the Persian king Yazdegerd II, discerning their Christianity as evidence of weakness, with its concept of "turning the other cheek," decided to crack down. All Armenians must convert to Zoroastrianism, Persia's

A ninth-century church stands on the shore of Lake Sevan, Armenia, amid the ruins of a larger building. In 701, in a similar church at Nakchivian, most of Armenia's nobility perished at the hands of their Muslim conquerors.

state religion, or face exile, torture, even death, he ruled. He erred. The Armenians did not turn the other cheek, and in the resulting showdown, sixty thousand defiant Armenians faced two hundred and twenty thousand heavily armed Persians at the Plain of Avarayr. The Armenian leader, Vardan Mamikonean, addressed his men in words that would echo far beyond Armenia through all the Christian centuries:

> Do not be afraid of the multitude of the heathen. Do not turn your backs to the fearsome sword of a mortal man. For if the Lord puts victory in our grasp, we shall destroy their power, so that the cause of truth may be exalted. And if the time has come to end our lives in battle with a holy death, let us accept it with joyful hearts—provided only we do not mingle cowardice with valor and bravery.

In the realm of heroic mythology, such an appeal should be followed by an Armenian victory. It was not. After a vigorous fight, the Armenians lost the battle, and Vardan lay dead. But Armenia's faith was not dead. The indefatigable little nation patiently, painfully, and very effectively continued to resist until Persia learned an elementary lesson: you cannot defeat a mountain people in the mountains. By 484, as Persian casualties rose and Zoroastrian fervor fell, cooler heads prevailed. If the Armenians wanted to be Christians all that much, why not let them? That year, the Treaty of Nvarsak guaranteed religious freedom to Armenia.

It didn't last a century. In 572, another Persian king, Chosroes I, goaded into war by Byzantium, turned on the Armenians and demanded they abjure their faith. When the Persian governor began building a Zoroastrian fire-temple, a clear breach of the treaty,

rebellion brewed anew. The governor reacted violently. He had a bishop publicly clubbed, called in two thousand troops, and then found them confronting even more seditious Armenians, all proclaiming: "As long as one Armenian remains alive, no fire-temples would go up in Armenia." So Chosroes dispatched fifteen thousand more. He would "exterminate all who dare resist," he warned. Twenty thousand Armenians took the dare. "In the name of the Lord Jesus Christ," they roared, and proceeded to decimate the Persian force. They reported their victory to Constantinople, enclosing the governor's head by way of documentation.

Victory, however, did not mean peace. Quite the reverse. Armenia became the battleground between the two gigantic belligerents, alien to the Persians because it was Christian, alien to the Byzantines because it was Monophysite, the wrong kind of Christian. "A knavish and indocile nation," fumed the Byzantine emperor Maurice, "a source of constant trouble." He ordered many Armenians transported to Thrace. "If they die there," he declared, "it will be but the death of so many enemies." The Armenians saw the irony, as many fled into Zoroastrian Persia for refuge.

When, twenty years later, the emperor Heraclius offered the Armenians a doctrinal compromise on Monophysitism, they rejected it firmly, bringing on Byzantine persecution so severe that when the Arabs arrived in 640, the Armenians saw them as liberators. So at first they were. But in 701, with the Byzantines finally driven out and the Arabs in charge, things changed. How drastically they had changed became evident that night in the church at Nakchivian. Vulnerable little Armenia seemed destined to play the pitiable role of the buffer state, perpetually placed between empires as hostile as they were powerful. Surrounded by Islam, Armenia's plight as a minority religion would last into the twentieth century, when one and a half million Armenians perished for their faith in a holocaust to be described in a later volume. ■

A fanciful early medieval depiction (top) of Constantinople, "New Rome," and a stylized, but more accurate sixteenth-century map (above), showing the Golden Horn, bisecting the imperial capital, and the Sea of Marmara to the south of the city.

He did more than visit; he stripped many Roman churches of their bronze statuary, hauling it all to Syracuse in Sicily, and for the next six years imposed such heavy taxes on North Africa and southern Italy that both verged on revolt. One day in 668, a bath attendant hit him over the head with a heavy soap dish, killing him in an apparent usurpation attempt. It failed. Constantine IV, his eldest son, arrived swiftly from Constantinople and summarily dealt with the conspirators.

All the while, the Muslim shadow across Asia Minor grew longer, darker, and ever closer to the capital. In 664, a Syrian raiding force actually wintered in Roman territory, a bad omen. Raids grew larger and deeper, until in the year of Constans's assassination, Chalcedon was sacked, and its attackers withdrew only to Amorium, 160 miles to the southeast, for the winter. This time, however, young Constantine IV led a task force to Amorium, which scaled the walls over the deep snow and killed every Muslim in the place.

The caliph Mu'awiya at Damascus could scarcely ignore such an affront, however, and having won his civil war, was free to embark on a crowning triumph. The time had come to capture the Christian capital, and perhaps the disreputable little barbarian Christian states beyond it as well. At sea, the Christians had no real navy left. Muslim land forces, although outnumbered four-to-one, or even ten-to-one, had invariably defeated the Christian empire's decaying army. Mu'awiya need only put a fleet on the Sea of Marmara, the 125-mile-long body of water between the Black Sea and the Aegean, sink the remnants of the Byzantine navy, and land an army in Constantinople's Golden Horn Harbor.

By now, the Muslims were operating virtually unopposed in Asia Minor, raiding city after city. In 669, the year after Constans's assassination, they attacked Sicily in force, carrying away, among other things, all the treasures Constans had amassed there for his new capital. In 670, two Muslim fleets moved through the Aegean and captured Smyrna, scene of the martyrdom of the saintly bishop Polycarp in the second century. (See earlier volume, *A Pinch of Incense*, page 58.) Then they transited the Hellespont,[5] and set up a base at Cyzicus on the south coast of the Marmara.

But they had seriously underestimated Constantine IV. Still in his late teens, he supervised the construction of a new fleet of very small, very fast vessels that could attack like terriers, inflict telling damage, and then dodge away from the heavier Muslim ships—a seaborne version of the tactic that won so many Muslim land victories. Furthermore, the Byzantines were experimenting with a new and terrible weapon. Their fleet included several larger ships with a kind of

5. The Hellespont is the ancient name for the forty-mile channel that links the Aegean Sea to the western end of the Sea of Marmara, which at its eastern end is linked to the Black Sea by the nineteen-mile-long Bosporus. Constantinople, now Istanbul, stands on the European side of the Bosporus, where it joins with the Marmara. In ancient times, the Marmara was known as the Propontis, the Black Sea as the Euxine, from the Greek word for dark or black.

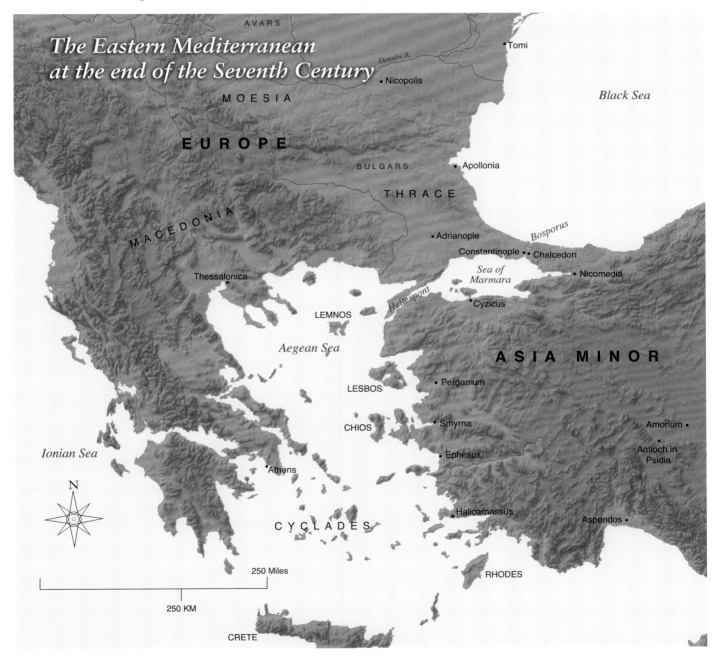

The Eastern Mediterranean at the end of the Seventh Century

spout protruding from the bow, which shot out an oily material intended to burst into flame on an enemy deck. Although not yet perfected, it was already spreading terror through the Muslim fleet.

Through the summer of 674, the Muslims patrolled the north coast of the Marmara without once attempting to land a soldier, and when winter came, retreated to their base at Cyzicus. So incessant were the Byzantine terrier attacks upon their fleet, and so increasingly effective the flaming oil, that this paralysis continued another two years. In 677, the Byzantine army in Asia Minor threatened the Muslim base at Cyzicus, leaving their fleet no option but to head for home, and it never got there. Caught by pursuing Byzantines at Syllaeum, off the south coast of Asia Minor, it suffered further grievous damage from the blazing oil, and then withdrew perforce into a ferocious storm that destroyed nearly all the remaining vessels.

The whole venture against Constantinople, in short, turned into one of Mu'awiya's few serious calamities, and forced him into an even more costly treaty. Constantine extracted from him payment of one pound of gold, one purebred horse, and one returned Christian slave for every day in the year. The treaty was to run for thirty years. The Byzantines wasted most of them.

Except, that is, in one regard: further development of their secret naval

The whole venture against Constantinople turned into one of Mu'awiya's few serious calamities, and forced him into a costly treaty.

weapon, which came to be known as "Greek fire," and is thought to have been discovered by a Christian Syrian architect named Callinicus. When the Muslims took over his homeland, Callinicus had made his way to Constantinople, where chemists and shipwrights worked to improve the incendiary potential of his invention, and perfect a way to project it. By the end of Mu'awiya's offensive, it had become the decisive weapon that saved the city. But the formula had to be kept secret—no mean trick in a city crawling with spies of every known nationality, which for the next forty years would be run by a succession of emperors whose incompetence still challenges belief.[6]

The Muslims had been learning, too. For one thing, they had discovered that Constantinople was not going to be another Antioch, Jerusalem or Alexandria, where theological feuds around the question of Monophysitism had so divided Christians that they could not unite to defend themselves. At Constantinople, they were not confused at all, and they knew by now what was at issue. If the city fell, the whole empire would become Islamic, the crosses would be stripped from the great churches, and most of them—beginning no doubt with mighty Hagia Sophia Cathedral itself—would become mosques. The Muslims, that is, were now up against an enemy as united in its religion as they were in theirs. So the capture of Constantinople—and captured it must be if Islam was to

6. The precise content of "Greek fire" is nowhere reliably recorded, although a tenth-century writer named Marcus Graecus leaves a treatise of instructions for making it: "Take pure sulfur, tartar, sarcocolla (Persian gum), pitch, dissolved niter, petroleum, and *huile de gemme* (probably a resin made from an undefined saline material); boil these ingredients together; saturate tow with the concoction, and set fire to it. The conflagration will spread, and can only be extinguished by urine, vinegar or sand."

An illustration from the Byzantine Scylitzes Chronicle *(left) showing noblemen boarding a* dromon, *the main warship of the seventh and eight centuries. The dromon was, in fact, a two or three-story battleship capable of carrying a crew of two hundred oarsmen and forty or more marines. The addition of weapons spewing Greek fire, shown below in another scene from the* Scylitzes Chronicle, *made the Byzantine navy a formidable opponent.*

succeed—would require the biggest fleet and mightiest army they could possibly assemble.

And second, of course, they must somehow find out how to manufacture this Greek fire. That would not be easy either, for every inquiry they made produced the same answer. It came, said the Christians, from God and the Virgin Mary, who didn't want the Muslims to have it.[7] Greek fire became the most closely guarded secret in all Christendom, and the most sought by Christendom's enemies.

With the death of Constantine IV, the downfall of the Heraclian dynasty accelerates. His son became Justinian II, whose yearning for personal glory was exceeded only by his incapability of achieving it. In exchange for amendments to the thirty-year treaty, for instance, he agreed to break up a Christian community known as the Mardaites, who for forty years had waged an effective guerrilla war against the Muslims in Asia Minor, often becoming a greater deterrent to them than the Byzantine army itself. Justinian moved most of the valiant Mardaites to the Danube region.

When the army protested the loss of these valuable allies, Justinian recruited a dubious contingent of barbarian Slavs instead, and led them against the Muslim army in Asia Minor. After two-thirds of the Slavs deserted to the Muslims, however, Justinian fled with the loyal third—all of whom he then executed because he was so furious with their faithless comrades. His two senior treasury officials meanwhile became so ruthless in their tax exactions that the populace rose against them, tied their feet together, and dragged them to death through city streets, then publicly burned their bodies. They next seized the emperor himself, slit both his nose and tongue, banished him to the Crimean Peninsula in the Black Sea, and proclaimed as emperor the individual who had led them in this rebellion.

7. In March 673, the year Mu'awiya's siege began, "a rainbow appeared in the sky," writes the historian Theophanes, "and all mankind shuddered. Everyone said it was the end of the world." Later interpreters had a different explanation: The rainbow hailed God's gift of Greek fire to the Christians.

This man, Leontius, inaugurated the first of seven imperial regimes that for two terrible decades would preside over the disintegrating empire while the Muslims made ready to finish it off. Leontius's regime, lasting three years, was distinguished only by the decision of the Roman governor of Lazica, on the Armenian frontier, to convert to Islam and take the province over with him. Leontius was succeeded by Apsimar, a general who headed a military revolt in southern Asia Minor, led his army against the capital, slit Leontius's nose, banished him to a monastery, and flogged and deported his senior officials.

Apsimar, declaring himself Tiberius III, launched an offensive against the Muslims in Syria. It failed. Armenia meanwhile rose in revolt against its Muslim masters. This too failed, and the Muslims, keen to discourage such conduct, burned the flower of the Armenian nobility to death in a church, along with their wives and children. (See sidebar, pages 260–261.) During his seven-year tenure, however, Tiberius did one thing well: He put his brother in command of the army on the Asia Minor front, and it inflicted two costly defeats on the Muslim forces, thereby delaying their planned attack on Constantinople.

Next followed one of the strangest and most tragic comebacks known to history. Justinian II, furiously brooding in his exile at Chersonesos, a semi-independent trading city on the Crimean Peninsula, plotted the recovery of his throne, split nose and tongue notwithstanding. Justinian was a man of great courage and relentless ambition, most historians agree, but by now was almost certainly insane. Fearing the wrath of the reigning emperor, Chersonesos's officialdom decided to assassinate him.

Apprised of the plot, Justinian fled the city and appealed for help to the wild and wily Khazars, who lived near the Black Sea's north coast. Their chief, the khagan, flattered that the direct descendant of the revered Heraclius should become indebted to him, offered him protection, and gave him his sister in marriage.

Emulating his namesake, Justinian the Great, the exiled emperor named his new wife Theodora. Tiberius, thoroughly alarmed, bribed the khagan to get rid of this unexpected challenger, and the khagan commissioned two officials to kill his newly acquired brother-in-law. But Theodora warned her husband, who invited the would-be assassins to dinner, one at a time, and personally strangled them.

Events now moved swiftly. Justinian commandeered a fishing boat, gathered the few officials who had remained loyal to him in exile, sailed along the Black Sea coast[8] and up the Danube, and there made a deal with the king of the Bulgars. For help in regaining his throne, he would bestow upon the Bulgar king the rank of caesar—an offer a barbarian king couldn't refuse. Thus Justinian marched on Constantinople at the head of a Bulgar army reinforced by other Slavs,

An eighth-century likeness of the vindictive and tragic Justinian II (below), from an architectural detail in the Piazza San Marco, Venice, Italy.

camped outside the walls, and declared that the rightful ruler, the descendant of Heraclius, had returned to claim his throne. The gates were mysteriously opened. Justinian took up residence unopposed in the Blachernae Palace—and unleashed upon the city a vindictive vengeance of appalling cruelty.

Tiberius was caught fleeing and brought back in chains. From his tranquil monastery the unfortunate Leontius was also dragged away. Both were paraded through the streets, then at the Hippodrome made to crouch before Justinian, who planted his feet on them. After this soul-satisfying ceremony, Justinian had them taken away and beheaded. Tiberius's brother, victor over the Muslims in Asia Minor, was returned to the city and hanged, together with all his senior officers. The patriarch was blinded and exiled to Rome. Special treatment was reserved for senior government officials, such as entertainment at a sumptuous official banquet, at the conclusion of which they were either hanged or decapitated.

Against Chersonesos, Justinian successively sent three fleets. The first brought the city's leaders to Constantinople, where they were publicly roasted on spits. The second, carrying thousands of Chersonese prisoners destined for death or slavery, sank in a storm. The third fleet had orders to burn the city to the ground and kill anybody left alive there, but turned instead against Justinian, proclaimed

Justinian successively sent three fleets against Chersonesos. The first brought the city's leaders to Constantinople, where they were publicly roasted on spits.

their Armenian commander Bardanes as the emperor Philippicus, and prepared to seize the capital. The timing of these massive naval expeditions is noteworthy; they occurred in 710 and 711, just when Muslim armies were crossing the Strait of Gibraltar to effect the conquest of Spain. The invaders made their crossings completely unresisted, because the Byzantines had no vessels to oppose them. Their ships were too busy wreaking Justinian's vengeance on Chersonesos.

With the arrival of Philippicus, troops previously loyal to the mad emperor deserted him. He was executed forthwith by a sword thrust, and Theodora was also slain. Their six-year-old son was sheltered by his grandmother in a Constantinople church, where he clung to the altar with a piece of the true cross in his hand and a number of relics hung about his neck. Thrusting aside the shrieking grandmother, an officer removed the sacred wood from the child's hand and laid it carefully on the altar. He next took the relics from his neck and hung them about his own. Finally, he carried the little boy to the church gate, stripped him, and cut his throat like a sheep's. Thus died the last representative of the house of Heraclius.

Philippicus, in his two-year reign, seemed more interested in the rewards of office than its duties. While he gained a reputation as a voluptuary, army morale sank perilously, and the Muslim takeover of Asia Minor began in earnest. In 712, they moved in force into Pontus and seized Amasya, only sixty miles from the Black Sea coast. The next year, they overran Antioch in Pisidia, the base for St. Paul's missionary work in eastern Asia Minor. By now, however, the army had had enough of Philippicus. The soldiers seized him after a bounteous morning banquet with his friends, blinded him, and replaced him with his secretary, Anastasius.

Anastasius was not long in office before alarming reports began coming in from Damascus, where the Muslims were said to be engaged in a vast military buildup, constructing siege equipment of all kinds. From Alexandria came information that timber was being imported from Lebanon, warships built by the hundreds, and crews trained. Clearly, a huge invasion was imminent.

Anastasius, who was no fool, immediately directed that the walls of Constantinople be repaired and strengthened, and stationed anti-siege equipment atop them. All citizens must provide themselves with a three-year supply of food, he ordered, or leave the capital immediately. He further ordered what a later generation would call a "preemptive strike," an attack on the Muslim shipyards and timber supplies. But the troops assigned to this task had politics of their

The troops informed Theodosius he was to be emperor. The man fled in abject fear; they tracked him down and declared him to be Theodosius III Augustus.

own. One of the key regiments ("themes," as they were called) assigned to the attack renounced its loyalty to Anastasius. Instead of attacking the enemy, they made for Constantinople to attack the emperor.

Their next move is close to incredible. Realizing en route that they had no replacement for Anastasius, they seized a minor official named Theodosius (he had an imperial name, at least) and informed him he was to be emperor. The man fled in abject fear to the mountains, but they tracked him down, took him along to the city, deposed Anastasius without harming him, and declared their terrified candidate to be Theodosius III Augustus. The Muslim buildup meanwhile continued unabated. What but a miracle could save Christendom now?

The Christians assuredly must have been praying for one, and what they received in response was a new and very different emperor. He is known as Leo the Isaurian. Isauria was the region in central Asia Minor where Paul and Barnabas had established some of their first missions nearly seven hundred years earlier. (Some accounts, however, make Leo a Syrian.) The chroniclers say that his given name was Conon and that his father, seeking a position for his son, presented Justinian II with five hundred sheep. In return, Leo was designated an imperial aide-de-camp.

But Justinian, growing suspicious of his new aide, sent him off as an emissary to the tribes beyond the Black Sea, where he intended him to be assassinated. Instead, after a number of hairbreadth escapes, Leo got back to Constantinople, where he found that Justinian himself had just been assassinated. His reputation for intrepidity established, Leo was given command of the defense of Asia Minor. This task he fulfilled so well that as the Muslim attack became ever more imminent, he became the obvious candidate to succeed the hapless Theodosius.

On March 25, 717, he was crowned Leo III, Theodosius having gratefully (and safely) abdicated. Leo had five months left to prepare for the most massive attack the city had ever confronted.

No adult in Constantinople was under any illusion as to what was in store. They knew there could be no question of surrendering without resistance, and therefore no hope of clemency if the Muslims were to take the city. The prospects in case of defeat were grim: slavery for able-bodied male survivors; rape and slavery for young women and for comely, pubescent boys; death for the valueless elderly. Everything marketable and movable in the empire's most opulent city would be hauled away—a staggering trove. To the defenders all this was the stuff of nightmare, but to the attackers, the stuff of fondest dreams. There had been no problem recruiting armies for the sack of Constantinople.

Then came the rumors. An enormous and heavily equipped Muslim army, tens, perhaps hundreds of thousands of men, was moving across Asia Minor unopposed. Men said that a fleet, far bigger than anyone could remember, was bound for Constantinople from Tarsus, birthplace of St. Paul. Meanwhile, Leo—cool, efficient, rational, and as always, wholly practical—made every day count.

On August 15, the rumors became hideously true. Crossing the Hellespont from Asia Minor, an army of eighty thousand men under Moslemah, brother of the caliph, Suleyman, came within sight of the city's four-mile long walls. The defenders looked on aghast as rank upon rank of heavily armed warriors appeared, and mammoth siege engines were dragged up. There were catapults to hurl great boulders at the ramparts. There were towers that would be worked forward to lean against the walls, whence screaming attackers could overtop them to slay the defenders.

The gates shortly opened, and an embassy from Leo emerged and paced towards the Muslim line. The emperor offered one gold piece for every person in

A six-sided silver Byzantine censer (left) from the seventh century, decorated with images of Christ and the Apostles. Used for burning incense, it would have been swung by three chains—now missing. Such vessels were rarely made of precious metal, but this one (now in the British Museum) was found near Kyrenia, Cyprus, together with a silver bowl, dish and spoons.

The jewel of Egypt

Wealthy and powerful, second city of the empire, the metropolis of Alexandria dazzles its conquerors

Nothing could have prepared Egypt's new Muslim overlords for the splendor, wealth, and sheer size of the metropolis of Alexandria. Founded by Alexander the Great in 331 B.C., it was the second city of the Byzantine Empire (after Constantinople itself), and the conduit through which flowed much of the trade between the Mediterranean, Africa and the Orient.

With the flowering of the empire under Justinian, a large number of new churches were built during the sixth century that reflected the power and wealth of the orthodox church. By the time of Heraclius, a century later, the Coptic patriarchate had become just as powerful, and even wealthier. It maintained its own trading fleet, and formed the most powerful institution in the city.

Alexandria was noted for its intellectual, artistic and cultural life. The study of Christian theology flourished there, and students from all over the empire attended its faculty of medicine. It was a center of craftsmanship in glass and metal, and the Alexandrian school of sculpture was foremost in the world.

As the Mediterranean's busiest port, shipbuilding was a major industry. In addition to large and small merchant vessels, the shipwrights of Alexandria built great battleships—floating fortresses that could carry a thousand men. The city also produced the best ropes in the world; made from a special hemp developed in Egypt.

In 290 B.C. a great lighthouse was built at the harbor entrance, to aid navigation. One of the Seven Wonders of the Ancient World, it

The slanting roof (left) of the spectacular new Library of Alexandria, which opened in the fall of 2002. The original disappeared after the Muslim conquest, and by some accounts contained seven hundred-thousand scrolls and books. The ornate front cover of this Coptic Gospels (below) dates from the time of the Muslim conquest, and survived at the Monastery of St. Michael at Fayoum, Egypt. The great port was also known for its fine hemp ropes, and shops specializing in rope and string (opposite page, top) can still be found there.

contained a huge mirror that reflected light (from a meticulously tended fire) that could be seen thirty-five miles offshore. The lighthouse was damaged by several earthquakes, but stood until 1480—when it was finally demolished to build a fort on the same site.

Equally famous was Alexandria's great library, containing seven hundred-thousand scrolls, and held to be the greatest repository of knowledge in the ancient world. It was partially destroyed during a fire begun by troops of Julius Caesar in 48 B.C., but more yet was lost during the fourth century. That it no longer existed in the twelfth century is fact, but who finally destroyed it is a question that perplexes historians even today.

One story suggests that the caliph, Umar, when asked what should be done with the library, ordered "if what is written in [the books] agrees with the Qur'an, they are not required: if it disagrees, they are not desired. Destroy them therefore." And they did. For six months the books were used as fuel, to heat the city's public baths. ■

The medieval Qait Bey Fort (left) was begun in 1480 on the site of the great Lighthouse of Alexandria, one of the Seven Wonders of the Ancient World. Built in 290 B.C., the lighthouse was damaged by a series of earthquakes before its stones were used as a foundation for the fort. A twentieth-century Alexandrian boat builder works on a fishing vessel (opposite page, bottom). The city once produced huge warships for the Egyptian, Roman, and later Byzantine and Muslim navies.

9. There is no direct evidence that Greek fire was used by land troops in the siege of Constantinople, but four pieces of circumstantial evidence make it highly probable. First, after the initial assault, Moslemah did not attack the walls again; something must have seriously deterred him. Second, he built a heavy breastwork of unmortared stones, distant from the walls, to shelter his troops—again, from "something." Third, historians agree that Greek fire was intended for use by land troops. Fourth, the accounts attribute the victory to God, of course, but also to the skill of the Christian technicians and army engineers.

Constantinople if the attacking army would withdraw, a generous and very costly gesture that would weigh heavily on his people, if accepted. But Moslemah was a realist. His men had been recruited with far greater spoils in mind. Anyway, how could the fleets of ships now on their way to the Sea of Marmara be turned back? Furthermore, this extraordinary offer must mean Leo figured he couldn't win. Moslemah haughtily rejected it, and ordered the attack.

To deafening cheers from the Muslim ranks, the big rocks crashed into the walls. The more daring assailants dashed in, to hurl up their grappling hooks. The siege towers lurched forward. Then, from the walls came a ghastly phenomenon: some kind of oily material that poured down on the most advanced attackers, bursting into flame and seemingly flying about everywhere. Men shrieked in pain and fled frantically, but the fire itself clung tightly to them, and nothing would extinguish it.

Next came another horror. Stones, catapulted back from the wall tops, smashed into the siege towers and seemed to burst, spreading the same flaming substance and completely destroying them. Strange arrows, carrying a kind of pouch, and raining down on the ranks of the Muslim cavalry and infantry, also spewed flaming oil that splashed far and wide. Men and horses panicked and ran insanely as their flesh burned away.[9]

Moslemah, sizing up the attack as hopeless, quickly signaled a retreat. As his men fled back to the Muslim line, another cheer went up, this one from the Christians. Islam's supposedly invincible army, hitherto universally victorious in almost everything

While Moslemah's men built a massive breastwork behind which his troops were able to take cover, he reluctantly concluded the attack was hopeless.

it undertook, was fleeing in terror from its first assault on the Christian capital.

But the siege had only begun. While Moslemah's men built a massive stone breastwork behind which his troops could take cover, he reached a reluctant conclusion. He must starve the city into submission. How he proposed to accomplish this became plain two weeks later. Constantinople awoke on the morning of September 1 to find that the familiar Sea of Marmara had become overnight a moving forest of ships' masts, a fleet that stretched as far as the eye could see, small vessels and large, eighteen hundred in all. Aboard it, they would later discover, were another eighty thousand soldiers, under the command of an admiral named (like the caliph) Suleyman. How could such an armada ever be stopped?

Leo was studying this fleet from a somewhat different perspective—looking for spouts on the bows of the lead vessels, and catapults on their decks. The outcome, he knew, depended on a single question: Had the formula been safeguarded? Had the Muslims acquired Greek fire? He had seen no sign of it in their army. Now he could see none in their navy. So the secret had been kept, a triumph of counterespionage. His deplorable predecessors had somehow accomplished this one thing—and it was the only thing that mattered.

Next day, the Muslims found out why. They divided their huge fleet. Half was to sail through the Bosporus to its junction with the Black Sea and block supplies from principal centers like Chersonesos in the Crimea and Trebizond on the south coast. The remaining ships would blockade it from the west, cutting off access from the Aegean. But as the first big vessels began rounding Seraglio Point at the entrance to the Golden Horn harbor, their captains noted a surprising change. The great chain that crossed the harbor mouth from towers on either side, to block enemy vessels from entering, had been dropped. The harbor was wide open. Was this some kind of trick?

As the swift current on the point swirled their vessels about, the gruesome explanation was revealed. Out of the harbor like a pack of wolves came a squadron of little vessels, biremes with two tiers of oars, each equipped with some kind of launching device. Though the Muslims didn't know it, the emperor himself was in one of them. The hundred or more soldiers aboard each big Muslim vessel grasped their scimitars and waited to pounce upon the much smaller Christian crews. But the little ships abruptly stopped short of them, and from them flew some kind of projectile.

Muslim captains who had heard accounts of Mu'awiya's siege forty years before may have guessed what this was. But it now came far more accurately, far more lethally, bursting into flame on their crowded decks, and spreading a raging fire upward into the rigging and in a wide arc all around. The men, their very skin on fire, went berserk. Many dove into the sea, only to find that the water would not put the fire out; when the substance again touched air, it burst into flame once more. Within perhaps an hour, twenty vessels had burned and sunk. Others were wrecked as they crashed crazily into each other. Some had been abandoned and captured. The rest escaped back to the Marmara. This left the path to the Black Sea still open, and through it, Christian vessels day by day brought tons of supplies into the capital.

Moslemah pondered his preposterous situation. He had enough men and

An Islamic cemetery nestles in the shadow of Constantinople's massive Theodosian walls (below). Now the Turkish city of Istanbul, large sections of its Byzantine walls remain, a reminder of its fierce resistance to Muslim conquest.

A flotilla of Byzantine ships, armed with Greek fire, spread panic among the Muslim vessels, and within an hour had destroyed twenty enemy warships. This nineteenth-century engraving shows the fearsome impact of Constantinople's secret weapon—which is still shrouded in mystery.

ships to take the city five times over, and more on the way, but he couldn't get near the enemy's vessels, nor attack the enemy's walls. Dumbfounding as it might seem, the sensible thing was to call off the whole expedition, but the consequence to Muslim prestige, he knew, would be devastating. What was to be done? Plainly, he must consult his brother.

About then, the next blow fell. The caliph Suleyman was at Tarsus, in personal command of a replacement contingent being trained there to reinforce the invasion troops. On October 8, however, his digestive system failed, and he suddenly died.[10] The withdrawal decision was therefore up to his successor, Umar II, a man as strong on theology as he was weak on warfare. Umar's decision was to not decide, which prolonged the siege into the winter—an eventuality for which the besiegers, having expected a swift victory, seemed to have been utterly unprepared.

The seaborne fighters were put ashore, and the fleet set at anchor. Soon the snow arrived, something many recruits from Arabia, Persia, Syria and Egypt had

Snow arrived, which many Muslims had never seen. It came and it stayed . . . and stayed . . . and stayed. For over three months it lay on the ground.

10. Caliph Suleyman's appetite for food was so spectacular as to find its way into Islamic history. At the time of his death, he had just eaten two baskets of eggs and figs, swallowing them alternately, and finished up with some marrow and sugar. The historian Edward Gibbon records that during a pilgrimage to Mecca he reputedly once ate, at a single meal, seventy pomegranates, a young goat, six chickens, and a huge quantity of grapes.

11. There are two Greek accounts of the Siege of Constantinople, that of the eighth-century monastic historian Theophanes, and that of Nicephorus, patriarch of Constantinople. Both men were born about thirty years after the siege. Their two accounts describe the mutiny of the captive Christian crews, each providing different, though not conflicting, details. This reconstruction draws on both.

never before seen. It came and it stayed . . . and stayed . . . and stayed. For more than three months of this unusually severe winter, according to the records, bare ground could not be seen. At the same time, while Constantinople dined frugally but adequately, the besiegers themselves suffered mortally from the starvation they planned to inflict upon their enemies. Before long, the hundred and fifty thousand Muslim troops had eaten all their horses and camels, and were subsisting (says one account) on a mixture of boiled human flesh and excrement. Disease spread, the death toll rose into the thousands, and among the dead was the admiral Suleyman, commander of the Muslim fleet.

Finally the spring of 718 came, and with it a supply fleet from Alexandria, some four hundred ships in all. Many began making their way through the Bosporus by night. It was then that another development heartened the defenders, although how it happened can only be conjectured.[11] The sentries at the entrance to the Golden Horn likely heard the splash of oars from a small boat out on the bay, since even a slight sound will travel far over calm water at night. Then they must have realized it was not one small boat but several, maybe a dozen, maybe more—a veritable squadron of little boats. What could this be? The Muslim army would not attack in rowboats, and whoever it was seemed remarkably noisy, for soon voices could be heard.

Many voices, it seemed, calling something in unison. It was Greek—they were definitely speaking Greek. Then words became discernible: "Long live the emperor!" As the little boats reached shore, the Byzantine guards doubtless stood alert with swords drawn. The men tumbled out, and with them came their story.

They were Christians, they said, pressed into slavery on the Muslim vessels. Having long planned to escape at Constantinople, they had overcome their guards and dumped their officers into the sea. These few had escaped in the ships' boats, while the rest took charge of the ships, and were awaiting orders from shore. The thought may have dawned on some Byzantines that most or all of these men must be Monophysite Christians. But what did that matter now?

Their liberated vessels were now drifting out there in the dark, they said. Very quickly, the agile Byzantine fireboats went into action, guided by the Christian mutineers. The seized ships were taken over; their former crews, now freemen, rowed them into the Golden Horn as prizes of war. Meanwhile, Greek fire wreaked a further toll on the rest of the Muslim fleet.

From this incident came another dividend. Leo now knew how many Muslim ships there were, what they were carrying, how they were armed, and also that another Muslim fleet, in fact the third, was sailing in from North Africa. He seems, from subsequent events, to have discovered something else, namely that the late caliph's replacement army was said to be nearing Constantinople, with no reason to expect an attack. Leo acted immediately. A task force dispatched across the Bosporus confirmed this intelligence and ambushed the army, claiming uncounted casualties and routing the rest. Thus, the Muslim thousands lost to cold, disease, starvation and Greek fire were not replaced. Further, the Byzantine force established fishing stations on the opposite shore to ensure the city a daily supply of fish.

When the third fleet arrived, 360 ships this time, it anchored on the Marmara's south coast and stayed there. It had been ordered to reinforce the Black Sea squadron, but its commander judged the risk too high. Some ships from the second fleet had made it through and were blockading the Black Sea approach to the city, but this, too, availed them little because Leo had one card left to play, and it would prove decisive.

The Bulgars, who had launched an ineffective attack on Constantinople after the assassination of Justinian II, had for some time been engaged in treaty talks with Leo's emissaries. By the spring of 718 they reached agreement, and soon a motley army of Bulgars and Slavs advanced southward against what remained of Moslemah's army, still camped outside the city walls. Moslemah marched north to meet them near the city of Adrianople, 125 miles to the northwest, scene of the empire's decisive loss to the barbarian Visigoths 340 years before. (See earlier volume, *Darkness Descends*, chapter 3.) Here Moslemah suffered a major defeat. Thus the barbarians, having first beaten the empire at Adrianople, now played a decisive role in saving it there.

This reversal, coupled with a false rumor (spread by Leo) that the fearsome Franks were also on their way to save the Christian capital, caused Umar to make up his mind. He ordered his troops to retreat. On August 15, 718, one year to the day after their arrival, the Muslim soldiers departed, transported across the Hellespont by the remainder of their navy. Yet even this was not the end. As the still considerable fleet sailed into the Aegean, a fierce and unseasonable storm drove much of it onto the rocks. On the south coast of Asia Minor, an even worse storm reportedly sank all but ten vessels. Then a small Byzantine force that had been shadowing the Muslim ships closed in and sank five. So only five ships reached Tarsus—of the approximately twenty-five hundred that descended so confidently on the Christian capital the year before.

Military historian J. F. C. Fuller (*The Decisive Battles of the Western World*) estimates that in all, two hundred-thousand men took part in the siege, and about thirty thousand survived it. "The fall of Constantinople would have

By the end of the seventh century, the glittering shrine of the Dome of the Rock (below, this page), built by the caliph Abd al-Malik, dominated the Jerusalem skyline. Muslims believe it marks the spot where Muhammad ascended to heaven on his Night Journey, but its construction on the Temple Mount--in the heart of the holiest city of Christians and Jews--was clearly a powerful political statement. Its great dome was originally covered in gold, and the foundation stone was encircled by sixteen arches from different churches in Jerusalem that had been destroyed in the final and fatal conflict between Persia and Byzantium. There is no little irony in the fact that this oldest and greatest monument to Islamic conquest was designed by Byzantine architects. The dome was restored and recovered in gold in the 1990s, at the expense of King Hussein of Jordan.

remodeled the entire history of the East," he writes. "Beyond question, the Muslim repulse was one of the great decisive events in Western history."

J. B. Bury calls the failure of the siege "ecumenical," implying that it pivotally affected all history. Harry Turtledove, in the introduction to his translation of Theophanes, says that if Constantinople had not survived, "the history of the world would have been incalculably different." Such a defeat for the Muslims, observes C. W. C. Oman (*The Byzantine Empire*), "was well calculated to impress on their fatalistic minds the idea that Constantinople was not destined by Providence to fall into their hands." It would stand as a Christian bastion against Islam for another 735 years.

Other conclusions can be drawn. One is the fact that the Christian victory was one of technology over mere mass and multitude. So thoroughly did the Byzantines safeguard the formula for Greek fire that to this day, no one is altogether sure what it was, though it must have been based on naphthalene. Equally significant is the fact that the Muslims had seen Greek fire in its early stages forty years earlier, but fatally underestimated its possibilities. They would soon demonstrate themselves every bit as intelligent as Christians (and frequently more virtuous), but never did they give the same attention to the physical sciences as would the Christians. This would tell against them right through to the twenty-first century.

The chronic weakness of the Christians was becoming similarly plain: what an old Anglican prayer calls "our unhappy divisions."[12] Almost every historical account agrees that Syria, Palestine, Egypt, and North Africa fell to the Islamic invaders because the populace had been so bitterly alienated by brutally zealous imperial efforts to stamp out Monophysite Christianity. But with Islam checked, the initiative now moved to the Christian side, and the story must next be told of how the Christians spread their faith northward and eastward, thereby laying the foundations of Western civilization. ■

12. This prayer "For the Unity of All Christian Peoples" first appeared in the Anglican *Book of Common Prayer* in the eighteenth century: "O God the Father of Our Lord Jesus Christ, our only Savior, the Prince of Peace: Give us grace seriously to lay to heart the great dangers we are in by our unhappy divisions. Take away all enmity and prejudice, and whatsoever else may hinder us from godly union and accord; that as there is but one Body and one Spirit, and one hope of our calling, one Lord, one Faith, one Baptism, one God and Father of us all, so we may henceforth be all of one heart and one soul, united in one holy bond of truth and peace, of faith and charity, and may with one mind and one mouth glorify thee; through Jesus Christ our Lord. Amen."

PREVIOUS VOLUMES IN THIS SERIES

VOLUME ONE:
The Veil is Torn
A.D. 30 to A.D. 70
Pentecost to the
Destruction of Jerusalem

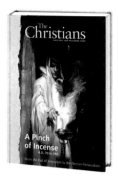

VOLUME TWO:
A Pinch of Incense
A.D. 70 to 250
From the Fall of Jerusalem
to the Decian Persecution

VOLUME THREE:
By This Sign
A.D. 250 to 350
From the Decian Persecution
to the Constantine Era

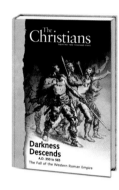

VOLUME FOUR:
Darkness Descends
A.D. 350 to 565
The Fall of the
Western Roman Empire

NEW CONTRIBUTORS TO THIS VOLUME

DEAN PICKUP is a graduate of the visual communications program at Edmonton's Grant MacEwan College with a major in design and digital media. He has worked on volumes 2, 3, 4 and 5 of the Christian History Project, and recently completed a redesign of volume 1. In addition to his illustrations and responsibilities for graphic design and page creation, he also created the original maps contained in this volume.

MIKE BYFIELD, formerly the editor of the Edmonton, Alberta-based *Report Newsmagazine* and business editor of *The Calgary Sun*, has been a journalist for twenty-five years. An avid reader of history, this writer also holds a college diploma in electronics technology and served in the U.S. Navy.

BIBLIOGRAPHY

Abraham, Gerald. *The Concise Oxford History of Music*. New York: Oxford University Press, 1979.

Ali, Maulana Muhammad. *Early Caliphate*. Lahore, India: Ahmadiyyah Anjuman Isha'at Islam, 1983.

Ali, Syed Ameer. *A Short History of the Saracens*. New Delhi: Kitab Bhawan, 1977.

Andrae, Tor. *Les Origines de l'Islam et le Christianisme*. Paris: Adrien-Maisonneuve, 1955.

Apel, Willi. *Gregorian Chant*. London: Burns & Oates, [1958?].

Aprem, Mar. *Nestorian Missions*. Trichur, India: Mar Narsai, 1976.

Atiya, Aziz S. *A History of Eastern Christianity*. London: Methuen, 1968.

Baali, Fuad and Ali Wardi. *Ibn Khaldun and Islamic Thought-styles, a Social Perspective*. Boston: G. K. Hall, 1981.

Barmby, James. *Gregory the Great*. New York: Pott, Young, 1879.

Barnes, Harry Elmer. *A History of Historical Writing*. New York: Dover Publications, 1962.

Beaucamp, Joelle and Christian Robin. "Le Christianisme dans le peninsule arabique." In *Travaux et Mémoires (Centre de Recherche d'Histoire et Civilisation de Byzance)*, v. 8: 45-61. Paris: Éditions E. de Boccard, 1973.

Bede the Venerable, Saint. *Bede's Ecclesiastical History of the English People*. Oxford: Clarendon Press, 1969.

Bell, Richard. "The Origin of Islam in its Christian Environment." In *Gunning Lecture, Edinburgh University, 1925*. London: Frank Cass, 1968.

Bishai, Wilson B. *Islamic History of the Middle East: Backgrounds, Development, and Fall of the Arab Empire*. Boston: Allyn and Bacon, 1968.

Bradley, Ian. *Celtic Christian Communities: Live the Tradition*. Kelowna, B.C.: Northstone Pub., 2000.

Browne, Edward Granville. *A Literary History of Persia*. Cambridge: Cambridge University Press, 1956-1959.

Browne, Laurence E. *The Eclipse of Christianity in Asia: From the Time of Muhammad till the Fourteenth Century*. New York: H. Fertig, 1967.

Browning, Robert. *Justinian and Theodora*. London: Thames and Hudson, 1987.

Bury, J. B. *A History of the Eastern Roman Empire from the Fall of Irene to the Accession of Basil I. (A.D. 802-867)*. London: Macmillan, 1912.

Bury, J. B. *A History of the Later Roman Empire from Arcadius to Irene, 395 A.D. to 800 A.D.* Amsterdam: Hakkert, 1966.

Butler, Alfred J. *The Arab Conquest of Egypt*. Oxford: Clarendon Press, 1978.

Cahill, Thomas. *How the Irish Saved Civilization: The Untold Story of Ireland's Heroic Role from the Fall of Rome to the Rise of Medieval Europe*. New York: Nan A. Talese, Doubleday, 1995.

The Cambridge Medieval History. New York: Macmillan, 1911-36.

Cameron, Averil. *Continuity and Change in Sixth-Century Byzantium*. London: Variorum Reprints, 1981.

Carroll, Warren H. *A history of Christendom*. Front Royal, Va: Christendom College Press, 1987.

Chadwick, Henry. *The Church in Ancient Society: From Galilee to Gregory the Great*. New York: Oxford University Press, 2001.

Chamberlin, Russell. *Charlemagne: Emperor of the Western World*. London: Grafton, 1986.

Church, F. Forrester and Terrence J. Mulry, eds. *The Macmillan Book of Earliest Christian Hymns*. New York: Macmillan, 1988.

Colgrave, Bertram, trans. *The Earliest Life of Gregory the Great*. Lawrence: University of Kansas Press, 1968.

Coppee, Henri. *History of the Conquest of Spain by the Arab Moors*. Boston: Little, Brown, & Company, 1881.

Cutts, Edward Lewes. *Augustine of Canterbury*. London: Methuen, 1895.

Daniel-Rops, Henri. *The Church in the Dark Ages*. London: Dent, 1963.

Dickinson, Edward. *Music in the History of the Western Church*. New York: Charles Scribner's Sons, 1931.

Downey, Glanville. *Constantinople in the Age of Justinian*. Norman: University of Oklahoma, 1960.

Elishe. *History of Vardan and the Armenian War*. Cambridge, Mass.: Harvard University Press, 1982.

Fahmy, Aly Mohamed. *Muslim Sea-Power in the Eastern Mediterranean from the Seventh to the Tenth Century A. D.* New Delhi: S. Chad [1966 ?].

Fisher, D. J. V. *The Anglo-Saxon Age, c. 400-1042*. London: Longman, 1973.

Franzius, Enno. *History of the Byzantine Empire, Mother of Nations*. New York: Funk & Wagnalls, 1967.

Fregosi, Paul. *Jihad in the West: Muslim Conquests from the 7th to the 21st Centuries*. Amherst, N.Y.: Prometheus Books, 1998.

Frend, W. H. C. *The Rise of Christianity*. Philadelphia, PA: Fortress, 1984.

Fuller, J. F. C. *The Decisive Battles of the Western World: 480 BC-1757*. London: Granada, 1970.

Gabrieli, Francesco. *Muhammad and the Conquests of Islam*. New York: McGraw-Hill, 1968.

George, Judith W. *Venantius Fortunatus: A Latin Poet in Merovingian Gaul*. New York: Oxford University Press, 1992.

Gibb, H. A. R. *Mohammedanism: An Historical Survey*. New York: Oxford University Press, 1961.

Gibbon, Edward and Simon Ockley. *The History of the Saracens and the Rise and Fall of their Empire*. London: F. Warne, 1873.

Gibbon, Edward. *Decline and Fall of the Roman Empire*. www.ccel.org.

Glick, Thomas F. *Islamic and Christian Spain in the Early Middle Ages*. Princeton, NJ: Princeton University Press, 1979.

Glubb, John Bagot. *The Great Arab Conquests*. London: Hodder and Stoughton, 1963.

Goubert, Paul. "Les Rapports De Khosrau II Roi Des Rois Sassanide Avec L'Empereur Maurice." In *Actes du VIIe Congrès des Études Byzantines, Bruxelles 1948*. Nendeln: Kraus, 1966-1979.

Great Britain. Naval Intelligence Division. *Western Arabia and the Red Sea*. [London]: Naval Intelligence Division, 1946.

Greenslade, W.G. "The Martyrs of Najran." In *The Moslem World* 22: 264-275.

Gregoire, Henri. "An Armenian Dynasty On The Byzantine Throne." In *Armenian Quarterly* 1 (1946).

Hamadeh, Muhammad Maher. *Muhammad the Prophet: A Selected Bibliography*. Thesis. [Ann Arbor, Mich.], 1965.

Higgins, Martin J. "International relations at the close of the 6th century." In *Catholic Historical Review* 27 (October 1941).

Hitti, Philip K. *History of the Arabs*. London: Macmillan, 1946.

Hodgkin, Thomas. *Italy and Her Invaders*. New York: Russell & Russell, 1967.

Holt P. M., Ann K. S. Lambton and Bernard Lewis, eds. *The Cambridge History of Islam*. Cambridge: Cambridge University Press, 1970.

Howorth, Sir Henry. *Saint Gregory the Great*. London: John Murray, 1912.

Ishaq, Ibn. *The Life of Muhammad*. New York: Oxford University Press, 1967.

Jackson, Gabriel. *The Making of Medieval Spain*. London: Thames and Hudson, 1972.

John, bishop of Ephesus. *The Third Part of the Ecclesiastical History of John, Bishop of Ephesus*. Oxford: Oxford University Press, 1860.

Kaegi, Walter Emil. *Army, Society, and Religion in Byzantium*. London: Variorum Reprints, 1982.

Kennedy, Pringle. *Arabian Society at the Time of Muhammad*. Calcutta: Simla, Thacker, 1926.

Kidd, B. J. *A History of the Church to AD 461*. Oxford: Clarendon Press, 1922.

Kritzeck, James. *Peter the Venerable and Islam*. Princeton, NJ.: Princeton University Press, 1964.

Lane-Poole, Stanley. *The Moors in Spain*. London: T. Fisher Unwin, 1888.

Lang, David Marsh. *Armenia, Cradle of Civilization*. Boston: Allen & Unwin, 1978.

Latourette, Kenneth Scott. *A History of Christianity*. New York: Harper & Row, 1953.

Latourette, Kenneth Scott. *A History of the Expansion of Christianity*, v.2 *The Thousand Years of Uncertainty*. New York: Harper & Brothers, 1937-45.

Latourette, Kenneth Scott. *The History of Christianity*. Berkley: Blackie & Sons, Glasgow, 1929.

Lewis, Bernard. *The Arabs in History*. London: Hutchinson University Library, 1958.

Livermore, H. V. *The Origins of Spain and Portugal*. London: George Allen & Unwin, 1971.

Louth, Andrew. *Maximus the Confessor*. New York: Routledge, 1996.

MacKay, Angus. *Spain in the Middle Ages: From Frontier to Empire, 1000-1500*. London: Macmillan, 1977.

Markus, R. A. *Gregory the Great and His World*. New York: Cambridge University Press, 1997.

Mason, Arthur James, ed. *The Mission of St. Augustine to England According to the Original Documents*. New York: Macmillan, 1897.

Maurice, Emperor of the East. *Maurice's Strategikon: Handbook of Byzantine Military Strategy*. Philadelphia: University of Pennsylvania Press, 1984.

McGuckin, John Anthony, trans. *At the Lighting of the Lamps: Hymns of the Ancient Church*. Fairacres, Oxford: SLG, 1995.

Menander, Protector. *The History of Menander the Guardsman*. Liverpool: Cairns, 1985

Moberg, Axel, ed. and trans. *The Book of the Himyarites: Fragments of a Hitherto Unknown Syriac Work*. Lund: C. W. K. Gleerup, 1924.

Muir, William. *Annals of the Early Caliphate: From the Death of Mahomet to the Omeyyad and Abbaside Dynasties A.H. XI-LXI (A.D. 632-680) from Original Sources*. Amsterdam: Oriental Press, 1968.

Muir, William. *The Life of Mohammad: from Original Sources*. Edinburgh: J. Grant, 1923.

Newark, Timothy. *The Barbarians: Warriors & Wars of the Dark Ages*. Poole, Dorset: Blandford, 1985.

Newman, John Henry. *Certain Difficulties Felt by Anglicans in Catholic Teaching*, v. 1. www.newmanreader.org.

Nicephorus, Saint. *An Eyewitness to History: The Short History of Nikephoros our Holy Father the Patriarch of Constantinople*. Brookline, Mass.: Hellenic College, [1989?].

Nutting, Anthony. *The Arabs: A Narrative History from Mohammed to the Present*. New York: New American Library, 1965.

O'Leary, De Lacy. *Arabia before Muhammad*. London: K. Paul, Trench, Trubner, 1927.

Paul, the Deacon. *History of the Lombards*. Philadelphia: University of Pennsylvania Press, 1974.

Petersen, Joan M., trans. and ed. *Handmaids of the Lord: Contemporary Descriptions of Feminine Asceticism in the First Six Christian Centuries*. Kalamazoo, MI: Cistercian Publications, 1996.

Pettersen, Alvyn. *Athanasius*. Harrisburg, PA: Morehouse, 1995.

Piguelevskja, N. "Les Rapports Sociaux a Nedjran." In *Journal of the Economic and Social History of the Orient* 4(1): 1-14.

Pipes, Daniel. *In the Path of God: Islam and Political Power*. New York: Basic Books, 1983.

Pirenne, Henri. *Mohammed and Charlemagne*. Cleveland, OH: World Pub., 1957.

Quasten, Johannes. *Music and Worship in Pagan & Christian Antiquity*. Washington, D.C.: National Association of Pastoral Musicians, 1983.

Read, Jan. *The Moors in Spain and Portugal*. Totowa, NJ: Rowman and Littlefield, 1975.

Reinaud, Joseph Toussaint. *Muslim Colonies in France, Northern Italy, and Switzerland*. Lahore: Sh. Muhammad Ashraf, 1964.

Rodinson, Maxime. *Mohammed*. New York: Pantheon Books, [1971].

Saunders, J. J. *A History of Medieval Islam*. New York: Barnes & Noble, 1965.

Sawyers, June Skinner. *Celtic Music: A Complete Guide*. [s.l.]: Da Capo Press, 2000.

Sellers, Robert Victor. *The Council of Chalcedon: A Historical and Doctrinal Survey*. London: S.P.C.K., 1961.

Shah, Irfan. "The Conference at Ramla." In *Journal of Near Eastern Studies* 23 (1964): 115-131.

Shahid, Irfan. *The Martyrs of Najrân*. Brussels: Société des Bollandistes, Subsidia Hagiographica 49, 1971.

Shinnie, P. L. *Meroe, a Civilization of the Sudan*. New York: F. A. Praeger, 1967.

Simeon, of Beth Arsham. "Letter of Simeon of Beth Arsham." In *Moslem World* 36(3), 1946: 205-16.

Simocatta, Theophylact. *The History of Theophylact Simocatta*. New York: Oxford University Press, 1986.

Smith, Sidney. "Events in Arabia in the 6th century AD." In *Bulletin of the School of Oriental and African Studies* 16 (1954): 425-68.

Sozomen. *Church History*. www.ccel.org.

Ste. Croix, G. E. M. de. *The Class Struggle in the Ancient Greek World: From the Archaic Age to the Arab Conquests*. Ithaca, N.Y.: Cornell University Press, 1981.

Stewart, John. *Nestorian Missionary Enterprise*. Edinburgh: T. & T. Clark, 1928.

Stratos, Andreas N. *Studies in 7th-century Byzantine Political History*. London: Variorum, 1983.

Stratos, Andreas N. *Byzantium in the Seventh Century*. Amsterdam: Adolf M. Hakkert, 1968.

Thomas, Charles. *Christianity in Roman Britain to AD 500*. Berkeley: University of California, 1981.

Trimingham, J. Spencer. *Christianity Among the Arabs in Pre-Islamic Times*. New York: Longman, 1979.

Turtledove, Harry, trans. *The Chronicle of Theophanes*. Philadelphia, PA: University of Pennsylvania Press, 1982.

Turtledove, Harry. *The Immediate Successors of Justinian*. Thesis (Ph.D.), University of California, Los Angeles, 1977.

Vasiliev, A. A. *History of the Byzantine Empire, 324–1453*. Madison: University of Wisconsin Press, 1958.

Wallace-Hadrill, J. M. *The Barbarian West, 400–1000*. Malden, MA: Blackwell, 1996.

Watt, W. Montgomery. *Muhammad: Prophet and Statesman*. [London]: Oxford University Press, 1961.

Whitby, Michael. *The Emperor Maurice and his Historian: Theophylact Simocatta on Persian and Balkan Warfare*. New York: Oxford University Press, 1988.

PHOTOGRAPHIC CREDITS

INDEX

Subsequent volumes bring the Christian story to the end of the twentieth century

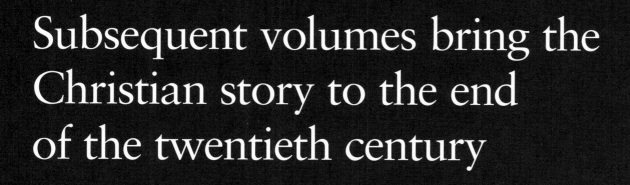

For additional copies of this book, or others in this series:

Write: Box 530 • Pembina, ND 58271 USA   or
10333 - 178 St • Edmonton, AB T5S 1R5 Canada
Call toll-free in North America: **1-800-853-5402**
On line: **www.christianhistoryproject.com**